"I am pleased to endorse this work, in which Kiwoon Lee guides us to understand more clearly how Paul's First Letter to the Thessalonians shaped the recipients' sense of identity and moral vision. Christian scholars and pastors will not only learn from Lee's skilled analysis, but also be moved to imitate in their own Christian communities the apostle Paul's doctrinally shaped approach to ethics."

—ROBERT L. PLUMMER, professor of biblical studies, The Southern Baptist Theological Seminary

"This study is an important contribution to our understanding of how Paul forms the identity and ethos of the Thessalonian Christians. Its novelty lies in focusing on how this process is influenced by prominent notions and echoes from the Hebrew Scriptures—an issue that has not received adequate attention from scholars before."

—FRANCOIS TOLMIE, professor in New Testament Studies, University of the Free State

"With a renewed angle on Paul's Jewish background, Kiwoon Lee explores the nature and purpose of 1 Thessalonians' discourse within the larger narrative of Israel as God's people. In his multi-layered analysis, Lee illuminates for today's Christians the letter's potential shaping of self-understanding and ethos. It is a welcome resource for theological students and clergy."

—ELNA MOUTON, professor emerita of New Testament, Stellenbosch University

"In light of 1 Thessalonians' social and historical setting and in connection to key redemptive themes of the Hebrew Scriptures, Kiwoon Lee provides a close reading of the apostle's discourse, i.e., a careful study that is exegetically robust, theologically enriching, and devotionally edifying. This is a must-read for all who desire to deepen their understanding of the First Letter to the Thessalonians and the formative thrust of Pauline theology."

—JOHN J. R. LEE, associate professor of New Testament, Midwestern Baptist Theological Seminary

"The construction of a people's identity was a topic of ancient reflection which holds currency for today's church as a global and multicultural community. Was identity linked with ethnicity and culture as with the Greeks or was it a matter of legal status not tied with ethnicity as with the Romans? Kiwoon Lee's study unfolds the way Paul unpacked the vexed question of who constituted 'the people' in a thorough exploration of 1 Thessalonians. This book is an essential read for anyone studying 1 Thessalonians and identity studies."

—GENE GREEN, professor emeritus of New Testament, Wheaton College and Graduate School

"In this important study, Kiwoon Lee considers the rhetorical nature and background of 1 Thessalonians, focusing particularly on the identity and moral formation of the nascent Christian community. In contrast to those who explain identity exclusively in sociological terms, he emphasizes the theological character of their identity and the role of the Old Testament in unpacking the meaning of the letter. Scholars will profit from this careful study that interacts extensively with current scholarship on the letter but also roots the letter in the historical context of the Jewish and Hellenistic world."

—THOMAS R. SCHREINER, professor of New Testament interpretation, The Southern Baptist Theological Seminary

Identity and Moral Formation in 1 Thessalonians

Identity and Moral Formation in 1 Thessalonians

KIWOON LEE

WIPF & STOCK · Eugene, Oregon

IDENTITY AND MORAL FORMATION IN 1 THESSALONIANS

Copyright © 2024 Kiwoon Lee. All rights reserved. Except for brief quotations in critical publications or reviews, no part of this book may be reproduced in any manner without prior written permission from the publisher. Write: Permissions, Wipf and Stock Publishers, 199 W. 8th Ave., Suite 3, Eugene, OR 97401.

Wipf & Stock
An Imprint of Wipf and Stock Publishers
199 W. 8th Ave., Suite 3
Eugene, OR 97401

www.wipfandstock.com

PAPERBACK ISBN: 978-1-6667-7890-8
HARDCOVER ISBN: 978-1-6667-7891-5
EBOOK ISBN: 978-1-6667-7892-2

01/11/24

All Scripture quotations taken from the ESV® Bible (The Holy Bible, English Standard Version®), copyright © 2001 by Crossway, a publishing ministry of Good News Publishers. Used by permission. All rights reserved.

Contents

Acknowledgments | vii

Abbreviations | ix

1 | Introduction | 1
2 | Paul's Conceptual World as Anomalous Diaspora Jew | 24
3 | The Thessalonians in a Pluralistic Religious Environment | 62
4 | Formative Effect of Identity Markers: An Exegesis of 1 Thess 1:1—2:12 | 91
5 | Discursive Function of Scriptural Echoes in 1 Thess 4–5 | 145
6 | Conclusion: Transformative Power of 1 Thessalonians for Present-Day Readers/Audiences | 200

Appendix I | 215

Appendix II | 218

Author Index | 245

Scripture Index | 251

Acknowledgments

THIS BOOK IS A revision of my doctoral dissertation, which I wrote at Stellenbosch University in the Western Cape of South Africa. It is a great honor to have this book published by Wipf & Stock. I give praise to God who has bestowed upon me his wonderful wisdom, love, and strength throughout my years of study. All glory belongs to God alone!

I wish to express my gratitude to my lovely wife, Sunyoung Park. I deeply appreciate her for walking the journey of God's discipline with me all the time. Her dedication, love, encouragement, support, and prayers for me are the sources of my strength, sustaining my life.

I would like to express the deepest appreciation to my supervisor, Prof. Elna Mouton, whose guidance was a pivotal moment in my academic journey. Prof. Mouton's profound academic insight and passion for viewing the world through the lens of the Bible inspired me to always keep the transformative power of God's Word in mind. Additionally, I am immensely grateful to my academic advisers in the United States of America, Prof. Douglas J. Moo (Wheaton College Graduate School) and Prof. Robert L. Plummer (The Southern Baptist Theological Seminary). Their instruction in the exegetical skills of the New Testament and their broadening of my understanding of biblical theology during my time at these institutions served as a profound model that I aspire to follow. Furthermore, I would also like to express my deep gratitude to the professors at Chongshin University and Chongshin Theological Seminary who played an essential role in shaping my early years in theology. Without their guidance and nurturing care, I would not have been able to embark on my academic journey.

I wish to express my gratitude to my family, in particular, my parents (Tae Eui Lee and Oak Soon Kwak), my parents-in-law (Sung Kyun Park and Soon Oak Lim), my brother and his wife (Ki Young Lee and Yeon Jin Jung), and my brother-in-law and his wife (Jong Won Park and Mi Kyung Jun). My family has patiently waited for me, and they did their best to support me in many ways. My academic journey of almost ten years (2009–2018) would have been nothing without my family's prayer and loving support. At the time of writing my thesis, there were only two of us—my wife and I—but now we have become a family of four with the addition of our two sons, Kangmin and Yumin. I also want to express my love and gratitude to my beloved sons.

Particularly, I cannot find the proper word to express my earnest gratitude to my father, Tae Eui Lee (1950–2016). While I was writing this thesis, my father passed away on March 15, 2016. I remember that in his lifetime my father gave all to my family through his sacrificial love. How deeply I am missing you . . . It was not easy to overcome the sadness and longing for him during my years of research, but 1 Thess 4:13–14 comforted me and gave me a genuine hope for our future encounter in Christ's parousia:

> Οὐ θέλομεν δὲ ὑμᾶς ἀγνοεῖν, ἀδελφοί, περὶ τῶν κοιμωμένων, ἵνα μὴ λυπῆσθε καθὼς καὶ οἱ λοιποὶ οἱ μὴ ἔχοντες ἐλπίδα. εἰ γὰρ πιστεύομεν ὅτι Ἰησοῦς ἀπέθανεν καὶ ἀνέστη, οὕτως καὶ ὁ θεὸς τοὺς κοιμηθέντας διὰ τοῦ Ἰησοῦ ἄξει σὺν αὐτῷ.

Abbreviations

Abbreviations of ancient texts come from the SBL Handbook of Style.

BIBLIOGRAPHIC AND GENERAL

ABD Freedman, D. N. (ed.) [1992] 2008. *Anchor Bible Dictionary*. 6 vols. New Haven; London: Yale University.

AGRW Ascough, R. S. & Harland, P. A. & Kloppenborg, J. S. (eds.) 2012. *Associations in the Greco-Roman World: A Sourcebook*. Waco: Baylor University.

ANF Roberts, A. & Donaldson, J. & Coxe, A. C. (eds.) 1951. *The Ante-Nicene Fathers*. 9 vols. Grand Rapids: Eerdmans.

BCE Before Common Era

BDAG Bauer, W. [1957] 2000. *A Greek-English lexicon of the New Testament and other early Christian literature*, rev. by F. W. Danker, W. F. Arndt, and F. W. Gingrich. 3rd ed. Chicago: University of Chicago Press.

BDB Brown, F. & Driver, S. R. & Briggs, C. A. 1977. *Enhanced Brown-Driver-Briggs Hebrew and English Lexicon*. Oxford: Clarendon Press.

BDF Blass, F. & Debrunner, A. 1961. *A Greek Grammar of the New Testament and Other Early Christian Literature*. Translated and edited by R. W. Funk. Cambridge: Cambridge University Press; Chicago: University of Chicago Press.

CD The Damascus Document

CE Common Era

EDNT	Balz, H. R. & Schneider, G. (eds.) 1990. *Exegetical Dictionary of the New Testament*. 3 vols. Grand Rapids: Eerdmans.
ESV	English Standard Version
ISBE	Bromiley, G. W. (ed.) 1988. *The International Standard Bible Encyclopedia*. 4 vols. Grand Rapids: Eerdmans.
IT	Edson, C. (ed.) 1972. *Inscriptiones Graecae. Vol. 10: Inscriptiones Thessalonicae et Viciniae*. Berlin: de Gruyter.
JB	The Jerusalem Bible
LSJ	Liddell, H. G. et al. [1843] 1996. *A Greek-English Lexicon with New Supplement*. 9th ed. Oxford: Clarendon Press.
LXX	The Septuagint (Ancient Greek translation of the Hebrew Scriptures)
MHT	Moulton, J. H. & Howard, W. F. & Turner, N. [1906] 1976. *A Grammar of New Testament Greek*. 5 vols. Edinburgh: T & T Clark.
MM	Moulton, J. H. & Milligan, G. M. 1926. *The Vocabulary of the Greek Testament: Illustrated from the Papyri and Other Non-literary Sources*. London: Hodder and Stoughton.
MT	Masoretic Text
NA28	Aland et al. (eds). 2012. *Nestle-Aland Novum Testamentum Graece*. 28th ed. Stuttgart: Deutsche Bibelgesellschaft.
NASB	New American Standard Bible
NEB	New English Bible
NIDNTTE	Silva, M. (ed.) 2014. *New International Dictionary of New Testament Theology and Exegesis*. 5 vols. Grand Rapids: Zondervan.
NIDOTTE	VanGemeren, W. A. (ed.) 1997. *New International Dictionary of Old Testament Theology & Exegesis*. 5 vols. Grand Rapids: Zondervan.
NIV 2011	The New International Version (2011)
NLT	New Living Translation
NT	The New Testament
NPNF	Scharff, P. (ed.) 1889. *A Select Library of the Nicene and Post-Nicene Fathers of the Christian Church*. Vol. XIII. New York: Christian Literature Company.

NRSV   The New Revised Standard Version
OT   The Old Testament
SEG   Supplement Epigraphicum Graecum (Leiden: Brill; et al., 1923–)
TDOT   Botterweck, G. J. & Ringgren, H. & Fabry, H. (eds.) 1977–2012. *Theological Dictionary of the Old Testament*. 15 vols. Translated and edited by J. T. Willis, G. W. Bromiley, D. E. Green, and D. W. Stott. Grand Rapids: Eerdmans.
TNDT   Kittel, G. & Friedrich, G. (eds.) 1964–1976. *Theological Dictionary of the New Testament*. 10 vols. Translated and edited by G. W. Bromiley. Grand Rapids: Eerdmans.

JOURNALS

AJT   *The American Journal of Theology*
ANRW   *Aufstieg und Niedergang der römischen Welt*
AThR   *Anglican Theological Review*
BASOR   *Bulletin of the American Schools of Oriental Research*
Bib   *Biblica*
BJRL   *Bulletin of the John Rylands University Library of Manchester*
BTB   *Biblical Theology Bulletin*
CBQ   *Catholic Biblical Quarterly*
CTJ   *Calvin Theological Journal*
CP   *Classical Philology*
ETL   *Ephemerides Theologicae Lovanienses*
EvQ   *Evangelical Quarterly*
ExpTim   *Expository Times*
HTR   *Harvard Theological Review*
HvTSt   *Hervormde Teologiese Studies*
JBL   *Journal of Biblical Literature*
JETS   *Journal of the Evangelical Theological Society*
JHS   *Journal of Hellenic Studies*
JR   *Journal of Religion*

JRS	*Journal of Roman Studies*
JSJ	*Journal for the Study of Judaism in the Persian, Hellenistic and Roman Period*
JSNT	*Journal for the Study of the New Testament*
LTQ	*Lexington Theological Quarterly*
Neot	*Neotestamentica*
NovT	*Novum Testamentum*
NTS	*New Testament Studies*
RevExp	*Review & Expositor*
RB	*Revue Biblique*
RTR	*Reformed Theological Review*
SBJT	*Southern Baptist Journal of Theology*
SBL	*Society of Biblical Literature*
TLZ	*Theologische Literaturzeitung*
TynBul	*Tyndale Bulletin*
ZAW	*Zeitschrift* für die alttestamentliche Wissenschaft
ZNW	*Zeitschrift* für die neutestamentliche Wissenschaft und die Kunde der älteren Kirche
ZPE	*Zeitschrift* für Papyrologie und Epigraphik

TRACING THE ARGUMENT

A	Alternative
Ac	Action
Bl	Bilateral
Cf	Comparison
Csv	Concessive
Exp	Explanation
G	Ground
Id	Idea
Mn	Manner

ABBREVIATIONS

P	Progression
Pur	Purpose
Res	Result
S	Series
T	Temporal
+	Positive
-	Negative
∴	Inference

1

Introduction

WITH THE EMERGENCE OF the early church, as Christian communities began to be differentiated from previous belief systems and values in the first-century Mediterranean world, the need arose to reconsider issues of "who we are" and "how we should live." As many gentiles became the followers of Jesus Christ by Paul's mission, his gospel preaching brought about a collapse (or at least a reinterpretation) of the boundaries between Jews and Greeks, slaves and free men, and male and female in those communities (1 Cor 12:13; Gal 3:28). People who came from diverse social, cultural, and religious settings now gathered as new faith communities in Christ. Particularly after the gentiles' conversion "from idols to the living and true God" (1 Thess 1:9), the communities of Christ followers were supposed to go through the unprecedented transition of redefining their social boundaries and acquiring a new sense of belonging together. Paul was responsible for illustrating to these newly established communities the nature of their newly gained identity as well as their changed social and religious position in the circumstances of the world around them.[1]

This study on the first letter to the Thessalonians—probably one of the earliest Pauline letters to a gentile community—invites contemporary readers to understand the initiatives underlying the shaping of the early Christian communities. Examining Paul's formative discourse in this letter holds particular potential in enabling us as twenty-first-century readers to

---

1. In reality, Paul never refers to the word that pertains to the modern concept of "identity." The term "identity" originated etymologically from the Latin adverb *identidem*, which means "over and over again, repeatedly." The roots of this word have gradually evolved to mean existing "side-by-side with those of 'likeness' and 'oneness'" (Owens & Samblanet 2013:227; cf. Oxford English Dictionary).

appreciate how he helped to mold the early Christian community's *identity* and *ethos*.[2]

In the process of Paul's formation of the community of believers, his major strategy was likely using the ancient story of Israel as a hermeneutical lens through which God's overarching vision of including gentile converts within the progressive story of redemption is emphasized (Hays 2005:148; see also Rosner 2013:164). The moral sphere of the new converts might be primarily defined by the "symbolic shape and texture" attributed to the prominent story of the covenant community of ancient Israel (Meeks 1993:32). Thus, Scripture seems to have played a (trans)formative role in the beliefs and lives of early Christian communities. Paul's use of important concepts from Scripture seems to have enabled ancient audiences, and continues to invite subsequent readers, to perceive their distinctive identity and ethos as Christ followers in the social world around them.[3]

1.1 MOTIVATION

This prospect is argued to be directly related to the dynamic ethical nature and purpose of Paul's letter. To consider some potential ways of resolving the moral crisis, it is meaningful to select and examine the first letter to the Thessalonians in this dissertation. Compared to other Pauline letters, 1 Thess includes extensive moral advice, which is aimed at encouraging and

---

2. The modern English words "ethos" and "ethics" have their etymological origin in the Greek term ἔθος. One should differentiate between ethos and ethics: "[E]thos refers to the standards of character and conduct people use in the living of the practical moral life, while . . . ethics is the critical, intellectual discipline in the service of the moral life" (Mouton 2002:44; cf. Birch & Rasmussen 1989:38). Admittedly, it is hard to identify the meaning of "ethics" in light of the usages of the term ἔθος in the NT, since this word never indicates "any particular pattern of conduct or any particular set of moral principles" as our modern understanding of it does (Furnish 1968:208). While this Greek word never occurs in the Pauline letters, a similar word, ἦθος (habit or custom), which is used in early classical Greek, appears once in 1 Cor 15:33. This term is already found in Aristotle's writing: "virtue of character (ētkos) is a result of habituation (ethos)" (Aristotle, *Eth. nic.* 2.1). For Aristotle, one cannot be persuaded to have good character through rational argument; rather, one's character is shaped by discipline and good habits (Meeks 1993:7). In the NT this word can be understood in two ways: "a usual or customary manner of behavior (habit or usage)" or a "long-established usage or practice common to a group (custom)" (BDAG, ἦθος).

3. According to Thompson (2011:44), the intrinsic relationship between the indicative ("is") and imperative ("ought to") can be rephrased in terms of the correlation between identity and ethos. While Meeks (1993:213; see also Mouton 2002:46) does not mention the term "identity" in dealing with Christian morality, the statement, "[m]aking morals and making community are one dialectical process," denotes that early Christian communities' identity awareness and moral formation could not be separated.

exhorting the Thessalonian believers to live in a way that will please God (1 Thess 4:1–2). As Meeks (1993:18) remarks, this letter "aims to reinforce a variety of things that Paul has taught the new Christians of Thessalonica about the behavior and the dispositions appropriate to people who have been 'chosen' and 'called' by God." Many commentators and scholars also notice the paraenetic features of the letter, particularly in 1 Thess 4–5. A common misinterpretation, however, has been that 1 Thess 1–3 merely serve as a theological basis for Paul's paraenesis in 1 Thess 4–5, making a sharp distinction between these two sections. As Beverly Gaventa (1998:48) argues, such a distinction may be ambiguous, since Paul's theological statements and ethical exhortations are indivisibly intertwined. First Thessalonians 1–3 implicitly exhort the audience to be examples for other Christian communities (1:6) and to demonstrate their love to one another (3:6, 12). Paul's moral exhortations in 1 Thess 4–5 also contain explanations of how their way of life was supposed to be in accordance with their new identity in Christ.

1.2 PROBLEM STATEMENT

The majority of scholars who have recently studied the generic nature of this letter, and the author's purpose in writing it, have done so in the light of Hellenistic rhetorical practices. For these rhetorical critics, deciding on rhetorical genre, style, and form was regarded as essential in identifying and understanding Paul's argumentation in his letters.[4] In the process of examining Paul's rhetorical strategies in 1 Thessalonians, particularly with reference to persuading them to adopt moral behavior, rhetorical critics focused on Paul's letters in light of Hellenistic rhetorical conventions and their relevance for his rhetorical argumentation (Long 2005:180). Recent scholars have increasingly engaged in identifying the particular genre of his letters in light of Hellenistic speech (e.g., judicial, deliberative or epideictic), and splitting the letter into rhetorical parts (e.g., *exordium, narratio, probatio* and *peroratio*).

---

4. *The Thessalonians Debate*, edited by Donfried and Beutler (2000), dealt with methodological considerations, which respectively investigated the pros and cons of epistolary and rhetorical approaches, as well as their compatibility. Wanamaker (2000:284, 286; cf. Watson 1997:426) critiques the view that "formal literary analysis is theoretically not interested in the purpose or meaning of the text but only in uncovering formal features." He suggests that rhetorical analysis can contribute to clarifying the function of each part within the whole letter as well as the author's intention and strategy. Nevertheless, many rhetorical critics have overlooked a benefit of epistolary approach that "at least attempt[s] to discover what a letter is mainly about and how a letter has been constructed according to its purpose" (Luckensmeyer 2009:9; cf. Green 2002:74).

However, questions remain about whether and how Hellenistic rhetorical categories can be an adequate hermeneutical lens for understanding 1 Thessalonians. Even if the importance of their contributions is acknowledged, to what extent has considering its rhetorical environment contributed to shedding light on Paul's argumentation? *What are the interpretative rewards of these scholars' attempts to read Paul in light of the ancient rhetorical environment?* Furthermore, what is the result of focusing on Paul's literary production in a Hellenistic context? Specifically, recent rhetorical critics seem merely to represent a single aspect, such as the formative influence of a specific literary and rhetorical milieu on the composition of Paul's letters. In my estimation, this approach has neglected appreciating the multifaceted nature of 1 Thessalonians and does not (adequately) account for *historical*, *textual*, and *discursive* (or *rhetorical*) aspects of the text.

1.2.1 APPROPRIATING HELLENISTIC RHETORICAL CONVENTIONS IN READING PAUL'S LETTERS

One might raise the question of whether Paul himself consciously adopted a "rhetorical arrangement" composed of *exordium, narratio, partitio, transitus, probatio* (Reed 1993:304–8). Some scholars raise the issue of whether adopting Hellenistic rhetorical conventions can be regarded as a feasible approach towards identifying Paul's writing purpose and his argumentation.[5] Green (2002:71) raises a similar concern:

> Did Paul and his associates really have these rhetorical categories in mind when they composed the letters? Is this a 'good fit,' or one that is forced upon the letter? But beyond this concern we must ask if it is legitimate to analyze the *letters* of the New Testament using the categories of *oral rhetorical discourse*.

Even if there are similarities between 1 Thessalonians and Hellenistic rhetorical categories, one should take into consideration the point that "the social setting of the Pauline letter is not the same as the social setting envisioned for any of the standard forms of rhetorical address discussed in the ancient handbooks of rhetoric" (Martin 1995:36). Even ancient rhetoricians hardly appropriated rhetorical techniques in their letter writing (e.g., Cicero, *Fam.* 9.21.1). Epistolary theory, which presumes that letter writing

---

5. Reed (1997:13) remarks that defining the genre and style of Paul's letter in light of Hellenistic rhetorical practice is controversial. Dealing with Paul's letters as speeches *only* characterized by the conventions of rhetorical handbooks is untenable, since in terms of structure the nature of rhetoric does not exactly correspond to the epistolary form (Classen 1993:286).

implies the use of rhetorical effects "in the same manner as a dialogue" recently attracted the attention of some scholars (Malherbe 1988:2). However, even though one might concur that rhetoric in a letter is not abnormal, "[i]t is probably mistaken to suppose that the New Testament epistles are essentially speeches in literary form and so justify the application of rhetoric based on the oracular nature of their form" (Bird 2008:376). Applying formal Hellenistic rhetorical categories to analyzing the Pauline letters might therefore be controversial (Porter 1993b:115–6; cf. Stamps 1995:144–5; 1997:233; Green 2002:72; Weima 1997b:463). Porter (1997:251–2; cf. Classen 1993:269–70; Reed 1993:294–6) also finds sparse evidence that letters were regarded as "a part of rhetoric," pointing out that applying rhetorical handbooks and other ancient sources to letters is the error of *anachronism*:

> Even though rhetorical features are found in other ancient writings besides speeches (e.g., Longinus and Dionysius of Halicarnassus), so far as I know letters—primarily because of their sub-literary status (literary letters are excluded from this)—were never analysed or examined in this way by the ancients or considered to be part of rhetoric or of the body of rhetorically influenced literature.

For rhetorical critics, further identifying how an author selected ancient rhetorical forms was a significant means of appreciating the rhetorical function of each unit in a letter. By making a connection between "a text" and "the art of ancient rhetoric," their construction of the rhetorical situation could be confined to a certain interpretive purpose based on correspondence between the text and the art of classical rhetoric (Stamps 1993:198).

Moreover, as Reed (1993:308) points out, although there is a parallel between each epistolary unit (opening, body, and closing) and the rhetorical arrangement, their similarities are not formal but functional. In addition, in each epistolary section it is possible to contain various possibilities for communicating meaning. The Hellenistic rhetorical arrangement might provide a single framework for reading Paul's letters (Reed 1993:307). Admittedly, understanding Paul's writing as having an oratorical nature enables epistolary analysis to maintain coherency. Moreover, it can help us conceptualize the function of the author's *ethos* and *pathos* as well as the audience's response to the development of the author's argumentation (Krentz 2000:310–1). Nevertheless, structural analysis based on Hellenistic rhetoric can be inclined to focus on the specific techniques of the speaker's persuasion and argumentation. One must ask questions about the reasons for using a particular rhetorical model to understand how the art of persuasion and the effect of the author's discourse work. Specifically, why do scholars of rhetorical criticism confine their studies to Aristotelian rhetoric or to other related rhetorical models? For this reason Porter (1993b:107) suggests extending the limited range of "rhetoric" into universal categorization:

> One need not confine oneself to any particular model, because the claim being made is that rhetoric is a universal category, one not necessarily confined to the specific set of techniques that developed in the Graeco-Roman world . . . It may be true that the ancient Greek rhetoricians conceptualized and elucidated their theories more clearly than any other cultural expression of the categories of rhetoric; it simply does not follow that analysis must follow the patterns established by them.

To this end, it could be proposed that establishing the author's argumentation should be based more on linguistic factors than confining and designating each unit to serve a particular rhetorical format.

1.2.2 LIMITATIONS OF UTILISING RHETORICAL CRITICISM?

Based on the above observation, I wish to point out some limitations of reading Paul's discourse in the first letter to the Thessalonians merely through the lens of Hellenistic literary and rhetorical conventions.

First, recent rhetorical critics seem to constrain Paul's argumentation to particular rhetorical characteristics and conventions when deriving interpretive conclusions. I wish to argue in this study that, in order to appreciate Paul's argumentation, a broader text-oriented analysis is primarily required to establish the correlation between smaller units and the larger discourse. This may enable one to investigate "the overall communicative function(s) of the text" (Johanson 1987:6). I contend that, if one fails to notice how the interrelation of each literary unit forges a coherent narrative, the deep reasoning of Paul's discourse cannot be established in its own right. Through analysis of Paul's discourse, I hope to demonstrate how Paul was informed by the social, cultural, religious environments of the Thessalonian believers. Moreover, analysis of the text may enable one to get a grasp how the apostle responded to their situation by introducing a new perspective to resolve the issue.

Second, rhetorical critics seem to adhere strongly to the presupposition that Paul's moral exhortation was configured in the Hellenistic environment, which is the Thessalonian audience's familiar sociocultural context regarding moral persuasion. In my view, this trend led many scholars to overlook the formative role of Paul's Jewish tradition and his own conceptual world in his constitution of the early Christian communities' identity and ethos.

Hence, many scholars have underestimated (the implied rhetorical effect of) Paul's moral exhortations within their larger Jewish canonical context despite the texts' dialogue with the Hebrew Scriptures. They have missed taking Paul's dominant historical context, i.e., his Jewishness, into consideration as an essential hermeneutical point in his discourse.[6] Overemphasizing one specific aspect of Paul's cultural context could be detrimental to another aspect. Rhetorical critics' concentration only on Hellenistic Paul does not necessarily allow a modern audience to reinterpret the full scope of the text in an analogous way. I thus believe that Paul's Jewishness should be included in the discussion of his discourse in 1 Thessalonians (cf. Hays 1996:306–7; Furnish 1968:34). In my view, Paul's broad sociocultural context should be taken into account to appreciate his transformative discourse among the newly established Christian community in Thessalonica.

Third, another challenge that rhetorical criticism has confronted us with is its methodological limitations in appropriating a text (such as 1 Thessalonians) in new circumstances. Recent rhetorical studies on 1 Thessalonians have focused very much on the production of the letter in the light of its Hellenistic background. Inasmuch as the interest of these commentators is to investigate the formative process of Paul's letters, from the methodological perspective there has been little consideration of how the interpretive outcome would affect the Christian community of today. So these interpretation strategies might run the risk of not being capable of resolving modern Christian ethical issues. In this regard, Smit (1990:16–28) notices significant agreement in recent biblical scholarship on the need for re-appropriating Scripture today. He insists that modern readers of the Bible are responsible for interpreting these texts within the broader context of a contemporary life-centered human praxis. For Smit, scholars should acknowledge their public accountability in the sociopolitical milieu. In addition, Wuellner (1987:449) argues that, whether pertaining to classical or new rhetoric, the purview of rhetorical criticism must go beyond the

6. My earlier encounter with biblical exegesis at Wheaton College Graduate School helped me to explore OT echoes, allusions and quotations in the NT. As I struggled to understand the continuity and discontinuity between the OT and the NT (e.g., Paul's understanding of Mosaic Law), on the one hand, Daniel Block's exegesis class on the book of Deuteronomy led me to read Deuteronomy with its immediate context in mind, rather than moving too quickly to read it in light of the NT. On the other hand, Douglas Moo's exegesis class on Romans helped me to understand OT echoes, allusions and quotations in Romans from the perspective of Christ's fulfillment of the law (1 Cor 9:21; Gal 6:2; Rom 10:4). At that time, the opportunity to write an exegetical paper on Romans 10:5–8 (Paul's reinterpretation of Deut 30:12–14) led me to pay more attention to the functioning of the Hebrew Scriptures in the Pauline letters; especially in asking, "How did a Pharisee who lived in a Hellenistic Jewish milieu integrate the OT into his thoughts and writings in his Gentile mission?"

perspective that language merely reflects a certain reality. The approach is expected to be a "dynamic process" overcoming the previous ethos of rhetorical criticism as merely focusing on style and form, i.e., "figures of speech" (Wuellner 1987:462–3). Quoting Perelman and Olbrechts-Tyteca (1969:513), Wuellner (1987:449) envisages the task of responsible rhetorical critics as also appreciating "the social aspect of language,[7] which is an instrument of communication and *influence on others*" (italics mine).

1.2.3 RESEARCH QUESTIONS

Thus, by exploring (aspects of) the above-mentioned issues, the study attempts to respond to the following major research questions:

- If the multifacetedness of 1 Thessalonians has been neglected in (recent) scholarship, can the discursive thrust of the letter and the urgent need that it addresses, be identified more satisfactorily through careful discourse analysis?
- If yes, is it possible to determine how Paul's discourse in 1 Thessalonians (on the identity and ethos of early Christian communities) was influenced by his conceptual (Hellenistic and Jewish) world?
- Once these questions have been attended to, the study wishes to explore Paul's response to these influences as reflected by dynamic processes of re-interpretation in 1 Thessalonians, particularly in 1:1—2:12 and chapters 4–5.
- The project is particularly interested in the functioning of probable echoes from the Hebrew Scriptures in Paul's response to the situation of (so-called gentile) Christian communities in first century Thessalonica.
- The study concludes by transitioning from the examination of 1 Thessalonians to the exploration of the insights that Christian communities today can derive from the letter within present-day (moral) contexts.

---

7. Porter (2015:142) argues that the sociolinguistic aspect of discourse in New Testament studies has been ignored: "Texts, as we know, are written by authors to readers. These authors and readers occupy particular sociological space, and hence in their writing and reading they are sensitive to social groups and social contexts. This is an element of discourse analysis that has not been given the kind of attention that it deserves." The rhetorical critics' focus on the literary and rhetorical environment of the Hellenistic world played a crucial role in clarifying Paul's argumentation in his letters. Nobody can refute that it is surely a valid point that Paul's letter should be viewed in the light of his contemporaries' modes of communication. But based on Porter's remark, it seems that in accessing to rhetorical nature of Paul's document, the social and cultural aspects of Paul's discourse have been less emphasized.

1.3 HYPOTHESIS

This study intends to address particular limitations in recent studies of 1 Thessalonians by drawing attention to the way that Paul's foundational (Jewish) conceptual and narrative world influenced his identity- and ethos-building discourse among early (mainly gentile) Christian communities. The focus of the study is not simply to explore *what* scriptural echoes or themes Paul used. Instead, it wishes to go beyond a thematic approach by dealing with Paul's discourse as a multilayered communicative act between him and the Thessalonians. This entails investigating (a) *how* a particular or anticipated exigency inspired Paul to adopt scriptural echoes, and (b) *how* these notions function in the dynamic process of persuasion. Specifically, in order to account for the multi-faceted nature and purpose of the letter, the study explores the following aspects:

- The *formative* influence of social, cultural and religious occasions (from the perspective of both Paul and the Thessalonians) in Paul's discursive strategy;
- The *informative* (linguistic) elements in the text;
- The *(trans)formative* force of Paul's discourse in reorienting the audience's perspective and self-identity to the gospel of Jesus Christ;

In order to enable proper understanding of the rich yet complex levels of Paul's discourse in 1 Thessalonians, the study investigates the ways in which Paul's scriptural world constituted these discursive layers. It therefore deals with the way that Paul's discourse functions with respect to identity building and moral formation in the Thessalonian believers' community. In the process, four main hypotheses were explored.

First, while the importance of rhetorical aspects and the implied effect of Paul's language cannot be denied, a broader definition of the notion of "rhetoric as the art of persuasion" is required. I do not wish to underestimate the contribution of rhetorical criticism to reading 1 Thessalonians. Rather, in order to develop such a broader definition of rhetoric, I suggest that "discourse" and "discursive" be utilized in the study rather than "rhetoric" or "rhetorical." I choose the former word pair to avoid confining Paul's argumentation to a Hellenistic rhetorical environment.[8] This is because, in my view, the development of Paul argumentation probably relied on his

---

8. Schreiner ([1990] 2008:35) admits the usefulness of applying Greek rhetorical schemas to Pauline letters, but warns against overemphasizing this aspect. He points out that without careful investigation of the text, identifying the basic genre does not guarantee comprehension of Paul's argumentation in each letter.

capacity to freely appropriate imagery from various social, cultural, and religious contexts for his discursive purpose.

Second, I explore Paul's Jewishness as a significant hermeneutical presupposition with regard to clarifying his argumentation in 1 Thessalonians (Watson [2004] 2016:1). Yet it has been a controversial issue as to what kind of Jew Paul was in the context of Hellenistic Judaism. Rather than determining Paul's ability to adapt to the Hellenistic sociocultural environment, I constructed Paul's conceptual map by comparing his thought and ideological background to that of his contemporary diaspora Jews. I also explored the possibility of Paul's utilization of concepts from the Hebrew Scriptures in his argumentation.

Third, I contend that 1 Thessalonians can be characterized as apocalyptic discourse. Its major strategy is to comfort the Thessalonian believers who faced conflict with their fellow citizens. As a result of their conversion, the conflict might have occurred between the Thessalonian believers and their neighbors. Consequently, such social harassment would inevitably have caused suffering to the new converts (Weima 1997a:90; Barclay 1993:514). Subsequent sociocultural and religious pressures might have urged Paul to assert their self-recognition as God's eschatological people within an apocalyptic scenario. The conflict between Thessalonian believers and their fellow citizens might have been the most probable occasion (exigency) for Paul's employing the language of apocalyptic discourse. In connecting a plausible historical context to Paul's apocalyptic language, "apocalyptic symbols and social dislocation continually maintain and reinforce each other in a complex dialectic" (Barclay 1993:519). In order to resolve the Thessalonian believers' frustration and struggling with this affliction, Paul seems to have deliberately reconfigured Israel's Scripture and apocalyptic expectations. Particularly, Paul's echoing of Scripture seems to play a major role in affirming the community's identity and reinforcing their belief, self-understanding as the people of God, communal solidarity and eschatological hope in the midst of persecution and suffering.[9] In order to

---

9. In terms of appreciating intertextuality in Pauline letters, there are different literary modes of reference to OT texts: echoes, allusions, and quotations. Particularly, "echo" and "allusion" are distinctions based on the degree of explicitness of intertextual references. While the notion of allusion is presupposed by authorial intention and an identifiable source, Beetham (2008:24) defines scriptural echo as a "subtle, literary mode of reference that is not intended for public recognition yet derives from a specific predecessor. An author's wording may echo the precursor consciously or unconsciously and/or contextually or non-contextually." In fact, in the case that the volume of the echo is subliminal, it would be hard to determine the legitimacy of the intertextual reference. The seven criteria suggested by Richard Hays are therefore helpful to identify "the presence and meaning of scriptural echoes in Paul": (1) *Availability* to the author and/

present this argument, the possibility that the audience was familiar with the Hebrew Scriptures needs to be substantiated. It seems probable that the Thessalonian church in Paul's time consisted predominantly of gentiles. Although there is a possibility that a Jewish population lived in Thessalonica, the letter does not tell us as to whether Jews were included in the community of Jesus followers. Nevertheless, the chances seem to be good that the audience was familiar with these Scriptures in light of Luke's report on Paul's regular teaching τῶν γραφῶν in the synagogue (Acts 17:2).

Fourth, I will further take into consideration the (trans)formative power of Paul's identity and ethos-building discourse in this letter within present-day contexts.

1.3.1 RECONSIDERING THE TERM "RHETORIC"

It is suggested that interpreters use the first-century Hellenistic rhetorical framework carefully and in a limited way because, as Krentz (2000:318) points out, "we do not press New Testament texts into categories not designed for them, nor act as though Paul does not write Greek as one at home in the culture of the early Roman Empire." In this regard, I wish to propose that Paul's letters do not display a "formal" rhetoric, but a "functional" rhetoric (Bird 2008:379; Reed 1993:308). In other words, it is important to understand how each unit of a letter functions as a particular rhetorical device in order to reveal how the author's argumentation flows throughout the letter. It is not necessary to compare the form of Paul's letters to the conventions of Hellenistic rhetoric here. As Weima (1997b:462) remarks, Paul employs "rhetoric as the art of persuasion" inasmuch as he uses "a variety of literary or so-called rhetorical devices that are universally practised in the everyday use of language." Lategan (1993:397) also understands the term "rhetoric" in a broader sense:

> There is no need to impose a rhetorical framework, which was originally designed for speech, on letters by categorizing them as 'speech at a distance' or 'deferred speech'. The specific nature of epistolography should rather be respected for what it is. Written communication with its accompanying feature of the presence/absence of the writer and reader has its own mysteries

or original readers; (2) *volume* determined by the degree of explicitness in repeating words or phrases; (3) *recurrence* of citation or allusion to the same scriptural passage; (4) *thematic coherence* in the same letter of the Pauline corpus; (5) *historical plausibility* that Paul's audience understood; (6) *history of interpretation* that attests other readers' hearing of the same scriptural echoes; (7) *satisfaction* of intertextual connection between texts (Hays 1989:29–32).

and fascination and should be studied in its own right . . . This provides all the scope for rhetorical analysis of letters in the broader sense of the word.

Scholars have found it difficult, from the perspective of ongoing debates, to establish the compatibility of (ancient and new) rhetorical and epistolary approaches to the genre and form of 1 Thessalonians. I do not intend to discuss the methodological compatibility of these approaches here. Rather, bearing the advantages of both in mind, I will concentrate on the implied persuasive and transformative force in Paul's letters, with specific attention to the means by which he motivates a particular audience in a particular context (cf. Mouton 1996: 281).

In rethinking Paul's letters from a "literary-rhetorical perspective," Stamps (1993:200) notices that the nature of letters is characterized by *discourse*: a communicative act between sender and receivers. By providing some (historically informed) knowledge and insight, an author attempts to persuade the audience to take certain actions and to maintain an affinity with him. Stamps' argument is supported by Norman Petersen's view that Paul's narrative world structures and plots his letter writing (Stamps 1993:201; cf. Petersen 1985:15). Indispensable elements in narrative, according to Petersen, are events and points of view (temporal and spatial). They are all recognized as playing a role in clarifying "the entextualised literary-rhetorical situation" (Stamps 1993:202; cf. Petersen 1985:11–13):

- "[T]he actions/events/situations which particularize the relationship between the letter parties embedded in the letter text."
- "The elements of plot and point of view . . . [that] enable these kernel statements about the situation to be listed or plotted chronologically from the temporal perspective of the time of writing."

According to Stamps (1993:203), comparing the textual and chronological sequence associated with those narrative components helps interpreters to recognize "how the plot of the story of the relationship between the letter parties assists the letter's message or informational intent and reinforces the statement of the letter's purpose." In this sense, it is important to establish a primary storyline of the communication between Paul and his audience by tentatively constructing discursive exigencies in first-century Thessalonica. In 1 Thessalonians the entextualized discursive (rhetorical) situation can hopefully be elucidated by exploring how the discursive (rhetorical) situation was established by provisionally constructing the historical situation.

1.3.2 PAUL AS ANOMALOUS DIASPORA JEW

Adolf von Harnack ([1901] 1904:179) asserts in his book *What is Christianity?* that "Paul's rabbinical theology led him to corrupt the Christian religion ... It was Paul who delivered the Christian religion from Judaism ... It was he who confidently regarded the Gospel as a new force abolishing the religions of the Law." These notions have contributed to an anti-Jewish atmosphere of scholarship in the field of Pauline studies and led many scholars to address the question of Paul's Jewishness. Recently scholars have recognized the environment of Paul's ministry as a largely Hellenistic world, assuming thereby that he was mainly influenced by Hellenistic philosophy (e.g., Stoicism and the popular Hellenistic philosophers), as well as religious cults. In addition, many scholars have concentrated on how studying the Hellenistic rhetorical environment may contribute towards understanding Paul's rhetoric with regard to the community's moral transformation. These scholars postulate that since Paul spent his early childhood in the city of Tarsus—a center of Hellenistic culture—he was a fluent Greek speaker and equipped with a high level of rhetorical expertise (Malherbe 1970, [1977] 1983, 1983, 1985, 1986, 1987, 1988, 1992, 2000; Roetzel 1999:11–14; Schnelle 2005:75–81).

In reality it is impossible to reduce the complexity of Paul's thought to a mere confrontation between two major sociocultural worlds, namely Hellenism and Judaism. An enquiry into Paul's Jewishness can therefore not be answered reductively, since one must raise the question of what kind of Jew Paul was in the context of first-century Hellenistic Judaism. Scholars' portrayals of Paul's Jewishness are varied, mainly categorizing him as a member of groups such as transformed Jews, faithful Jews and radically Hellenized Jews (Bird 2016:12–25). In this study I follow John Barclay's view that Paul may be regarded as "an anomalous Diaspora Jew." Barclay (1995:90) understands that Paul grew up in a Jewish diaspora family and that his (new) theological views were shaped in the geographical and social milieu of his mission fields for the gentiles. Scholars agree that Paul was probably a Hellenized Jew to the same degree that his contemporaries would be. Hellenization in Paul's time represented a wide and complex blend or spectrum of social, cultural, and geographical influences and interactions in the Mediterranean world. Hellenization of the Jews, in particular, has to be understood in a nuanced way. Barclay (1995:93–97) proposes that Paul's conceptual world be explored in the light of (1) the degree of his social integration into the Hellenistic world ("assimilation"), (2) the degree of his cultural exposure, especially to the educational environment ("acculturation"), and (3) the degree to which his susceptibility of acculturation shaped his stance towards a Jewish heritage ("accommodation") (see 2.2; 2.3).

1.3.3 FIRST THESSALONIANS AS IDENTITY- AND ETHOS-BUILDING DISCOURSE

This study suggests that the first letter to the Thessalonians was deliberately designed within an apocalyptic eschatological framework—*not only to affirm the Thessalonian community's new identity but also to encourage their holiness in the midst of a religiously pluralistic society* (see 3.2.2; 3.2.3). I hypothesize that the following elements seem to encourage interpreters to read the letter within the frame of reference of apocalyptic discourse.[10] First, apocalyptic eschatology cannot be confined to apocalypses *per se*,[11] but rather reflects the belief of God's future intervention, reversal of the present world's absurdity, judgment over the wicked, and vindication of God's chosen people at the eschaton (Hanson [1992] 2008:280–1).[12] Specifically, I

---

10. Carey (1999:4–5; cf. Murphy 2012:8–14; Gupta 2016:94–95) lists ten characteristics of apocalyptic literature that could at least be considered as requirements for apocalyptic discourse: (1) "The narration of *visions* and/or audition sent by God to the visionary;" (2) "*Heavenly intermediaries*, usually angels, interpret these visions and auditions;" (3) "Intense *symbolism*, reflecting earlier traditions and archaic cultural myths, often populates the visions;" (4) "Most formal apocalypses—including all of the Jewish ones—are *pseudonymous*;" (5) "An urgent expectation of the imminent end of this world age and the inauguration of a *new aeon*;" (6) "The imminent eschaton is preceded by *cosmic catastrophes*;" (7) "Many apocalyptic texts imply various levels of dualism, whether of people (the righteous versus the wicked), cosmic powers (God versus Satan), or time periods (this age versus the age to come);" (8) "Such a dualistic perspective implies a measure of *determinism*;" (9) "*Ex eventu prophecy* ... results from the combination of pseudonymity with determinism;" (10) "*Cosmic or astronomical speculation* marks many apocalyptic texts." Although not all of these categories are applicable to our reading of 1 Thessalonians, this study will explore which of them may be identified in the first letter to Thessalonians.

11. According to Hanson (1976:29; cf. ABD 1:280–1), "Apocalyptic eschatology is neither a genre, nor a socioreligious movement, nor a system of thought, but rather a religious perspective [on Israel], a way of viewing divine plans in relation to mundane realities."

12. Some scholars argue that, because of the absence of Jewish apocalyptic notions in 1 Thess, Paul was likely to have shared Hellenistic philosophical traditions of eschatology with them (Cancik 2000:84–85; Ascough 2004:526–7; e.g., Lucretius, *De rerum natura*. 2.1150–2). However, many scholars agree that apocalyptic eschatology mainly originated from the prophets' eschatological tradition in the Hebrew Scriptures. Admittedly, one should not avoid considering the ancient Near Eastern and Mesopotamian (external) influences on the formation of a Jewish apocalyptic genre in both pre-exilic and post-exilic periods (Murphy 2012:15–19). But at least the prophetic and wisdom traditions are an important (internal) feature of Jewish apocalypse (Murphy 2012:19–21). Hanson (ABD 1:281) views prophetic eschatology and apocalyptic eschatology are inextricably

postulate that the apocalyptic perspective reflects the author's interpretation of an actual situation. It can be taken for granted that the Thessalonian converts were confronted with threats by their neighbors. In this circumstance Paul could have viewed the conflict as an apocalyptic phenomenon of the end time. As Barclay (1993:516) has suggested, "Paul had provided them with an apocalyptic perspective which correlated well with the social alienation they experienced." Second, at least apocalyptic dualism between two ages ("this age" and "the age to come") and between God's chosen people and those who cannot escape from God's wrath seems to provide a relevant hermeneutical framework for interpreting the letter. Through appropriating apocalyptic dualism, Paul appears to raise the issue of who belongs to God and who does not. Intensive use of identity markers implies a division between insider and outsider groups (1 Thess 1:4, 6, 9; 2:7–12, 19; 5:5).

In the process of establishing Paul's larger discourse, considering the religious and political contexts of first-century Thessalonica will hopefully enable a nuanced appreciation of the dynamic relationship between the text and the (historical) circumstances of its audience. Specifically, I posit that the Thessalonian believers lived in a religiously pluralistic environment, in which the imperial cult and worship of local gods were crucial to social and religious life. In this milieu, the Thessalonians' conversion from worshiping idols to God and placing their faith in Christ might have caused social conflict or alienation from their neighboring non-believers.

First, it is well known that the city of Thessalonica rendered patronage services to Rome, as a part of the imperial cult. The Christian community's faith in and loyalty to another king, Jesus, would therefore necessarily endanger them. The Thessalonians served the Roman benefactor (i.e., the emperor) as the object of religious devotion or honor (Donfried 2002:36; Green 2002:41–42). According to Weima (2002a:407), the imperial cult had two significant functions: (1) to "ensure the ongoing favor of the current Roman emperor by visibly demonstrating the city's allegiance to his leadership";

---

intertwined: "Periods and conditions permitting members of the protagonist community to sense that human effort would be repaid by improved fortune tended to foster prophetic eschatology, that is, the view that God's new order would unfold within the realities of this world. Periods of extreme suffering, whether at the hands of opponents within the community or those of foreign adversaries, tended to cast doubts on the effectiveness of human reform and thus to abet apocalyptic eschatology, with its more rigidly dualistic view of divine deliverance, entailing destruction of this world and resurrection of the faithful to a blessed heavenly existence." Even though Paul never produced any document in the apocalyptic genre, his perspective might be framed by Jewish apocalyptic thinking. (De Boer 2000:357–66). In my view, *parousia* in 1 Thessalonians, is depicted as a key 'apocalyptic eschatological' event for the Thessalonians by which at the eschaton, the cosmic power opposed to God would be defeated, his people would be vindicated, and finally, divine sovereignty over the world would be revealed.

(2) to "sustain Roman rule over the local populace by stressing the divine nature of the emperors as well as the benefits the city enjoyed under their rule." In Acts 17:5–7 the reason for the Thessalonian citizens' accusation of the believers is related to this political and religious milieu.[13] In this account Luke wrote that certain Jews and a mob of wicked people accused Jason and some of the other brothers before the city officials (πολιτάρχας). They might have been accused of violating "Caesar's decree" because of their faith in another king, Jesus.

Second, recently excavated archaeological resources may indicate that participation in religious dedications to the gods was an essential part of the Thessalonians' social life (Weima 2014:9–23). In fact, Paul did not describe any concrete practices of the cult of local gods in his letter, except for the implication in 1 Thess 1:9 ("you turned to God from idols to serve the living and true God"). Nevertheless, recent studies have demonstrated that there was an inseparable relationship between the religious life in Thessalonica and the local cults of Dionysus, Egyptian deities, and Cabirus. These findings may help to elucidate the nature of the Thessalonian converts' suffering as well as the conflict with their fellow citizens (see 3.2.3.4).

Once the discursive (rhetorical) situation of the text has been established, Paul's strategy for resolving this urgent situation will be investigated. I hypothesize that Paul's echoing Scripture functioned in his mind to affirm the audience's awareness of their identity and moral character in the midst of a plurality of religious/political loyalties and suffering/alienation of various kinds (cf. Mouton 2002:90). My hypothesis is that the faith and mindset of early Christian communities were shaped as their exposure to significant Old Testament narratives, concepts, and echoes (cf. Mouton 1997:248). Based on Luke's report in Acts 17:1–2, I assume that Paul's use of Scripture is conscious and deliberate, and presented with the expectation that his audience would recognize its significance. For Paul, Scripture played a discursive role in distinguishing the new converts from their surrounding

---

13. The majority of scholars are careful to use the book of Acts as a significant resource for constructing the background of 1 Thessalonians (Donfried 2002:72; Malherbe 2000:57–62; Wanamaker 1990:6–8). It has been refuted that the composition of Luke's account purports to be accurate historical facts (Haenchen 1971:109–110; Conzelmann [1963] 1987:xxxvi–xl). In reality, ancient historiography was used to focus on propagating a certain notion or value. So scholars tend to view Luke's narration of some historical facts in a loose sense, regarding him primarily as a theologian (e.g., Dibelius, Conzelmann, Haenchen, and Bultmann). However, in dealing with Luke's account of Paul's personal background, I think that even though Luke's main goal is not to present Paul's biography in detail, he plausibly reflects actual information in describing the apostle Paul's life/thought and the Thessalonians' circumstances (Bruce 1976:285–98; Marshall 1980:43). For this reason, I argue that Luke's report could be at least a significant extant source for establishing the rhetorical situation in first-century Thessalonica.

world, confirming their identity as God's people within the eschatological context. By utilizing Scripture, Paul fostered a sense of solidarity, bringing himself and his audience together as part of God's extended family. As a united community, they shared in the privilege of Christ's ultimate fulfillment of the covenant.

1.3.4 MEANING OF PAUL'S DISCOURSE FOR TODAY

In exploring 1 Thessalonians the study will engage the following question: *How can this New Testament document assist a modern audience towards making ethical (social) decisions?* In other words, how can subsequent readers make the journey from their existential socio-ethical challenges to those biblical texts, and from the dynamics of those texts back to the here and now via the many layers of interpretation through centuries? Unfortunately, recent biblical scholarship has fallen short of appropriating Paul's ethical discourse to address today's ethical dilemmas (cf. Gustafson 1984:151). As Mouton (2002:172) points out, after the Enlightenment, Christian ethics and biblical studies have been treated as separate academic disciplines instead of being viewed as inextricably intertwined. Certainly, this issue remains hermeneutically significant as long as the Bible is regarded as authoritative for the lives of Christian communities.

1.4 METHODOLOGY

As I have argued, current rhetorical approaches to 1 Thessalonians are inclined to focus on specific techniques of the speaker's persuasion and argumentation in light of the first-century Hellenistic literary and rhetorical environment. I raise the question as to why one particular rhetorical model rather than another has gained credibility in determining the art of persuasion and the effect of the author's discourse (cf. Porter 1993b:107; 1997:253–5). In view of the limitations of this approach, as argued above, I wish to suggest discourse analysis as an alternative useful tool for discerning Paul's argumentation throughout 1 Thessalonians. In fact, discourse analysis as New Testament hermeneutics is an undeveloped field as yet and there is no agreed definition of what the approach entails (Wallace 1996:xv; Porter 2015:133). Nevertheless, this approach may enable interpreters to appreciate the author's communication act by considering connections between the role of speaker/author, recipients/audience and the text itself. In doing so, this approach presupposes the dynamic interrelatedness of syntactics, semantics, and pragmatics to derive a larger discourse as a coherent piece of communication (Reed 1996:231, 232, 234, 236; cf. Porter 1997:254). Going beyond the rules of ancient rhetoric's designation of each literary unit, this approach helps interpreters to explore "the history behind the text, the world of the text, or the reading community in front of the text" (Green 1995:175). I motivate this hypothesis by describing the unique characteristics and contribution of discourse analysis.

1.4.1 UTILIZING DISCOURSE ANALYSIS

As pointed out (see 1.2.1), the discussion based on appealing exclusively to rhetorical analysis may have fallen into the error of producing a one-sided understanding of Paul's composition of 1 Thessalonians. As Beale (2003:24–25) notes, the rhetorical approach has discerned the cultural context of Paul's persuasive techniques solely from Hellenistic rhetorical conventions. To overcome such an interpretative limitation, Beale suggests utilizing discourse analysis to gain fuller access to this letter. For him, an advantage of utilizing discourse analysis is that interpreters could identify the author's major argumentation "through a logical analysis of the development of the propositions in each unit and then tracing the logical development of the themes from paragraph to paragraph and attempting to discover the main point of the entire epistle."[14] Just as Beale's methodological consideration indicates, in most cases, discourse analysis in biblical studies has been identified with a linguistic analysis of written texts.[15] Certainly, it is essential to explore how written texts are linguistically structured and what their original meaning could have been.

A structural analysis will, therefore, form an essential part of my reading of 1 Thessalonians. Yet, it may be methodologically too narrow to confine the nature of discourse analysis to examining linguistic elements in the text (cf. Reed 1997:18). As Joel Green (1995:176; cf. Osborne 2006:150) points out, the process of New Testament interpretation requires readers to consider "the broader contexts and sets of relationships in which communication must be understood." He suggests three levels of relationships

---

14. There are few recent publications that deal with a discourse analysis of 1 Thessalonians (see Johanson 1987; Sterner 1998). This study does not provide all the details of the textual analysis but will demonstrate how the author's argumentation is developed by tracing given texts.

15. Recently, NT scholars have treated text linguistics and discourse analysis as the same enterprise (cf. De Beaugrande 1981:26, cited in Reed 1997:18). Guthrie's definition reflects this trend: "a process of investigation by which one examines the form and function of all the parts and levels of a written discourse, with the aim of better understanding both the parts and the whole of that discourse" (2001:255).

in utilizing discourse analysis: (1) "discourse within the narrative itself"; (2) discourse between the speaker/author and original recipient/audience; (3) discourse between the original text and subsequent readers. "Discourse" has to be understood as a collective term for broader, complex systems and structures, often of competing social practices. This has in fact been emphasized in recent research on the term "discourse." Accordingly, discourse is formulated within a social and cultural context—an immediate situation in which the audience is involved. A speaker uses language that reflects his or her unique conceptual world or perspective and deliberately designs discourse in order to bring about a desired effect. Discourse analysis will, therefore, be utilized in this study while being mindful of the inseparable relation between a written text and its social embeddedness. Exploring a biblical author's discourse through such a multi-dimensional approach is meant to enable later audiences/readers to appreciate an ancient speaker/author's message within a specific social context.

A significant contributor to the theory of discourse analysis, Jeffrey Reed, recently made remarkable progress in laying the foundations for implementing its major principles. In his work Reed (1997:24-33) elaborates four core aspects of modern discourse analysis to be taken into account in reading New Testament documents. These features, discussed below, will be crucial for this study.

According to Reed (1997:25), discourse analysis firstly examines the roles of speaker/author and audience in producing and consuming the communicative act (cf. Green 1995:178-9). Green (1997:26) explains how both parties are involved in the creation of a discourse. On the one hand, the speaker/author formulates the textual output responsibly. Indeed, production of texts reflects the author's/speaker's particular sociocultural context and ideological background. On the other hand, analyzing discourse entails an interpretation of the audience's understanding of the speaker/author's discourse and their own (putative) response to it. Reed (1997:27, quoting Brown and Yule, 1983:24) confirms that the audience also partially contributes to determining the nature of the discourse:

> We shall consider word, phrase, and sentences which appear in the textual record of a discourse to be evidence of an attempt by a producer (speaker/writer) to communicate his [or her] message to a recipient (hearer/reader). We shall be particularly interested in discussion how a recipient might come to comprehend the producer's intended message on a particular occasion, and how the requirement of the particular recipient(s), in definable circumstances, influence the organization of the producer's discourse.

Second, discourse analysis identifies the meaning of a text by exploring it at a linguistic level, namely at the level of words, sentences, paragraphs, and larger textual units. It involves establishing the meaning of a text by probing beyond the level of individual sentence structure. Sentences must be understood in their broader literary context (Osborne 2006:151). Hence, it is essential to see that sentences constitute paragraphs while creating meaning within a larger literary unit. In this way, each sentence and paragraph finally contributes to shaping a larger coherent discourse.

Third, discourse analysis regards discourse itself as "a mode of action" in a specific social context (Fairclough 1992:63, cited in Reed 1997:30). It examines the social function of a communicative event (and should therefore take social context into account). Reed (1997:30; cf. Fairclough 1992:63; Porter 1995:28) elaborates on this tenet: "Discourse is not simply a set of propositions (logical, literal, conceptual or cognitive) with a certain factual content, but rather social, communicative interaction between communicants."

The fourth tenet is that discourse analysis seeks to construct a cohesive and coherent piece of communication by combining the linguistic units in a given text.

1.4.2 DISCOURSE ANALYSIS AS MULTI-DIMENSIONAL METHODOLOGY?

As the next step in constructing a methodological framework for reading 1 Thessalonians, I wish to relate discourse analysis to the major categories of linguistics, i.e., three semiotic modes of texts, namely their *syntactic, semantic* and *pragmatic* dimensions (Morris [1938] 1955:79–137; Hellholm; 1980:18–52; Schenk 1984:19–20; cited in Reed 1997:33).[16] These modes do not work separately but rather function together as "structural, historical, and dialectic levels of communication" (Mouton 2002:29). In this sense, the dynamic nature of discourse analysis may be described as multi-dimensional. Specifically, reading Paul's first letter to the Thessalonians multi-dimensionally will elucidate the rich yet complex nature and intention of the text by bringing together insights from three sophisticated levels of analysis: the "linguistic-structural dimension" of the text, the "interrelation between

16. With reference to the work of Plett and Rousseau, Mouton (2002:29) defines these modes as follows: (1) the syntactic mode "describes the relation between written language signs," (2) the semantic mode "focuses on the relation between the signs and that to which they refer, i.e., the 'meaning' of words, phrases, sentences, and larger literary units," and (3) the pragmatic mode has to do with "the relation between signs and their interpreters."

the author's ultimate commitment and socio-cultural world," and the "communicative persuasive power of the text" (Rousseau 1986:48–51; Mouton 2002:29).

The potential benefits of such an encompassing approach seem to be numerous. First, discourse analysis goes beyond examining language solely on the basis of its grammar, since larger discourse units are more than the accumulation of individual lexical units (Nida et al. 1983:80–82; cf. Green 1995:180; Porter 1995:25; Reed 1996:231; 1997:27; Runge 2010:3–16). To appreciate the linguistic-structural dimension of written communication, the interaction between bottom-up and top-down analysis will be considered. Reed (1996:232) argues that, at a text-linguistic level, analyzing a text begins "at the bottom with morphology, moving up through words, phrases, clauses, sentences and paragraphs/sections/pericopes (i.e., sequences of sentences and embedded sequences of sentences) until reaching the top—namely, the discourse." This process is also reversed to read smaller units in the light of a larger discourse. The study will thus include lexical studies, syntactical discussions, structural analyses and the identification of specific literary devices from the bottom to the top. In this process, examining the linguistic units aims at illustrating the formation of the larger discourse and thereby identify what a speaker/author emphasizes.[17] In particular, tracing Paul's argument will be valuable in demonstrating how each literary unit contributes to constructing a larger discourse and elucidating the central thrust of the author's argumentation at the top level.

Second, a potential reward of examining a variety of components of linguistic units is ultimately to discern that the communicative event is a social phenomenon. Thus, one should not overlook the impact of the first-century Mediterranean world, the author's unique conceptual world, and the audience's particular circumstances. Specifically, considering Paul's unique cosmological *perspective* shaped by the Hebrew Scriptures helps interpreters construct the rationale for his selection of a specific word/expression and

17. While this study does not engage in the technicality of linguistics, the concept of markedness and prominence is significant in understanding "the phenomenon of linguistic highlighting, whereby some feature of the language of a text stands out in some way" (Halliday 1973:113). Westfall (2005:33) remarks that, "[m]arkedness is concerned with the hierarchical nature of lexical and grammatical categories." She agrees with Stephen Wallace's observation that prominence is related to linguistic categories (aspect, mode, tense, voice and nominal expressions): "linguistic categories such as verbal categories can be ranked according to salience or prominence" (see Wallace 1982:214). Westfall (2005:34) remarks that markedness occurs in a certain context in associated with other emphatic elements. Thus, examining language at discourse level takes a complex process such as identifying the function of each linguistic category, repetition, uniqueness, and use of distinctive discourse marker leads one to observe the prominence of themes and major perspectives.

composition of the document. On the other hand, in order to understand the dynamic process of discourse formation, I will explore how Paul specifically combined layers of scriptural notions and apocalyptic elements in the specific historical situation of Thessalonica. I am particularly interested in the political and religious factors that may have caused Paul's selection of vocabulary and concepts pertaining to his scriptural/conceptual world in the discourse of the letter. I hope that this exploration at least provides a clue to Paul's discursive strategy in resolving the crisis among the Thessalonians.

Third, constructing the occasion that might have influenced the author's writing will help interpreters to identify some clues as to how the original author's discourse was supposed to have an impact on the audience. Quoting Fairclough's observation of the persuasive power of discourse, Reed (1997:30) clarifies that the nature of discourse analysis has nothing to do with the "abstract formalisms of language," but rather the "*communicative functional role of language*" (emphasis added). Interpreters are therefore challenged to focus on how the author interweaves specific vocabularies, metaphors and literary devices while aiming to achieve a certain pragmatic effect. A brief discussion of the implied pragmatic effect of this text in the conclusion of this study will explore the (trans)formative potential of Paul's discourse.

To sum up: taking into account that reading a text is a communicative act (Green 1995:178), this study investigates textual/intertextual, socio-historical, and pragmatic dimensions of 1 Thessalonians. These aspects will constitute a major part of each chapter's discussion. I will construct the major thrust of Paul's discourse by considering the influences of his (the speaker/author's) conceptual world as well as the audience's social world in the production of the letter. Exploring the (broad) social, cultural, and religious worlds of both Paul and the Thessalonians forms a crucial part of the study (chapters 2 and 3) and will precede a structural analysis of the text (chapter 4). In the latter I conclude that the direction of Paul's discourse is towards building a strategy for resocialization of the new converts. In the paraenetic part of the letter, in particular, the volume of scriptural echoes seems to be higher and constitute the nerve of his identity- and ethos-building discourse.

1.5 POTENTIAL VALUE OF THIS STUDY

This dissertation's first contribution to current discussions on Paul's first letter to the Thessalonians is to suggest an alternative way of understanding the letter, hoping to overcome some of the weaknesses and limitations of recent (rhetorical) approaches to the letter. Scholarly debates between epistolary and rhetorical analysts have tended to confine themselves to the nature of argumentation in the first-century Hellenistic literary and rhetorical environment. Hoping to overcome limitations of previous studies, this study aims at enabling modern readers to rediscover 1 Thessalonians through establishing its thematic coherence based on discourse analysis.

Another potential value of the study is to identify probable scriptural themes echoed throughout 1 Thessalonians. Identifying probable echoes in Paul's discourse will hopefully enable contemporary readers to appreciate and re-appropriate the discursive impact of Paul's use of Scripture.

In the current climate scholars often neglect to consider how Paul's discourse in the first century may continue to shape modern audiences' identity awareness and ethos. This study is aimed at exploring the (trans) formative force of Paul's discourse, also towards renewing Christian communities of the twenty-first century. Having a better understanding of the dynamic identity formation processes in early Christian communities will hopefully assist modern Christian audiences in finding a solution to the problem of their (often) lost memory of "who they are" and "how they ought to live."

2

Paul's Conceptual World as Anomalous Diaspora Jew

To UNDERSTAND THE SOCIAL setting and nature of Paul's composition of 1 Thessalonians, most of all, the author's conceptual world is to be constructed. This chapter therefore seeks to examine the social, cultural, and religious backgrounds that influenced Paul. Specifically, this chapter explores what sort of Jew Paul was in the context of the first century. This examination will provide an opportunity to overcome the weaknesses of rhetorical criticism's assumption that Paul was a person assimilated into the Hellenistic world. The commentators who utilize the rhetorical approach have delved particularly into the influence of literary or rhetorical forms and styles on Paul's letter writings.

In search of Paul's Jewishness, this chapter draws attention to the significance of identifying Paul's scriptural ideas underlying the conceptualization of the letters. In writing the first letter to the Thessalonians, Paul's own narrative world seems to play a significant role in the formation of the early Christian communities.[1] In so doing, he attempts to enable the audience

---

1. Lau (2011:41) perceives the link between biblical narrative and its contribution to identity formation as follows: "Modern literary approaches to biblical narrative highlight the literary devices encoded in a text, which link and configure the selected events of the story into a coherent whole. Since these narratives are written from a particular point of view, they express the attitudes and values of an author. Yet they also shape the identity of a reader." Although his articulation of the interrelatedness between narrative, identity and ethics comes from a different text and context, Ricoeur (1990:187) notices the potential transformative power of discourse by illustrating its domino effect: "[E]vents, which are said to be 'epoch-making,' draw their specific meaning from their capacity to found or reinforce the community's consciousness of its identity, its narrative identity, as well as the

to be aware of their distinctive identity in comparison to others religious groups from the surrounding world. After having established some gentile Christian communities, Paul's primary and urgent task was not only to create a new identity from mindsets and morality that were rooted in pagan society but also to project his "vision of a new community" characterized as followers of Jesus of Nazareth (Punt 2011:1). Even in the letters where direct quotation from the Hebrew Scriptures is not found, his identity-building and moral formation are mainly carried out through his appropriation of significant scriptural notions. In this way, Paul integrates the gentile converts into the larger narrative of God's covenant community (cf. Punt 2011:1).

Identifying Paul's concrete conceptual world is not a simple matter, because of his complex and broad ideological background rooted in both Hellenistic and Jewish sociocultural settings. In addition, scholarly studies of the Thessalonian correspondence have focused on comparisons between these letters and contemporary literature of the Hellenistic world. Recent scholarly discussions on Paul's ideological background unfortunately resulted in revitalizing the dichotomy between the (so-called) "Hellenistic" Paul and the "Jewish" Paul. On the one hand, emphasizing Paul's Hellenistic roots could underestimate the influence of the conceptual map of the Hebrew Scriptures on Paul's discourse. On the other hand, if one concentrates only on Paul's Jewishness without considering his pre- and post-Damascus perspectives, the problem of one-sidedness may manifest. Understanding Paul in the light of a single sociocultural context may indeed be problematic.

In this chapter I argue for an appreciation of Paul's conceptual world vis-à-vis a wide spectrum of diaspora Jewish beliefs and convictions in the period before and after his encounter with Jesus of Nazareth.

2.1 A HISTORICAL SURVEY OF PAUL'S IDEOLOGICAL BACKGROUND

In the search of Paul's conceptual world it has been acknowledged that the apostle is indebted to various streams of thought and culture amidst the socio-political complexity of the first-century Mediterranean world. Thus, it might be naïve to even endeavor to ascertain the most plausible background to Paul's conceptual world. As Furnish (1968:25–67) stated, it might be profitable rather to consider the diverse foundations of Paul's thought in understanding how the Hebrew Scriptures, Jewish (Rabbinic) tradition/

identity of its members. These events generate feelings of considerable ethical intensity, whether this be fervent commemoration or some manifestation of loathing, or indignation, or of regret or compassion, or even the call for forgiveness."

literature, Hellenistic sources and conventions, and ultimately Jesus' teachings influenced him. In addition, as Martin Hengel (1974) argued, first-century Judaism could not be separated from Hellenism. Hengel (1989:11, cf. 1974:103–6) surmises that there was "an independent Jewish Hellenistic culture in Jerusalem and its environs."[2] But one should not neglect that the *piece de resistance* is that Paul's exhortation is based on his unique soteriology, which was formulated by "the encounter with Christ, the experience of the Spirit, all within the framework of a fervent eschatological expectation" (DeSilva 1995:564; cf. Seifrid 1992:19).

2.1.1 THE DICHOTOMY BETWEEN A HELLENISTIC AND A JEWISH PAUL

In spite of Paul's diverse and complex sociocultural background, debates and discussions concerning Paul's ideological background are still in progress, and the pendulum has been swinging between the two major matrices of the Hellenistic world and Judaism. Scholars have attempted to determine the most influential background of Paul's writings. But their examination has yielded diverse results, depending on their presuppositions and perspectives on Paul's biographical and educational background. At the outset of this chapter, it is necessary to provide an overview of how New Testament scholars in the nineteenth century initiated the debate on whether the cultural milieu of Paul was mainly that of Judaism or Hellenism. I consequently present a brief historical survey of the ways in which the scholarly stance on the Hellenistic Paul developed during the twentieth century.

2.1.1.1 F.C. BAUR

In the nineteenth century some scholars began to concentrate on tracing the historical development of Christianity. Their interest in the area naturally led them to delve into identifying the relation of "a movement deriving from Jewish followers of a Jewish teacher" to the Hellenistic sociocultural

---

2. In the discussion on encounters between Jewish and Hellenistic thought in the early Hellenistic period, Martin Hengel (1974; 1989) demonstrates how Hellenistic culture impacted Palestinian Jews. In this period, he argues, the Greek language played a major role in the process, alongside Hebrew and Aramaic. "[A]rchaeological, inscriptional, numismatic" data shed light on "the presence of a multilingual society in Palestine during the first century A.D" (Wilson 2000:479). As Greek language and nomenclature were widely known in the Palestine region, it is suggested that Greek education naturally or forcefully infiltrated Judaism, even in the Jewish upper classes, in the process of the assimilation of Judaism in the Hellenistic environment (Hengel 1974:103).

milieu within which this movement had to negotiate its new identity time and again (Meeks 1972:273). In the post-Enlightenment period Ferdinand Christian Baur (1792–1860) played a crucial role in triggering the controversy as to whether Paul's background was oriented towards Judaism and/or Hellenism. Many scholars agree that Baur's dichotomous understanding of Hellenism and Judaism can be attributed to his reading of Paul with regard to a Hegelian dialectic (Martin 2001:33; Meeks 2001:19). In his pursuit of the synthesis of two different worlds, the thesis can be Judaism, Palestinian Jews, the Jerusalem Church and Jewish Christianity; the antithesis can be Hellenism, Hellenistic Jews/Christians, and gentile Christianity. Consequently, what Baur strived to resolve the tension between these two parties as the synthesis was "early Catholicism" (Meeks 2001:19).

2.1.1.2 THE HISTORICAL RELIGIONS SCHOOL

The so-called historical religions school (*Religionsgeschichtliche Schule*) was launched in the theological faculty at Göttingen in the 1890s. According to Meeks (2001:20), scholars argued that "neither the biblical and legal tradition of Israel nor the intellectual culture of classical Greece" could provide the decisive indication for understanding the beginning of Christianity. He remarks that rather, they regarded that "oriental" influences such as apocalypticism (e.g., outbreak of cosmic war and catastrophic change of the world) in Judaism and the mystery religions and Gnosticism in Hellenism affected Paul's thought as the prototypes of pre-Christian religions.

The era of F. C. Baur and the historical religions school was characterized by a transition in understanding Paul's background in terms of purely Jewish categories to acknowledging Hellenistic views. Such a tendency governed German scholarship for a long time (Lüdemann 1872:29). In *Die Anthropologie des Apostels Paulus* (1872), Lüdemann initiated the debate as to whether the origin of Paul's understanding of human nature came from Judaism *and* Hellenism. He located Paul's thought in the transition (Übergang) from a purely Jewish consciousness to a Hellenistic dualism (1872:29). Otto Pfleiderer provided answers to questions raised by Lüdemann regarding where the various elements that constituted Paul's 'anthropology' came from (Riches 1993:35). In his book *Primitive Christianity: Its Writings and Teachings in their Historical Connections* (1906) Pfleiderer described Paul's theology as embodying the coexistence of two incompatible thought patterns. He argued that the tension between individual streams of thought was left unresolved and they were introduced into Paul's theology (Riches 1993:35; Martin 2001:36). Moreover, in his work *Kyrios Christos*

(1913) Wilhelm Bousset described a trajectory of how the early Palestinian community's understanding of the Son of Man dogma was developed and integrated into the Hellenistic Christian community's belief system. To Bousset, common knowledge of Hellenistic mystery religions led the Hellenistic communities to form a new perception of Christ (Bousset [1913] 1970:31–56; 138–52). He attempted to clarify the Hellenistic Christian community's attitude to the title "Lord" in the light of its usage in the cultic context of Hellenistic culture. In so doing, Bousset understood that "cultically orientated Hellenistic Christianity" was the point of departure for Paul's theology.

2.1.1.3 GUSTAV ADOLF DEISSMANN

A prominent Berlin scholar of the nineteenth and early twentieth centuries, Adolf Deissmann (1866–1937) contributed significantly to "the contextualizing of the social world of early Christianity and to the understanding of the linguistic matrix of the LXX and New Testament" (Horsley 2007:72). His book *Light From the Ancient East* (1908) examined the Hellenistic background of early Christians in light of newly discovered ancient inscriptions, papyri and archaeological relics. Deissmann (1926:5–7) pointed out that previous scholars' interests had been limited to explicating Paul's theology, literary questions about the authenticity of Paul's letters, and historical constructions of the relation between the book of Acts and Paul's letters. Instead, he suggested that the apostle's thinking be explored from the perspective of his specific social contexts and religious history. Rather than focusing on Hellenistic classical literature, Deissmann (1908:8) devoted attention to "non-literary written memorials of the Roman Empire" around the period of the rise and development of early Christianity. Based on common cultural elements, similar customs and parallel expressions from ancient non-literary material, Deissmann described the way in which common linguistic, social, religious, and cultural denominators were shared by the Hellenistic world and early Christianity.

2.1.2 STUDIES OF PAUL'S HELLENISTIC BACKGROUND

In the nineteenth century the German scholars' understanding of "Hellenistic influence" on Paul's thinking seems to have been confined to a few themes, or merely discussed in broad terms. However, the next phase of the studies of "Hellenistic Paul" expanded the scope of questions to include how studying his Hellenistic background could help us to understand the nature of Paul's writings. Since the 1970s in particular, numerous scholarly publications on the influences of Hellenistic philosophy and rhetoric on Paul have accomplished remarkable advances.

Before surveying recent contributions, I provide a brief historical survey in this section of some supporters in this camp from a time when studies concerning the so-called "Hellenistic" Paul were not yet systematic or flourishing. Particularly, I survey studies of "the social setting of the Pauline texts" and of the correlation between Paul's writings and Hellenistic "rhetorical structure, style, and argumentation" (rhetorical criticism) (Engberg-Pedersen 1995:xiv).

2.1.2.1 RUDOLF KNOPF

Rudolf Knopf, a German scholar who specialized in studying Christian communities of the post-apostolic period, published his monograph *Paul and Hellenism* in 1914, which paved the way for more recent studies on the "Hellenistic Paul." While Knopf (1914:513) articulates Paul's Jewishness, he presupposes that "in Paul's day Hellenism had affected Judaism, or at least the Judaism of the Diaspora." Knopf's first task was to substantiate Paul's fluency in *Koine* Greek,[3] the formative years of his youth in a Hellenistic environment, his use of Greek rhetorical devices, and his familiarity with Hellenistic philosophies. In response to Albert Schweitzer, who gradually gained influence in criticizing the *religionsgeschichtliche* school's premise, the second part of Knopf's argument attempts to substantiate a strong connection between Paul and Hellenistic religions. In this process, his appeal was based on newly recovered inscriptions and papyri in his time (e.g., *Mithrasliturgie*, the hymn of Isis, and so on).

After Knopf's monograph, however, the discovery of the Nag Hammadi codices (1945) and the Dead Sea Scrolls (1946–1956) led many scholars to delve anew into the relationship between Judaism and Paul. This phenomenon led to a gradual dwindling of studies on the "Hellenistic Paul" (Engberg-Pedersen 1995:xvi).

2.1.2.2 ROBERT M. GRANT

Nevertheless, Knopf's work remained influential, particularly in North American circles, where scholars continued to explore Hellenistic elements

---

3. Deissmann (1908:66) argued that *Koine* ('common') Greek was a single international language under the unified Hellenistic world.

in the Pauline letters. In fact, in North America remarkable advances were made in this area. Robert M. Grant (1949, 1952, 1961; see also Schoedel & Wilken 1979), for example, pioneered a wide range of studies on the early church. His focus included the study of Gnosticism and Origen, with specific attention to the Hellenistic background of the church fathers. Grant's best illustration of Hellenistic influence on Paul's thinking was probably his admission that while Paul's materials were Jewish, his method was "self-consciously Greek" (1961:63). For example, in his study of the letter to the Galatians, Grant (1952:224) argued that Paul's criticism of Judaizers' observing Jewish festivals was based on the Stoic philosopher Posidonius' theory that the pure monotheism of Moses was corrupted by his successors. In doing so, he suggested that Paul's use of Greek philosophy functioned as *praeparatio evangelica* in his debate with Judaizers. For instance, Grant (1952:223, 225) argued that Paul used Greek rhetoric as "a theoretical justification of his rejection of the Jewish Law" in relating Gal 3:1 to "a magical 'spell' in Pseudo-Demosthenes" and 4:24–25 to the Greek rhetorical terms ἀλληγορούμενα and συστοιχεῖ.

In fact, Grant (1952:226; 1961:60–61) did not refute the idea that "Jewish and Hellenistic elements are almost inextricably woven in [Paul's] thought and expression." But he devoted himself to finding Hellenistic elements (e.g., Paul's acquaintance with Greek rhetoric and his use of few Hellenistic philosophical themes) in the Pauline letters. His contribution was to lay a significant foundation for the next development in portraying the Hellenistic heritage implicit in Paul's composition of the letter as well as in his theological thinking.

2.1.2.3 ABRAHAM J. MALHERBE

Abraham Malherbe was a South African-born scholar whose work focused on similarities between Hellenistic moral philosophy and the views expressed in Paul's letters. By employing a sociological approach to the New Testament, he molded a new hermeneutic that understood Paul's writings in the context of a Hellenistic social setting (1970, [1977] 1983).

Specifically, Malherbe (1985:6–7) argued that Paul's style in 1 Thessalonians relies on the popular philosophers in his day. He showed that Paul built up his communities by alluding to, or reinterpreting, the moral philosophers' method of education. They developed an "extensive system of pastoral care which aimed, through character education, at the attainment of virtue and happiness" (Malherbe 1985:7). Malherbe ([1977] 1983:19) contended that the most appropriate literary resources in the construction of the social setting of Paul's time would be the works of Dio Chrysostom. More specifically, Malherbe (1970:216-7; 1985:7-9; 1986:24-26; 2000:156) noticed that 1 Thess 2:1-12 has remarkable similarities with Dio Chrysostom's *Oration 32.11-12, 77/78.38*, which describes an ideal philosopher's way of using *topos* as rhetorical strategy:[4]

Dio Chrysostom	The Apostle Paul
καὶ ταῦτα ἀκούων Ὁμήρου τε καὶ τῶν ἄλλων ποιητῶν ὑμνούντων ἀεὶ τὸν ὄχλον ὡς χαλεπόν τε καὶ ἀπειθῆ καὶ πρὸς ὕβριν ἕτοιμον, τοῦ μὲν οὕτω λέγοντος (Or. 32:22) ἄνδρα δὲ λαβεῖν καθαρῶς καὶ ἀδόλως παρρησιαζόμενον (Or.32.11)	ἀλλὰ προπαθόντες καὶ ὑβρισθέντες, καθὼς οἴδατε, ἐν Φιλίπποις ἐπαρρησιασάμεθα ἐν τῷ θεῷ ἡμῶν λαλῆσαι πρὸς ὑμᾶς τὸ εὐαγγέλιον τοῦ θεοῦ ἐν πολλῷ ἀγῶνι (1 Thess 2:2)
ἄνδρα δὲ λαβεῖν καθαρῶς καὶ ἀδόλως παρρησιαζόμενον (Or. 32.11)	ἡ γὰρ παράκλησις ἡμῶν οὐκ ἐκ πλάνης οὐδὲ ἐξ ἀκαθαρσίας οὐδὲ ἐν δόλῳ (1 Thess 2:3)
ἀλλὰ κολακεία καὶ ἀπάτη κρατεῖ παρ' αὐτοῖς (Or. 32:26) καὶ μήτε δόξης χάριν μήτ' ἐπ' ἀργυρίῳ προσποιούμενον (Or. 32:11) εἰ δ' ὡς φιλόσοφοι ταῦτα πράττουσι κέρδους ἕνεκεν καὶ δόξης τῆς ἑαυτῶν (Or. 32:10)	Οὔτε γάρ ποτε ἐν λόγῳ κολακείας ἐγενήθημεν, καθὼς οἴδατε, οὔτε ἐν προφάσει πλεονεξίας (1 Thess 2:5) οὔτε ζητοῦντες ἐξ ἀνθρώπων δόξαν οὔτε ἀφ' ὑμῶν οὔτε ἀπ' ἄλλων (1 Thess 2:6)

In carrying out this comparative study, Malherbe (1970:217) demonstrated that the major point of using negative and antithetic terms in 1 Thess 2:1-12 is to appeal to his genuineness in presenting the gospel without deceitfully presenting himself as a philosopher.

Malherbe (1983:238) argued that Paul adopted popular philosophical traditions and hortatory devices that were familiar to his first audiences in Thessalonica. Malherbe found similarities to Paul's speeches by listing his frequent uses of traditional material such as *topoi* on the moral life: (a) reiteration of the phrases καθὼς οἴδατε (1:5; 2:2, 5; 3:4), καθάπερ οἴδατε (2:11),

---

4. Malherbe (1992:320-5) played a pioneering role in investigating the reinterpretation of *topoi* (as used by Hellenistic moral philosophers) in the NT. Assuming that the early Christians shared common topics and values with their contemporaries in the first-century Mediterranean world, he takes for granted the biblical authors' use of *topoi* and their descriptive functions in the NT writings (Robbins 2004:119-20). He concentrates on the development of "specific *topoi*" to the status of "common *topoi*" in this social, religious and cultural environment (Robbins 2002:12-13).

or οἴδατε (2:1; 3:3; 4:2; 5:2); (b) a similarity between "a model to be imitated" in ancient paraenesis (1:6); (c) the occurrences of hortatory speech (2:3, 12; 3:2, 7; 4:1, 2, 6 10, 11, 18; 5:11, 12, 14); (d) appealing to the philophronetic element, which was used in ancient letters to bridge the gap the relationship between an author (Paul) and his audience (the Thessalonians);[5] and (e) adopting the moral philosopher's conventional use of parental metaphors for moral exhortations (Malherbe 1983:240–2; cf. 1992:321–4).

However, among all the Hellenistic hortatory traditions, Malherbe (1983:246–8) focused on the difference between the popular philosophers' use of "a model to be imitated" and Paul's use of "μιμηταί." He remarked that, while philosophers were hesitant about persuading their audience to follow their examples, Paul confidently regarded the Thessalonians as imitators of him and the Lord, and as his coworkers (1 Thess 1:6–7). In addition, the philosophers believed that the reliability and credibility of their rhetoric were established through the consistency of their speech and their conduct. For Paul, however, such attitudes are based on the gospel of God as seen in 1 Thess 2:2, 9 (Malherbe 1983:247–8).

2.1.3 THE RISE AND DEVELOPMENT OF RHETORICAL CRITICISM

Malherbe's approach has been well-regarded among New Testament scholars. Along with other major scholars, his contribution brought about a *renaissance* of rhetorical criticism. In 1970 a portent of the prevalence of rhetorical analysis had already appeared before its formal appearance in academic discussions (Olbricht 1990:217). Even before rhetorical criticism began to draw much scholarly attention, a form-critical scholar, Boers (1976:140–58), already critiqued previous limited interpretations of the formal structure of 1 Thessalonians and structured each part of the letter based on the conventions of Hellenistic letter-writing. In so doing, Boers' form-critical reading appears to be aligned with Malherbe's understanding

---

5. Malherbe (1983:241) regards chapters 1–3 as the "philophronetic" section of 1 Thessalonians, which is an ancient author's attempt to bridge the gap between the writer and the recipients by expressing intimacy. Thus, the unit 2:1–12, as part of *philophronesis* (chapters 1–3), plays a role in the preparation for the exhortation in chapters 4–5. Dividing this letter into broadly two parts (1 Thess 1–3 and 4–5), Malherbe (2000:156) notices that the implicit paraenesis in 1 Thess 1–3 is reiterated and expanded in the explicit paraenesis in 1 Thess 4–5: "impurity: 2:3/4:7; love: 2:8/3:12; 4:9; 5:13; labor: 2:9/4:11; blamelessness: 2:10/5:23; individual attention: 2:11/5:11; exhortation: 2:12/5:11; charging: 2:11/4:6; comfort: 2:12/4:18; 5:14 and God's calling associated with the moral life: 2:12/5:23–24."

that this letter consists of philophronesis and paraenesis (Walton 1995:237; see Malherbe 1983:239). Even if Boers' study cannot be labelled with the technical term "rhetoric," some scholars used his work to develop a rhetorical approach to 1 Thessalonians (Olbricht 1990: 217; see Jewett 1986:69–70; Koester 1979:44). Moreover, Betz's monumental article, "The Literary Composition and Function of Paul's Letter to the Galatians" (1975), and his commentary on Galatians ([1979] 1989), played a significant role as forerunners for rhetorical analysis of the Pauline letters. Many scholars since then have applied Betz's approach to Paul's letter "according to Graeco-Roman rhetoric and epistolography" in reading 1 Thessalonians (see also Malherbe 1988).[6] Even though the emphases of different scholars are diverse in terms of identifying the genre of the letter and Paul's employment of rhetorical techniques, their outcomes led many to perceive 1 Thessalonians as the best example of intensive use of Hellenistic rhetoric. In this section, I selectively survey the work of a few significant contributors to the study of Paul's Hellenistic background.

2.1.3.1 GEORGE A. KENNEDY

George Kennedy, a North American scholar of classical rhetoric and literature, discusses and clarifies the rhetorical nature of Paul's writings in light of the Hellenistic letter form. Kennedy (1984:10) contends that, even if the fact that Paul was formally schooled in Greek rhetoric is equivocal, he was explicitly aware of the commonly circulated ancient handbooks of rhetoric. For Kennedy, the rhetoric in Paul's time was not only generally applied to every "oral and written communication," but was also used to persuade Paul's Greek-speaking communities. In order to appreciate implicit Hellenistic rhetorical features of the New Testament, Kennedy (1984:33–38) suggests various steps in practicing rhetorical criticism, namely: (1) determining the rhetorical unit; (2) defining the rhetorical situation; (3) identifying the rhetorical problem; (4) considering the arrangement of material in the text; and (5) reviewing and analyzing the rhetorical impact.

6. Betz (1975:377) analyzed the Galatian letter's literary structure based on the ancient epistolary framework. His methodology presupposes that Paul intended to overcome limitations of "the actual delivery of the speech" in his letter-writing. Since the letter itself is less efficient than real rhetorical speech with regard to communication, Paul was challenged to bring about the expected effects of persuasive rhetoric through "a lifeless piece of paper." In proposing that the epistle to the Galatians is an "apologetic letter," Betz (1975:356–77) contended that Paul's line of reasoning in Galatians was communicated by the use of epistolary elements: the prescript (1:1-5), the *exordium* (1:6–11), the *narratio* (1:12—2:14), the *propositio* (2:15-21), the *probatio* (3:1—4:31), the *paraenesis* (5:1—6:10) and the postscript (6:11–18).

By applying this series of rhetorical practices to 1 Thessalonians, Kennedy (1984:36) substantiates his view that Paul's writing is characterized by a *deliberative* style, which intends to affect the audience's decision about pursuing certain actions.⁷ His appreciation of the rhetorical features of 1 Thessalonians is firstly carried out in the division of rhetorical units (1:2–10, 2:1–8, 2:9—3:13, and 4:1—5:22) (1984:142-4). My brief reference to Kennedy's work is an attempt to ascertain the legitimacy of acknowledging Paul's utilizing Greco-Roman handbooks of rhetoric, even if this might represent a fresh approach to 1 Thessalonians. According to Watson (2008:44), however, Kennedy's reliance on rhetorical theory in handbooks alone may bring about an unbalanced understanding of the New Testament. In addition, he observes that Kennedy's over-dependence on Hellenistic rhetoric can restrict interpreters from appreciating "the benefits of modern rhetoric, which is more highly conceptualized and complete" (see also 1.2.1).

2.1.3.2 ROBERT JEWETT (NEW RHETORIC)

The concept of "New Rhetoric" was initiated by I. A. Richards ([1936] 1965:7–10), whose enquiry sought to understand how language works in discourse (Aune 2003:318). While studies based on Hellenistic rhetoric focused on classifying the speaker's act of persuasion, identifying the "partly unconscious factor in appeal" is a significant supplementary concept (Aune 2003:318). The scholars who are involved in the New Rhetoric "draw attention to the social context of human communication, thereby placing the

---

7. It has been a controversial issue whether this letter's style could be described as *deliberative* or *epideictic* or *paraenetic*. Some scholars regard the rhetorical genre of 1 Thess as *epideictic* rhetoric, which is used to convince an audience to take hold of or confirm a certain perspective in the present, especially in the context of celebrating (praising) or denouncing (blaming) some characteristics of someone or something (Jewett 1986:71; Hughes 1990:97; Witherington III 2006:23). Another rhetorical style according to which this letter may be categorized is *paraenesis* (Stowers 1986:94–106; Aune 1987:206). Malherbe (2000:83–85) compared 1 Thessalonians to Hellenistic paraenetic letters, showing common characteristics such as: (1) antitheses between good and bad models (e.g., Seneca, *Ep.* 52:8; cf. 1 Thess 1:5; 2:1, 2, 5); (2) the presence of an authoritative/philosophical teacher (e.g., Seneca, *Ep.* 6:5–6; cf. 1 Thess 2:1–12); (3) describing oneself as an example or model (e.g., Pliny, *Ep.* 7.7; cf. 2.6; cf. 1 Thess 2:13–16); and (4) the theme of remembrance (e.g., Seneca, *Ep.* 11.9; cf. 1 Thess 3:3–4). I argue that one cannot confine 1 Thess to a single rhetorical style, since all these styles are found in the letter. Yet, if I have to choose from these categories, I would say that 1 Thess belongs predominantly to the *deliberative* rhetorical genre. Throughout the letter Paul attempts to persuade the audience to take a certain kind of action (Kennedy 1984:19, 142; Wanamaker 1990:46). Paul drew the audience's attention to their "self-interest and future benefits" so as to convince them to stand fast in the Lord as seen in 3:8.

insights and tools of classical rhetoric within a larger framework accessible to modern social science" (Jewett 1986:64). Thus, New Rhetoric does not merely apply the formal logic of Hellenistic ancient rhetoric, but seeks to understand the effect of a speaker's argumentation in relation to the audience (Aune 2003:318).

Robert Jewett, a New Testament professor formerly at the University of Heidelberg, revisited rhetorical approaches to 1 Thessalonians in his book *The Thessalonian Correspondence: Pauline Rhetoric and Millenarian Piety*. Jewett (1986:65–66) argued that the New Rhetoric, as a synthetic approach to classical rhetoric and linguistic theories, provides a holistic delineation of the communication environment of the Hellenistic world. His research is meaningful inasmuch as it complements the limitation of Kennedy's study. Jewett (1986: 64) pointed out that Betz's methodology was oriented towards Hellenistic classical rhetoric, and its typical forms and literary approach. For him, Betz's orientation to those approaches neglects the point that "the potential of rhetoric" could construct the audience's circumstances and establish their correlation to the texts. Jewett's contribution to rhetorical criticism was to draw scholars' attention away from purely speaker-oriented rhetoric to the overall communication circumstance and process involving both speaker and audience.

However, his views were not received without criticism. In my view, Jewett's discussion of genre and structure mentioning some rhetorical terms seemed to reiterate the findings of previous studies. Jewett's way of identifying "the speaker's 'construction' of the audience" seems to give priority to the influence of Hellenistic rhetorical conventions rather than establishing the logical flow/argumentation in the author's discourse itself. Such analysis endeavors to infer the author's essential message and the "larger rhetorical framework of the audience and the circumstances" in light of Hellenistic rhetorical structures (Jewett 1986:67). This approach seems to suggest that Paul's ideas can be clarified by relying "on ancient ways of analysing argumentation" (Thurén 2002:79; cf. Porter 2010: 10). Furthermore, as Olbricht (1990:218) points out, although Jewett's discussion of the genre and structure of 1 Thessalonians relied on citing some classical rhetorical principles, his construction of the circumstances of the Thessalonian believers did not devote sufficient attention to "invention and proofs."

Unfortunately, as New Rhetoric scholars employ classical theory, they also run the risk of one-sidedness and of confining Paul's argument to a particular culture's rhetorical conventions. Thus, Jewett's enquiries into the genre and use of the ancient epistolary theory could not enable him to fully construct the broad social milieu of the Thessalonian congregation. At this point, it is important to question the extent to which an approach oriented to literary criticism could elucidate the Thessalonians' situation and social setting.

2.1.3.3 BRUCE C. JOHANSON

Right after the publication of Jewett's book in 1987, Bruce Johanson suggested a balanced approach between text-linguistics and rhetorical analysis. His doctoral dissertation, *To All the Brethren: A Text-Linguistic and Rhetorical Approach to 1 Thessalonians* (Johanson 1987:81–153), seems to be a mixture of rhetorical criticism and discourse analysis. Johanson (1987:6; 39–41) pointed out the limitations of epistolary form criticism and previous rhetorical analysis, since those approaches overlooked "a sufficiently rigorous and concerted text-centered analysis." For this reason he attempted to read 1 Thessalonians "as an act of communication in its initial communicative context" (1987:3), establishing interconnected relations between smaller and larger literary units to establish the letter's unity.[8] Johanson (1987:41) raised a question about the adequacy of rhetorical criticism's tendency to date to adopt Aristotle's classification of three rhetorical genres—forensic (judicial), deliberative (political) and epideictic (ceremonial):

> While forensic, deliberative and epideictic characteristics may appear more or less prominently in such discourse, depending on the particular exigence(s) occasioning Paul's letters, it is doubtful whether any of them can be adequate generic categories strait across the board.

However, even if Johanson was cautious about Paul's letters being straitjacketed into a Hellenistic epistolary framework, he employed the Hellenistic epistolary term "exordium-like" (Johanson 1987:160). In his great concern to establish coherence between 1:2—3:13 and 4:1—5:24, he viewed the expanded thanksgiving section as typical of Paul's use of *exordium/narratio*-like strategies (cf. Malherbe 1983:241). For him, mentioning of something that the Thessalonians are lacking in their faith in 3:10 and transitional prayer in 3:11–13 are his rhetorical strategy for subsequently connecting to the paraenetic section (4:1—5:24).

---

8. Olbricht (1990:218–19), criticized the inductive nature of Johanson's study. For Olbricht, while commending Johanson's dedicated ways of immersing himself in the text, critiqued him for overlooking the presupposition that "writers typically have some [rhetorical] vision of the whole before they set out to write." But, in my estimation, one's view can vary according to the extent to which one acknowledges the methodological cogency of appropriating practices from the rhetorical conventions.

Johanson (1987:161-3) suggested that the grief and perplexity caused by the unexpected death of some community members was the rhetorical exigence that constituted the section. According to him (1987:189), this circumstance led Paul to console and correct the recipients without reproof, which may be seen as "a rhetorical situation"—a significant clue towards identifying the occasion and purpose of the letter:

> While consolation was obviously a major aim of the informative and argumentative features of the passage, the simultaneous presence of dissuasion from the incipient doubts and perplexity occasioning the non-Christian type of grief reflected in 4:13 indicates that the main aim could not have been only consolation (4:18; 5:11) pure and simple.

Johanson (1987:189) thus described the rhetorical nature of 1 Thessalonians as being close to the deliberative genre.

In a positive sense, his employing a textual-linguistic approach on the basis of rhetorical criticism (which explores syntactic, semantic, and pragmatic dimensions of a text) has contributed to recognizing the unity among the different units of 1 Thessalonians to a larger extent than previous rhetorical critics have done. Particularly, Johanson (1987:163) identifies a ring composition in 1 Thessalonians (1:2—2:16, 2:17—3:13 and 4:1—5:24). In so doing, he demonstrates Paul's major "persuasive concern" throughout the letter within "the general rhetorical-functional relation[ship]" between chapters 1–3 and 4–5.

2.1.4 PRELIMINARY CONCLUSION

Scholarly investigations into Hellenistic social settings of the Pauline letters and rhetorical criticism based on the epistolary framework have contributed significantly towards portraying a comprehensive picture of the so-called "Hellenistic Paul." Understanding Paul in relation to Hellenistic culture and its literary environment has now become a prerequisite for Pauline studies. However, while scholars also noticed dissimilarities between Paul and Hellenistic elements, they were not yet able to fully appreciate the socio-cultural complexity of Hellenistic and Jewish influences on Paul's thinking. Most Pauline scholars seem to have a standardized portrait of Paul as one who was proficient in Hellenistic rhetoric. If, however, Paul's Jewishness and the extent to which his mind had been Hellenized are not considered in nuanced ways, one can easily separate those Hellenistic and Judaistic influences. Unfortunately, one also may then end up viewing the scope of Paul's thinking in a one-sided way. It is to this issue that I now turn.

2.1.5 A HISTORICAL SURVEY OF JEWISH INFLUENCES ON PAUL

Studies on the formative role of Paul's Jewishness in his teachings have drawn less attention, because of the tendency in recent scholarship to regard his Hellenistic roots as the dominant conceptual influence in his mind, as has been argued in this chapter.[9] Adolf Von Harnack ([1928] 1995:44) argued that "Paul did not give the Old Testament to the young churches as the book of Christian sources for edification." This was attributed to Paul's giving priority to the gospel of Jesus Christ, taking the Hebrew Scriptures' subordinate role and relative validity for granted ([1928] 1995:48–49). Von Harnack surmises that it was only at the end of the first century CE that Christian communities began to publicly read these Scriptures. According to Von Harnack's evaluation of Paul, Paul's appeals to the Hebrew Scriptures with regard to the gospel impacted negatively on its authority in the process of edifying the early churches. Harmerton-Kelly (1990:74–75) also denied the "constructive role" of the Mosaic law in Paul's ideology by observing that the Old Testament "provides corroborative sanction at best and that only on the margin." Malherbe (1992:332) admitted to paying less attention to Hellenistic Jewish texts as an influential moral environment for Paul's ethical teachings, but states that "in many respects Paul had no Jewish antecedents for the way he appropriated elements from the [Hellenistic] moralists." Furthermore, many scholars have doubted that Paul's ethical teachings are rooted in the Hebrew Scriptures. Rosner (1999:4–8; 2013:24) sets out eight reasons to substantiate this view:

- Paul's negative articulations of the Mosaic Law (e.g., "the law came in to increase trespass" in Rom 5:20).
- Paul's statements on the abrogation of the Torah (e.g., circumcision, food laws, the Sabbath, etc.).
- Paul's haphazard and atomistic appeal to Scripture in his moral admonitions.
- Paul's use of the Hebrew Scriptures is regarded as inappropriate for gentile Christian churches as guidance for Christian ethical life.

---

9. On the long list of scholars who argue that the Torah has no formative role in Paul's ethics, see Rosner 1999:4.

- Many scholars doubt the Pauline authorship of 2 Timothy, which states, "All Scripture is breathed out by God and profitable for teaching, for reproof, for correction, and for training in righteousness" (2 Tim 3:16).
- Jesus' words and other non-Jewish ethics were considered to be more influential in the formation of Pauline ethics.
- Other significant factors, such as "eschatology, the Spirit, love, and social conditions" shaped Paul's ethics.
- The Hebrew Scriptures were infrequently quoted in Pauline ethical teachings.

Since Albert Schweitzer attempted to shape a pivotal framework for understanding Paul's faith within widespread Jewish beliefs and conceptions, some scholars endeavored to establish the correlation between Paul's ethical exhortations and his Jewish background. Even though there has been disagreement amongst scholars with regard to whether Paul uses the Hebrew Scriptures as a formative source in his paraenesis, some scholars have attempted to find the traces of Paul's Jewishness, approaching this through three salient perspectives: (1) Paul's Jewish background; (2) Jewish *apocalypticism/eschatology*; and (3) the *halakhic* tradition.

2.1.5.1 PAUL'S JEWISH IDENTITY AND FORMAL EDUCATION

Paul's autobiographical statements evidently enunciate his own Jewish identity and probable upbringing in a strict Jewish educational setting (see Acts 22:3; 23:6; 26:4, Rom 9:3-5; 11:1, 2 Cor 11:21-22; Gal 1:14; Phil 3:4-6). I deem it necessary to explore some texts where Paul acknowledges his Jewish identity, as well as some key texts that substantiate his Jewishness.

Acts 22:3 is a key text in the discussion about whether Paul's conceptual world was indebted to Hellenistic or Jewish culture and education. Paul states:

> "ἐγώ εἰμι ἀνὴρ Ἰουδαῖος, γεγεννημένος ἐν Ταρσῷ τῆς Κιλικίας, ἀνατεθραμμένος δὲ ἐν τῇ πόλει ταύτῃ, παρὰ τοὺς πόδας Γαμαλιὴλ πεπαιδευμένος κατὰ ἀκρίβειαν τοῦ πατρῴου νόμου, ζηλωτὴς ὑπάρχων τοῦ θεοῦ καθὼς πάντες ὑμεῖς ἐστε σήμερον."

Carson and Moo (2005:356) notice that there are two different interpretations of this verse, depending on where punctuation divides the sentences. On the one hand, one can read the second participle ἀνατεθραμμένος only in association with the phrase πόλει ταύτῃ and separate it from the subsequent phrase, παρὰ τοὺς πόδας Γαμαλιὴλ. Then Luke adds that, while Paul was born in the city of Tarsus, he was brought up in Jerusalem (see ESV, NASB, NIV 2011, NLT).[10] In this case, the Greek conjunction δέ establishes a contrast to the previous phrase, "born in Tarsus in Cilicia." Also, the demonstrative pronoun ταύτῃ may refer to Jerusalem, where Paul defended himself in front of the crowds. This interpretation suggests that Paul was born in Tarsus but moved to Jerusalem in his early childhood.

On the other hand, if one connects the participle to the phrase παρὰ τοὺς πόδας Γαμαλιὴλ, it would imply that Paul moved to Jerusalem for his rabbinic education (which would probably have started in his early teens) after receiving a primary Hellenistic education during his childhood in the city of Tarsus (see GNT, NRSV).

In my view, it is more natural to put the punctuation mark after the phrase δὲ ἐν τῇ πόλει ταύτῃ (cf. Van Unnik 1962:44; Haenchen 1971:624–5; Bruce 1977:43; Carson & Moo 2005:356). Aernie (2011:32–33) criticized some scholars' rendering of γεννάω by which they imbue the term with the meaning "growing up," although it simply indicates "to give birth to, *bear*" (BDAG, γεννάω §2). Moreover, in Acts 22:3, the participles "born," "brought up," and "educated" most likely indicate three stages of Paul's early life (Carson & Moo 2005: 356). Recent scholars suggested that the pattern in which Paul uses three consecutive participles (γεγεννημένος, ἀνατεθραμμένος and πεπαιδευμένος) is similar to "a fixed biographical formula common in Greek writings" (Polhill 1992:458).[11] Van Unnik (1962:19–45) used a plethora of Hellenistic texts that demonstrate the triad formula ("born," "brought up" and "educated") as "*a fixed literary unit*" to come to the following conclusions:

- The verbs, ἀνατρέφω and παιδεύω may not be rendered as identical concepts.[12]

---

10. Cf. Munck (1967:217); Haenchen (1971:624–25); Marshall (1980:353–4).

11. Conzelmann ([1963] 1987:186) finds Arrian's *Bitynica* frag. 1.2, to be an example of a Greek biographical formula: "Νικομήδειον γάρ [τι] τὸ γένος αὐτοῦ ἐν ταύτῃ τῇ συγγραφῇ διορίζει, ἐν αὐτῇ τε γεννηθῆναι καὶ τραφῆναι καὶ παιδευθῆναι" (italics mine).

12. The verb ἀνατρέφω, which occurs only in Luke-Acts, means "the rearing of a child." The same usage of this verb is found in illustrating the childhood of Jesus and Moses (e.g., Luke 4:16; Acts 7:20, 21; Kremer, EDNT 1:94), where the term "denotes the idea of nurturing or rearing a child with respect to feeding and physical care" (Aernie 2011:32). Likewise, παιδεύω has a wide range of meanings between "train" and "discipline" (G. Schneider, EDNT 3:3). Paul seems to have used this word to articulate his own involvement in the study of the Law of the ancestors, which might have been based on Rabbinic and Pharisaic exegetical methodologies (Bertram, TDNT 5:619).

- In terms of the degree of growth, rather, the verb παιδεύω contains a higher notion than ἀνατρέφω (e.g., Eusebius, *Hist. eccl.*, 6. xix. 5–9).
- In most Hellenistic documents, ἀνατρέφω used to be carried out in the parental home.
- The term ἀνατρέφω refers to the entire childhood phase until mental maturity is reached.

Given the three distinctive meanings of ἀνατρέφω, one may conclude that Paul spent his childhood in Jerusalem while being raised by his parents.

Even if this fact is substantiated, such data cannot decisively determine whether Paul's formal education was in a Hellenistic or Jewish cultural milieu. Many scholars have tended to blur the distinction between Hellenistic and Jewish influences based on the fact that even the Jewish education and way of life in Jerusalem had been heavily Hellenized for a number of centuries (Hengel 1989:75–78; Murphy-O'Connor 1996:46; Johnson 2009:26–31; cf. 2 Macc 4:13). Admittedly, the complexity of Paul's background should be seriously considered. However, this does not allow us to imagine Paul as merely an amalgamated or syncretistic figure, regardless of whether Paul's own perception of his ethnic and social status is taken into consideration or not.

At the same time, one cannot overlook Paul's remarkable autobiographical statement in Phil 3:5, in which he rebukes the Judaizers' boasting of their Jewish credentials in support of the message of Christ's superiority (Silva 2005:149). Paul's articulation of five significant Jewish qualifications presents his prior adherence to Judaism as representing the Jew *par excellence* (see Lightfoot 1913:146; Stegner 1993b:503–11; Hawthorne 2004:184–6; Silva 2005:150–2). First, Paul's circumcision on the eighth day (περιτομῇ ὀκταήμερος) indicates that he was born and brought up by strict Jewish parents who circumcised their son on the right day designated by the Hebrew Scriptures (Gen 17:12; Lev 12:3). Second, Paul acquired his Jewish status not by conversion but by birth (ἐκ γένους Ἰσραήλ).[13] Third, he belonged to the distinguished and highly regarded Benjaminite tribe, which was faithful to the Davidic kingdom when the new monarchy (of King Jeroboam) arose and separated the nation (O'Brien 1991:370–1; Hawthorne 2004:184–5; see 1 Kgs 12:21; Rom 11:1; Phil 3:5). Fourthly, his ethnicity was purely Hebrew (Ἑβραῖος ἐξ Ἑβραίων).[14] Fifth, the pre-Damascus Paul lived as a Pharisee who not only observed the commandments, including the oral

---

13. The term, Ἰσραήλ as a genitive of apposition refers to γένος (Hawthorne 2004:184).

14. "A Hebrew, the son of Hebrew" (Zerwick [1974] 1996:599) or "Hebrew born of Hebrew parents" (JB).

law, but was also eager to avoid even an accidental transgression of the law. Hawthorne (2004:185) summarizes well the ideas expressed in this section thus far:

> Although Paul himself was born outside of Palestine (in Tarsus) and therefore could rightly be labeled a Hellenist, he in essence rejects this label, because not only was he the son of Pharisees (Acts 23:6), who saw to it that he was educated precisely in the ways of the Jewish law in Jerusalem under a Hebrew teacher (Acts 22:3), but he himself gladly adopted the Hebrew language as his own language (Acts 21:40; 22:2) and accepted the customs and manner of life of his forefathers (Acts 26:4-5). Paul claims, therefore, to be a Hebrew of Hebrews, one belonging to the elite of his race, tracing his ancestry beyond Tarsus to Palestine.

Nevertheless, even this illustration regarding Paul's ethnic and educational background cannot fully describe his unique status in the first-century Mediterranean cultural milieu, or the way in which such settings played a formative role in Paul's thinking. For this reason, a more in-depth examination of Paul's major conceptual world and sociocultural setting as a diaspora Jew is required (see 2.2).

2.1.5.2 JEWISH APOCALYPTIC PERSPECTIVE AND PAUL

Scholars notice that one of the prominent streams in ancient Jewish thought is "apocalypticism." This Jewish worldview "characterized segments of early Judaism from c. 200 B.C. to A.D. 200, and which centered on the expectation of God's imminent intervention into human history in a decisive manner to save his people and punish their enemies" (Aune 1993:25). In the light of Paul's Jewishness and a widespread perception of an apocalyptic perspective in Judaism, there is general agreement among New Testament scholars that Jewish apocalyptic eschatology was probably central to Paul's thought (Davies [1948] 1955; Dodd 1951:25-26; Beker 1980:143-4; De Boer 2000:366-7). As De Boer (2000:367) acknowledged, for example, Paul maintained the continuity between his pre-Christian understanding of "the apocalyptic-eschatological two-ages dualism" and the apostolic message.

Many Pauline scholars have observed that apocalyptic notions are central to the understanding of 1 Thessalonians. Jewett (1986:168) notices that "[n]owhere in the later Pauline letters does one encounter so thorough a concentration on the apocalyptic future as the centre of faith." More specifically, since Paul concentrates on the Thessalonian believers eagerly awaiting the *parousia* of Jesus Christ (1:6-10; 3:11-13; 4:17-18; 5:23), the parousia of the Lord "is the central theme in Paul's *homilia*" (Collins 1993:170). Meeks (1983b:693) argues that three confirmations of apocalyptic thinking can be identified in 1 Thess 4:13—5:11: (1) the apocalyptic description of "[t]he word of the Lord" in 4:16; (2) the sudden and unexpected coming of the day of the Lord in 5:2; (3) the admonition in the dualistic perspective to alert "the children of light" who are contrasted with "the children of darkness" in 5:4-8.

If it is so, what was Paul's intention in appropriating an apocalyptic perspective and thought? Going beyond merely identifying the discussion of the apocalyptic nature of Paul's thought, recent studies take into consideration the correlation between Paul's apocalyptic perspective and his ethical teachings.

2.1.5.2.1 JEWISH APOCALYPTIC PERSPECTIVE AND ETHICS

Schweitzer (1931:1-18) played an integral role in introducing a reading of Paul in the light of Jewish beliefs, especially Jewish *apocalypticism* and eschatology. He argued that Paul derived his thought world from a scheme of apocalyptic mysticism that presented the world as divided into "this age" and "the age to come." Riches (1993:43) comments that Schweitzer thought that Paul's mysticism was closely associated with his expectation of the imminent coming of eschaton. For instance, Riches mentions that Schweitzer thought that the Spirit of Christ is identified with "the heavenly power of life that is preparing the believers for their existence in the resurrection state"; for him, the Spirit is a significant and compelling reason for the moral life. Schweitzer ([1933] 1949:182) further stated that "(a)ny profound view of the world is mysticism, in that it brings men into a spiritual relation with the Infinite. The view of Reverence for Life is ethical mysticism. It allows union with the Infinite to be realized by ethical action."

Davies ([1948] 1955:98) followed Schweitzer's theological understanding that Paul's mysticism "is derived from the eschatological concept of the community of God in which the elect are closely bound up with one another and with the Messiah" (Schweitzer 1931:101). One of their tasks was to refute the notion that Paul's mysticism was based on Hellenistic mystery religions. Davies ([1948] 1955:90-91) opposed the views of Bousset and Reitzenstein, who compared the death and resurrection of Christ and those of Greek and Egyptian gods (Attis, Osiris, or Dionysus) for a number of reasons. First, the sources used by the scholars raise the problem of anachronism. Second, biblical authors never mentioned the Hellenistic mystery religions of the second century. Third, in contrast to the individualistic feature of the union with Greek gods, the union with Christ implies a communal aspect. Fourth, Christ cannot be a mere counterpart of the Greek gods, since the gods of Hellenistic mysticism "were not rooted and grounded in history as was the Jesus whom Paul knew as the Risen Lord" (Davies [1948] 1955:90). Fifth, while the union with the Greek gods indicates "absorption in the divine" through the union with Christ, personal identity is preserved. Sixth, Paul's terminology, such as salvation, mystery, wisdom and knowledge, cannot be directly deduced from Hellenistic mysticism.

From another perspective, Davies identified potential Jewish sources in the Pauline letters. Particularly, with regard to identifying the sources of Pauline ethics, following Daube's argument, Davies ([1948] 1955:131–6) posited that three Jewish writings—*Pirke Aboth*, *Mishnah Demai*, and *Derek Eretz Rabba*—can be regarded as "the kind of code material that lies behind the hortatory section of the Pauline" letters.

Furthermore, Davies ([1948] 1955:111–2) understood that Christ's return and the end of the world were dominant expectations of early Christian communities. For example, according to Davies, some Thessalonians neglected their own work and responsibility because of their fervent expectation and (mis)understanding of Christ's imminent parousia. Especially, he remarked that in 1 Thessalonians the issue was that Christ's second coming became an excuse for idleness and lack of concern about morality. According to Paul, this attitude of lethargy and disregard for morality in this church needed to be addressed through the eschatological gospel of Christ's second coming. A distinct feature of Paul's apocalyptic perspective is associated with the events of Christ's death, resurrection and his parousia. Davies ([1948] 1955:136) argued that the word of Jesus mainly constituted Paul's hortatory sections based on the close connection between Jesus' ethical teachings and the Jewish didactic tradition.

2.1.5.2.2 RECENT STUDIES ON APOCALYPTIC DISCOURSE

Recently, many scholars have paid attention to the discursive (rhetorical) function of Paul's apocalyptic language in the life of the early Christians. Three significant scholars—Wayne Meeks, Duane Watson, and Charles Wanamaker—delve into the apocalyptic characteristics of Paul's discourse. Though each scholar's emphasis falls on different aspects, they complement one another in the pursuit of tangible contours for grasping the nature of apocalyptic discourse. They together contributed to paving a constructive way towards the development of an ongoing discourse concerning the function of apocalyptic language, especially in 1 Thessalonians.

2.1.5.2.2.1 SOCIOLOGICAL FUNCTION OF APOCALYPTIC DISCOURSE

Meeks played an important role in introducing an interpretation of 1 Thessalonians as apocalyptic discourse. He argued that apocalyptic eschatological language in this letter purported "social control, not only the control of belief" (Meeks 1983b:689). For him (1983a:700), apocalyptic beliefs had the following sociological functions in the faith communities with whom Paul communicated:

- "To emphasize and legitimate boundaries between the Christian groups and the larger society;"
- "To enhance internal cohesion and solidarity;"
- "To provide sanctions for normative behaviour;"
- "To warrant innovations over against the Jewish norms and structures from which Christianity emerged;"
- "To resist, on the other hand, deviant behavior that led to disruption of the Christian community;"
- "To legitimate the leadership of Paul and his associates against challenges;"
- "To justify radical interpretation of scripture and tradition."

Meeks's reading of this letter as apocalyptic discourse complemented Malherbe's argument. Both argued that Paul's Jewish apocalyptic perspective and language of dualism (heaven/earth, this age/the coming age, and worshiping God/idolatry) in 1 Thess 4–5 serve a *paraenetic* function. The doom of the final judgment with Christ's second coming seems to have been intended to provoke, uphold and consolidate appropriate and acceptable behavior among the audience (Meeks 1983b:694; cf. 2000:474). Meeks (1983b:688; 1983a:171–80) provided a potential correlation between the apocalyptic nature of Paul's discourse and millenarian movements.

Scholars who acknowledge the potential contribution of social anthropology to New Testament studies endeavor to find a fresh understanding of early Christianity in the light of recent theories of millenarian movements (Gager 1975:20–21; Meeks 1983b:688; Wanamaker 1987:2). Apart from Jarvie's identification of four characteristics of a millenarian movement, Gager

(1975:21) suggested five criteria that enabled the early Christian movement to be characterized as apocalyptic: (1) the imminent promise of heaven on earth; (2) overturning the present social order; (3) a terrific release of emotional energy; (4) the fleeting lifespan of the movement; and (5) the essential role of a messianic, prophetic, or influential leader. A millenarian movement begins when persons and groups are frustrated in their attempts to gain social power and by "the existing scheme of social transaction" (Meeks 1983b:688; see also 1983b: 172). On the other hand, central leaders in such a movement compensate for their frustration not only by articulating apocalyptic beliefs but also by realizing that the group's values and beliefs can be reinforced in creating "a plausibility structure" or "mazeway" (Wanamaker 1987:3). In so doing, Meeks (1983b:688) argues, a group can gain social power in the new social order: "The apocalyptic myths, radical as they may be in 'nihilating' the existing world—that is, the 'symbolic universe' of the dominant society—may therefore serve a 'conservative' and constructive function for the believing group."

Nevertheless, even if apocalyptic discourse is socially motivated, it is mostly hard to construct such a social setting from the text (Rowland 2010:347). Apocalyptic discourse may (often) be regarded as a projection of an author's conceptual world, not necessarily as reflecting a historical reality (cf. Aune *et al.* 2000:53; Murphy 2012:13, 310-2). Hence, readers should devote themselves to carefully construct the social reality of the time, and then to establish the relevance to the author's perspective.

2.1.5.2.2.2 RHETORICAL ASPECT OF APOCALYPTIC DISCOURSE

Duane Watson's survey on Paul's methodology in appropriating apocalyptic language/discourse was somewhat different from that of Meeks. Watson concentrated intensively on Paul's rhetorical strategy in 1 Thessalonians. In structuring the letter according to Hellenistic epistolary format, Watson (1999:65-79) demonstrates comprehensively how apocalyptic elements are integrated into the rhetorical purpose of each section. For example, in the *exordium* (1:2-10) the Thessalonians' conversion occurred by God's heavenly signs with power and the Holy Spirit. They were exempted from the wrath of God and would finally encounter hope in Christ (1:9-10). The commendation of the gentiles' transformation in Christ indicates the author's intention to shape a good affinity with the audience and bring about pathos through rhetoric (Watson 1999:64). Watson (1999:71) further argues that the *narratio* section (2:1—3:10) contains apocalyptic notions such as calling into the kingdom of God (2:12), Satan's obstruction of Paul's visit to the Thessalonians (2:17–18), and an apocalyptic-laden expression, ἐπὶ πάσῃ τῇ ἀνάγκῃ καὶ θλίψει (3:7). Analogous to Meeks's argument, Watson understood the *peroratio* (5:23–28) as Paul's illustration of an apocalyptic scenario and imminent eschatology in 4:13–18 in order to establish "the ethos or authority of that scenario" (Watson 1999:73).

However, as we have seen, rhetorical arrangement based on Hellenistic epistolary theory cannot be applied systematically to the first letter to the Thessalonians (see 1.2.1). Although the suggested genre is "apocalyptic discourse," Watson's understanding of apocalyptic discourse seems not to be differentiated adequately from rhetorical approaches to the letter. His attempt seems to be an amalgamation of the rhetorical analysis influenced by Hellenistic epistolary theory and apocalyptic discourse. Additionally, Watson should provide further clarification on how Paul's Jewish apocalyptic perspective was adapted and integrated into the widespread convention of letter writing. Furthermore, with regard to identifying the rhetorical style of 1 Thessalonians, Watson (1999:63) confines the rhetorical function of Paul's apocalyptic vision and hope to epideictic rhetoric. For Watson, Paul's rhetoric does not intend to persuade the audience to take a specific action (or moral responsibility). Rather, giving a comfort to the persecuted community, he encourages and strengthens them to adhere to their beliefs and values. In my view, however, this argument may not be persuasive to those scholars who regard 1 Thessalonians as deliberative or paraenetic rhetoric. Finally, Watson's approach overlooked various aspects of apocalyptic language such as "theological, political, and social constructs underlying the rhetoric of the letter" (Luckensmeyer 2009:39). To understand the implications of Paul's apocalyptic language, it is necessary to explore how the author's apocalyptic eschatology is involved in interpreting the social, political, and religious circumstances of the audience.

2.1.5.2.2.3 APOCALYPTIC *TOPOI* IN 1 THESSALONIANS

In his article "Apocalyptic Discourse, Paraenesis and Identity Maintenance in 1 Thessalonians," Wanamaker (2002) elaborated on previous studies of 1 Thessalonians as apocalyptic discourse. Wanamaker (2002:137) identified resemblances between the paraenetic section of the letter (1 Thess 4–5) and characteristics of apocalyptic discourse, since this part of the letter provides direction on how the believers are to be "kept blameless at the coming of our Lord Jesus Christ" (1 Thess 5:23). A prominent feature of Wanamaker's argument is that the concept of apocalyptic *topoi* is central to the development of apocalyptic discourse, having explored its discursive (rhetorical) function rather than only its form and content. For him, "the *topoi* of apocalyptic dualism, apocalyptic determinism, and apocalyptic suffering and vindication" (2002:136) permeate the letter. Wanamaker (2002:137) regarded apocalyptic *topoi* as a foundational resource, particularly in the paraenetic section embedded in Paul's ethical discourse in 4:1–12 and 4:13—5:11.

Apocalyptic *topoi* can be categorized as *rhetorical topoi* that offer the thrust of the narrator's argumentation and "schemes of thought" (cf. Thom 2003:566–7). According to Carey (1999:11), "the resources of apocalyptic discourse function as what the ancient rhetoricians called *topoi*, or flexible resources for persuasion." However, Carey seems to differentiate loosely between *topoi* and theme or idea. Expanding Carey's definition of apocalyptic discourse, Robbins (2002:11) adopts a fixed phrase, "apocalyptic *topoi*," to account for the operation of *topoi* behind argumentative discourse for persuasion. Particularly, Robbins (2002:13, quoting Peacock [1986] 2004:37) remarks that "Aristotle's insight that enthymemes are the 'substance' of persuasion itself has been expanded in modern times to an awareness that a 'cultural system can be envisioned as a set of major premises . . . from which its more specific minor premises can be derived.'" Robbins (2002:14) elaborates that *topoi* are embedded in enthymematic argumentation inasmuch as *topoi* play a persuasive role in delivering discourse based on one's recognition of pattern. He explains:

> The experience of "recognizing the pattern" gives credibility to the *topos*, evoking a conviction that the pattern is "sure" (based on a "sign") or "probable" (based on a "likelihood"). This credibility undergirds enthymematic argumentation, which moves in an inductive-deductive-abductive manner. Thus, a *topos* is not simply a probable or sure "idea" or "theme"; it is "a nexus for enthymemes."

In other words, (re)employing *topoi* per se is an *act of communication* to promote change in the audience's beliefs and behavior.

Concretely, Paul's utilization of apocalyptic *topoi* functions to sustain the Thessalonians' newly gained identity in Christ and simultaneously encourage their moral responsibility and adherence to the Christian faith and virtues (Wanamaker 2002:132). Here, a major strategy adopted by Paul is to establish the Christians' distinctive identity with regard to their sociological position (Wanamaker 2002:140–3).[15] Wanamaker (2002:13; citing Jenkins

---

15. Nevertheless, one must be careful "when specific theory is treated as a transcultural control that may not itself be questioned" (Carson & Moo 2005:71). It has been expected that social scientific perspectives would enrich the understanding of biblical

1996:20) notes that one's social identity is determined through "an ongoing and, in practice simultaneous, synthesis of (internal) self-definition and the (external) definitions of oneself offered by others." In adopting and reinterpreting apocalyptic language, Paul formulated social dialects, "which both reflect and shape their [the communities'] peculiar interpretations of the world" (Barclay 2016:207).

However, even if he and his audience lived in social settings in which the concept of *topoi* was naturally perceived and used, the specific kind of apocalyptic *topoi* Paul appeals to remains vague. In addition, one has to distinguish between Paul's use of apocalyptic *topoi* and their conventional use at the time.

2.1.5.2.3 PAUL AND THE HALAKHIC TRADITION/ NOACHIDE COMMANDMENTS

Recently, scholars have devoted attention to the issue of whether Paul's moral exhortations were indebted also to the halakhic tradition of interpretation of Jewish law (Weima 2014:247-8). According to Tomson (1990:19), *halakah* can be defined as "the tradition of formulated rules of conduct regulating life in Judaism." He elaborated as follows on its three aspects: the "classic literary genres of Rabbinic literature," "a legal system which develops in comparable ways to other systems yet distinct from them," and "the whole of traditional behavioural rules of the Jewish people." It was regarded as a central nerve to the whole system of Jewish life, belief, and custom. Particularly, it is significant that *halakah* or the halakhic tradition also resonates in Paul's paraenesis directed towards gentile believers (Tomson 1990:62; see also 55-95).

Scholars from the so-called radical New Perspective on Paul have focused specifically on his appeal to the Noachide (or Noachian) Commandments as universal requirements for all of humanity, including non-Jewish converts (Davies [1948] 1955:113-5; Tomson 1990: 273; Segal 1992:198-201; Bockmuehl 2000:167-172, 2005:96-100, 2008:343-5; Nanos 2009:14).

---

passages, "putting living flesh upon the sometimes dry bones of textual analysis, adding color and perspective and allowing us to see the world, characters and message of the NT with greater vigor" (Berding 2003:22). I do not regard texts merely as "socially and culturally conditioned documents" as May (1991:1) remarks. In response, I claim that the reading of 1 Thessalonians should involve more than merely applying sociological theory to the paraenetic part in chapters 4-5, and more than recognizing "the dialectic between social reality and ideas" (cf. Wanamaker 1987:1). Paul defines the identity of Thessalonian Christians within an apocalyptic scenario not based merely on sociological terms, but also and mainly on the theological redefinition of his inherited resources.

Segal (1992:195) has argued that the Noahide Commandments in the Rabbinic tradition are attributed to two significant Old Testament passages, which have to do with all humanity:

> In rabbinic midrash, the Noahide Commandments include monotheism, avoidance of murder, organizing courts and promulgating justice, avoiding incest, theft, blasphemy, as well as avoiding eating the flesh of living creatures and, sometimes, recognition that the Lord, the God of Israel, is the one true God. All of these ideas can be derived from the Noah story in Genesis, if they are read together with the rules for sojourners, principally in Leviticus 17–26. These two passages are associated because they point to the origin of the laws for the legal treatment of resident aliens.

Davies ([1948] 1955:115) proposed Paul's familiarity with the Noachide Commandments based on his argument regarding the universality of God's moral requirements among all of humanity in Rom 1:18–32. Here, Paul articulated the view that natural knowledge of God leads to the universal moral law of the creator. However, the issue of anachronism can be raised since the Noachide Commandments were not given shape until the second century CE (Bockmuehl 2000:167; Wilson 2007:6; Du Toit 2015:6). Because of this problem, scholars explored their proximate form (e.g., *Jub.* 7:20–21) rather than making a direct connection between Paul and the Noachide Commandments (Tomson 1990:62–68, 208–16; Bockmuehl 2000:168; Segal 1992:195). According to Bockmuehl (2000:150), the Noachide Commandments might have been a *topos* which "in rabbinic thought governs relations between Jews and non-Jews." In this way it may (also) be regarded as "the *rationale* of New Testament ethics."

For these scholars, general (or universal) moral precepts, such as "the prohibition of idolatry, sexual abuse and bloodshed," were significant principles resonating in the Pauline letters (Tomson 1990:50). Even though evidence is scarce, they assume that Paul's ethical teachings in 1 Thessalonians allude to the halakhic tradition (Tomson 1990:91–92; Bockmuehl 2000:135). Examples are the prohibition of sexual immorality (1 Thess 4:3) and the tradition of economic self-sufficiency from Rabbinic Judaism (1 Thess 4:11–12). In addition, Weima (2014:248–9; see 5.2) observed Paul's probable appeal to Jewish moral tradition in the paraenetic section of chapters 4–5: (1) the occurrence of technical terms, "to receive" and "to walk," which were often used in rabbinic tradition; (2) the concept of "pleasing God" as the purpose of human life; (3) Paul's echoing of Old Testament texts in 4:8–9; (4) "holiness" as an essential character of God's new covenant people; (5) the influence of Jewish practice in using the vocative "brother" (4:1,6, 10); and (6) the virtue of making a favorable impression on outsiders; these appear throughout the Hebrew Scriptures (e.g., Exod 32:12, 25; Num 14:14–16; Deut 9:25–29; 1 Kings 20:28) and in non-Christian Jewish literature of the Second Temple period.

Nevertheless, for a number of reasons it is uncertain whether echoes of the halakhic tradition are indeed to be found in Paul's ethics. First, the association between Paul and later rabbinic tradition remains merely conjecture because of sparse evidence and its anachronistic relation. Second, one may raise questions about the differences of shared moral values between the halakhic tradition for the gentiles and a universal moral standard. For instance, does the prohibition of sexual immorality exist only in halakhic tradition? Third, Paul did not make the boundary between the Jews and the gentiles (Rom 3:22; 10:12; 1 Cor 1:24; 12:13; Gal 3:28; cf. Horrell 2005:18). Fourth, representatives of the radical New Perspective on Paul do not seem to overcome the apparent distance between Paul's understanding of himself as "no being . . . under the law" (1 Cor 9:20) and his former thinking on Torah as a follower of Judaism (Horrell 2005:18). Fifth, even though 1 Thessalonians was written to gentile Christians, Paul's potential use of the halakhic tradition can be applied consistently to other letters (inter alia) addressed to Jewish Christians (e.g., Rom 2:17; 3:9; 16:3, 7, 11). As Horrell (2005:18–19) mentioned, "nowhere does Paul state that his ethical teaching applies only to Gentile converts, while Jewish Christians must obey the whole law." Instead, without making a distinction between gentiles and Jews, Paul states that whoever is "in Christ" is presented as the genuine descendant of Abraham.

2.1.6 PRELIMINARY CONCLUSION

Thus far my discussion has focused on three perspectives that seem to point significantly to Paul's Jewishness. His Jewish background can be substantiated based on Luke's report in Acts 22:3 and the autobiographical statement in Phil 3:5, his Jewish apocalyptic perspective, and the halakhic tradition with respect to the gentiles. From these arguments, it can provisionally be deduced that Paul's Jewish apocalyptic worldview and appropriation of Scripture formed important building blocks for his teaching on identity and moral formation among gentile Christian communities.

Nevertheless, one has to be careful about describing Paul's Jewishness only from the perspective of first-century Judaism. Such an approach runs the risk of considering Paul's ideological background merely in light of the dualistic framework of Hellenism and Judaism. In an attempt to avoid being reductionist, any discussion on Paul's Jewishness also needs to include his status as a diaspora Jew, particularly in the light of sociocultural perspectives beyond the above-mentioned two delineations of Paul's background. It will also be crucial to consider the extent to which Paul appropriated his Jewish traditions as the apostle of Christ after his encounter with Jesus of Nazareth on his way to Damascus.

2.2 PAUL AS AN ANOMALOUS DIASPORA JEW AND THE CONCEPT OF IDENTITY

Recent scholarship has indicated that various forms of Judaism existed in the first-century Palestinian region (Longenecker 1964:28; Safrai & Stern 1976:161–6; Stegner 1993a:212). In order to understand the nature of Paul's Jewishness, one has to be mindful of the geographical and sociocultural milieu in which he grew up. Barclay (1995:90) contributed as follows to our understanding of Paul's sociocultural context:

> Paul as a Jew has to work within the same social parameters and had to define and practice his Christian mutation of the Jewish tradition alongside other Diaspora Jews. Thus, whatever his birthplace or early environment, Paul's social context invites us to compare him with the range of viewpoints and practices current among Diaspora Jews.

This observation enables us to postulate Paul's stance and position as part of the Jewish diaspora. Barclay (1995:93) argues that this may happen through a synthetic consideration of the degree of *assimilation, acculturation,* and *accommodation* with regard to processes of Hellenization. At least, these criteria potentially enable us to appreciate various aspects that Paul could have experienced within the spectrum of Hellenization of the Jews. In so doing, one may acquire a more comprehensive picture of Paul's Jewishness in his time and social setting. Particularly, constructing Paul's conceptual map (as a Hellenistic Jew) in the light of a particular social, cultural, and religious milieu enables us to understand his unique characteristics and viewpoints better.

2.2.1 JEWISH IDENTITY IN THE JEWISH DIASPORA

Diaspora Jews can be classified in a variety of ways according to the degree of assimilation, acculturation and accommodation they went through with regard to Hellenization (Collins 1986:7–10; Kraabel 1992:25–28; Barclay 1995:92–103; 1996:82–102; Thompson 2011:19–20). Taking into account the broad spectrum of those considered diaspora Jews will prevent us from making an excessively sharp distinction between Paul's Jewishness and the Hellenistic social setting. Specifically, through this, one may determine the degree of Paul's integration into and cultural exposure to the Hellenistic world by comparing him with other diaspora Jews. In the following section Barclay's analysis of three broad categories of Hellenization of the Jews (*assimilation*, *acculturation*, and *accommodation*) will be employed to identify Paul's social, cultural, and religious position.

2.2.1.1 ASSIMILATION INTO HELLENIZATION

Maintaining one's Jewish identity as a foreigner in a pluralistic gentile world might have caused social tensions and dissonance with indigenous people, because of the Jews' repudiation of pagan worship (Collins 1986:7; Barclay 1995:94; 1996:82; Gruen 2004:59). Yet it seems that adaptation to the new cultural environment had started to occur. It was found that various elements of the migrants' life such as interracial marriage and interaction with the multicultural society emerged and that a new generation gradually arose. Assimilation took place in a similar manner where the Jews participated socially in the Hellenistic world. This process depended on the degree of adherence to Judaism in the Hellenistic world, and openness to pagan society. According to Barclay (1995:95), "the degree to which Jews in the Diaspora were socially aloof from, or socially integrated" could have varied according to their attachment to the social structure of the environment:

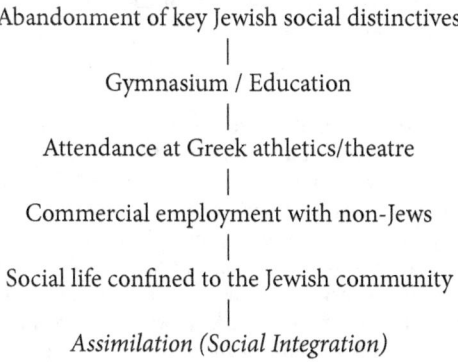

The range of adaptation of diaspora Jews to a syncretistic gentile society may have ranged from the cultural customization of their ancestral religion to the renouncement of their belief and conviction (Kraabel 1992:27).

Even though Greek-speaking diaspora Jews might have gone through the process of external "Hellenization," many of them were not absorbed into Hellenistic syncretistic religions but remained faithful to the Torah and maintained their Jewish identity (Hengel 1980:101; Thompson 2011:19–40). Some Jews' adherence to their own tradition was expressed even in association with Hellenistic philosophical language and concepts (Hengel 1980:102; Collins 1986:9; Thompson 2011:27; see *Let. Aris* 16; *Aristob.* 4:3–4, 7–8). On the other hand, there were also diaspora Jews who forsook Judaism. Philo's nephew, Tiberius Julius Alexander, renounced his own Jewish intellectualism, since the issue of divine providence was problematic for him (Wolfson 1948:82; Collins 1986:9; Kamesar 2009:23; cf. Josephus, *Ant.* 2. 100).[16]

2.2.1.2 ACCULTURATION INTO HELLENIZATION

Barclay also employed the concept of "acculturation" to indicate the diaspora Jews' educational and cultural exposure to Hellenistic society. As the Hellenistic period began after Alexander's conquest of the Mediterranean world, with propagation of the idea of "Greek by παιδεία (education)" as a significant slogan, the Greek educational system and gymnasium played a significant role in maintaining and undergirding Hellenistic culture (Hengel 1974:66; Safrai & Stern 1976:162). Despite limited access to the Greek education system, as the gymnasium accepted only Greek students, opportunities for instruction gradually opened up to some prominent male Jews during the Ptolemaic period (Hengel 1974:67).

However, the problem for the Jews was that the gymnasium was associated with Greek deities. Festivals of the religious cult required the involvement of young students in expressing gratitude to their indigenous gods as benefactors. This was, however, incompatible with Jewish monotheism and adherence to the Torah (Hengel 1974:67; Safrai & Stern 1976: 162).

---

16. According to Wolfson (1948:73–80), Philo sets out three patterns to describe diaspora Jews as apostates. First, "the weakness of flesh" led some diaspora Jews astray as Philo illustrates: those who abandon the holy laws are "willing to sell their liberty for luxurious eating, for strong wine, for sweetmeats, and for beauty, for pleasures of the belly and of the parts below the belly." Second, their apostasy was attributed to "the vulgar delusion of social ambition." To accumulate financial assets, having business relationships with the gentile partners, naturally led some diaspora Jews to join gentile communities. Mingling with those business partners was often accompanied with "cordial reception" of the gentile customs. Third, "an unconscious shifting of intellectual interest" brought about separation from Judaism. Philo illustrates that philosophy was the Alexandrian Jews' intellectual concern, saying, "in accordance with which custom, even to this day, the Jews hold philosophical discussions on the seventh day, disputing about their national philosophy, and devoting that day to the knowledge and consideration of the subjects of natural philosophy." According to Wolfson (1948:81–82), as diaspora Jews increasingly had social interaction with non-Jews, Jews turned their attention to the fields of arts, sciences, and philosophy in forsaking their traditional religious training.

Occasionally, the Jewish upper class amongst the diaspora communities compromised by adopting polytheistic beliefs in Greek gods. Some Jewish names kept appearing "in the list of ephebes of Greek cities, which usually end with a formula of dedication to Hermes and Heracles" (Hengel 1974:68; cf. Wolfson 1948:79). On the other hand, there were some Hellenistic Jews in Alexandria who did not attend the gymnasia and maintained their ancestral belief (Safrai & Stern 1976:162).

Depending on the extent to which the Jews were open to attending Greek education, the degree of familiarity with Greek literature, rhetoric or philosophy varied among them. The possibility of diaspora Jews equipped with Greek education and fluency in the Greek language suggests a wide spectrum of acculturation. This idea is substantiated by Barclay (1995:96) in terms of the following categories:

Scholarly Expertise
|
Familiarity with Greek literature, rhetoric, philosophy, and theology
|
Acquaintance with common moral values
|
No facility in Greek
|
Acculturation (Language/Education)

2.2.1.3 ACCOMMODATION INTO HELLENIZATION

Deciding on the degree of a diaspora Jew's Hellenization based on the level of assimilation and acculturation per se might lead to a superficial conclusion. For this reason, Barclay (1995:97) prefers the concept of "accommodation" to shed light on "the type and degrees of fusion between the Greek and Jewish heritages" in the process of Hellenization.

Acculturation does not necessarily occur concurrently with accommodation, as one sees in the case of Philo of Alexandria. Philo's stance with regard to accommodation can be located at the top of the scale of Hellenization. He was educated in a Greek gymnasium and was familiar with Greek rhetoric, literature, and philosophy. Most notably, his application of Hellenistic allegories to the interpretation of Scripture tends to relativize the historical dimension of those Hebrew texts and to generalize the stories of ancient Israel (Termini 2009: 123; Barclay 1995:100). However, the degree of accommodation in the case of Philo is not as high as the degree of his acculturation. Philo articulated the superiority and eternal value of the Torah, which is regarded as the backbone of Jewish tradition and which had to be made known to all people (*Mos.* 2.12, 14–15, 17, 25–27, 43–44). The significance of Torah was even expressed through Hellenistic allegory. Philo illustrated the significance of the Decalogue by using Stoic philosophy's four passions (Harrington 2010:607). Moreover, in 4 Maccabees the author's first statement governs the rest of his argument: "[h]ighly philosophical is the subject I propose to discuss, namely, whether devout reason is absolute master of the passions, and I would strictly counsel you to give earnest attention to my philosophical exposition" (1:1).[17] Through tripartite association—philosophy (e.g., 7:21), reason (e.g., 5: 31), and law (e.g., 5:18; 6:21; 7:15, 21), the author indicated that philosophical rule is not incompatible with Jewish belief in God and a pious life (7:21–23). Moreover, Jason, a member of the Jewish diaspora community from Cyrenaica, wrote five books to summarize 2 Maccabees. In the process he used the techniques of Hellenistic historiography and rhetoric to authenticate his account of the Maccabean revolt (Hengel 1974:95–96).

Because of the complex relationship between acculturation and accommodation, it is necessary to figure out to what extent diaspora Jews accepted Judaism in relation to Hellenistic culture. Barclay (1995:97) categorizes this process in terms of three scales of accommodation:

Submersion of Jewish cultural uniqueness		
Reinterpretation of Judaism preserving some uniqueness		Integrative
	↑	
Antagonism to Graeco-Roman culture		Oppositional
	↓	
Accommodation (Use of Acculturation)		

2.3 PAUL AS DIASPORA JEW

An important advantage of Barclay's coordinates of assimilation, acculturation, and accommodation is that it prevents one from confining Paul to a single sociocultural milieu (whether the Hellenistic or Palestinian world). A comparison between Paul and his contemporaries not only sheds light on

---

17. See *Old Testament Pseudepigrapha* volume II (Charlesworth [1983] 2011:544).

his pre-Christian status but also leads to an awareness of their contribution to shaping his conceptual world.

However, given the complexity of "hybrid" or "liminal" personalities, even Barclay's encompassing framework can probably not (fully) cover the multifaceted social strata of diaspora Jews in the first century CE. Barclay's three scales are merely meant to be a convenient tool for providing preliminary conjectures. How then can one locate Paul amidst the variegated stances of Jewish diaspora with reference to these scales? How does one determine the "degree" of Paul's Hellenization?

With regard to Paul's assimilation into Hellenization, his social integration into the Hellenistic world may first be viewed as occurring along the borderlines of perspectives of both Jews and Greeks. On the one hand, Paul was not assimilated into widespread moral perception in Hellenistic society, as is clear from his prohibition of its common practices, such as sexual immorality and idolatry (1 Cor 5:9–11; 6:12–20; 10:14).[18] Particularly, Paul's opposition of idolatry implies that he never appeared as "an ephebe in a Greek gymnasium," nor as "a civic official" associated with cultic ceremonies in honor of Greek gods (Barclay 1995:104). Even though it is impossible to have a clear or definitive picture of Paul's assimilation into Hellenistic thinking and practices, we may hypothesize that he probably confined himself to the "strong and self-confident" Jewish diaspora community (Frey 2007:294). According to Stegner (1993b:505), the Jewish school in Paul's day taught wisdom and the Torah for the young people of the Jewish upper classes, in an attempt to "preserve Judaism from assimilation to Greek learning and language." He (1993b:505) states that in Paul's day, six- or seven-year-old (Jewish) boys learned the Pentateuch in elementary schools, and young men were educated in the interpretation of the Hebrew Scriptures. Considering Paul's educational background in this light raises another question with regard to whether diaspora Pharisaism existed in his day. Several scholars deny the possibility that Paul had a Pharisaic education outside Palestine. There seems to be no Pharisee who lived permanently as a diaspora Jew, since—from a Jewish perspective—it is difficult to observe Torah in a pagan world (Hengel 1991: 29–31). If my discussion of Luke's account of Paul's educational background is tenable (see 2.1.5.1), it is plausible to assume that Paul was born outside Palestine in the Jewish diaspora but obtained his Pharisaic education in Jerusalem from his early childhood. Thus, the degree of Paul's assimilation into Hellenization may be estimated as a mid-point in the scale of assimilation. As Barclay (1995: 104) conjectured, "[t]he intimate associations which Paul enjoyed with Gentiles

---

18. The Hellenistic world tolerated promiscuity, since marriage was regarded merely as a family match. Outside of marriage it was tolerated/expected that men would engage in relations with prostitutes, female slaves, or concubines (Weima 2002a:419).

who were not, in Jewish terms, law-observant set him high on the scale, not indeed fully assimilated, but certainly higher than Philo."

Second, the level of Paul's acculturation into Hellenization may be appreciated by conjecturing to what extent Greek rhetoric and moral philosophy permeate Paul's knowledge and the stylistic features of his paraenesis. With some evidence that Greek rhetorical skills (e.g., chiasmus, litotes, alliteration, oxymoron, etc.) and philosophical elements are indeed found in Paul's writings, recent scholars conclude that "Paul received at most a secondary Hellenistic education" (Yamauchi 1993:386). Certainly, as has already been discussed, it cannot be disputed that Hellenistic rhetoric and epistolary skills were commonly practiced in Paul's day, and that Hellenization might have been the common cultural phenomenon of the first-century Mediterranean world. In addition, some highly acculturated diaspora Jews, such as Aristeas, Aristobulus, Philo, and the author of 4 Maccabees, are "more conversant with the philosophical currents of thought than Paul" (Barclay 1995:106; see 1996:138–49, 150–3, 369–80).

However, the mere occurrence of Hellenistic rhetoric and philosophy in Paul's writings does not necessarily mean that he embraced those traditions "for his own use," or received any formal education of letter writing, elementary rhetorical practice and philosophy (Litfin 1994:139; Barclay 1995:107).[19] Moreover, the degree of acculturation into Hellenization seems not to be high enough to have deeply infiltrated Paul's conceptual framework, Barclay (1995:105–6) remarks:

> It does not seem that Paul had more than a rudimentary knowledge of Greek literature or philosophy either. The allusions to Greek literature in his letters are extremely sparse and in any case only what were common proverbial sayings . . . The use of philosophical tags could signal merely *superficial acculturation* (italics added).

Hengel (1991:58) argues that although Paul (as a Greek-speaking diaspora Jew) seems to have obtained "a certain basic training in rhetoric" and basic "rhetorical art" in his earlier childhood at a Jewish Hellenistic school, such education can probably not be considered equivalent to "the *Attic-style* school rhetoric of the time" (italics added). For Paul, the LXX most plausibly

---

19. Even if Paul could read Hellenistic philosophy, his intentional allusion to Hellenistic literature is unlikely. Norden (1898:496–7) observes that: "daß Paulus z. B. etwas von Platon gelesen haben könne, wage ich nicht zu bestreiten (so sehr sich mein subjektives Gefühl dagegen auflehnt), aber was nützen uns solche problematischen Urteile? . . . nicht einmal Anklänge sind weder an Platon noch an irgend einen anderen hellenischen Schriftsteller nachgewiesen worden, den was man als Beweise oder Anklänge auszugeben pflegt, erweist sich bei auch nur flüchtigem Zusehen als ganz und gar nichtig."

not only was his primary textbook from his early childhood but also played a major role in constituting his knowledge and conceptual map than any classical Greek literature or philosophy (Hengel 1991:37).

Third, the question of how cultural fusion could have occurred in Paul's mind may be answered by exploring two phases in his life—pre- and post-Damascus. At least Paul's fluency in Greek and familiarity with Hellenistic culture seems not to have affected the awareness of his Jewish identity in profound ways. As Frey (2007:294) points out, Paul belonged to a community that had a self-confident recognition of Jewish identity among various diaspora Jews:

> [I]t must be assumed that not wide-ranging assimilation but the awareness of the religious otherness and the cultivation of a strong diaspora-Jewish identity were decisive for the climate in which the young Paul grew up and got his primary education. Here are the roots of the strong rejection of any kind of iconic and polytheistic cults and the emphatic monotheism, which was no less characteristic for the later Apostle.

If Frey's notion is right, the level of Paul's accommodation into Hellenism may be located near the bottom of Barclay's accommodation scale.

However, the level of Paul's accommodation after the Damascus Road incident could even have been higher than before he became a follower of Christ, embracing a wide range of the social, cultural spectrum. Paul did not only reinterpret Judaism "from a new vantage point, created by his Christology" but also attempted to integrate Jews and gentiles into solidarity in Christ (Barclay 1995:109; e.g., Rom 1:16; 1 Cor 1:22–24). Paul's eradication of ethnic dualism ("Jews" and "gentiles") indicates that his perspective towards gentiles was transformed from the perspective of a fervent Judaizer to that of the apostle of Christ/a Christian missionary. After his encounter with the resurrected Christ, Paul underwent a profound shift in his perspective on Jewish tradition. It is evident that he became receptive and open to reaching out to the gentiles. His rhetorical question in Gal 2:14 ("If you, though a Jew, live like a Gentile and not like a Jew, how can you force the Gentiles to live like Jews?") pointed out the inconsistent attitudes of Peter regarding requirements for gentile conversion, as well as those of the Jewish Christian leadership in Antioch (Moo 2013:152). It was, for example, not problematic for Paul to eat with gentile Christians, since he understood Jewish dietary laws no longer to be effective for those who are *in Christ* after his encounter with the resurrected Christ on the way to Damascus (e.g., Rom 14:14, 20; cf. Gal 2:18).[20] Moreover, Paul rejected the practice of 'Jewish

---

20. Neusner ([1973] 1979:86; 1982:534) found that, "[o]f the 341 individual Houses'

only' table fellowship, since it functioned to create a distinction between the Jewish community and the gentiles, which could endanger the unity in Christ amongst the early Christian communities (Smith [1992] 2008:303: cf. Douglas 1972:78–80).

In my estimation, particularly, the frame of "Paul's universalizing hermeneutic" seems to have been beneficial in bringing about a crucial and unprecedented transformation of the sociocultural division of these two ethnic groups. In dealing with Paul's universalistic hermeneutic and theology as a whole, I believe that the salvation-historical perspective of Abraham's promises (Rom 4; Gal 3) could provide a significant key. As Moo (2007:74) illustrates, in those texts, "Paul's task, then, was to explain how the gospel he proclaimed, which brought Gentiles into the people of God on equal footing with believing Jews, could be squared with these Abrahamic promises." Moreover, Moo (2007:77) shows the continuity between Israel and Church in dealing with the theological implication of Paul's analogy of olive tree (Rom 11):

> Paul views Gentiles who are experiencing the messianic salvation as belonging not to a new body discontinuous with Israel but to Israel itself. True, this is not simply national Israel ... But ... the church is not so much a replacement for Israel or even a "new" Israel; it is the continuation of "Israel" in the era of fulfilment.

Likewise, in 1 Thessalonians, Paul's reconfiguration of the election of God's people in the Jewish Scriptures functions as the ground for the inclusion of Thessalonian believers into the people of God. This seems to serve as a hermeneutical presupposition for his entire discourse.[21]

Hence, attention must be devoted to the notion of identity as a major thrust in Paul's formation of Christian communities. This is reiterated by Thompson (2011:16):

> Ethical instruction in the Diaspora was inseparable from the establishment of Jewish identity. This identity protected Jewish communities from assimilation by demarcating them from the surrounding society ... Communities express their distinctive

---

legal pericopae [of Hillel and Shammai], no fewer than 229, approximately 67 per cent of the whole, directly or indirectly concern table-fellowship." Pharisaic table fellowship in and around Paul's day required "ritual purity" and "food restriction" in order to protect one from violating observance of the law (Neusner [1973] 1979:89). Observing food laws and ritual purity among the Pharisees were boundary markers that differentiated them from others (Neusner [1973] 1979:89; 1982:536).

21. At the same time, we need to assume that Paul's negative statement about the Jews in 1 Thess 2:14–16 does not nullify his universalistic hermeneutic.

identity with a code of conduct that distinguishes them from others. Through all of Paul's letters he weaves a thread of terminology that establishes a shared identity among converts who come from a variety of backgrounds. He appeals to this identity as the basis for his instructions . . . ethics is the expression of our identity.

2.4 CONCLUSION

Previous studies that attempted to fit Paul into a certain ideological world have (often) produced a one-sided picture of the apostle's thinking, thereby limiting the hermeneutical potential of his writings. Approaching Paul in the light of the notion of an anomalous diaspora Jew holds the potential to clarify that he could adapt to either of the two great cultural settings of his day, namely Hellenistic thinking and Judaism. As Bird (2016:28) observed, Barclay's categorization contributes to our understanding of the formation of "a social space for a unified body of Jewish and Gentile Christ-believers." On the other hand, a significant argument for being anomalous can be attributed to Paul's new understanding of Scripture, yielded after his encounter with Jesus of Nazareth. His salvation-historical understanding and apocalyptic interpretation of Christ's death and resurrection opened his eyes anew, so that "[t]he story and symbols of Judaism were now redrawn around Jesus the Messiah and his followers, who constituted the renewed Israel of an inaugurated eschaton" (Bird 2016:28). Based on Paul's belief in God's new creation in Christ, both continuity and discontinuity are applicable in his self-construal of Jewish identity. In Paul's view, the ethnic and religious qualifications according to Judaism are no longer valid in defining the people of God. Rather, identity has now to do with having faith in Christ, beyond sociocultural constraints. In this way, Paul relativizes the ethos of being the people of God "in relation to a new Christ-given and Spirit-endowed identity" (Bird 2016:52). In 1 Thessalonians Paul appropriated foundational principles regarding the identity and ethos of ancient Israel in his teaching to the Thessalonian faith communities. In so doing, Paul integrated the gentile converts into God's meta-narrative of salvation, in which Christ's work has now become the crux.

3

The Thessalonians in a Pluralistic Religious Environment

THE PREVIOUS CHAPTER OF this study focused on Paul's Jewishness, especially his conceptual map as an anomalous diaspora Jew. An attempt was made to establish and undergird this study's hypothesis that Paul's Jewishness played a formative role in his paraenetic discourse. Yet in Paul's case communication would not occur unilaterally, that is, only from his perspective as a Jewish speaker. Discourse can be regarded as entailing a communicative act that is created through interactions between author and audience, reflecting their common memory of, and perspective on, a specific event (cf. 1.4.1). According to Hester (2002:138), discourse takes place in "a variety of social settings, institutions, and disciplines, each of which have coding systems understood by members of those entities, and for which the use of a coding system can both generate and elaborate knowledge." Even though it is not possible to construct the entire reality an audience was/is confronted with, the language selected by the author of a text may—albeit only partially—reflect relevant political and religious contexts of their society as well as shared experiences of the speaker and audience.

Information about the historical context of the city of Thessalonica per se is absent in the text itself. However, without constructing the historical context of a text (albeit provisionally), it may be difficult to establish its discursive exigency or specific occasion. Since it is not always possible to figure out what sorts of situations led the author to adopt a specific language and connotations, some data from extra-biblical sources are inevitably useful. Recent scholarship has noted the distinctiveness between historical and discursive (rhetorical) situations (Wuellner 1987:456;

1990:124–6; Fiorenza 1987:388). Even though a "historical situation" itself may not be identified with "rhetorical situations," the interrelatedness between these two should not be neglected.[1] When one pays attention to a Pauline text, questions regarding the reason(s) why Paul might have employed such specific language and expression should be raised. Though one should be careful not to allow extra-biblical information to impose the interpretative process of a text, the audience's social, cultural, and religious contexts should be constructed in order to estimate its relation to textual clues. As Kittredge (1998:101) argues, a discursive (rhetorical) situation can be established by acquiring "information from outside the text in order to gain a more accurate picture of the audience for the letter." In this sense, constructing a probable "historical situation" for 1 Thessalonians is crucial in as far as it was reflected, (re)arranged, and integrated into Paul's establishing the discursive (rhetorical) exigency in the letter.

This chapter will make use of extra-biblical resources from the Thessalonica of Paul's day in the attempt to construct and understand the nature of the persecution the Thessalonians were experiencing. Essentially, it is likely that Paul perceived and reinterpreted the audience's actual circumstances in light of Jewish apocalyptic eschatology. In Paul's view, the chief discursive exigency in 1 Thessalonians is probably an *identity crisis* and *ethical dilemma*, which were precipitated by the believers being alienated from their social group. This investigation aims at constructing the discursive exigency of this letter.

---

1. The relation between historical and discursive (rhetorical) situations has been controversial (see Martin 2010:79–87). But I argue that a close link between these two should be taken into account with regard to Paul's establishing a discursive exigency. The text itself provides limited clues regarding what happened to Paul and his communities. With such partial information, an interpreter's goal is not only to construct the "historical situation" of the text, but also to figure out how that situation is reflected and embedded in the discourse of the text. In this regard, Stamps (1993:199) argues that the "[discursive or rhetorical] situation [is] embedded in the text and created by the text which contributes to the rhetorical effect of the text." In other words, as Christopher Stanley (1990:488) explains, "(t)he 'rhetorical situation' . . . includes not only the particular historical situation within which a given dialogue between speaker and hearers (or author and readers) takes place, but also the speaker/author's *perception* of that situation as one that requires change, a change that the speaker/author feels can (perhaps) be brought about by verbal argumentation of a particular sort." For this reason, both situations should be regarded as distinct but related to each other. This distinctiveness may help the interpreter to imagine how a particular historical context could have informed the author's perception of the exigency that motivates the entire discourse.

3.1 THE THESSALONIANS' MORAL INTEGRITY IN THEIR PRESENT REALITY

The Thessalonians' calling "to walk in a manner worthy of God" can be understood in Paul's presenting both present and future aspects of God's kingdom. In 1 Thess 2:12 he notes: "[W]e exhorted each one of you and encouraged you and charged you to walk in a manner worthy of God, who calls you into his own kingdom and glory." Many scholars seem to acknowledge that the notion of God's kingdom is only future-oriented. But the Thessalonians might also have been reminded that their present participation in the kingdom of God prompts their holiness.

It is controversial whether the participle (καλοῦντος) in 1 Thess 2:12 denotes the continuing nature of God's kingdom. While it is hard to decide whether Paul refers to the present or future aspects of God's kingdom, because of his few references to it, the majority's view is that this term supports the future coming of the kingdom (Hendriksen 1955:68; Marshall 1983:75; Green 2002:138). Certainly, one cannot argue that the present tense itself denotes the present aspect of Paul's eschatology, since elsewhere Paul uses the aorist tense of this verb (Rom 8:30; 1 Cor 1:9; Gal 1:6; 1 Thess 4:7) to indicate God's calling to conversion (Wanamaker 1990:107). Since this participle's grammatical function as a substantive describes God as "the caller," it can connote timelessness (Best 1986a:108; Bruce 1982:37). In this sense, one should consider both the present and future reality of Paul's eschatology with regard to the understanding of God's kingdom in 1 Thess 2:12. The present exhortation to the Thessalonians for upright conduct is not merely oriented to God's calling into the future kingdom; rather, their current affiliation with the present reality of the kingdom should lead to moral alertness. Donfried (1987:179) describes how the new converts who had turned from their idols to God were living in between the present and future: "Already now, partially and proleptically, through Christ and his gospel, God's rule and glory have broken into this transient world and are at work in them." If both present and future aspects of the kingdom of God are maintained, in understanding this verse Paul describes the effectiveness of God's calling as operating from the beginning of the new converts' life to the day of the *parousia* (cf. Best 1986a:108; Wanamaker 1999:107). In examining the absolute juxtaposition of present and future eschatological realities in this letter, Seifrid (1999:61) emphasizes that the fullness of salvation has already been given to believers in the present time through Christ.

In 1 Thessalonians Paul's apocalyptic eschatology seems to be a significant basis for his exhortations (see 1.3.3; 2.1.5.2.2). His use of eschatological language and portraying an apocalyptic scenario cannot be separated from the exhortation to moral uprightness. The entire paraenetic section of 1 Thessalonians addresses instructions on holiness (4:3–8). Specifically, in 1 Thess 5:1–11, Paul elucidates the detailed aspects of God-pleasing ethos mentioned in 4:1–2. By employing apocalyptic and dualistic language, this paraenesis effectively articulates the moral responsibility associated with the new identity that the Thessalonian believers are encouraged to embrace within their prevailing environment.[2]

A prominent feature of Paul's apocalyptic eschatology is that he interprets the existential reality that implicitly confronts the Thessalonian audience. It is difficult, however, to correlate apocalyptic thinking with specific social situations, because of its hypothetical nature. I therefore argue that apocalyptic language in 1 Thessalonians provides, at least in part, some clues to understanding the probable tension between the congregation and their fellow citizens. This is supported by Still (1999:197), who explains the occasion for Paul's concentration on apocalyptic language: "[T]he apocalyptic motifs of 1 (and 2) Thessalonians may be viewed as Paul's theological response to the hostile social relation that he and his converts had experienced/were experiencing with non-Christians." In fact, the apocalyptic setting of Paul's discourse in the paraenetic section may probably be attributed to political and religious conflicts between the new converts and their fellow citizens in first-century Thessalonica. Paul construes the conflict and the audience's alienation from society in the light of his "symbolic world of apocalyptic," which is characterized by the dualistic framework between insiders and outsiders (Barclay 1992:54). Here, it is crucial to notice Paul's social dialects that are "special forms of speech which both reflect and shape their peculiar interpretations of the world" (Barclay 2016:207). For instance, Paul's prominent use of the language of belonging, and his consistent contrasts between two antithetical concepts (God's chosen one and gentiles [1:4, 9; 4:5]; insiders and outsiders [πρὸς τοὺς ἔξω, 4:12; οἱ λοιποί, 4:13; 5:6]; and holiness and impurity [4:7]) may be considered as important clues towards constructing a *Sitz im Leben* of suffering in the Thessalonian community. These antitheses are based on the function of apocalyptic dualism to solidify the community's self-recognition of their elected status in Christ, as well as their moral values. Here Paul seems to make a connection

2. Here one may ask why Paul used Jewish traditions that might have been incomprehensible to gentiles. Stanley (2008:133) argues that Paul's community came from a Hellenistic background and would not (necessarily) have been familiar with reading and understanding the Hebrew Scriptures. However, in order to describe the Thessalonians' identity as distinctive from the rest of the world, it came naturally for Paul to remind them of the narrative that forms the origin of their existence. In this regard, Thompson (2014:42) explains how the gentile community's new identity is in continuity with that of ancient Israel.

between his conceptual map and the audience's suffering, thereby affirming the "normality" of the community's persecution while resolving the issues of alienation they may be dealing with (cf. Barclay 1992:56). By locating the audience in the apocalyptic scenario of Christ's parousia, Paul urgently motivates the Thessalonians to develop self-awareness and to actualize a morality that is different from that of the gentile society (see 5.5).

3.2 PERSECUTION AND THE THESSALONIAN BELIEVERS

In appropriating the term θλῖψις (1:6; 3:3, 7) with reference to the situation the Thessalonians were experiencing, Paul illustrates that their ongoing suffering is not unexpected but *destined* (NIDNTTE 2:463; Best 1986a:135).[3] In the light of Paul's apocalyptic perspective, suffering was "part of the catechism" that solidified the boundary between the faith community and larger society (Meeks 1983b:692). For this reason, the social harassment evoked by the converts' rejection of *the Roman imperial cult* and *local religions* in Thessalonica is not abnormal. Rather, the persecution that threatened to undermine the community's foundational faith and identity in Christ was not only an arena in which God's chosen people were to demonstrate their faithfulness but also a painful yet rewarding means of solidifying their beliefs and community values.

The persecution that the Thessalonian believers were confronted with can obviously be ascribed to the fact that ancient Thessalonica was "a religiously pluralistic environment" (Weima 2014:10). Particular political and religious environments relating to idol worship (cf. 1 Thess 1:9) might have caused Paul to exhort the community to differentiate their identity and life from those of the rest of the world. Paul's consistent use of particular boundary markers differentiated the Thessalonian community from outsiders. Paul urgently requested those who were alienated from society to see themselves as God's chosen people and to give concrete expression to their holiness in the midst of tribulation and suffering. In fact, it is impossible to fully construct the complex political and religious reality of first-century CE Thessalonica in this limited space. Yet by examining various conflicting factors in that particular political and religious milieu (with *Jewish agitators, the Roman imperial cult*, and *the local religious cults*), I attempt to cast some light on the probable nature of the persecutions that the Thessalonian believers

---

3. This term refers to the afflictions of God's people in the Hebrew Scriptures (cf. Ps 34:19 [33:20 LXX]; Dan 12:1).

were enduring. I wish to construct these sociohistorical settings so that they may finally aid in establishing the discursive exigency in 1 Thessalonians.

3.2.1 IN CONFLICT WITH JEWISH AGITATORS

After Paul left Thessalonica, opposition towards the newly established community continued to undermine the believers' faith and communal solidarity in Christ. While it is difficult to know how the community would have felt after their abrupt separation from Paul, Paul's apology seems to have been necessary since, as Donfried (2002:44) notices, he "had to leave Thessalonica hurriedly after a brief stay due to the opposition originally mounted by the Jews of the city but which had quickly spread to the non-Jewish population." In consideration of Paul's overcoming the difficult situation in the community, scholars raise a question as to whether 1 Thess 2:1-12 reflects the historical context. Specifically, scholarly debate has revolved around determining whether or not the antithetical statements in 2:1-12 are used for Paul's self-defense against the opponents' accusation (see 4.4.1).

Some scholars have paid little attention to, or neglected, the connection between Paul's antithetical statements in 2:1-12 and the potential opponents' persecution mentioned in 2:13-16 (Schlueter 1994:51-53). In this respect, Donfried (2002:182; see also Aune 1987:206) agrees with Aune that Paul's articulation of contrasting ideas is a rhetorical technique that amplifies his thinking, refuting the possibility of actual conflict in Paul's antithetical statements. Pearson (1971:87) also repudiates the historical context of this passage and argues that Paul sets up a hypothetical context, saying that.

> [T]his is a theological *topos*, revealing his eschatologically oriented theology—about the apostle and his congregation undergoing 'tribulation' (θλίψις, 1:6, recapitulated at 3:3), but that the Thessalonian Christians were actually suffering systematic persecution in the apostolic period is very much in doubt.

Wanamaker (1990:109; see Wuellner 1979:181) regards the rhetorical feature of 2:13-16 as a digression. "Digression" is understood as follows by Wuellner: "Digressions in the *narratio* were often intended to lay the basis for subsequent argumentation or to provide a transition to the next issue to be discussed ... the digression has a parenetic function as well." I wish to argue, however, that the use of the rhetorical technique of digression has to take this pericope's polemical context into account. Holtz (2000:77; cf. Weima 2014:167) claims that 1 Thess 2:13-16 cannot be discussed without considering the immediate context of the new converts having received God's word in the midst of suffering at the hands of their fellow citizens.

I suggest that one of the major causes of the Thessalonian conflict was the Jews' jealousy of Paul's success in attracting some gentiles to the community of Christ followers (cf. Acts 17:5–6). According to 1 Thess 2 and Acts 17, both the Jews and citizens of Thessalonica appeared to be engaged in the persecution of Paul and the believers. These texts do not provide information concerning a concrete cause as to how these ethnic groups were involved in the conflict. But significant clues that seem to reveal persecutors' identity are the New Testament hapax legomenon συμφυλέτης in 2:14 and the phrase "by hindering us from speaking to the Gentiles that they might be saved" in 2:16. Paul describes the similar situation of the Thessalonian believers and Judean churches in 2:14 by making a parallel between συμφυλετῶν and Ἰουδαίων. To clarify the identity of these fellow countrymen as potential opponents to the faith community, one must reflect on the meaning of this hapax legomenon. The term can be defined as "one who is a member of the same tribe or people group" (BDAG, συμφυλέτης) or "the same tribe" (LSJ). However, many dictionaries do not sufficiently indicate whether this word is used in an ethnic or geographical sense. Some scholars argue that the term συμφυλέτης indicates the believers' non-Jewish compatriots, therefore distinguishing between Jews and gentiles (Still 1999:220; Malherbe 2000:168). However, in Koine Greek, this term seems to lose its particular implication of ethnicity (Riesner 1998:352; Tellbe 2001: 115).[4] In *Hermias* 8, for example, συμφυλέτης indicates "the same school" (see Sophocles, *Greek Lexicon of the Roman and Byzantine Period*, 1033). If Jews could be included in Paul's using συμφυλέτης and a collusion between the Jewish opponents and a mob of Thessalonian citizens (Acts 17:5) is considered, one cannot avoid the question of whether Jews resided in the city of Thessalonica in Paul's day. In fact, there are some inscriptions that prove their residency in the city. Unfortunately, the date of inscriptions concerning the existence of a Jewish community did not come from the first century.[5] Nevertheless, one of the most reliable pieces of evidence can be found in Philo's work (*Embassy* 281). He reports that Jewish communities were found throughout the Roman provinces:

> It, as I have already stated, is my native country, and the metropolis, not only of the one country of Judaea, but also of many,

---

4. Tellbe (2001:115) provides some evidence that the term συμφυλέτης is used in a non-ethnical sense.

5. For archaeological evidence that Jews lived in Thessalonica after the first century, see Weima (2014:21–22).

> by reason of the colonies which it has sent out from time to time into the bordering districts of Egypt, Phoenicia, Syria in general, and especially that part of it which is called Coelo-Syria, and also with those more distant regions of Pamphylia, Cilicia, the greater part of Asia Minor as far as Bithynia, and the furthermost corners of Pontus. And in the same manner into Europe, into Thessaly, and Boeotia, and Macedonia, and Aetolia, and Attica, and Argos, and Corinth and all the most fertile and wealthiest districts of Peloponnesus.[6]

Considering Thessalonica's significant status as the largest city in Macedonia, it is reasonable to assume that a sizable Jewish population resided there, despite the absence of explicit mention (Weima 2014:20–21; see Green 2002:46; Purvis 1976:121–3; Nigdelis 1994:304–6). Thus, it is reasonable to conclude that there were some Jews who "were free citizens of Thessalonica" while the majority of these fellow citizens seem to have been gentiles (Lightfoot 1904:32).

The driving out of the apostles from Thessalonica, according to Acts 17:5–10, and continuous persecution of the Thessalonian converts, could thus have originated from Thessalonian Jews who took pride in their ethnic privilege. Tellbe (2001:110) suggests two main reasons why the opposition to Paul and the Thessalonians was triggered: (1) "Paul's identification of the eschatological Messiah with Jesus from Nazareth as crucified and risen from the dead" (see also Brown 1997:463); (2) the gentile converts' participation in the apostle's mission. With regard to the specific reason(s) for the Jewish community's jealousy towards the apostles, Polhill (1992:361) suggests that for the Jews, some God-fearing gentiles who attended the synagogue could justify their residence in the gentile city, and the gentiles probably financially supported the Jews. In this situation, through Paul's gospel ministry, the fact that the gentiles who attended the synagogue began to participate in the believers' community would have been enough to evoke the Jewish jealousy. As Luke reported, Jewish jealousy of the apostles was a major cause for the opposition and their creating a mob brought about great hostility towards the gospel movement. Given that the Jews community had limited influence in Thessalonica during Paul's time, their strategy of persecution appeared to have resulted in the formation of an easily provoked mob (ἀγοραῖος) (Keener 2014:2546–7).[7] But the term ζηλόω can also refer to "typical Jewish fervor" (Popkes, EDNT 2:100). By comparing Paul with other diaspora Jews

---

6. This is Yonge's translation (see Yonge 1995:782–3).

7. In the book of Acts, we see a regular pattern of Jewish instigation of gentiles to persecute Christian communities (e.g., 13:50; 14:2, 5, 19; 17:5, 13; 21:27).

regarded as transgressors of the law from the viewpoint of traditional Judaism, Still (1999:153–85) finds examples of Jewish jealousy from some other disputes between Paul and the Jews (e.g., different views on "circumcision" in Gal 5:11, 6:12 and "the dietary law" in 1 Cor 8–10).

As indicated above, a geographical rendering of συμφυλέτης does not exclude the possibility that certain Jews in Thessalonica hired a mob to agitate the citizens in opposition to the new converts. In this sense, one cannot discount the possibility of Jews playing an active role in the persecution (1 Thess 2:13–16; Tellbe 2001:115; cf. Weima 2014:168).

3.2.2 IN CONFLICT WITH THE ROMAN IMPERIAL CULT

Under Roman governance, the city of Thessalonica gained special status through their loyalty to Rome as a free city (*civitas libera*) in the first century (Hendrix 1984:30–31). One cannot explain the rise and fall of ancient Thessalonica without considering its relationship with Rome. The special privilege granted by the Roman Empire led ancient Thessalonica to honor its supreme benefactor (i.e., the Roman emperor). This honor was expressed through their fidelity to the Roman imperial cult.[8] In first-century Thessalonica the imperial cult was at the center of citizens' religion, since it was a means not only of ensuring their benefactor's favor but also of maintaining the authority of the Roman government (Hendrix 1984:253, 303–8; Green 2002:41–42; Donfried 2002:35–38; Weima 2002a:407). Moreover, celebrating the imperial cult "was a political and diplomatic act that was intimately intertwined with the economic realities of the relationship between Thessalonica and Rome" (Green 2002:41). During this era some Thessalonians' conversion in turning from idols to the God of Israel would be incompatible with the sentiments of the imperial cult. The community who served Christ as their true Lord could not compromise their beliefs and convictions with the (for them) false vision of *Pax Romana*. Such a stance would result in the endangering of Thessalonica's privileged status and relationship with the Roman emperor (Weima 2014:108; cf. Boring 2015:74).

---

8. The funerary inscription *Res Gestae Divi Augusti*, which displays Augustus's numerous achievements on a monument, urged the Thessalonians as well as other cities to express thanksgiving and loyalty to Augustus, who brought them economic prosperity, political stability and various benefits (see Sherk 1988:41–50). The relationship between Rome and Thessalonica revolved around mutual benefit. According to Hendrix (1984:253), from 142 BCE to 41 CE, "Rome's assumption of responsibility for Macedonia's security and the escalating expansion of a provincial magistracy often bent on increasing its revenues meant that the city's well-being depended on its ability to attract and sustain influential Romans' commitments and favors."

3.2.2.1 THE ROMAN IMPERIAL CULT

In the ancient world the distinction between honoring and deification of the Roman emperor was nebulous, since "the altars dedicated to Caesar in this [Thessalonica] and other cities, the divine titles, the temple, and the priesthood all point to the presence of genuine religious sentiments" (Green 2002:42; see also Ferguson 1993:197–9). In the ancient perception of the divine status of a Roman emperor, "[D]ie Trennlinie zwischen Gottheit und Mensch war unscharf" (Clauss 1999:30; see also Gordon 2011:42). In response to the promise of Roman imperial propaganda, i.e., peace and security (cf. 1 Thess 5:3), the Thessalonians acknowledged the divine status of Julius Caesar and erected a temple in which "an imperial 'priest and *agonothete*'" served (Tellbe 2001:83). Significant evidence that the imperial cult flourished in the ancient city of Thessalonica comes from ancient coinage from the city at the end of first century BCE. While the front side of the coin portrays "the laureate head of Julius Caesar with the legend ΘΕΟΣ," its reverse side depicts the "bare head of Octavian with the legend ΘΕΣΣΑΛΟΝΙΚΩΝ" (Donfried 2002:140; see also Harrison 2011:55).

Caesar Claudius, who was most likely ruling the Roman Empire in the days when this letter was sent to the Thessalonians, did not officially encourage the practice of the imperial cult for himself. A significant Roman historian, Cassius Dio (Roman History VII, 60.5.4), reported its manifestation in this way:

> Claudius "further forbade any one to worship him or to offer him any sacrifice; he checked the many excessive acclamations accorded him . . . all the temples and all the other public buildings had become filled with statues and votive offerings, so that he said he would consider what to do even with them."

However, he enabled the state to worship his *Genius* (Gradel 2002:164).[9] The deification of Claudius did not occur until after his death (Fishwick 2012:341–9), but the emperor's high position was confirmed by his *Genius* as the *paterfamilias* of the whole Roman Empire (Gradel 2002:187; Várhelyi 2010:188).[10] As a result of articulating his status of *paterfamilias*,

---

9. The Latin term *Genius* indicates the divine nature that is congenital in every person and place (see http://www.perseus.tufts.edu/hopper/text?doc=Perseus%3Atext%3A1999.04.0059%3Aentry%3D%2319459&redirect=true).

10. This notion helps with regard to considering the political tensions between emperor and senators. As Várhelyi (2010:189) points out, "[i]t is likely that genius worship was perceived to be less offensive than the direct worship of a living emperor, and therefore it served as a convenient compromise that helped senators avoid recognizing the emperor himself as god."

the relationship between the *paterfamilias* and *clientes* was established and this implicitly instigated the practice of the imperial cult. Interestingly, Claudius's tactic in acquiring the supreme position as Emperor was clever inasmuch he associated the acquisition of the title *paterfamilias* (on January 12, 42 CE) with his deification of Livia and Augustus (January 17, 42 CE). In so doing, he might have claimed his own true heirship from Augustus (Gradel 2002:187). Moreover, though the Emperor did not take the lead in a systematic arrangement of the imperial cult, much evidence of his veneration as emperor is found in various regions: temples to Claudius in Cos and Prusa and a head sculpture of Claudius in the temple of Athena in Priene to corroborate that Claudius used to be deified (Price 1984b:249, 258, 266).[11] Intriguingly, the portrait of Claudius "was incorporated into Greek religious practices, became an object of honour or cult, and was also a place of asylum, by analogy with statues of gods" (Allamani-Souri 2003:110). A remarkable feature of the emperor's statues found from Thessalonica (also similar to other statues from other regions of Greece, such as Megara and Olympia) is that he is described as Zeus, holding the scepter in his right hand and an accompanying eagle—symbol of the gods—next to his support (Allamani-Souri 2003:114–6).[12]

3.2.2.2 A CAUSE OF SEDITION OF THESSALONIAN CITIZENS IN ACTS 17:6–8

In pursuing the maintenance of the *Pax Romana*, any disturbance by Jewish people would have been a politically sensitive issue to Claudius. First, when conflicts arose between Greek and Jewish inhabitants of Alexandria, Egypt, Claudius sent a letter to the city to endorse the traditional privileges of the Jews in the city (Bruce 1962:311). In this letter Claudius also prohibited the influx of Jews into the city to prevent further conflict between Greek and Jewish residents, saying that "I bid the Jews . . . not to introduce or invite [other] Jews who sail down to Alexandria from Syria or Egypt, thus compelling me to conceive the greater suspicion; otherwise I will by all means take vengeance on them as fomenting a general plague for the whole world" (Bell 1924:29). Second, Claudius's warning "to show what a benevolent prince can be when turned to just indignation" in the letter to

---

11. With reference to Price (1984a:81), Harrison (2011:58) notes that Claudius was honored as "Tiberius Claudius Caesar Sebastos Ge[r]manicus god manifest (θεὸν ἐπιφανῆ), saviour (σωτῆρ) of our people too."

12. See also the statue of the emperor Claudius (no. 1759). National Archaeological Museum of Athens, Athens, Greece.

Alexandria was put into action through his expulsion of the Roman Jews: "Since the Jews constantly made disturbances at the instigation of Chrestus, he expelled them from Rome" (Suetonius II, 25.4).[13] In this regard, when Paul and his coworkers came to Thessalonica, their gospel preaching and some Thessalonians' conversions might have been noticed by the city officials and other citizens, because their ministry in Thessalonica caused a disturbance among the Jewish population. In the light of Luke's report in Acts 17:7, the Thessalonian citizens regarded Jason and some Christians to have "turned the world upside down" and accused them of violating "the decrees of Caesar."[14] The disturbance of the Jews because of Paul's preaching in Thessalonica could have reminded city officials and citizens of the reason for the Jewish expulsion by Claudius's edict (Bruce 1962:322).[15]

13. Some recent scholars argue that the term "Chrestus" mentioned by Suetonius does not indicate Christ but unknown riots in Rome (France 1986:40–42; cf. Levick 1990:121). However, I leave it open that Suetonius could have had the Christ in mind who founded Christianity, and his influence on the subsequent agitations of his followers (Bruce 1962:316). According to Van Voorst (2000:31–39), the term (Suetonius referring to "Chrestus" was a more common Roman name than "Christus") might have been attributed to a similar pronunciation among iota, eta, and epsilon-iota at that time. He concludes that Suetonius most likely made a mistake by altering "Christus" with "Chrestus."

14. Weima (2014:33) categorizes the possible basis of the mob's charges against Paul and Silas into four types: treason [*maiestas*], Jewish messianic agitation, violating oath of loyalty to Caesar, and prediction of a change of ruler and points out the weakness of each argument. I agree with Weima's claim that the fourth option is the most plausible one (see also Judge 1971:3–5, 7; Riesner 1998:357; Green 2002:50) and that the third option should be refuted (e.g., Jewett 1986:125; De Vos 1999; 156–7; Witherington III 2006:7; Furnish 2007:28). According to Judge (1971:6), an oath dated to 3 BC from Paphlagonia, *Documents . . . Augustus and Tiberius* (315), states that "I swear . . . that I will support Caesar Augustus, his children and descendants, throughout my life, in word, deed and thought . . . that in whatsoever concerns them I will spare neither body nor soul nor life nor children . . . that whenever I see or hear of anything being said, planned or done against them I will report it . . . and whomsoever they regard as enemies I will attack and pursue with arms and the sword by land and by sea. . ." Judge is skeptical that this document could be the foundation for the fellow citizens' accusation against Paul, since in the case of ignoring this oath, the reports would be delivered not to the local authorities, but directly to Caesar. According to another part of the same document (311, 2), when Stlaccius Maximus was accused by the Cyrenaean ambassador under the pretext of removing statues bearing Augustus' name from public places, the emperor detained him until his investigation was finished. In the light of this evidence, if Paul was charged with violating the oath of loyalty to Caesar, the jurisdiction of dealing with this case did not belong to city officials but to the Emperor (Judge 1971:5–7; Weima 2014:33).

15. When Claudius' edict was published, Christianity began to be distinguished from Judaism under the rule of Claudius. Though the edict was directed against Roman Jews, the final greeting in Rom 16:3–15 substantiates that Jewish *Christians* were also banished from Rome (Riesner 1998:191).

A major charge against the Christians was that they were patrons of Paul and Silas, who taught that "there is another king, Jesus." Most likely, "the decree of Caesar" refers to Augustus's edict that prohibited predictions of his health and death (Judge 1971:3).[16] The term δόγμα, which is a reminder of the edict in Acts 17:7, is also found in Cassius Dio's statement that in 16 CE Tiberius banned predictions of the emperor's death (Cassius, Roman History VII, 57. 15. 8):

> But as for all the other astrologers and magicians and such as practised divination in any other way whatsoever, he put to death those who were foreigners and banished all the citizens that were accused of still employing the art at this time after the previous *decree* by which it had been forbidden to engage in any such business in the city (italics mine).

Specifically, predicting an emperor's death was heavily punished in Roman and other provinces, since chances were that this act was associated with usurpation of the throne (Riesner 1998:357).

The politarchs of Thessalonica could have recognized that Paul's apocalyptic message contained some subversive elements that went against the emperor's royal and divine authority (see Acts 17:7). At the same time, it is likely that the Thessalonians' faith in another king, Jesus, collided with the ideology of the imperial cult, the expression of the citizens' ultimate loyalty to their benefactor. In this political context the politarchs could have surmised that the conflict would not only be offensive to the decrees of Caesar but also endanger Thessalonica's privileged status in relation to the Roman Empire.

Many scholars in the past have doubted the existence of Thessalonian "politarchs" in Paul's day, since the title did not occur in Greek literature except for Luke's account in Acts 17:6-8 (Schuler 1960:90).[17] However, studies of the inscriptions from Macedonia found much evidence to support the idea that the politarchs were "the chief administrative officers"

---

16. Augustus seemed to have believed that astrology could predict one's life. By attempting to foresee his own destiny through the stars, he might have relieved "suspense by revealing the date himself" but also might have prevented others' investigation of it (Judge 1971:3).

17. Aeneas Tacticus, in the fourth century BC, used another morphological form, πολίταρχος (cf. πολιτάρχης in Acts 17:6). But this was different from the term that Luke employed inasmuch as those with the title πολίταρχος played a military role in a city (Horsley 1994:99). An excavated inscription dated 2 CE from the Golden Gate (i.e., Vardari Gate on Thessalonica's western wall) includes the title "politarch" with lists of civic officials. This inscription is currently exhibited in the British Museum (see: http://www.britishmuseum.org/research/collection_ online/collection_object_details.aspx?objectId=398975&partId=1).

in Thessalonica (Schuler 1960:94; Tellbe 2001:116).[18] While one may not be able to illustrate in detail what sort of authority the politarchs wielded, scholars commonly note from Luke's report in Acts 17:6-9 that city officials had *judicial authority* (Schuler 1960:91; Tellbe 2001:117; Green 2002:22).[19] Tellbe (2001:118) states that, while the Thessalonian politarchs were officially independent without the interference of a Roman proconsul, "*they still functioned more or less as agents of Roman rule and administration.*" Based on this fact, the politarchs were responsible not only for maintaining the peace and harmony of the city in dealing with the disturbance that arose from Paul's ministry, but also for ensuring that "the decree of Caesar" would be preserved (Schuler 1960:91; Judge 1971:5; Horsley 1994:117; Riesner 1998:357). The fact that the Thessalonian politarchs were disturbed by the crowds' accusation against Jason and his friends (Act 17:7-8) was attributed to their loyalty to their Roman benefactors and devotion to the *imperial ideology* (Tellbe 2001:118).

3.2.2.3 ANTI-ROMAN IMPERIAL IDEOLOGY?

Some Thessalonian converts' families and neighbors might have been socially stigmatized because they denied participation in the imperial cult. If we assume that some of the language used by Paul in 1 Thessalonians may be regarded as reflecting anti-Roman sentiments by politarchs and fellow citizens, the issue of rebellion against Roman imperial ideology might have been raised amongst the citizens.

With regard to the question of how to deal with the interrelation between Christian and Roman terminology, Oakes (2005:302-7) suggests four interpretative options. Firstly, he suggests that Rome and Christianity share

18. It is controversial as to when the title of politarchs was established in the region of Macedonia. Did it originate from the monarchical period or did the Romans introduce it to the city? According to Schuler (1960: 93), chances are good that before the Roman colonization of Thessalonica, the municipal officials in the monarchical period already existed, bearing various titles (epistates, hypepistates and dicasts). But after Romans began to rule this region, the position of politarchs "at least was basically altered by them" (Schuler 1960:96). For a list of the occurrences of the title politarchs in the region of Macedonia, see Schuler 1960:96-98; Horsley 1994:102-10.

19. According to Schuler (1960:90-91, 98; see also Horsley 1994:118; Tajra 1989:34), the politarch as a civil administrator was widespread in the four regions of Macedonia. They came from the upper classes and social elite. Their number was different from city to city, but in the late first century BCE Thessalonica probably had five to six politarchs. The term of office (magistracy) was not to exceed one year and they could take the position for successive terms. Tellbe (2001:117) remarks that the roles of politarchs were "chief administrative and executive officers of the city, responsible for virtually all aspects of city life."

the Hellenistic tradition. Secondly, he notes that Rome influenced Christianity. Thirdly, Rome collided with Christianity. And finally, Christianity opposed Rome. While these options do not bring us to a full understanding of why Paul selected the specific terms that were also used in the imperial context, they at least provide a clue as to the disturbance and outrage that were attributed to their fellow citizens. Indeed, Harrison (2011:66), whose views could be categorized as accepting the third or fourth options, argues that Paul's "alternate eschatology was a blend of traditional Jewish apocalyptic and . . . a radical subversion of the Augustan age." He contends that Paul's use of eschatological terms, εἰρήνη (1 Thess 1:1; 5:3, 23), ἐλπίς (1 Thess 1:3; 2:19; 4:13; 5:8), εὐαγγέλιον (1 Thess 1:5; 2:2, 4, 8, 9; 3:2), σωτηρία (1 Thess 5:8, 9), and χαρά (1 Thess 1:6; 2:19, 20; 3:9), conveys a political overtone to counteract Roman imperial ideology, especially the eschatology of a Roman imperial gospel.[20] Moreover, the term παρουσία (1 Thess 4:15) is mentioned to indicate a visit of an emperor or officials (LSJ). The word ἀπάντησις (1 Thess 4:17) refers to the civic reception of a ruler's triumphant entry into the capital of the Empire (i.e., Rome) (LSJ; Harrison 2011:60).

However, one must be careful in determining whether these terms had merely political connotations, since the literary context itself does not clarify whether Paul intended to react to or oppose the Roman emperor. For example, the term παρουσία also occurs in Jewish literature, indicating the coming or presence of God, the last day, and the messianic figure (NIDNTTE 3:647–57). Moreover, with regard to the usage of ἀπάντησις elsewhere in the New Testament, the term refers to "action of going out to meet an arrival" rather than having a specific political meaning (LSJ; cf. Matt 27:32; Acts 28:15). Nevertheless, while one should not easily conclude that Paul simply conveys political overtones in using these words, the city officials and citizens might have been aware that Paul used this term in his message about Christ's coming. Oakes (2005:317) does not rule out the possibility that the politarchs and fellow citizens in Thessalonica could have construed Paul's message in a political sense. But he explains that "[i]t is probably given to them by the unexpectedly weighty apocalyptic of v. 16 [1 Thess 4:16] . . . [t]he two terms may become political translations of apocalyptic into a form understandable to a Greek audience: political hook on which the audience can hang the apocalyptic imagery."

---

20. Harrison (2011:67–68) argues that "Augustan apotheosis traditions" were widespread in Paul's day. The belief is based on Augustus being viewed as an immortal and transcendental existence. Augustus was perceived as a god whose place was in heaven and who continued to rule the world even after his death, sustaining the political and social stability of the Roman Empire.

Allegiance to the Roman Empire was central to the city's survival. In this sociopolitical milieu the new converts in Thessalonica were stigmatized by their fellow citizens since the believers were involved in Paul's destabilizing message of the gospel (e.g., prediction of change of emperor) against Roman imperial ideology. Hence the city's authorities and citizens might have kept an eye on these potential traitors. Indeed, from the perspective of the citizens, Paul's teaching of the kingdom of God might have been threatening to Thessalonica's privileged relationship with the Roman Empire. As Donfried (1987:188) remarks, Paul's use of this political term, i.e., the kingdom, "may well have served as a catalyst for the animosity he and his co-workers aroused in Thessalonica."

To conclude, in light of our provisional construction of the life of Thessalonian citizens in Paul's time, one may assume that Paul's new converts were at least situated within the complicated web of its political milieu. For them, allegiance to the Roman emperor was part of everyday life. Their conversion probably caused conflict with the civic communities, since it meant the rejection of allegiance to the Roman benefactor (De Vos 1999:176). Thus, the Thessalonian believers were regarded as a potential risk that could impair the relationship between Thessalonica and Rome.

Yet there is another potential cause for their social alienation that should be examined—their rejection of local gods may also have resulted in social discrimination against them.

3.2.3 IN CONFLICT WITH LOCAL RELIGIOUS CULTS

Recent scholars have endeavored to construct the social identity of the ancient Thessalonians from newly found inscriptions from the city of Thessalonica. Based on the evidence from these inscriptions, scholars have found that many voluntary associations were linked to local religious cults.[21] These associations worshiped Dionysos, Egyptian gods (Isis and Serapis) and many other deities (e.g., Aphrodite, Demeter, Zeus, Asclepius, Herakles, etc.). According to Nigdelis (2010:20), the number of religious associations was greater than professional ones.[22] He elaborates that many professionals belonged to religious associations, since in so doing they most probably

---

21. At least sixteen inscriptions were found in ancient Thessalonica that demonstrate the existence of voluntary associations in the first and second centuries CE (Ascough 2014:10–11; see also AGRW 47–59). Thirty-nine associations were mentioned in forty-four inscriptions of the Roman period from the second and third centuries CE. (Nigdelis 2010:14).

22. He adds that it is ambiguous to put them in a single category, since the former were made up of professionals in similar businesses.

created more opportunities for the prosperity of their businesses or cooperation with others in a similar business. Within this religious framework, for instance, merchants could find more opportunities to secure economic benefits through cooperation with others than they could in professional organizations.

While information on local religions is not mentioned in 1 Thessalonians, recently excavated epigrams and inscriptions are used as significant data to construct Thessalonica's religious environment. According to Green (2002:32–34), some epigrams from Thessalonica demonstrate that the ancient city worshiped multiple deities and held the belief that the gods were benevolent in providing for their personal needs or malevolent in causing tragedy in their lives. In one such source Antipater of Thessalonica (see Gow & Page 1968a:19) dedicates himself to a statue of Aphrodite in the expression of his desire for a woman. Also, Philip of Thessalonica offers a sacrifice for the recovery of the emperor (Augustus or Caligula):

> Archer and spyer of wild life, daughter of Zeus and Leto, Artemis, whose lot is cast in the mountains' dwelling-places, dispatch this very day that hateful sickness away from the best of Emperors, as far as the Hyperboreans. For Philip will offer the smoke of frankincense above your altars, and will make splendid sacrifice of a mountain-roaming boar (see Gow & Page 1968a; cf. 1968b:331).

Furthermore, Philip's listing of the dedication of various kinds of workers (e.g., a fisherman, farmer, goat-herd, cook, carpenter, hunter, and weaver) to gods denotes how these ancient peoples perceived the gods as playing a significant role in the success of their life and business (see Gow & Page 1968a:303–13). On the other hand, ancient peoples were afraid of the gods' malevolent characteristics that caused personal misfortune and calamity. Antipater of Thessalonica (see Gow & Page 1968:1.51) describes how an athlete who is on the way home from Olympia dies when he hit by lightning from Zeus. In addition, when Antipater mentions a bridegroom's death, he questions whether a cause of his death could have been "[a] curse upon that envious flame, whether unwilling Hymen kindled it, or Hades willing" (see Gow & Page 1968a:51). Such ancient beliefs demonstrate that "the gods were just as much a part of the fabric of life as the air" (Ascough 2014:12).

Scholars of ancient Thessalonica mostly recognize three significant cults among the local gods—Dionysus, Egyptian and Cabirus—that prevailed in first-century Thessalonica. The aim of this section is not to provide detailed historical information on these cults. Rather, I will briefly illustrate some features of these cults, since it is crucial to understand why their immoral elements from Paul's perspective were incompatible with the Thessalonians' new faith in Christ.[23] These local religious cults in Thessalonica most likely underpin Paul's reference to the Thessalonian Christians' previous life: "For they themselves report concerning us . . . how you turned to God from idols to serve the living and true God" (1 Thess 1:9). "For this is the will of God, your sanctification: that you abstain from sexual immorality; that each one of you know how to control his own body in holiness and honor, not in the passion of lust like the Gentiles who do not know God" (1 Thess 4:3-5).

3.2.3.1 THE DIONYSUS CULT

The existence of Dionysiac associations undoubtedly denotes that their religious belief in this deity has to do with defining their social identity. Since Thessalonica was founded in the third century BCE by king Cassander of Macedon, the cult of Dionysus became the religious center of the city (Edson 1948:160; Weima 2014:11). As a state cult, worshiping Dionysus continued after General Cassander founded the city and he became the most popular deity (Edson 1948:160, 164). Significant evidence that this deity was venerated in this city can be found in an inscription estimated to be from the early period of Thessalonica. It reads: "This city, to Dionysus, from the city leaders, Aristandros, son of Aristonos, Antmachos, son of Aristoxenos" (IT 28, cited in Weima 2014:11). Further evidence for the pervasiveness of the worship of Dionysus is that both the priests of Dionysus and *hydroskopos* (water diviner or water seeker) were linked to the municipal cult of the deity in the region of Macedonia (IT 503, cited in Weima 2014:11; Edson 1948:164). The *thiasoi*, which were private or official religious associations, gathered to worship the diverse aspects of Dionysus's nature (Nigdelis 2010:14-15).

While it is impossible to construct the practices of ancient Thessalonians within the Dionysus cult, one could conjecture that the cult was accompanied by ecstatic dance and musical instruments (Rice & Stambaugh 1979:195-8). Plutarch (*Mor.* 527D) elaborates on the practice of the festival of Dionysus. "First came a jug of wine and a vine branch, then one celebrant dragged a he-goat along, another followed with a basket of dry figs, and the phallus-bearer came last." Throughout ancient times this deity has been regarded as "first and foremost the god of wine and intoxication" and the cult was characterized by "madness or ecstasy (mania)" (Hornblower *et al.* 2012:462).

---

23. In the ancient world ethics had nothing to do with religions and belonged to the domain of philosophers (Malherbe 2000:240; Green 2002:35).

A remarkable feature is that participants worshiped the phallus, a significant symbol of the Dionysus cult:

> Dionysus was the only god manifested by and through the penis, the figurative representation of which occupied a place of central importance in his cult and in the greatest of his festivals. Dionysus, who appeared in the form of a phallus and instituted a phallus procession in which the whole city took part, clearly has things to tell us about the penis, about how, as a god, he himself acted through and on the phallus, about his sexual strategies with regard to obstinately chaste Maenads, about the satyrs whose sexual energy was so exuberant, and also about the pleasure derived from sex in everyday life by both men and women. (Sissa & Detienne 2000:232)

In the Dionysus cult ancient peoples regarded the male phallus as symbolically "the power of generation" to provide and sustain life (Sissa & Detienne 2000:240; Otto 1965:165–7). However, the sexual symbol is not a mere expression of a life-providing power but also has to do with provoking sensuality (Donfried 2002:24). This god inspires drinking wine and encourages the experience of sexual pleasures brought by Aphrodite who "is the symbol of sexual licence and the patroness of the prostitutes" (Green 2002:35; cf. Sissa & Detienne 2000:238). The phallus cult is a significant potential background for Paul's exhortation to avoid sexual immorality in 1 Thess 4:3–8.

3.2.3.2 EGYPTIAN DEITIES

In the early third century BCE the cult of Isis and Serapis began to spread over various regions of Greece, including Macedonia (Griffiths 1970:41). Ancient people might have felt attracted to Egyptian gods since, in contrast with the Greek gods, these deities were not far from the worshipers and were conscientious about meeting their personal needs (IT 100, 120, cited in Weima 2014:14). For Greek initiates, the most appealing element of Egyptian beliefs (particularly, the Isis cult) was that immortality, salvation and eternal joy could be attained by devoting themselves to a moral life including strict fasting and knowing the goddess' divine nature (Green 2002:45; Tzanavari 2003:239). Ancient people were attracted by Egyptian gods since the Egyptian gods "control[led] destiny and [we]re in a position to alter it," while Greek gods suffered from the consequences of fate and destiny (Tzanavari 2003:239). The popularity of Egyptian gods (Serapis, Isis, Osiris, Harpocrates and Anubis) in this city was established after archaeologists found a temple of Serapis and a great number of inscriptions in 1939 (IT 3, 15, 16,

37, 51, 53, 59, 61, 73, 75–123, 221–2, 244, 254–9, cited in Weima 2014:13). Religious associations that worshiped Egyptian deities were the second largest group in Thessalonica. Participants in the cult presented themselves as "συνθρησκευταί κλείνης θεοῦ μεγάλου Σαράπιδος (worshipers of the great god Sarapis), θρησκευταὶ καὶ σηκοβάται θεοῦ Ἑρμανούβιδος (worshipers and religious officials of the cult of the god Hermanoubis), and ἱεραφόροι συνκλίται" (Nigdelis 2010:16–17, 36–38). A combination of the terms ἱεραφόροι (bearers of holy vessels) and συνκλίται (dining companions or fellow banqueters) indicates that their social relations were also involved as they participated in the state cult of the Egyptian gods (Edson 1948:184; Weima 2014:15). Since the meetings of religious associations cost money, people in ancient times needed a patron to support their cults and banquets. An inscription dating from approximately the first century BCE to the first century CE shows that thirteen members of the association for Anubis, which is depicted as having a dog's head, express their devotion to Aulus Papius Chilon who established their meeting place (οἶκος) (AGRW 2012:45).

The phallus also played a significant role in the cult of Osiris, an Egyptian god. According to a myth narrated by Plutarch (*De Iside et Osiride*. 358A–B, 365C), the body of Osiris is cut into fourteen pieces which are then scattered. Isis, the wife of Osiris, finds them, except for his phallus, because it was eaten by a pike. Isis then makes another phallus and consecrates it, after which the Egyptians observe a festival which was held in Plutarch's time. Interestingly, Osiris is identified with Dionysus as Herodotus mentions that "Osiris is, in the Greek language, Dionysus" (Herodotus 2.144; see also Plutarch, *De Iside et Osiride*. 364D, cited in Weima 2014:12). Identifying their own god with foreign gods might be attributed to the ancient Greeks' radical openness towards new deities and cults (Aune 2000:919). According to Weima (2014:12), the close link between these two deities could be attributed to the fact that they both suffered from dismemberment of the phallus.

3.2.3.3 THE CABIRUS (OR CABIRI) CULT

Cabirus "was chief, the tutelary deity of Thessalonica" (Edson 1948:192). But it is intriguing that the name of Cabirus (singular) or Cabiri (plural) is not mentioned in the inscriptions of voluntary associations in Thessalonica (Ascough 2011:157). Because of the paucity of evidence, scholars are confronted with difficulties in constructing the way that Thessalonians venerated Cabirus and identifying the cult's origin and nature.[24] Hendrix

24. Donfried (2002:26–27) shows that the scholarly discussion of the Cabirus cult's

(1987:26, cited in Weima 2014:18) remarks on the uncertainty of the cult: "[t]he Kabiros temple at Thessalonica has not been found, and until new material or literary evidence is discovered, the nature of the Thessalonian cult ritual and its 'legend' cannot be determined more precisely." Thus, one must be careful about using any bit of data to shed light on the nature and practice of the Cabirus cult in this city.

Nevertheless, Cabirus was one of the most significant deities and his cult was widespread throughout ancient Thessalonica. Edson (1948:189–91; see also Donfried 2002:27) provides two pieces of substantial evidence for the connection of Thessalonica and the island of Samothrace, from where this deity originated. One inscription that includes the names of Augustus' priest and agonothete (president who presided over the games in ancient Greece, see ἀγωνοθέτης in LSJ), who came from Thessalonica and visited the island of Samothrace in order to participate in the cult of Samothracian deity between 37 BCE and 43 CE (Edson 1948:189–90). Another inscription found by F. Chapouthier in 1926 records lists of novices from Thessalonica (Edson 1948:190). Edson (1948:190) concludes that this evidence shows that some of the upper classes in this city were interested in the Samothracian cults by the time of Augustus' reign.

Numismatic and archaeological evidence since the first century CE demonstrates how deeply the Cabirus cult was rooted in Thessalonian citizens' daily/religious life (Weima 2014:17–18). First, the coinage of Thessalonica from the Flavian period (from the reign of Vespasian [69–79 CE]) shows the centrality of the Cabirus cult in the city (Edson 1948:190; Hendrix 1987:25–26; Tzanavari 2003:229). On the imperial coinage of Thessalonica, one side bears the portrayal of the ruling emperor or imperial family members, and the reverse side includes the image of Cabirus (Edson 1948:191–2). On the reverse, Cabirus appears full body, beardless, shouldering a hammer (see Tzanavari 2003:229). Second, while it is after the time of Paul writing the first letter to the Thessalonians, the centrality of the Cabirus cult in Thessalonica can also be attested by three inscriptions, according to Tzanavari (2003:230). First, an inscription dated to 3 CE describes the deity as "the most holy ancestral god" (Edson 1948: 193; IT 199 cited in Weima 2014:17). Second, Cabirus, carved on a grave stele in 2 CE alludes to the cult's orgiastic nature. Third, an inscription dedicated to

---

nature is in dispute. Edson (1948:188–9) argues that the Cabirus cult came from the island of Samothrace. On the other hand, Hemberg (1950:209–10) argues that the Cabirus cult began before the Diaspora of Samothrace came to Thessalonica. While there was a Cabiri (plural) cult in the regions of Thebes, Delos, Imbros, Lemnos and Samothrace, the Thessalonian citizens worshiped a Cabirus (singular).

the god by an influential family from Thessalonica is found at Agios Mamas in Chalkidiki.

Moreover, some Christian writers, such as Clement of Alexandria and Firmicus Maternus, reveal its widespread presence in Thessalonica. Notably, some documents specifically describe the Cabirus cult with regard to its origin and nature. In the *Exhortation to the Heathen*, written in 180-190 CE, Clement of Alexandria (see ANF 2:176) describes the mysteries of the Corybantes (i.e., Cabiric), which can be condensed into the concepts of "murder and funeral."[25] In this myth two elder brothers kill the third one whose name is Cabirus and cover his dead body with a purple cloth, crown him, and carry the corpse by hanging it on the point of a spear, and then they bury him under the foothills of Olympus. Clement continues to write that these two fratricides take a box that contains the phallus of Bacchus and stay at Etruria as exiles, teaching their myth "and presenting the phallic symbols and the box for Tyrrhenians to worship." Firmicus Maternus also describes the same myth of the Cabirus cult, observing the connection between the cult and parricide in *The Error of the Pagan Religions*, written in the fourth century CE. The dead one "is the same person that the Macedonians worship in their fatuous superstition. He is the Cabirus, the bloody one to whom the Thessalonians once offered supplications with bloody hands." It is, however, not certain from these witnesses whether Thessalonian citizens in Paul's day worshiped the Cabirus cult.[26] Yet early Christian literature witnesses to the cult's significance in Thessalonica and the incompatibility with the believers' spiritual and moral life (cf. Tzanavari 2003:229).

3.2.3.4 IDENTITY CRISIS AMONGST THE THESSALONIAN CHRISTIANS

One consequence of conversion to the true and living God (1:9-10) was that *philia* networks with fellow citizens were threatened or broken (Smith 1995:99). McNeel (2014:90) observes that "[e]arly Christians across the

---

25. Hendrix (1987:26) explains that although Clement states that the Corybantes were called Cabiric, he does not link this legend to the Cabirus cult. Rather, for Clement, the cult has relevance to "the teaching of piety associated with *virilia* of Dionysos."

26. Weima (2014:18) insists on a careful use of these Christian literary sources in clarifying the custom of the Cabirus cult in first-century Thessalonica. First, one must find an explanation of the relationship between Cabirus and Dionysus (i.e., Bacchus) with regard to their death and dismemberment of the phallus. Second, the blood sacrifice mentioned by Firmicus is not an illustration of a unique feature of the Cabirus cult inasmuch as Christian apologists commonly point out that blood sacrifice was a major characteristic of pagan religions.

empire risked losing family and social contracts, business partners, and even patronage relationships as a result of their conversion."[27] Moreover, Green (2002:47) remarks that adopting a new deity was not an issue since the Hellenistic world was a polytheistic society. Rather, the problem was that converts "abandoned those gods who were considered to be patrons of both their families and city (cf. 1 Thess 1:9)." Consequently, the Thessalonians' conversion caused social alienation from the larger society, which was accompanied by issues of incompatibility. Here one may ask about the nature of the sufferings that new converts had to experience after their social links were severed. What was the intensity of the persecution or to what extent was the Thessalonian community's life hampered by discrimination from their fellow countrymen?

3.2.3.4.1 SOME COMMUNITY MEMBERS' DEATH AS CAUSE OF THEIR CRISIS?

Recent scholars have explored the nature of the persecutions experienced by the Thessalonians in more depth. Specifically, it has been debated whether the intensity of the persecution was severe to the point of causing the death of some community members. Does Paul's mention of "those who fall asleep" in 1 Thess 4:13-18 denote the deceased as a result of intense persecution? Many scholars believe that identifying the historical issues behind the dead in Christ (4:16) is significant. In connecting Paul's mention of the dead in Christ to martyrdom, they corroborate the view that some new converts were most likely martyred because of their faith in Christ (Donfried 1985:349–52; 2000:41–43; Pobee 1985: 113–4; Collins 1993:112; Riesner 1998:386–7; Witherington III 2006:139; Boring 2015: 101). The proponents of this theory provide three possible "proofs" that the death of the Thessalonian converts has to be attributed to severe persecution by fellow citizens.

However, their argument suffers from a lack of substantial evidence. First, Donfried (2000:42) suggests that the parallel between Luke's account of Stephen's martyrdom (Acts 7: 60) and Paul's use of the term κοιμάω in 4:14 indicates that some Thessalonian converts died as a result of grievous persecution. However, this term is also used in contexts in the book of

---

27. Barclay (1995:515) explains that the conversion to Christianity meant abandoning the familial responsibility to practice ancestral traditions. The common belief of the society in gods was that "Civic peace, the success of agriculture, and freedom from earthquake or flood were regularly attributed to benevolence of the gods." Thus, such a disrespectful attitude to familial responsibilities was prohibited in first-century Thessalonica, since it associated with the idea of contempt for the gods and their consequent wrath directed at the ungrateful.

Acts and the Pauline letters where death had nothing to do with martyrdom (De Vos 1999:160; see Acts 13:36; 1 Cor 7:39, 11:30, 15:51). Second, Pobee (1985:113–4) suggests that the phrase διὰ τοῦ Ἰησοῦ in 4:14 modifies the preceding substantial participle τοὺς κοιμηθέντας. He argues that the preposition διὰ conveys attendant circumstances of the death of some Thessalonians by persecutions and explains as follows:

> [O]ur phrase οἱ κοιμηθέντες διὰ τοῦ Ἰησοῦ refers to the Christians who died in their zeal for Jesus as was demonstrated by their patient endurance of persecution, before the Parousia of Christ. The attendant circumstances of the death were the persecutions raging in the church of Thessalonica.

However, it has been a matter of debate whether the prepositional phrase, διὰ τοῦ Ἰησοῦ is linked to τοὺς κοιμηθέντας (those who have fallen asleep) or the main verb ἄξει (he will bring).[28] One cannot derive the possible historical background of some believers' death by persecution through identifying the function and meaning of this prepositional phrase. But I contend that the phrase διὰ τοῦ Ἰησοῦ modifies the following verb ἄξει (Marshall 1983:123; Nicholl 2004:31; Weima 2014:318). Paul's focal point in this verse is providing assurance to those who grieve over deceased believers of their future status in Christ. While Paul does not directly make mention of the resurrection of "those who have fallen asleep," such a concept is embedded in his reference to God's bringing the dead with Christ (Marshall 1983:123). As Weima (2014:319) remarks, here "the apostle is thinking specifically about the resurrection of Christ as the means by which believers are resurrected and able to be with Jesus at his return." In 4:14 Paul does not intend to clarify the cause of the death of some believers, but provides a consolation for those who grieve for the deceased concerning their future fate and status. Third, Donfried (1985:350; 2000:43) suggests extra-biblical evidence that "the Paphlogonian oath of loyalty to the Caesarian house," which is dated to 3 BCE, required not only the reporting of disloyalty but also physical punishment of those who violated the oath (see footnote 14 in Chapter 3). However, the degree

---

28. Even if the phrase, διὰ τοῦ Ἰησοῦ is connected to the participle, many commentators understand that the phrase διὰ τοῦ Ἰησοῦ implies a sense of relationship, i.e., "in Christ" (De Vos 1999:160; Still 1999:216; see NIV); i.e., the deceased Christians are in relationship with Jesus. However, some commentators refute the view that the Pauline formula "in Christ" can be equivalent to this prepositional phrase since the implication of agency in using διὰ cannot be dismissed (Wanamaker 1990:169; Weima 2014:319). In the protasis in 4:14 Paul spells out the essence of Christian faith, i.e., Jesus died and rose again. This context clarifies that the prepositional phrase διὰ τοῦ Ἰησοῦ indicates Jesus "as the mediating link between His people's sleep and their resurrection at the hands of God" (Milligan 1908:57).

of persecution might have varied according to circumstance and there is a considerable time gap between the Paphlogonian oath and 1 Thessalonians. In addition, it is simply a conjecture that death is an obvious consequence of severe persecution. Admittedly, one could lean towards the possibility of severe persecution that results in the death of some believers. Still (1999:216) is disinclined "to dismiss out of hand the possibility that some of Paul's converts were victims of physical violence and that perhaps on the rarest of occasions such opposition might have culminated in death." Even if one might determine a possible correlation between persecution and the death of believer, our text does not provide any certain clues of this (Bruce 1982:98; Luckensmeyer 2009:215).

The issue of whether severe persecution caused the death of believers is no longer regarded as a significant point for scholarly discussion. Rather, consensus has been reached by recent scholars regarding the reason for the community's affliction and tribulation. The Thessalonian converts could at the least have experienced social harassment and ostracism, which was most likely not accompanied by martyrdom (Barclay 1992:53; Weima 2014:309). But few scholars devote attention to the specific nature of the Thessalonians' social harassment or ostracism.[29] Investigation based on nebulous assumptions leads interpreters into the danger of pure conjecture. Nevertheless, identification of the social position of Paul's audience and the nature of their suffering is not utterly impossible, since recent studies provide sufficient historical evidence for constructing the Thessalonians' social world. In understanding the nature of the social alienation experienced by the converts, it is significant to note that the majority of the community members were manual workers.[30] The understanding of the audience's social status may be

---

29. Luckensmeyer (2009:173) rightly states that "the *crux interpretum* is the problematic horizon of the Thessalonians' life-situation and Paul's attendant solution by way of consolation."

30. Recent studies demonstrate that Paul preached the gospel to his fellow manual workers in Thessalonica while being involved in the same trade with them. Hock (1979:440–4) argues that the setting of Paul's evangelistic ministry was a workshop in the light of the ancient conventional setting for intellectual discourse. According to Luke (Acts 18:3), Paul was a σκηνοποιός. Paul might have made his living by tentmaking, following the Pharisaic custom that studying Torah in practicing a trade was regarded as a rabbinic ideal model (Hock 1979:439). In fact, it is difficult to identify what precisely Paul used to handle as σκηνοποιός because tent-making requires many processes (e.g., preparation for patches, stitching, and so on). But patristic documents and modern studies reveal that Paul was a leather worker (Michaelis, TDNT 7:394; BDAG, σκηνοποιός; Hock 1979:441). Thus, it is plausible to say that Paul cut off and stitched leather together to make tents, while he was sitting with manual workers (cf. Hock 1979:441). 1 Thess 2:9 (Μνημονεύετε γάρ, ἀδελφοί, τὸν κόπον ἡμῶν καὶ τὸν μόχθον·νυκτὸς καὶ ἡμέρας ἐργαζόμενοι πρὸς τὸ μὴ ἐπιβαρῆσαί τινα ὑμῶν ἐκηρύξαμεν εἰς

a significant foundation for shedding light on the nature of the persecution (contra Barclay 1992:56). In the ancient Mediterranean world self-identity was perceived in the light of social belonging. In this regard, separation from their associations, consisting of the people in the same business, not only meant a loss of self-identity but also endangered their ordinary life in various ways.

3.2.3.4.2 IDENTITY CRISIS (SOCIAL ALIENATION) AND ETHICAL DILEMMA AMONG THE THESSALONIANS

The new Thessalonian converts went through an *identity crisis* brought about by their loss of self-recognition and social belonging. In his letter, Paul does not offer any indications regarding the social class or occupations of Thessalonian believers. Nevertheless, recent scholars suggest that the majority of Paul's community consisted of *manual workers*, just as in other Roman urban sites (Best 1986a:176; Meeks 1983a:64–65; Jewett 1986:120; Ascough 2000:314–5; 2014:9–10; Weima 2014:29). They lived in a social context in which veneration of the local gods could not be separated from the belief that patron deities protect one's business and cause it to flourish. Nigdelis (2010:34–35) claims that participating in voluntary associations was essential to maintaining Thessalonica's public life and social identity:

> Living in a city in which political and social life was dominated by a minority of aristocrats, and having few opportunities to play an active role in local politics as individuals, the Thessalonians ... sought new collective identities as members of groups, organized on the model of the polis. *These identities were built upon common elements linking the members, such as religious convictions, possibilities of professional cooperation, solidarity* ... when they joined associations, the Thessalonians—or at least most of them—aimed at being reintegrated into the life of the city as active citizens through a new collective identity (my italics).

After conversion, the Thessalonian believers realized that their new belief was not compatible with their previous participation in religious associations, which gathered in the name of local deities. As new converts broke radically from their previous perspectives and lifestyles, the characteristics of the local gods and the lifestyle of worshipers were viewed as immoral (Green 2002:35).

ὑμᾶς τὸ εὐαγγέλιον τοῦ θεοῦ) might be understood in this regard (Ascough 2000:314).

In the sociocultural milieu in which the frenzied, Bacchic, and sensual nature of the local cults might have been natural and widespread, ethical dilemmas were another major issue for the newly converted group. Donfried (2002:30) claims that, in the paraenetic section of 1 Thess 4–5, Paul warns against committing sexual immorality, so as to differentiate the converts' moral behavior from that of their Thessalonian fellow citizens, which was most probably associated with the orgiastic and phallic cult. Jewett's understanding of the nature of sexual immorality is similar to Donfried's, but he elaborates on Paul's exhortation in 1 Thess 4:1–8 through the lenses of apocalyptic framework and a social-scientific study of millenarianism (cf. Johnson-DeBaufre 2010:85). According to Jewett (1986:130), this Bacchic frenzy of the cults was expressed as an egalitarian vision of millennialist movements in that people could engage in sexual intercourse with anyone regardless of social status:

> The presence of both male and female participants in this scene indicates an egalitarian emphasis that is consistent with the details Hemberg discovered about the inclusion of slaves and strangers as honored initiates in various Cabiric temples; slaves dedicated their chains or their writs of manumission to Cabirus, indicating that he was the god of the "suppressed population."

In this potential social atmosphere Paul inserts the unprecedented paradigm for the new gentile converts that ethics and religion cannot be separated in the Christ followers' mindset. This notion that holiness, as proper moral behavior, is a natural consequence of having faith in Christ is a major thrust throughout the paraenetic section of the letter (4:1—5:22). The transformed lifestyle of the Thessalonian converts was expressed by Macedonian believers' witnessing their total commitment to "the living and true God" and anticipation of Christ's coming (1:9–10).

In this pluralistic religious milieu, furthermore, proclaiming monotheism could be regarded as atheism. Though it was normal for the ancient Greeks to accept new deities, worshiping one deity at the expense of abandoning others would have been regarded "as disruptive or even subversive" (Still 1999:255). For the Greeks, worshiping the deities had nothing to do with building moral character; rather religion, social, and political life were inextricably woven together. As Wilken (1984:58 cited in Still 1999:256) notes: "Piety towards the gods was thought to insure the well-being of the city, to promote a spirit of kinship and mutual responsibility, indeed, to bind together the citizenry." According to Hellenistic culture, a close link between "social exclusiveness" and "religious exclusiveness" may be regarded as a possible reason for the Thessalonian converts' hardship and alienation from their fellow citizens (Still 1999:257).³¹ The fact that Christians refused to participate in the cults caused society to brand them as "dangerous atheists," since neglecting the gods was believed to result in bringing divine wrath down upon the civic community (Barclay 1993:515; De Vos 1999:156; Still 1999:256–60).³² Ascough (2014:14–15) also illustrates the meaning of being an atheist in the ancient world, namely that serving one single god "was a denial of the full range of the gods" and the ignorance of other gods meant taking "the risk of alienating them or even inciting their wrath." From the Roman religious perspective, furthermore, the Thessalonians' conversion to "monotheistic exclusiveness" might have meant ignoring the local deities' benevolence as well as threatening the Roman *pax deorum* (De Ste. Croix 1963:24, cited in Still 1999:257).³³ Withdrawal from participating in the local cults aroused public indignation since the Christians' atheism, as evaluated by outsiders, would reverse the deities' goodwill in protecting their life and sustaining their provision.

3.3 CONCLUSION

In the complex political and religious milieu of first-century Thessalonica, societal antipathy towards the exclusive sect of Christ followers conceivably led to discrimination and harassment by their fellow countrymen. I argue that turning from idols to the God of Israel meant a rejection of both the imperial cult and the cults of the local deities. Refusing to participate

---

31. Since religion and politics are integrated in ancient peoples' perception, atheism was most likely regarded as having a politically subversive intention (De Vos 1990:156). Indeed, the Christians' refusal to participate in the Roman imperial cult meant they could be charged with atheism (ISBE 4:113).

32. Barclay (1993:515) gives an example from ancient sources that Christians were branded as "atheists" (e.g., Justin, 1 Apol. 5–6 [ANF 1:164]; Tertullian Apol. 10–11 [ANF 3:26–28]; Apuleius, *Metam.* 9.14).

33. The *pax deorum* ("peace with the gods") indicates the Roman Empire's religious goal for maintaining a harmonious relationship between men and gods (Johnson 2013:5116–7). The *pax deorum* was fulfilled under these conditions: "deities must be placated by sacrifice and prayer"; (2) "all vows and oaths must be fulfilled exactly"; (3) "the city must be preserved from hostile influences by the ritual of *lustratio*"; and (4) "strict attention must be paid to all outward signs of the will of the gods" (Aune 2000:921). According to Johnson (2013:5116), the Roman Stoic Cicero (*Nat.d* 2.3.8) set out examples of how failing in reverence towards the gods could result in severe disasters. Livy believed that making an unacceptable sacrifice (Livy 6.1.12) and violating religious regulations (Livy 2.36.6) endangered the *pax deorum* through military defeat (Livy 6.1.12), disease (Livy 3.6.5), or pestilence (Livy 5.14.3–4). The notion of the *pax deorum* is related to the Roman imperial cult, since the gods played a significant role in supporting and protecting the emperor (Aune 2000:921).

in deifying the emperor might have jeopardized Thessalonica's privileged status in its relationship with the Roman Empire (Weima 2014:108; cf. Boring 2015:74). Consequently, their fellow citizens were seriously concerned that the Christian believers could debilitate "the foundations of established order and custom" of their society (Dunn 1996:228).

On the other hand, as the converts were separated from their pagan society, the ordinary life of the Thessalonian believers might have been threatened. Certainly, since such political and religious conflicts probably caused the community to suffer social alienation by their fellow citizens, they lost their sense of belonging in society. Hence, Paul's discourse seems to have been intended to encourage those who were dejected in their persecution to effect a (trans)formation of the audience's self-understanding as well as of their daily ethos of living in that community.

4

Formative Effect of Identity Markers

An Exegesis of 1 Thess 1:1—2:12

THIS CHAPTER DEALS WITH how Paul appropriates the chosen status of ancient Israel when he defines the Thessalonian believers' new identity. Paul appropriates the election and calling of Israel to describe the early churches' new identity and ethos in Christ (see Grindheim 2005:169–97). The background of Paul's identity awareness was discussed in chapter 2, where it was argued that Paul's conceptual world and his thought need to be considered in light of his unique identity and *ethos* as a diaspora Jew. Paul grew up in a diaspora Jewish family and learned the Hebrew Scriptures from his early childhood. Even after his encounter with Jesus of Nazareth on the road to Damascus, the Hebrew Scriptures were central and authoritative in his thought. Paul manifests the corporate aspect of early Christian communities by echoing the narrative of God's chosen people in the Hebrew Scriptures (e.g., calling, election and holiness).[1] Even though physical/ethnic connotations of family/kinship metaphors were abrogated in Christ, "Paul brings his Gentile churches into Israel's story, establishing the identity that is the basis for moral conduct" (Thompson 2011:55).

---

1. For example, the thrust of Deut 7:6–11 is that God's election of Israel is not based on their ethnic superiority over other nations but rather on God's love and faithfulness to the oaths that were made with their ancestors. The Israelites were thus encouraged to be responsible for the covenantal relationship with God by living lives worthy of their high calling, as well as adhering to the principles of moral accountability (e.g., loving neighbors, actualizing social justice, etc.) in the ancient Near Eastern world (Grindheim 2005:12; Müller 2012:36; cf. Deut 14: 2; Amos 3:2a; 5:7, 11a).

Scholarly contributions towards understanding the perception of identity in the first-century Mediterranean world through modern social theory can help interpreters to appreciate the nature of group identity and the formation of Christian community. The scholars who utilize social theory have attempted to trace Paul's way of shaping communal ethos in the light of how ancient Mediterranean people understood themselves. This approach has the potential to reveal how sociocultural factors might have influenced on shaping early Christian communities' identity. However, some scholars tend merely to emphasize external influences on group identity and how those influences motivate behavior. Formation of the community's identity is more than a sociological phenomenon.

Hence, the necessity arises to clarify Paul's attempt to shape the gentile community's identity formation by analyzing the text as well. An interpretation of a biblical text can compensate for the limitations of social scientific analysis. Our investigation of textual communication cannot merely involve a linguistic, literary, and grammatical analysis of the text, nor can it only be an *eisegesis* that forces a text into a specific unnuanced social-scientific understanding of the first-century Mediterranean world. Rather, such a multifaceted approach may be used to substantiate how Paul established a communal *ethos*, i.e., group identity, through selecting and arranging static forms (viz. grammar and lexicon) that "reveal the thrust or direction of a text as an author's attempt to guide the readers' thoughts and actions toward a certain goal" (Mouton 2002:32). To explore how identity and its function as Paul's primary ethos are apprehended in the text, this chapter carries out an analysis of Paul's discourse in 1 Thess 1:1—2:12. In this process, tracing the flow of Paul's discourse and identifying its major thrust help us gain a deeper understanding of this part (see Appendix I). Establishing possible links from smaller literary units (words, phrases, sentences) to larger units (paragraphs, chapters) may provide important clues towards the logical development of the author's thinking (see 1.4.1).

4.1 SOCIAL "IDENTITY" IN THE FIRST-CENTURY MEDITERRANEAN WORLD

Recently, many New Testament scholars have utilized social-scientific approaches to explore the concept of "belonging" and group dynamics in the first-century Mediterranean world. Since ancient societies were group-oriented, group identity and family relations (both real and fictive) were noteworthy for individuals' self-recognition. As Van der Merwe (2006:537; cf. Esler 2000:149–57; Robbins 1996:101) elucidates, in the ancient world individuals "were socially minded, attuned to the values, attitudes and beliefs of their in-groups. Because these people were strongly embedded in a group, their behaviour was controlled by strong social inhibitions along with a general lack of personal inhibition." Based on this conception, scholars particularly demonstrate how the distinctive identity of early Christian communities was established.

Some New Testament scholars utilize the social identity theory of Henri Tajfel, former professor of social psychology at the University of Bristol, in understanding a group's valued distinctiveness. They argue that a group's identity and behavioral norms are established through social comparison in relation to outgroups. Moreover, Esler (2000:160) identifies two aspects of the dynamic relationship between sociocultural milieu and group belonging. First, various social situations led an individual member to define his or her identity, as well as to perceive "the clarity of the sense of belonging to the group, the extent of positive or negative evaluations attached to membership and the emotional investment in the fact of belonging and in such evaluations." Second, social situations motivate individual members to behave according to their communal identification. Regarding social identity as group norm, Esler (2000:160) appropriates Tajfel's view to illustrate the connotation of social identity in 1 Thessalonians and how norms play a pivotal role in maintaining and confirming group identity. Though ethics is not equal to group norms *per se* but part of them, his argument substantiates how ethics is placed "within a new framework of group identity" by deriving communal consensus with regard to the appropriateness of behaviors. For Esler (2000:162–73), his theory succeeds in showing how the social identity of the audience of 1 Thessalonians, and its pertinent ethics, were developed in conflict with the "agonistic nature" of their social-cultural environment. In this regard, Horrell (2005:92–93) indicates how identity awareness motivates and solidifies group belief and behavior. He argues that this happens when a narrative, through constructing a specific symbolic world, functions to shape identity in a particular social context. Establishing identity thus lays the foundation for the worldview, moral values and praxis of a group. For Horrell (2005:94), such a notion may serve as an alternative way of resolving the paradoxical relationship between the indicative and the imperative:

> Since social identity is constantly in process, as it were, reinforced or transformed over time, then there is certainly a clear logic in *urging someone to be who they are, to act in ways congruent with their (current group) identity*, particularly when there is perceived to be some threat to the viability of the group's identity, or to its boundaries or integrity (italics mine).

Furthermore, Paul's kinship/family metaphors based on the first-century milieu (both Hellenistic and Jewish worlds) have recently become an increasingly important topic of concern. While Paul develops the image of "fictive" or "alternative" family relations, particularly to indicate his affinity with the Thessalonians, the main effect of emphasizing these relationships is the creation of a sense of group belonging and of the community's distinctive identity in relation to outsiders (Sandnes 1994:81–82; Aasgaard 2004:306–8; Thompson 2011:56–57; McNeel 2014:25). As is widely known, kinship was a "primary means to structure social life" in the Hellenistic culture (Moxnes 1997:17). Maintaining a member's identity and role in relation to the family code of honor and dishonor/shame was a particularly significant social value to people in the Hellenistic world. As Moxnes (1997:28) remarks, "[f]amily is the main source of honour, and consequently it becomes important to uphold the family honour, to behave according to the family honour." A code of honor and dishonor/shame in the first-century Mediterranean world was a means of enhancing feelings of family belonging and solidarity. While individuals who embodied their family values by maintaining its honor were rewarded, shameful behavior dishonored the family and was therefore disapproved of (DeSilva 1996:51).

According to Osiek (1995:1; cf. Harland 2002:389), family in the first-century Mediterranean world was defined as "the entire network of people related to each other by blood, marriage and other intimate social ties, such as clientage." Similarly, for Paul, forming family-based networks is foundational to fostering solidarity and membership in the communities he interacted with. His use of family metaphors could have reflected the inclusive characteristics of ancient families with regard to their structure and affinity among the family members (Martin 2003:207).[2] In order to define relationships in the community, reinterpreted or appropriated notions of conventional kinship are probably reflected in his discourse. He

---

2. Ancient families differed from those of the modern world. Thus, one cannot typify the family in Greco-Roman society as merely a nuclear family, or conjecture some idealized portraits of just the Roman *familia* (Garnsey & Saller [1987] 1990:129). As Joubert (1995:214) remarks, it was more inclusive than the modern concept of family. The *familia* in the Roman Empire "was also used with reference to the kin as well as to the property or family estate...[t]he familia thus included more than just the nuclear family." In first-century contexts the circumstances with which the family unit was confronted varied according to political and economic conditions, and it is important to note that there were various types of families in the Greco-Roman period. Because of the high rate of child mortality and the short life span of adults in the ancient world, one should not idealize a typical ancient family as including all family members. For example, since many children grew up in single-parent families, older siblings often played an important role in parenting the younger ones (Aasgaard 2004:40; Paddock 2008:85).

needed to redefine each member's relationship in the new community that was "composed of those who were alienated from their closest relatives" (Thompson 2014:43, 47–48). As the previous chapter discussed, the crisis of losing their social identity and sense of belonging after their conversion away from the idols might have led Paul to identify the need to explicitly define the Thessalonians' newly established identity, as well as the relationship between the community members. Paul employs kinship metaphors in shaping the distinctive community of Christ followers in 1 Thessalonians, not only to encourage those whose relationships with their families were severed as a result of their conversion, but also to reinforce their solidarity as a group (cf. Horrell 2005:139). Family/kinship metaphors supplement the notion of God's election as significant identity marker. Paul invites the gentile believers into ancient Israel's narrative world, regarding them as true siblings/family in Christ. Campbell (2008:36) notes that "Paul's own experience and understanding of family life in Judaism provided him with the raw material for such a theological conception." Both metaphors and concepts not only imply the establishment of communal solidarity, but also function to undergird the community's value by "adopting a code of conduct that distinguishes them from others" (Thompson 2011:62).

4.2 BELIEVERS' IDENTITY AND MORALITY IN THE FIRST-CENTURY MEDITERRANEAN WORLD

In my view, one of the primary functions of the New Testament writings was not only to shape the identity of audiences as Christ followers but also to encourage them to live in accordance with their calling. Meeks (1986:12) argues that Christian practices and customs in the first century CE were an essential part of recognizing their newly established identity in relation to Jesus of Nazareth (e.g., "the churches of God," "the holy ones," "children of God," "slaves of Christ," "brothers and sisters," "those for whom Christ died"). Along these lines, Mouton (2002:44) states that "[t]he essential aspect of the early Christians' moral life is their *identity awareness*, the *self-understanding* within which ethical requirements or directives were embedded."

For Paul, theological reinterpretation of Israel's redemptive history may serve as the essential framework for his definition of the identity of newly converted gentile communities. He could utilize the concept of "the people of God," which was a core identity marker for both Jews and Christians, as "a group ethos for his communities, a collective identity as the basis for the 'ought'" (Thompson 2011:44). Paul (re)interpreted God's chosen people in accordance with his primary salvation-historical perspective. The apostle's theological understanding of the gentiles as God's true people in the new era of Christ's fulfillment of the Hebrew Scriptures could serve as a foundational motif for defining the identity and moral life of the community (cf. Thompson 2011:65). If "Paul uses Scripture primarily to shape his understanding of the community of faith," Israel's Scripture might serve as a *great textual precursor* for Paul's symbolic universe and teachings (Hays 1989:96).

In the process of shaping identity formation, the memory of God's gracious election of ancient Israel, and its conceptual extension to Christ, could provide essential hermeneutical keys for interpreting Paul's writings (cf. Lieu 2004:67–75; Yee 2005:190–212; Campbell 2008:6). In asking how early Christian identity was constructed,[3] Judith Lieu (2004:7) describes the early Christians as textual communities, since "texts play a central part not just in the documentation of what it meant to be Christian, but in actually shaping Christianity."[4] But a particular story that the ancient Israelites struggled with in maintaining their identity as the people of God is *(re)appropriated* for the formation of Christian identity (for both an individual and community) and is *retold* and *remembered* in a new sociocultural milieu (Lieu 2004:67–68). In most cases, Paul's use of specific vocabularies and the deliberate design of his exhortation may have resulted from a "radical redefinition" of the social and ethnic boundaries of Jewish communities.

On the other hand, a process of shaping identity involves resocialization, transforming "some of the most fundamental relationships, values, perceptions of reality, and even structures of the self" (Meeks 1986:13). In the New Testament writings, the obligations of community members are not articulated as "the patterns of euergetism or reciprocity that were common in the contemporary world" (Lieu 2004:165). But these authors envisaged an ideal family that practices mutual obligation for those who came from different social classes and ethnic backgrounds and thereby would reinforce

3. According to Lieu (2004:11–12), discussing Christian identity in the first and second century and probing its nature in the light of the term "identity" could be anachronistic, since it is a recently invented word even if the *phenomenon* could have existed without the word. Hence, she suggests considering "ideas of boundedness, of sameness and difference, of continuity, perhaps of a degree of homogeneity, and of recognition by self and by others," since those ideas were intricately related to the various aspects of what we refer to as identity.

4. Her argument is based on Stock's definition of "textual communities," which indicates that "a group experience based on the interpretation of texts and organized as sectarian behavior was framed within a larger political and theological debate" (see Stock 1983:150). Modifying Stock's idea of "textual communities," Lieu (2004:29) redefines the Christian community as "a group that arises somewhere in the interstices between the imposition of the written word and the articulation of a certain type of social organization. It is an interpretative community, but it is also a social entity."

the solidarity of community members. Having gained a new and equal status in Christ, the believing communities refashioned and appropriated the notion of ἀγάπη as their own "cardinal virtue" (Lieu 2004:165–166). Especially Paul's family/kinship metaphors were particularly unprecedented in as far as they were appropriated to establish and affirm mutual love and unity among community members who had had nothing to do with each other before their conversion (1 Thess 1:3; 3:6, 12; 5:8, 13).

4.3 IDENTITY-BUILDING DISCOURSE IN 1 THESS 1:1–2:12

For Paul's early gentile believers, how did he enable the newly established communities of Christ followers to perceive their self-awareness in the ancient world in concrete terms? How did Paul shape the community's distinct identity and ethos in his gospel ministry to the gentiles? I suggest that appreciating the discursive features of this letter is crucial in understanding such a dynamic process. Although some scholars have argued that Paul adheres strictly to the basic form of Hellenistic letters, he was free to adapt the letter form to suit his strategy and purpose (Hagner 2012:462). A remarkable feature of 1 Thessalonians is that it was designed to be read out loud and heard by the whole congregation (cf. White 1988:99; Collins 2000:329–32; Johanson 1987:66; see 1 Thess 5:27). The most significant benefit of examining the discursive nature of this letter is uncovering the logical development of each literary component—from the level of *word* to *sentence* to *paragraph* to *the larger discourse* as a whole. In this process, one may cautiously examine how a prominent idea develops in each phase. Furthermore, an exploration of the discursive features of Paul's letter could complement the shortcomings of previous studies of rhetorical criticism that tended to confine Paul's letter writing to Hellenistic rhetorical conventions.

This section aims to zoom in on how each identity indicator is interwoven in Paul's discourse. Specifically, exploring significant identity indicators probably enable us to identify Paul's discursive strategy to shape communal ethos. Paul seems to use markers that seem explicitly and implicitly to derive from God's act of choosing ancient Israel.[5] In identifying the thrust of

5. Thompson (2014:23) argues that, of all Paul's letters, 1 Thessalonians may be his initial attempt to explain the formation of the Christian community's identity as God's chosen people: "Paul's task is unprecedented in antiquity. The creation of a corporate identity for converts whose only common interest was the conviction that Jesus suffered, died, and was raised from the dead (cf. 1 Thess. 4:14) separated the believers from the communities from which they had come—the family, the clan, the tribe, the civic assembly (*ekklēsia*)—and brought them together with those whom they did not choose."

Paul's employment of identity markers, an analysis of 1 Thess 1:1—2:12 will show that these markers motivate the process of resocialization of the community, imbuing their communal ethos with a corporate and theologically reinterpreted identity (cf. Campbell 2008:70).

4.3.1 STRUCTURE OF 1 THESSALONIANS

As I begin to engage in the exegetical work, a consideration of the overall structure of 1 Thessalonians is required to grasp the flow of Paul's argumentation. For the purpose of my analysis of 1 Thess 1:1—2:11, I regard the structural division of this letter, based on Hellenistic epistolary convention, to be the following (cf. Weima 2014:56-58):

A. Opening (1:1)

B. Thanksgiving (1:2-10)

    1. God's election of the Thessalonians (1:2-5)

    2. Imitating Paul and the Lord / a model for all believers in Greece (1:6-10)

C. Body (2:1—3:13)

    1. Paul's self-defense of his own integrity for community formation (2:1-12)

    2. The Thessalonians' suffering (2:13-16)

    3. Paul's desires for visiting the Thessalonians and his thanksgiving (2:17—3:11)

    4. Paul's transitional prayer (3:11-13)

D. Exhortation/Paraenesis (4:1—5:22)

    1. Introduction (4:1-2)

    2. Holiness: sexual purity (4:3-8)

    3. Love for one another (4:9-12)

    4. Comfort for the mourning believer (4:13-18)

    5. Awakeness in the day of the Lord (5:1-11)

    6. Exhortation to live as God's eschatological people (5:12-22)

E. Closing (5:23-28)

Studies of ancient letters reveal that Hellenistic letters consist of three major sections—introduction (including the author's name, recipients, a greeting, and health wish), body (beginning with disclosure formula), and conclusion (including greetings, wishes, and prayer). In view of this letter writing convention, many scholars have come to conclude that this basic form is also reflected in the composition of Paul's letters (Green 2002:73; cf. Doty 1973:27–47). In fact, Paul was not strictly tied to the formal structures of Hellenistic letter-writing. Marshall (1983:9) confirms this: "Paul remains broadly within the general pattern in order to compose a letter whose content is determined by the particular needs of this congregation." The larger structure of the Pauline letters reveals "that the apostle followed this basic outline with certain modifications" (Green 2002:73–74).[6]

Depending on one's observation of the way certain parts function (e.g., "thanksgiving" and "paraenesis"), the structural divisions could be varied from three to five major sections (Porter 2010:19–20). In this research I take it that this letter can be divided into five major parts, for the reasons outlined below. First, scholars unanimously agree that 1:1 is the opening of this letter. Second, given the grammatical and syntactical connections and ascertaining the function of some discourse formulae indicates Paul's thanksgiving section is 1:2–10. In 2:1 the consequent occurrence of the vocative, the emphatic "yourselves" and an appeal to what the audience already knew ([α]ὐτοὶ γὰρ οἴδατε, ἀδελφοί) indicate a shift to the beginning of the body of the letter (Sanders 1962:356; White 1971:94; Ellingworth & Nida 1976:19; Green 2002:74; Weima 2014:125). Third, I regard 2:1—3:13 as the main body. Paul's central focus is establishing an affinity with the Thessalonian believers (cf. McDonald & Porter 2000:420–1). But, in my view, this part of the letter was not merely to close the gap in the relationship between Paul and the community during his absence from them. Rather, as I will show the case of 2:1–12, this part also affirms the grounds for Paul's exhortation in the next part. Fourth, I view 4:1—5:22 as the paraenetic section. In my estimation, this part itself functions as Paul's imperative that is based on the concept of identity established in 1 Thess 1–3. Intensive occurrences of imperative and hortatory subjunctive moods characterize this part as the paraenesis (Johanson 1987:78; e.g., 4:18; 5:11, 13–22). In correlating eschatology and ethics, this paraenetic section focuses on exhorting the addressees to preserve ethical behavior by ἵνα clauses (4:1, 12, 13) and the

---

6. Compared to contemporary papyrus letters, Paul's letters have distinctive features with regard to form and contents (White 1988:96–100; Arzt 1994:30). Paul not only brings some Christian features into the epistolary genre, but also adapts Hellenistic epistolary conventions for his pastoral care to communities (White 1988:99; Arzt 1994:30–31).

infinitive clauses (4:3, 4, 6, 10, 11; 5:13). On the other hand, the section on Paul's moral exhortations cannot be separated from the body section, since the phrase λοιπὸν οὖν in 4:1 is a transitional marker from 1 Thess 3 to 4. Although the issue of contingency can be raised (see Luckensmeyer 2009:64), I will deal with this paraenetic section separately from the main body. The vocative ἀδελφοί in 4:1 and disclosure formula οἴδατε γάρ in 4:2 also demarcate the line between the main body and the paraenesis. Nevertheless, I believe that Paul's moral exhortations should not be regarded as appendices; rather, the section is integrated into the body of the letter (Green 2002:74). Fifth, there has been controversy about whether the closing section begins at 5:23 (Morris [1984] 2009: 107; Boers 1976:142; Doty 1973:43; Weima 1994:174–86; 2014:58, 379, 415; Collins 2000:334–6; Malherbe 2000:336–7; Green 2002:76; Hagner 2012:462; Shogren 2012:231–2;) or 5:25 (Marshall 1983:11; Johanson 1987:65–66; Lambrecht 2000: 165, 172; Beale 2003:175–7; Furnish 2007:122–3; Boring 2015:42). I view epistolary analysis as helpful to define the location of the peace benediction. Weima (1994:175; cf. Roetzel [1975] 1982:37–38) provides two major reasons for the former option (i.e., 5:23). First, Weima comments that "both the peace wish of Semitic letters and the health wish of Greco-Roman letters (to which the peace benediction is analogous) clearly belong to their respective letter closings and not to their letter bodies." Second, he mentions that "by including the peace benediction here in the letter closing, Paul creates an *inclusio* with the letter opening." Moreover, the consequent occurrence of the adversative conjunction, δέ in 5:23, the peace benediction, and the transition of the dominant mood from imperative to optative indicate that the conclusion of the letter begins from 5:23 (Weima 2014:379). The closing part wraps up Paul's major concern in his benediction, prayer-wish, encouragement, exhortation and final greeting. Finally, a major motif, their calling and responsibility as the eschatological people of God, reaches its climactic moment at the end of the letter.

Admittedly, some recent scholars who read Paul's letter based on Hellenistic rhetorical conventions raise the question as to whether a formal analysis of 1 Thessalonians can help us find answers about the purpose and function of certain passages (e.g., 1 Thess 2:1–12, 13–16; cf. Donfried 2002:168–70). Even with such an epistolary analysis, it is not easy to recognize the interrelatedness between literary units (Jewett 1986:68). At the same time, fragmenting texts into smaller literary units may prevent one from reading the text as a unified whole (Wanamaker 2000:284). However, I suggest that considering the discursive features of 1 Thessalonians in this research could supplement any deficiencies of epistolary analysis.[7] With regard to structuring 1 Thessalonians, utilizing epistolary analysis seems to be advantageous. It enables the researcher to construct an overview of the larger structure/outline of the letter in the light of the letter writing conventions of Paul's day. Furthermore, in contrast to the point that the rhetorical critics problematized, I rather contend that identifying small literary parts may contribute to a better understanding of the letter as a whole.

4.3.2 THE CHURCH OF THE THESSALONIANS

Paul addresses the community of the recipients as ἐκκλησία (1 Thess 1:1; cf. 1 Cor 1:1; 2 Cor 1:1; Gal 1:2, Philem 2).[8] In Hellenistic societies the term ἐκκλησία was characterized as referring to "a political phenomenon." In a democracy, for example, each member would play a role in making fundamental political and judicial decisions (NIDNTTE 1:135). Here Paul's appropriation of the term is to differentiate his recipients from the secular assemblies that existed in Thessalonica.[9] The phrase τῇ ἐκκλησίᾳ

---

7. Porter (2010:10; cf. Reed 1993:294–314) argues that it is possible to establish a relationship of mutual supplementation between the epistolary structure and the rhetorical characteristics of the Pauline letters. He (2010:11–12) draws attention to a significant contribution of the Prague Linguistics Circle (especially, Mathesius) to overcoming the gap between "structuralism" and "functionalism." First, they argue that a sentence is made up of formal and functional units. Second, the act of communication is established in ways that are associated with syntax. Third, "every organized communication represents a definable confluence of old and new material, which material is what constitutes the progress of communication." Fourth, each communicative element can be classified. In utilizing this principle, Porter (2010:15) further sets a theoretical basis for the understanding that each epistolary unit in Paul's letter has its own communicative function in the whole structure and finally organizes a larger communicative entity: "[t]hese meaningful units extend beyond the sentence in structure and encompass full semantic-pragmatic meaning, in terms of various larger complexes of organization." While Porter's "functional letter perspective" is in its initial stages, I believe it has the potential to advance the next phase of the studies of epistolary analysis.

8. In the opening section of 1 Thess Paul employs Hellenistic epistolary formula that consists of a threefold greeting formula (author, recipient, and greeting). While there is a controversy as to whether Silvanus and Timothy participated in the composition of 1 Thess, most commentators do not doubt that Paul is the single author of 1 Thess (Carson & Moo 2005:535; Furnish 2007:37; Weima 2014:65–68). The first person plural may be an "authorial plural" that can be used interchangeably with the singular pronoun (Malherbe 2000:88; cf. 2 Cor 1:1–14, 18, 24; 7:5–7; 7:12–8:8).

9. There are two objections to this understanding: (1) reading ἐκκλησία with political connotations; (2) occurrence of the phrase ἐκκλησία θεοῦ originates not from the LXX but from apocalyptic Judaism. First, Van Kooten (2012:523) opposes the idea that the NT employment of the term ἐκκλησία should primarily be understood against the background of the LXX. His major argument is that the term ἐκκλησία has political

Θεσσαλονικέων ἐν θεῷ πατρὶ καὶ κυρίῳ Ἰησοῦ Χριστῷ in 1:1 indicates the distinguished and re-socialized social status of the converted Thessalonians from the other ἐκκλησίαι of the city such as "voluntary associations, mystery cults, philosophical or rhetorical schools as well as the Jewish synagogue" (Thompson 2014:29;cf. Meeks 1983a:77–78; 85–86).

When Paul mentions the term ἐκκλησία, as most scholars notice, he probably has a rendering of the corresponding Hebrew word קהל in mind (i.e., the ancient Israelite congregation) (BDB, קהל; BDAG, ἐκκλησία §3.a). Trebilco (2011:440) argues that Hellenists (including Jewish Christians) who lived in Jerusalem and spoke Greek as their mother tongue chose the term ἐκκλησία for their self-designation because they perceived that their community stood in historical continuity with YHWH's assembly in ancient Israel. It is not disputed that ἐκκλησία originally indicated civic assemblies with political overtones. But Paul's reinterpretation of this term "enhanced its [conventional] use" (Trebilco 2011:445). Indeed, this community was not abruptly created out of vacuum. Paul's use of ἐκκλησία thus seems to refer to the roots of their communal story and existence according to the Hebrew Scriptures (Fee 2009:15; Weima 2007:68). Kraus (1996:154) rightly remarks that this epithet implies *continuity* in relation to the heritage of the Hebrew Scriptures:

> Paulus überträgt im 1 Thess Epitheta des alterstamentlichen Gottesvolkes konsequent auf die christliche Gemeinde. Damit zeichnet er die „Gemeinde der Thessalonicher in Gott, dem Vater und dem Herrn Jesus Christus," ein in den Rahmen der alttestamentlichen Gottesvolkvorstellung. Daraus wird man folgern dürfen: Die Kontinuität des Gottesvolkes bleibt in der Diskontinuität sichtbar.

---

implications, saying that "Paul wishes to contrast the Christian 'assembly of God' with the civic assemblies (ἐκκλησίαι) of the Greek cities in the Roman empires, as a parallel, alternative organization existing alongside the latter" (Van Kooten 2012:527; cf. Malherbe 2000:98–99). Second, out of 123 occurrences, קהל was translated as ἐκκλησία 73 times in LXX, and in the remaining occurrences it was rendered as συναγωγή. While the phrase ἐκκλησία θεοῦ appears only once in Neh 13:1, the phrases, ἐκκλησία κύριου or συναγωγή κύριου occur more frequently; when LXX indicates the people of God, συναγωγή was more often employed than ἐκκλησία (Thompson 2014:31). For these reasons, some scholars argue that the phrase ἐκκλησία θεοῦ did not come from LXX but apocalyptic Judaism (Roloff, EDNT 1:412; Thompson 2014:31). However, when one investigates the background of this term, it is necessary to pay attention to Paul's distinctive use of ἐκκλησία. Moreover, their choice of ἐκκλησία rather than συναγωγή might be ascribed to the fact that the latter was already used by the Jewish community (Trebilco 2011:440; Thompson 2014:32).

Furthermore, the gathering of Thessalonian believers may be regarded as a true local congregation of believers rather than a mere local expression of the universal church, connoting their distinctive identity from other Thessalonian citizens ἐκκλησίαι (Ellingworth & Nida 1976:2; Morris [1984] 2009:42; Donfried 2002:141). Paul's unusual employment of the partitive genitive Θεσσαλονικέων (people "of the Thessalonians") indicates "the church of the population" rather than "the church in the city" (1 Cor 1:2; 2 Cor 1:1; Phil 1:1) (Donfried 2002:139; cf. Thompson 2014:29). This grammatical structure shows that the community has a distinct identity from the rest of society.

A distinctive characteristic of community formation is attributed to the associational work of both God and Christ when compared to their surrounding world. The community's existence was defined by their relationship to both God and Christ. The phrase ἐν θεῷ rarely occurs in Pauline letters, since the phrase "in [the Lord Jesus] Christ" is more common. Even though it is difficult to decide whether the grammatical function of ἐν is instrumental or incorporative, these two understandings are not incompatible (Donfried 2002:143; Furnish 2007:38; Weima 2014:69). Some scholars suggest that the grammatical function of ἐν is instrumental, so it can be translated as "the assembly of the Thessalonians brought into being by God the Father and the Lord Jesus Christ" (Malherbe 2000:99; Best 1986a:62). Paul recognizes that God plays the ultimate role in shaping the Thessalonian community. God chose the Thessalonians (1 Thess 1:4), and in response to God's calling, the Thessalonians "turned to God from idols to serve the living and true God" (1 Thess 1: 9). On the other hand, the preposition ἐν could refer to more than a mere instrument, since God's major role in association with Christ not only called the community into existence but also established the relationship between the church and these divine persons (Fee 2009:15; Thompson 2014:33; cf. 1 Thess 1:5; 3:8; 4:17).

From the perspective of their neighbors, this community could have been considered as exceptional and foreign, since the heritage of the Thessalonians' identity was also rooted in faith in Christ. At the beginning of the letter, God and Jesus are presented in apposition, reflecting Paul's high view of Christ's person (Fee 2007:36; 55). According to Fee (2007:42), this belief was shared between Paul and the Thessalonian congregation inasmuch as the term κύριος in 1:1 reflects the translated the Tetragrammaton (יהוה) in the LXX. Paul's use of κύριος does not blur the distinction between God and Christ but rather indicates that "Christ as κύριος shares in the divine purposes and activities with God the Father" (Fee 2007:42). The opening section anticipates the essential communication of the letter. Paul sets the foundation of the Thessalonians' distinctive identity, which is theologically redefined by the two divine persons (God and Jesus Christ) who take the lead in the salvation history. The Thessalonians' faith in God and Christ might have been a major cause of social isolation, harassment, conflict and persecution directed towards the Christian community (see 3.2.1; 3.2.2; 3.2.3).

4.3.3 GOD'S ELECTION AS PAUL'S MAJOR DISCURSIVE THRUST

Despite the fact that the term ἐκλογή occurs only once in 1 Thessalonians (1:4), God's election of the Thessalonians seems to be the major reason for Paul's thanksgiving (1:2-10). In addition, this concept permeates the whole of 1 Thess 1:1-10.[10] Remarkably, in his naming the Thessalonians as God's elect and beloved brothers and sisters, Paul "recalls the frequently repeated statement in Deuteronomy that God 'loved' Israel and demonstrated his love for them by 'electing' their ancestors and eventually the Israelites themselves, among all the peoples of the earth, to be his own possession" (Thielman 1994:73).[11] When Paul defines gentile Christ followers, his strategy of resocialization serves to incorporate them into the "Jewish symbolic universe" of the Hebrew Scriptures (Campbell 2008:57–67; cf. Marshall 1990:262–5; Tellbe 2001:134–5; Grindheim 2005:184–5). Moreover, as Campbell (2008:60; cf. Stanley 1992:338) remarks, "the authority of scripture extends to his Gentile Christ communities," so that it seems to play a formative role in defining their newly established identity in Christ. Thus, Paul's view is that gentile converts belong to the culmination of God's redemptive story, in continuation with YHWH's calling and election of Israel. Thielman (1994:73) renders the gentiles' new identity as being based on God's covenantal relationship with God's chosen people:

> From the perspective of first-century Jews familiar with all of this [the covenantal relationship between God and Israel/calling for holiness], the most astonishing characteristic of the Thessalonian letters would have been Paul's assumption that the collection of uncircumcised Gentiles together with some God-fearers

---

10. In other Pauline letters this term occurs only in Rom 9–11 (9:11; 11:6, 7, 28), where Paul deals with Israel's status in God's divine plan. Paul does not fully articulate the issue of the gentile inclusion in 1 Thess yet. But it is remarkable that he uses the same term, ἐκλογή in his first letter, since this term anticipates his establishing the universal category of God's people that includes both Jews and Greeks (see Thompson 2014: 40, 121, 140–2; Elwell 1993:227; see also 2.3).

11. Remarkably, in the Hebrew Scriptures the notions that Israel is God's beloved one and that God chose them often occur together (Deut 4:37; 10:15; 33:12; Ps 60:5; Isa 41:8; 44:2; Hos 11:1).

and Jews in Thessalonica stood in continuity with God's chosen people as they are described in the Old Testament.

According to 1:1–10, the notion of *God's election* reflects a major motif of Paul's missionary project (Míguez 2012:91–93). In verse 4 this concept permeates both Paul's thanksgiving statement (vv. 2–3) and his subsequent narrative. In verses 6–10 the concept aims at reminding the audience both of their conversion and their exemplary role in the regions of Macedonia and Achaia (Fee 2009:19). God's election of the Thessalonians is not only a central cause of Paul's thanksgiving to God but also a major subject in the rest of his discourse in the first chapter. Furthermore, according to Furnish (2007:33), the notion of God's election of the Thessalonians is developed throughout the letter as Paul attempts to shape the Christian community's identity:

> The first direct theological assertion of the letter is about *election*, which Paul implicitly presents as an expression of God's love (1:4). He subsequently refers to this as God's *call* (2:12; 4:7), emphasizing the divine faithfulness (5:24). Because he is addressing Gentile believers, it is clear that he understands God's love and faithfulness to be universal in scope, inclusive of humankind as a whole. Conversion (accepting the gospel) means accepting not only one's election by the "living and true God" (1:9), but also God's call to holiness (2:11–12; 4:7; 5:23–24).

Also, the term ἐκλογή implies that the dawning of God's ultimate plan of salvation had already become a reality amongst these gentile believers (cf. Boring 2015:63–64). He mentions that this concept constitutes the texture of the whole letter in association with the notions of grace, calling, church, Holy Spirit, Christ, and even the eschatological language in the rest of the letter. In addition, Paul's use of this notion encompasses both the initial phase of shaping the believers' identity (their conversion) and their full-fledged status (as examples of the Christian life). The community's election is the essential foundation for his thanksgiving to God as well as his moral exhortation in this letter. Bassler (1993:14) also remarks that the concept of election "emerges as fundamental convictions through which Paul consistently interprets their world and motivates their behavior."

4.3.4 ELECTION AS MAJOR REASON FOR PAUL'S THANKSGIVING TO GOD (1:1–5)

Paul's thanksgiving to God for the Thessalonians (1:2–3) is expressed by mentioning them in his prayer, since he constantly remembers their work of faith, labor of love, and steadfastness in hope.¹² This section will not discuss this triad in detail.¹³ Suffice to say that the text informs its audience that the triad is the first cause for Paul's thanksgiving to God, since the participle μνημονεύοντες functions grammatically as causal in this case. During his earlier mission in Thessalonica Paul was abruptly separated from the community because of Jewish opposition to his gospel preaching (cf. Acts 17:5–6). Paul now constantly gives thanks (πάντοτε) since, notwithstanding the absence of their founder and persecution/social harassment from their fellow countrymen and the Jews, God continues to generate the three basic characteristics/virtues of the Christian life among them (Marshall 1983:51; Holmes 1998:48). However, even if the second group of genitives (faith, love, and hope) are significant in defining the nature of the Christian life, Paul's emphasis falls on the moral triad (work, labor, and steadfastness). In this grammatical construction Paul's thanksgiving focuses on the fact that the Thessalonians themselves actualized the expected Christian life. These characteristics mark their distinct life in their surrounding society.¹⁴ Paul's first thanksgiving that the Thessalonians' life attains "the vital, active character of Christian commitment" is deeply associated with his articulation of their privileged status, i.e., as God's chosen people (1:4). The perfect participle, εἰδότες (for we know), modifies Paul's statement of thanksgiving

12. In vv. 2–3 two participles, ποιούμενοι and μνημονεύοντες, modify the main verb εὐχαριστοῦμεν. The first participle ποιούμενοι in association with μνείαν may be rendered as an idiomatic expression, "to make mention" or "to speak to someone concerning another" (BDAG, μνεία §2; Bruce 1982:11–12; Shogren 2012:57; Fee 2009:20; Weima 2014:83). When it comes to the first adverbial participle (ποιούμενοι), it most likely functions as manner (Weima 2014:83). Thus, Paul's prayer cannot be separated from his thanksgiving, and the thanksgiving is concretely articulated by means of his mentioning the community in his prayer.

13. There are two major grammatical understandings of these consecutive genitives: (1) subjective genitive (MHT 3:211; Best 1986a:67–70; Wanamaker 1990:75; Malherbe 2000:108–9; (2) genitive of production/ producer (Morris [1984] 2009:43–44; Marshall 1983:51; Wallace 1996:104–6; Shogren 2012:59). In my view, these two grammatical functions are not incompatible, since the first term could be the result of the second term (Weima 2014: 85).

14. Though Paul does not elaborate on what the ethical triad concretely indicates, the long series of the combined concepts denotes "vibrant realities" of having a Christian identity (Shogren 2012:59). Faith is expressed by taking a specific action of missionary work (Malherbe 2000:108; Beale 2003:46) or living a holy life (Wanamaker 1990:75) or showing faithfulness to Christ (Furnish 2007:41; Weima 2014:86). Love is fully expressed through the labor for their community members (cf. 1 Thess 3:12–13; 4:9–12). Hope strengthens their steadfastness to keep reminding them of their Christian identity as the eschatological people of God. Here Paul articulates "a very specific hope in Christ's imminent return from heaven to bring about their deliverance" (Weima 2014:88; cf. Hendriksen 1955:47–48; Wanamaker 1990:76; Gaventa 1998:26; Green 2002:91; Furnish 2007:42).

(εὐχαριστοῦμεν τῷ θεῷ) in verse 2. Just as the grammatical function of the adverbial participle μνημονεύοντες is causal, Paul's employment of the second participle (εἰδότες) signifies that the fundamental ground for his thanksgiving is God's election of this gentile group. As tracing 1 in Appendix I shows, both Paul's remembering the fruitful result of his initial ministry and his conviction of the Thessalonians' election become reasons for his thanksgiving.

Significantly, Paul's employment of the two phrases ἀδελφοὶ ἠγαπημένοι ὑπὸ [τοῦ] θεοῦ and τὴν ἐκλογὴν ὑμῶν in verse 4 echoes the election tradition in the Hebrew Scriptures. This echo strategically integrates gentile converts into the story of Israel's election by God (Matera 2007:108). First, Paul's designation of the community as ἀδελφοί may also be unusual, since his kinship metaphors would not have been compatible with the hierarchical structures of other voluntary associations, which consisted of overseers and servants (Thompson 2014:19). It has been suggested that Paul's employment of this term comes from mainly Jewish practice (Malherbe 2000:110; Fee 2009:30; Weima 2014:89).[15] Paul frequently used ἀδελφός not merely to indicate members of the same religious group but to differentiate the community "from the ancient associations, in which the word was rare" (Thompson 2014:44; see 4.4.4).[16] Second, the implication of ἀδελφός may be clarified by the modifying phrase, ἠγαπημένοι ὑπὸ [τοῦ] θεοῦ.[17] Marshall (1990:262) illustrates the implications of the expression "beloved by God" as follows:

> Here we can see the actual process of extension of the term taking place; what once applied to Israel is now seen to apply to the church, and what formerly applied only to racial Israel is now extended to the Gentiles also. The significance of 1 Thess 1,4 is that Paul carries out this extension in application without, as it were, showing us the working or needing to justify it to his readers.

Moreover, according to Weima (2014:90; see also Thielman 1994:74–79, 89; Thompson 2011:44–45), Paul appropriates specific language that used to indicate Israel's privileged position, "being loved by God," to represent the gentile believers as "the renewed Israel" called by God. The perfect passive participle (ἠγαπημένοι) not only illustrates that God's love continues to be made known to the brothers and sisters, but also implies God's active role

---

15. Exod 2:11; Deut 2:4; 15:3, 12; Ps 22:22 (21:23 [LXX]); Jer 22:18; 31:34 (38:34 [LXX]); Zech 7:9; 1QS 6.10, 22; CD 6.20–21; Josephus, J.W. 2.122; Jos. Asen. 12:11; 13:1; Philo, Spec. Laws 1, 52; Virtues 103–4, 179.

16. For further discussion of Paul's use of this kinship metaphor, see 4.4.4.

17. Cf. Deut 33:12; Ps 60:5; Isa 44:2; Jer 11:15.

in calling the Thessalonians into the new reality unified in Christ (Boring 2015:58). Third, the next phrase, τὴν ἐκλογὴν ὑμῶν in verse 4, that echoes God's election of Israel, substantiates this idea more clearly. Though Paul's word ἐκλογὴν does not appear in the LXX, its verbal (ἐκλέγω) and adjectival form (ἐκλεκτός) convey the election tradition, i.e., one of the representative symbols of Israel's faith (Thompson 2014:35).[18] In this sense, the eventual occasion for Paul's thanksgiving to God is that the Thessalonians now become beloved brothers and sisters in Christ.

By appropriating Israel's tradition of being God's chosen people in the formation of this gentile community, in verse 5, Paul begins to shape the common ethos between speaker and audience, i.e., *the formation of their differentiated identity through the concept of God's election*. In illustrating the initiative phase of the formation of the Thessalonians' identity, Paul's appeal to the tradition of being God's chosen people by using ἐκλογὴν derives from the shared memory that both Paul and the Thessalonians had experienced the power of the gospel in the previous mission.

The major focus in verse 5 falls on the apostle's act of delivering the gospel rather than the Thessalonians' acceptance of it. Paul's preaching the gospel with a "great sense of certainty" is efficacious (Shogren 2012:65). Beale (2003:51) illustrates the nature of the effectiveness of Paul's ministry, saying that Paul's "word was effective because the power of God's Spirit had produced a great conviction of faith in preacher[s] and such conviction spilled over into the hearers" (cf. Fee 2009:34). In particular, I contend that Paul's discourse displays that the Holy Spirit is the major cause of God's election. Paul's appeal to the knowledge from what they experienced firsthand (καθὼς οἴδατε) in this verse indicates that the Thessalonians already recognized the work of the Holy Spirit in their receiving of the gospel. And yet, this discursive device purports to convince them of the genuineness and integrity of the previous missionary project.[19] Moreover, the construction οὐκ ... μόνον ἀλλά (not only ... but also) denotes the Thessalonians' conversion would not have been a result of oral persuasion alone (Fee 2009:32). The Holy Spirit is a true sign of Paul's preaching, differentiating his preaching from the charlatan philosophers and wandering preachers of his day (Boring 2015:64; cf. Acts 10:34–48; 11:15–18; 1 Cor 6:19; 12:3).

Furthermore, in tracing his argument in verses 4–5, Paul clarifies the meaning of God's election of the Thessalonians. The ὅτι clause in verse 5 concretely elucidates Paul's previous statement regarding the Thessalonians'

---

18. E.g., Deut 7:7–11; 12:5, 11, 18, 21; 16:6, 7, 11, 15, 16; 17:8, 10, 15; Isa 14:1 41:8–9; 43:10; 44:1–2; 49:7; 42:1; 43:20; 45:4; 65:9.

19. This idea will be developed in 1 Thess 2:1–12 (see 4.4).

election (τὴν ἐκλογὴν ὑμῶν). Here, God's election is concretely described as the logical and chronological sequence of the Holy Spirit's involvement in Paul's preaching of the gospel. The Spirit was involved both in the initiative phase of Paul's ministry and its fruitful result of shaping the Thessalonian community. In so doing, Paul reminds the audience that the Holy Spirit's active role in his previous missionary work resulted in the formation of their distinct identity (Fee 2009:32; cf. Best 1986a:73; Malherbe 2000:110).[20] Grindheim (2005:185) also maintain this connection by saying that "[t]he manner in which their election was effected . . . in power and in the Holy Spirit and in full conviction (1:5) . . . [t]heir election is made manifest through their receiving the word in persecution and joy in the Holy Spirit (1:6b)." Their identity as God's elect was not solely established through an oral communication of God's gospel but from "the power from the Holy Spirit that causes the spoken word to penetrate the hearts and minds of its hearers" (Weima 2014:95).[21]

20. Most major commentators on 1 Thess interpret this clause as "causal" (Morris [1984] 2009:46; Wanamaker 1990:78; Holmes 1998:49; Green 2002:93–94). However, the participle εἰδότες in v. 4 in association with ὅτι clause makes a normal construction of "knowing . . . that" (Fee 2009:31). In my view, this ὅτι clause could be understood as epexegetical (or explanatory) (Malherbe 2000:110; Fee 2009:31; Weima 2014:93).

21. It is difficult to decide the meaning of the third dative phrase, [ἐν] πληροφορίᾳ πολλῇ in v. 5, because we are confronted with a critical textual issue as well as the question of the relationship between the three nouns (δυνάμει, πνεύματι ἁγίῳ and πληροφορίᾳ πολλῇ). When it comes to the external evidence, both textual supports are substantial. While one may read "in power and in the Holy Spirit and in full conviction" (א A C P 048. 33. 81. 104. 326*. 945. 1739. 1881 vgst; see NA28), other possible textual support could be "in power and in the Holy Spirit and full conviction" (B D F G K L Ψ 0278. 326c. 365. 630. 1175. 1241. 1505. 2464 𝔐 it vgcl.ww sy(p); see NA28). While the former reading may emphasize that Paul's message results in the Thessalonians' conviction in accepting the gospel message (Best 1986a:76), the latter reading may focus on the audience's perceiving Paul's message in full assurance (cf. Hendriksen 1955:51; Fee 2009:29; Weima 2014:113). Fee (2009:28–29) argues that the error might have occurred because scribes deliberately produced grammatical consistency (i.e., maintaining the three consecutive ἐν phrases). If the preposition ἐν before πληροφορίᾳ in v. 5 is omitted, one must further identify internal evidence as to the interrelationship between these three nouns in this context (Fee 2009:33; Weima 2014:113). According to Fee (2009:33), in these prepositional parallels, the second compound phrase (in the Holy Spirit and full conviction) qualifies the first one ("in power"). The first noun "power" cannot necessarily be rendered as a "miracle" that is accompanied by the preaching of the gospel, as some commentators suggest (Marshall 1983:53; Wanamaker 1990:79; Green 2002:96). But, as Weima (2014: 95) remarks, the term δυνάμει most likely means "the power from the Holy Spirit that causes the spoken word to penetrate the hearts and minds of its hearers." At any rate, it is certain that the main focus of this series falls on Paul's apologetic concern in light of the last statement of v. 5b, which reads: "[y]ou know what kind of men we proved to be among you for your sake." While I prefer the understanding that the preposition, ἐν ("in") is omitted, I suggest that both textual

4.3.5 ELECTION AS MOTIVATION FOR THE THESSALONIANS' INFLUENTIAL ROLE (1:6–8)

In verses 6–8 Paul develops the election tradition to elucidate the consequential effect of the Thessalonians' conversion and their consequent reactions in actualizing their distinct life. Míguez (2012:93) remarks that "the election (a subjective fact) becomes imitation (an objective fact) and is transformed into data for others, thus providing a new alternative subjectivity (a model)." In verse 6 the conjunction καί indicates that Paul expands the notion that God chose the Thessalonian community, already mentioned in verse 4. With regard to the possibility that verses 6–10 are connected to the idea of God's elect, it is more natural to regard the function of καί as a coordinating conjunction.[22] So, the sentences are structured as parataxis (using καί with the Semitic style that comes from the usage of the Hebrew conjunction וְ) (Fee 2009:37; Weima 2014:97; see BDF § 458, 471).[23] Using καί in verse 6 as a coordinating conjunction does not simply reiterate the speaker's previous idea and statement but indicates more advanced concepts (see tracing 1, Appendix I). Hence, Paul most likely posits another cause for his thanksgiving that they imitated him and the Lord.

In verse 6, Paul's retrospective statement of his missionary project for establishing the community's identity now changes focus from his own ministry of gospel preaching (v. 5) to the audience's response to the gospel. After establishing the new identity of the Thessalonians in the initial setting of Paul's ministry,[24] in this transition Paul demonstrates that the Thessalonians' imitating the apostle and the Lord signifies their progression and maturity in their faith and life. The term μιμητής denotes "a characteristic quality or act of the person referred to" or "the example's entire way of life" (Larsson, EDNT 2:429). In the ancient world the idea of imitating a specific

---

variants could be convincing, since the Holy Spirit's divine working provides both Paul's preaching the gospel and the Thessalonian converts' receiving it with "inward assurance" (Morris [1984] 2009:46; cf. Schrenk, TDNT 4:179; Delling, TDNT 6:311).

22. The previous phrase in v. 5, "you know what kind of men we proved to be among you for your sake," could be a parenthetical statement (Green 2002:97; Fee 2009:37).

23. Fee (2009:37) structures vv. 4–6 in this way:
 Knowing your election
  that our gospel came (ἐγενήθη) to you . . . with power,
   (just as you know how we were toward you),
  and you became (ἐγενήθημεν) imitators of us and of the Lord . . .
(emphasis mine)

24. In v. 5 the phrase "our gospel came (ἐγενήθη) to you" denotes that Paul's previous missionary preaching had brought about the Thessalonians' newly established community.

model's value or conviction (e.g., philosophers, teachers, parents) was "a means of moral education" (Green 2002:97).[25] But it is not certain whether Paul employs this word in precisely this sense, since their imitation of Paul and the Lord is not directly linked to moral education but to persecution by being modified by the phrase ἐν θλίψει πολλῇ (Wanamaker 1990:81). Their imitation of Christ and Paul is differentiated from its general meaning in Paul's day.[26] The term θλῖψις ("trouble that inflicts distress, oppression, affliction, tribulation" in BDAG §1) informs modern readers of the ongoing situation of the Thessalonian community's persecution.[27] Here Paul does not merely state that the community faced opposition; rather, he establishes this literary setting of severe persecution to highlight the solid foundation of their Christian identity and beliefs. Paul places the Thessalonians' actual suffering within a theological framework and vindicates the genuineness of their Christian identity as this word is used to indicate "the mark of the true people of God" in LXX (Boring 2015:66).[28] As many New Testament texts also substantiate, suffering implies the genuine mark of Christian discipleship as well as the community's contextual suffering (Green 2002:98; Fee 2009:38–39; e.g., Matt 24:9; Mark 4:17; John 16:33; Acts 14:22; Rom 8:17; 2 Cor 1:4–5; Phil 4:14). In other letters by Paul, his referring to this paradoxical combination of suffering and joy represents an expression of the remarkable characteristic of the true followers of Christ (cf. Rom 5:3; 12:12; 2 Cor 7:4; 8:2).

By using a resultative conjunction, ὥστε, in verse 7, Paul shows "a chain reaction" that the community imitates him and the Lord, thereby becoming a model (τύπος) to all the believers in Greece (Lambrecht 1994:347). The locative extension indicates the effect of the gospel spreading from Thessalonica to the whole of Greece (Fee 2009:40–41):

---

25. E.g., Xenophon, *Mem.* 1.6.3; Epictetus, *Diatr.* 2.14.12–13.

26. I contend that the participle δεξάμενοι in v. 6 is grammatically temporal rather than instrumental. If one translates this participle in the instrumental sense, this verse might imply that the community imitates the Lord and Paul in the way that they received the word in the midst of suffering. However, this understanding is unwarranted. In the NT Jesus and Paul experienced much affliction in their ministry, but "they did not endure this in the specific context of 'receiving the word' as conversion" (Weima 2014:100). Therefore, it is natural to translate this phrase in a temporal sense, such as "after they received the word" or "when they received the word."

27. As I have already discussed in chapter 3, the Thessalonians' conversion and their abandonment of their indigenous gods and religious cults led to social harassment. Their serving another Lord might threaten their social and political associations with the Roman Empire and lead to conflicts with local religious sentiments.

28. See Exod 3:9; 4:31; Deut 4:29; 1 Kgdm 10:18; 4 Kgdm 19:3 (LXX).

Christ → Paul → Thessalonica → Macedonia and Achaia.

It is important to note how Paul gradually expands his designation of the community's identity and role from being God's elect (τὴν ἐκλογὴν ὑμῶν) in verse 4, to imitators (μιμηταί) of Paul and the Lord in verse 6, and consequently to a model (τύπος) for all believers in Greece in verse 7 (cf. the "Action-Result" relationship between v. 6 and vv. 7–10). In verse 7 there is a close relationship between the locative extension and the development of the Thessalonians' identity and role. Míguez (2012:92) delineates the larger discursive structure of 1:4–8 by observing the interrelatedness of each linguistic unit. And then he categorizes the key words under governing ideas ("election," "gospel," "word," "divulge" and "speak") and the audience's attitudes ("conviction," "imitate," "receive" and "becoming a model"). From the logical consequence in 1:4–8, suggested by Míguez, Paul illustrates a ripple effect of God's election from the city of Thessalonica to the regions of Macedonia and Achaia. Míguez's categorization does not appear to be based on specific criteria, but through this one could easily note that the reiteration and amplification of each significant idea occur at various levels (2012:92):

We know:
- of the election of the brothers and sisters loved by God
- how our gospel came to be not just in words
- it is power in the Holy Spirit and great conviction

You know:
- about the identity-imitation of the Thessalonians, Paul, the Lord
- about accepting the word
- about the severe suffering with the joy of the Holy Spirit

Therefore:
- you became a model for the believers in Macedonia and Achaia
- from you, in fact, the word of the lord resonates
- your faith in God has spread out everywhere

Therefore:
- it is not necessary to say anything to you.]

For Míguez, these levels include a cognitive organizer, an identity organizer, an ideological organizer, and the form of realization. I provide a table that is based on Míguez's discursive structure in 1:4–8. Míguez (2012:93) presents a multidimensional phase of identity development by demonstrating parallels of three different constituents at various levels:

	The subjective realization	The objective realization	The extension and gift
A cognitive organizer	We know	You know	Therefore (conclusion)
An identity organizer	Election	Imitation	Model
An ideological organizer	Our gospel	The word	The word of the Lord
The form of realization	Power and conviction	Suffering and joy	Spreading faith

Looking at the horizontal line in this table enables us to identify the epistemological transition that occurs from the subjective (receiver) to the objective (giver). The role of the Thessalonians as receivers is characterized by the passive position. Paul employs language such as "the chosen one" and "the imitator," which implies their dependence on their major predecessors, i.e., Christ and Paul. Paul gradually shifts the position of the community from their elected status to becoming imitators and then to being a model. In so doing, he demonstrates a process of the Thessalonians becoming "a new alternative subjectivity" that actively transmits the gospel to extend the fulfillment of God's election to other regions. The gospel preached by the apostle to the Thessalonians is accepted as "the word" and transmitted to their neighboring believers as the authoritative word of God (Míguez 2012:93).

Many scholars point out that one can easily be misled in rendering the term τύπος in verse 7 as merely referring to "example." It literally refers to a mold that was used for shaping or casting a certain form, such as the stamp or seal that makes an impression (Goppelt, TDNT 8:249). Thus, it is right to argue that Paul's description of the community as τύπος does not merely refer to "a model whose particular actions are to be *copied* as closely as possible" (Furnish 2007:45). Rather, its meaning is more inclusive. Boring (2015:66) states that the nature of this word is Janus-faced: "as it has been stamped or molded, so it stamps or molds others." This illustrates the sequence of how a model is concretely transformed into a viable example. This passage is concerned with the consecutive and resultative effect of being a model in the relationship between the Thessalonians and their predecessors (Paul and the Lord). The basis for Paul's representing himself as a model for his community is attributed to the fact that his life is stamped by the

Lord and, through Paul, the community became God's chosen people and a model in relationship with others.

Paul's use of this word can figuratively indicate a model or pattern of one's moral life (BDAG, τύπος §6b; Goppelt, TDNT 8:249–50; Weima 2014:102). In fact, when Paul uses the term τύπος, there is no hint as to whether he implies an ethical notion (NIDNTTE 4:507). The conjunction γάρ in verse 8 establishes the grounds for the newly converted community being regarded as τύπος (Sterner 1998:27). The Thessalonians' progression towards becoming a model amongst their neighboring believers is represented, first of all, in their playing a major role in sounding the gospel and their faith in God over all the regions of Greece (see tracing 1, Appendix I). It is remarkable that, except for verse 7, Paul does not indicate that his audience has communicated the gospel and played a role in being an inspiring model for other believers (Ware 1992:126; Weima 2014:102; cf. Martin 1995:62). Some scholars particularly assert that Paul's unprecedented reference to the word of the Lord being sounded forth through them denotes their evangelistic activity (Ware 1992:127; Lambrecht 1994:345–348; Shogren 2012:70). However, it is plausible that their becoming a model of the word of God is not merely attributed to their preaching of the gospel, but to their formative influence on other believers as well. I therefore focus on the "Action-Result" relationship between verse 6 and 7, in which Paul substantiates the Thessalonians' transformation from being imitators of Paul and the Lord to being a model to all the believers in Greece. In this regard, Marshall (1983:55) describes the fact that the Thessalonians became a model in relation to others "could be said to exercise a formative influence on the other Christians, just as they themselves were to imitate the formative example of Paul." Paul's central focus is evident in his consecutive use of the verbs with the prefix ἐξ (ἐξήχηται and ἐξελήλυθεν). This form indicates that their continuous propagation of the gospel (verbal means) and being exemplars of faith (non-verbal means) are intertwined (Weima 2014:105). I here provide Richard's chiastic structure of verse 8, bracketing the subject and antithetical statement by two verbs, which denote the Thessalonians' formative influence on other believers ([1995] 2007:70–71):

- A   Verb: ἐξήχηται
  - B   Subject: ὁ λόγος τοῦ κυρίου
    - C   Antithetical statement: οὐ μόνον ἐν τῇ Μακεδονίᾳ καὶ [ἐν τῇ] Ἀχαΐᾳ,
    - C'   Antithetical statement: ἀλλ' ἐν παντὶ τόπῳ
  - B'   Subject: ἡ πίστις ὑμῶν ἡ πρὸς τὸν θεὸν
- A'   Verb: ἐξελήλυθεν

Once they were receivers of the word of the Lord, but now they are recognized to be playing a role as faithful disseminators of the word who challenge their neighbors to appreciate the transformative power of the word of the Lord. The resultative conjunction ὥστε ("so that") in verse 8c indicates employing a sort of *paraleipsis*. This rhetorical technique is "a literary device allowing writers to address a subject that they outwardly claim does not need to be addressed" (Weima 2014:106). Paul's mentioning that "so that we need not say anything" in verse 8 is probably to commend the community's contribution to spreading the gospel message and their faith, as well as their formative role all over Greece.

In my perspective, the election of the Thessalonians by God is inseparable from their responsibility to represent God among the nations. Paul perceives the Hebrew Scriptures anticipated the inclusion of the gentiles into the people of God, and this anticipation finds fulfillment through the Thessalonians' election and their influential role as a model to all of Greece. In presenting this gentile community as an example, Paul prompts readers to recall ancient Israel's responsibility to serve as representatives of YHWH to all nations (cf. Bauckham 2003:36–38; Exod 9:16; 19:4–6; Josh 4:24; Ps 67:1–3; 106:8). But one must take into consideration the difference between God's election of ancient Israel and of the gentiles. As Plummer (2006:69) observes, while, in the Hebrew Scriptures, God's word and the Spirit came to particular members in the faith community for specified period of time, "a broader outpouring of the Spirit and word" would occur at the eschatological fulfillment. God's word and the Spirit now abide in the hearts of Gentile believers as a result of their faith in Christ's death and resurrection.

The Holy Spirit works in the calling and the gospel ministry of God's chosen people. At the same time, God's word is dynamically and effectively disseminated (cf. Plummer 2006:69). As seen in 1 Thessalonians, the Holy Spirit is described as the major source of joy in the Thessalonians' acceptance of God's word; meanwhile, the work of the Holy Spirit resulted in the Thessalonians' becoming a good exemplar to other neighboring believers in Greece (1 Thess 1:6–7).

The Hebrew Scriptures explain that God's election will not be confined to ancient Israel. Isaiah envisages the inclusion of the gentiles into God's chosen people: "bring my sons from afar and my daughters from the end of the earth, everyone who is called by my name, whom I created for my glory, whom I formed and made" (Isa 43:6b–7). When Paul mentions that "our gospel came to you not only in word, but also in power and in the Holy Spirit" (1:5), he implies that the prophetic expectation that the word of God and the Holy Spirit will come at the eschaton (cf. Joel 2:28–32) has been fulfilled in Paul's mission to the Thessalonians. As Fee (2009:33) remarks, in this verse the role of the Holy Spirit is significant in that it enables the gentiles to experience incorporation into God's chosen people. In other words, "the Spirit for Paul is the key to the present fulfillment of the eschatological inclusion of the Gentiles in the people of God" (Fee 1994:812; cf. Gal 3:1–6).

4.3.6 LXX-BASED LANGUAGE THAT ALLUDES TO ISRAEL'S IDENTITY (1:9B–10)

As the conjunction γάρ in verse 9 is closely connected to verse 7 (cf. tracing 1, Appendix I), Paul provides a second group of reasons for the Thessalonians becoming a τύπος to all the regions of Greece: (a) the neighbors' reports on the apostle's visit to the Thessalonians, and (b) how they converted from idols to the God of Israel. Here, in reminding readers of the initiation of the Thessalonian community, I suggest examining Paul's description of the conversion of the gentiles by means of the language of the LXX. In my view, in 1:9b–10 Paul establishes a theological foundation for how the gentile community came to be incorporated into the people of God. According to Furnish (2007:48), verses 9b–10 are filled with "scriptural concepts and idioms" that are derived from "both Hellenistic-Jewish and Hellenistic Jewish Christian circles." I wish to argue that typical language from the Hebrew Scriptures (such as "turn," "serve" and "the living and true God") is reiterated here, presenting the notion that the Thessalonians have been incorporated into God's chosen people. They demonstrate that Paul includes the gentile community in the narrative of God's drama of salvation (Boring 2015:70–76). As I conclude the exegesis of part of 1 Thess 1:1–10, I would like to point out that Paul's illustration of their identity and the contents of their faith can be indicated by his echoing of language from the LXX.[29]

The expression that the Thessalonians turned from idols to God echoes Israel's repentance of their idolatry in the LXX (Deut 30:2, 8, 10; 2 Chr 30:6, 9; Jdt 5:19; Hos 3:5; 6:1; Joel 2:12–13; Isa 45:22; Jer 24:7), as well as the gentiles' conversion in Hellenistic Jewish literature (*Jos. Asen* 11:7–11).

---

29. The controversial issue is that some scholars regard 1 Thess 1:9–10 as a pre-Pauline text, which Paul borrowed and adapted as a summary of missionary preaching, creedal formula and a baptismal hymn. As Weima (2014:115) well recapitulates, the proponents of this view argue that Paul's expressions, such as ἐπιστρέφω (to turn), "to serve God," "true God," ἀναμένω, which is hapax legomenon, "Son" in association with the parousia, ἐκ τῶν οὐρανῶν, ἐκ [τῶν] νεκρῶν, and ῥύομαι, are foreign to Paul's normal practice. However, my assumption is that these expressions may be attributed to Paul's own writing. It is not wholly invalid to call 1 Thess 1:9b–10 pre-Pauline in that Paul echoes the earlier election traditions of ancient Israel, which originated from the language of LXX (see Furnish 2007:48–49).

The two infinitives, δουλεύειν and ἀναμένειν, grammatically function to reflect how radical the nature of the Thessalonians' conversion was. Their conversion naturally resulted in a change in their lifestyle and identity to one that was characterized by "a new relationship to God and Jesus" (Marshall 1983:57).[30] This new identity inevitably brought about a "radical break with their previous way of life" as they were incorporated into the group of God's election (Weima 2014:108-9). Moreover, after their faith in Christ had become publicly known throughout the region of Greece, they were always exposed to persecution because they aligned "themselves with a new religion that was offensive to the surrounding culture" (Plummer 2006:136). In a religiously pluralistic world, Paul could analogously have set up a discursive exigency that reminded his audience of the context in which the Israelites were constantly confronted with the issue of idolatry.

In verse 9, Paul's description of the Thessalonians' conversion seems to be intentional, since the consequent expressions and ideas, such as "turning to God," "serving God," and the descriptions of God (ζῶντι καὶ ἀληθινῷ) are derived from the LXX. In this expression, Paul represents that after their conversion, the Thessalonians now share the prestige of Israel's chosen and beloved status of God's people. In the Hebrew Scriptures and Jewish literature conversion is expressed as "a turning to God" and "a turning to some quality of the moral life such as justice or the light" (Green 2002:107). Weima (2014:109) mentions that the Thessalonians' serving the living and true God commonly echoes Israel's "total commitment to God," which indicates both inward and outward expressions of their devotion to God. Noticeably, in the LXX, the term δουλεύω is common ceremonial language of the ancient Israelites for worship (NIDNTTE 1:769; e.g., Judg 2:7; 1 Sam 12:14; 2 Chr 30:8; Ps 2:11). This term connotes unbridgeable distance between the slaves (the Israelites) and God, and their reliance on God without implication of their servile status (NIDNTTE 1:769). According to Gupta (2010:156), in verse 9c, Paul not only employs the term δουλεύω in a conventional manner but also conveys the concept of servile status. Imbuing this term in 1:9c with the LXX's connotations, Gupta (2010:157) understands that "Paul's thought derives from a robust theology of exodus, liberation, and devotion to God

---

30. Many commentators claim that these two consecutive infinitive forms are grammatically "infinitive of purpose" (see Weima 2014:109; Malherbe 2000:120). While it is possible to take these infinitive forms as functioning as purposive or resultative, I prefer to view them as signifying the outcome of the Thessalonians' conversion. It does not make sense to accept the infinitive's purposive meaning, "the goal of conversion," since no one repents with a certain intention/goal/purpose in one's own mind. Instead, worshiping God and awaiting the parousia of Christ are the natural consequence of their response to the gospel.

as redeemer as prominent in Jewish tradition . . . This powerful event, then, lies at the heart of Israel's sense of devotion toward serving God as a master."

The first infinitive, δουλεύειν in verse 9c, is modified by the phrase, ζῶντι καὶ ἀληθινῷ. In this construction Paul clarifies the object of their commitment but also informs readers of the attributes of ancient Israel's God. Paul's discursive strategy is to connect the Thessalonians' faith in God with the narrative world of Scripture. Both ζάω and ἀληθινός, which derive from Semitic expressions, describe attributes of the ancient Israelites' God, whom the gentile community now serves with total commitment after their conversion ("living": Num 14:21, 28; Deut 32:40; 1 Sam 17:26, 36; Ps 30:2; Jer 23:56 Hosea 2:1; "true": Exod 34:6; 2 Chr 15:3; Ps 86:15; Isa 65:16). According to Malherbe (2000:121), in Hellenistic Judaism the epithet "true God" refers to God's role as creator of the world (e.g., Josephus, *Ant*. 11.55; *Sib. Or*. 5.495–9). Moreover, the most plausible echo of this verse may be found in Jeremiah 10:10, וַיהוָה אֱלֹהִים אֱמֶת הוּא־אֱלֹהִים חַיִּים ("But the Lord is the true God; he is the living God"). In this section the prophet warns against idolatry by making a contrast between idols and God, who is the everlasting king. Through these probable echoes, I wish to argue that Paul presents the Thessalonians' faith in the light of a salvation-historical trajectory from creation, to Israel's election in history, to realization of the gentiles' inclusion into the people of God, and ultimately to Christ's parousia.

In verse 10a, Paul shifts his focus to the Christ-centered notion in association with eschatology. The second infinitive ἀναμένειν (v. 10a), which occurs only once in the New Testament, indicates that the Thessalonians eagerly anticipated the parousia of Christ. Paul's use of this term reflects the LXX's notion that one awaits "faith and full assurance for God's righteous judgment, mercy, and salvation" (Malherbe 2000:121; e.g., Jud 8:17; Sir 2:6–8; Isa 59:11; Jer 13:1). Paul understands that the waiting for God's righteous judgment, mercy, and salvation would be fulfilled in the Son's returning at the eschatological time. In stating the Son's role in salvation in verse 10, Paul's use of the verb ῥύομαι echoes Isaiah's prophecy, "a Redeemer [ὁ ῥυόμενος] will come to Zion, to those in Jacob who turn from transgression" (Isa 59:19–20), and the coming of a redeemer is connected to the notion of coming of wrath, 59:19 [LXX].[31] Beale (2003:61) argues that this scriptural echo in employing terms from the LXX substantiates that

---

31. Some scholars argue that this is a pre-Pauline tradition, since the term ῥύομαι was never used for eschatological deliverance. Thus they argue that the fact that the verb σῴζω is used here could be evidence that 1:9–10 is pre-Pauline (Richard [1995] 2007:57). However, the occurrence of the verb ῥύομαι is not unusual, since Paul uses it when he refers to the notion of eschatology (e.g., Rom 7:24; 11:26; Col 1:13; Kasch, TDNT 6:1003; NIDNTTE 4:216; Lichtenberger, EDNT 3:215).

Paul deliberately describes this gentile community's new identity. He comments that "[t]he point of noticing this Old Testament background is that Gentiles who turn from their unclean idols to the true God fulfil part of the prophecy of Israel's salvation; they become the true Israel of God."

4.3.7 PRELIMINARY CONCLUSION

In 1 Thess 1:1–10, Paul articulates that major causes of his thanksgiving are God's election of the gentile believers in Thessalonica and their exemplary role and behavior all over Greece. In his expansion of their identity from their election to their role as imitators of Paul and Christ, Paul delineates the gentiles' origin and foundational tradition rooted in the narrative world of ancient Israel, especially with regard to their election and their representing the Lord. Wright (1992:268) contends that the ancient Israelites' calling is closely related to the salvation and restoration of the whole of creation. According to the Jewish perspective, the restoration of the entire world and fulfilment of the divine goal would be accomplished when the gentiles are incorporated into the people of God.[32] If Paul had this view in mind, it seems that echoes of the tradition of Israel's election and their calling among the nations are deliberately employed to illustrate the nature and origins of their newly gained identity.

4.4 FAMILY METAPHORS IN 1 THESS 2:1–12

Paul's establishment of the connection of the Thessalonians with Israel's story of its election in the initial stages of shaping the Christian community provides a significant theological motivation for elucidating the nature and origin of the community. Apart from describing the gentile converts' existential reality through the use of the vocabulary of ancient Israel, on the other hand, he also uses language from a sociological perspective, since their conversion resulted in distress and the loss of social networks and family relationships (Malherbe 1987:41; Thompson 2014:43). Since the

---

32. Wright (1992:267-8) investigates the notion of the gentile's inclusion into people of God in Second Temple Judaism and the later rabbinic understanding of the gentile's status. He explains that "[w]ithin the Jewish worldview itself, Israel's vocation is not compromised but is in a sense fulfilled when Gentiles come to join the people of God (like Ruth the ancestress of David), listen to his [God's] wisdom (like the Queen of Sheba), or otherwise share the life of his [God's] people. This theme is continued into the [S]econd [T]emple period, as can be seen in a book like *Joseph and Aseneth* . . . If the Gentiles, and the ultimate divine purpose for them, are ignored, then Israel's claim to be the one people of the one creator [G]od is itself called into question."

first-century Mediterranean world had a group-oriented culture, separation from society meant the loss of a sense of social belonging. Thus, the Thessalonians' social bonds to various groups would probably have been cut off (McNeel 2014:85). Kinship metaphors play a significant role in the Christian community's identity and ethos formation; as McNeel (2014:93; cf. Meeks 1983:86–88) has argued: "It is not surprising that when Paul wants to strengthen the identity of a congregation and solidify the bonds between members, he pictures the local congregation as a kinship group."

In these circumstances there are two major reasons why adopting kinship metaphors (nursing mother, brothers and sisters, and nurturing father) in 1 Thess 2:1–12 could have been an appropriate strategy for Paul to utilize in encouraging the new Christians. First, their feeling of a sense of alienation and frustration caused by Paul's abrupt leaving required affirmation of the relationship between him and the community (Malherbe 1987:51; Burke 2003:26). Second, in their social context, which greatly valued corporate identity, those who suffered the loss of social identity and a sense of belonging needed to be reorganized as a newly defined social community in relation to both the community itself and to those outside of it. By defining the relationship amongst the community members, Paul intended not only to shape the solidarity of the community, but also to encourage them to adhere to significant communal values. Noticeably, in 1 Thess 2:1–12 family metaphors are adopted in his self-defense to opponents. In this respect, it is necessary to examine what those metaphors connote, why they are employed in such a context, and how they function discursively in this pericope. These considerations will hopefully enable us to identify the purpose of Paul's discourse among this fledging community.

4.4.1 PAUL'S SELF-DEFENCE AND FAMILY METAPHORS

Paul aims to shape the community's solidarity against a potential "countering accusation of some kind" (Weima 1997a:85; 2014:131). This section will examine the existence of potential opponents who threatened Paul and the Thessalonian Christians, and the way they are reflected in Paul's use of discourse markers in the text. It is particularly necessary to probe Paul's repetitive use of antithetical statements ("not A but B") as a remarkable literary device. This discourse marker sheds light on the fact that Paul defends his own integrity in past missionary work, for which he has been criticized. As Still (1999:143) maintains, the connection between this literary device and the conflict at the city of Thessalonica is plausible:

> When these foregoing observations are coupled with the fact that talk of the apostles' [Paul, Silvanus, and Timothy] external conflict in Thessalonica permeates 1 Thessalonians 2 . . . the scales are tipped decidedly to the side of 2.1–12 being a Pauline apology. Paul's primary purpose in penning this passage, then, was to defend himself against actual (or at least potential) accusation, not to exhort his converts. Whatever parenetic intentions Paul had in writing 2.1–12, they should be judged secondary.[33]

In this section I contend that Paul's autobiographical statement plays an apologetic function in reaction to his accusers. This presupposition is significant, since his self-defense sets the grounds for reaffirming the trust between himself and the Thessalonians. For the persecuted Christians who have been alienated from the rest of society, Paul needed to demonstrate the veracity of his gospel preaching and instruction in the previous mission. He was challenged to respond to the accusation made against him during his absence from the Thessalonians. Only after defending himself, could Paul encourage and comfort the persecuted believers and shape their communal ethos as God's family called into God's kingdom and glory.

Malherbe's remarkable article, "'Gentle as a Nurse': The Cynic Background to I Thess II," points out close verbal parallels between Paul and a Hellenistic philosopher, Dio Chrysostom (see 2.1.2.3).[34] Malherbe (2000:134) argues that Paul presents himself as a model of the moral life in the later paraenetic section of the letter (1 Thess 4–5) to encourage the Thessalonians to imitate him. Malherbe's argument is based on Paul's employment of the tradition of popular philosophers in his day. So Paul intended to distance himself from the charlatans just as Dio Chrysostom presents himself as a true philosopher with the use of the same kind of vocabulary (Malherbe 1970:126–7; cf. 2.1.2.3). The fact that Dio Chrysostom did not respond to any personal accusation against him led Malherbe to conclude that Paul does not render any personal apology in 1 Thess 2:1–12 (1970:216). In his establishment of the intimacy between Paul and the Thessalonians in 2:1–12, Malherbe argues that 1 Thess 1–3 is a philophronetic section (see 2.1.2.3) which prepares his audience to follow the ethical teachings in the paraenetic part of the letter (1 Thess 4–5). He suggests that Paul's appeals to his authority and the integrity of his motives and ministry have nothing

---

33. Still (1999:143) remarks that even though many scholars do not agree with this view, the link between Paul's rhetoric and the actual conflict is still maintained by the majority of scholars and commentators (e.g., Marshall 1983:Weima 1997a:86–88; Bruce 1982:28; Holtz 2000:70–78; Kim 2005:524–7; Fee 2009:55–56).

34. In this article, Malherbe (1970:203) refutes the notion that Paul was "defending himself against specific charges that had been made against him" in 1 Thess 2:1–12.

to do with the actual accusation of opponents against the apostle (see also Walton 1995:244). Malherbe's argument has brought about a remarkable paradigmatic shift in understanding the function of 1 Thess 2:1–12, not as "apologetic" but as "exemplary or paraenetic" (Weima 2014:122).

However, as he proceeds with his argument in this passage, Paul implies the presence of opponents. Kim (2005:525) agrees with Winter's observation that Paul makes a sharp and succinct contrast to the Sophists' "seeking money, reputation, and praise by means of flattery and other deceptive rhetorical tricks." He notices the larger context in which Paul responds to the real situation that his opponents disparaged him as one of the charlatans. Thus, Kim (2005:526) understands that there is real urgency in the passage, not merely an allusion to the moral philosopher's words.[35] In addition, Weima (2014:122–4) provides five crucial points of evidence as to why the traditional understanding of 2:1–12, as Paul's apologetic argument, may be regarded as legitimate:

1. Paul's defensive tone in 1:2–10 signals his apologetics for the genuine character of his previous mission project in 2:1–16;

2. Paul defends his past ministry in 2:1–16 and his present absence from the community in 2:17—3:10. The sudden separation between Paul and the Thessalonians inevitably led him to use the apostolic Parousia—an epistolary convention that functions to enable the recipients/audience to experience the apostle's personal presence without his visit—in 2:17—3:10. In this part Paul's reassuring the Thessalonians of his love and concern towards them is linked contextually to his defense in 2:1–16;

3. The antithetical statements (οὐχ . . . ἀλλὰ . . .) substantiate Paul's self-defense in 2:3–4, 5–7;

4. The antithetical statements occurring elsewhere in 1 Thessalonians (1:5, 8; 2:17; 4:7, 8; 5:6, 9, 15) and especially the negative conjunctions occurring eight times (three times in 2:3–4 and five times in 2:5–6) indicate that Paul does not simply suggest himself as a model but responds to the opponents' accusation;

5. Paul appeals to the audience's first-hand knowledge of his character and ministry. Paul's discourse formulae that appealed to the Thessalonians' first-hand knowledge (e.g., [καθὼς] or [καθάπερ] οἴδατε, 2:1, 2, 5, 11; θεὸς μάρτυς or ὑμεῖς μάρτυρες καὶ ὁ θεός, 2:5, 10,

---

35. According to Kim (2005:526), 1 Thess 2:13—3:10 conveys Paul's sense of urgency that the Thessalonians' faith might have been shaken by "the temper" (ὁ πειράζων) in 3:5 (cf. 3:3).

μνημονεύετε, 2:9) function to characterize this pericope as Paul's own defense.

4.4.2 IMPLICATIONS OF PAUL'S ANTITHETICAL STATEMENTS

In 1 Thess 2:1, Paul begins his discourse by drawing the audience's attention. Here Paul emphasizes that his ministry in Thessalonica was never in vain (οὐ κενὴ γέγονεν) with a series of occurrences of the emphatic pronoun αὐτοί, the perfect indicative οἴδατε, and the vocative "brothers and sisters"[36] He appeals to the Thessalonians' past memory of his sincere preaching of the gospel of God (2:2, 8, 9), even in the midst of suffering and insults (including his suffering at Philippi; cf. Acts 16:16–24). The logical explanatory γάρ in verse 1 is closely connected to the preceding idea (thanksgiving for the election of this gentile community, being imitators of the suffering of Christ, and their role as missionaries and model to all the believers in Greece in 1 Thess 1) and the continuous occurrences of γάρ in verses 3 and 5 have the same grammatical function.[37] Paul's fruitful visit to the Thessalonians is emphasized by his reuses of the term εἴσοδος (2:1; cf. 1:9) to remind the Thessalonian community of his pure motivation for promoting the fruitfulness of God's gospel in this community. In particular, by appealing to their shared memory of the suffering (cf. 1:6) Paul defends that his arrival at the city did not aim at pursuing personal profit. The conjunction γάρ in verse 3 links to the previous verse, particularly the clause ἐπαρρησιασάμεθα ἐν τῷ θεῷ ἡμῶν

36.. There are chiefly three options for the translation of the term κενός in 2:1: (1) the first rendering can be that Paul was not "empty-handed" but brought something, such as the gospel message and the miracles (Hendriksen 1955:60); (2) the second interpretation indicates the results of Paul's mission in a fruitful sense (Furnish 2007:53; Fee 2009:57; Shogren 2012:90); (3) the third emphasizes the character of Paul's past missionary work in Thessalonica, which indicates this term as meaning "hollow, empty, wanting in purpose and earnestness" (Lightfoot 1904:18; cf. Marshall 1983:62–63; Morris [1984] 2009:51–52; Malherbe 2000:135–6). In the third option, Malherbe's contribution is unique, since he identifies the allusion to the Hellenistic philosophical tradition. According to him, (2000:135–6), the fact that philosophers' speeches are κενός as professional orators illustrates the character of their powerless speeches, which merely aim at pleasing and flattering others (e.g., Quintilian, *Inst.* 12.73–74; Dio Chrysostom, *Or.* 32.26). However, it seems to be that there is no obvious boundary between these two renderings. Bruce (1982:24) states that, "the character and results could not be separated." Green (2002:115) also mentions that "[s]ound character produced credible results."

37. While 1 Thess 2 is not Paul's thanksgiving section, it can potentially be an extension of 1 Thess 1 in making a close connection through γάρ. Nevertheless, the most remarkable feature is the transition of Paul's emphasis from the Thessalonians' elected status to Paul's contribution to it.

λαλῆσαι (Malherbe 2000:138). Here Paul reveals the context of his suffering that some opponents might attempt to use to undermine the veracity of ἡ παράκλησις.[38] Paul responds to the slanderers who attempted to weaken the foundation of Paul's gospel ministry by accusing him of flattery and greed. In so doing, he seeks to differentiate himself from the wandering charlatan philosophers whose life was not relevant to the ἀγών (Donfried 2000:44). In response to those who compared Paul's previous ministry to that of the charlatans, Paul suggests that his suffering was a natural phenomenon and a true mark in his gospel ministry.

Paul's statements of self-defense in this pericope were anticipated by his earlier mention of the term in 1 Thess 1:5 ("you know what kind of men we proved to be among you for your sake"). Moreover, Paul's using the antithetical statement (οὐ κενὴ γέγονεν, ἀλλὰ προπαθόντες καὶ ὑβρισθέντες) in 2:2 leads us to recognize his apologetic tone with regard to his integrity and sincerity in the past mission at the Thessalonica. Whether the negative section indicates the notion of "powerless" or "in vain" in 2:1, it cannot be refuted that Paul is responding to the opponents' negative accusation against him. Through a so-called "mirror-reading" of the text, recent interpreters have perceived that Paul strategically contrasts himself to the adversaries' wicked scheme that undermines the congregation's faith and their communal solidarity. Some scholars disprove identifying the existence of potential opponents through "mirror-reading," since deriving social conflict from the text that has no indication explicit of it could be considered eisegesis (Donfried 2002:194). Despite the risk of employing "mirror-reading," 2:1–12 can be viewed as an appropriate case that fits the practice of "mirror-reading" (Weima 1997a:93; cf. Barclay 1987:74; Carson 2014:99). If mirror-reading is applicable to this pericope, the accusers' charge against Paul may be presupposed sufficiently. Particularly, in tracing 2 (Appendix I), I indicate that the antithesis occurs intensively in 2:1–7. A series of Paul's antithetical statements presumably reflect that Paul had those in mind who falsely slandered his entry as "powerless" or "in vain" (2:1). Paul's opponents regarded his motivation as insincere, and such an attitude was attributed to *deceit*, *impure motives*, and *treachery* (2:3). For them, Paul seemed to win the Thessalonians by pleasing them (2:4) and flattery (2:5). Not only that, but the accusers criticized Paul for approaching this community with greed

---

38. According to BDAG, the term παράκλησις has various meanings (e.g., encouragement, exhortation, appeal, request, comfort, consolation). I argue that the most plausible interpretation is "Paul's act of preaching the gospel" (Schmitz, TDNT 5:795; Thomas, EDNT 3:26; Ellingworth & Nida 1976:24; Marshall 1983:64; Weima 2014:134). The definite article ἡ most likely modifies the previous mention of Paul's activity of preaching the gospel.

(2:5) and in pursuit of his own glory (2:6). While Paul does not set forth the opposite list of the vices, the positive halves of the antithetical statements affirm that his εἴσοδος is not self-motivated for his own profit. Rather, his visit to the Thessalonians is instead attributed to his pure motivation for preaching the gospel, which comes from God's entrusting the gospel message to him.

In attempting to prove his own innocent motivation for preaching the gospel in verse 3, Paul reminds the audience of the veracity of his παράκλησις. I maintain that by using this term, Paul gives a prophetic message of consolation and "fuses it with his evangelistic appeal, God's call/invitation to respond to this message" (Boring 2015:83). Paul's use of παράκλησις can be deliberate to express that he represents himself as the one who stands in the line of the prophetic tradition (cf. Holtz 1966:324; Myers & Freed 1966:40-53; Ellis 1970:57; Thompson 2014:154; see 5.2). In fact, since the usage of the term παράκλησις is varied, it is not easy to determine its meaning in 2:3 ("exhortation," "appeal" or "consolation"). The majority of commentators rightly understand that this noun can mean "appeal" inasmuch as παράκλησις indicates Paul's original communication of the gospel to the Thessalonians (Marshall 1983:64; Richard [1995] 2007:79; Green 2002:118; Fee 2009:59; Weima 2014:134).[39] Weima (2014:134) argues that Paul's preaching in previous missionary work was "an urgent 'appeal' to turn from idols to the living God and accept his Son as deliverer from the coming wrath." Green (2002:118) also remarks that this act of preaching the gospel in 2:3 was what Paul has done in the city.

But, in my view, Paul most likely emphasized the broad framework of the symbolic world of biblical prophecy to justify his pure motivation. According to Donfried (2000:136), Paul was influenced by "the normative criteria of the true prophet which involved not only the content of teaching as deriving from God, but also involves the moral behavior of the prophet as one accountable and acceptable to Yahweh." Tellbe (2001:109; see also Denis 1957:265-6) claims that the intensive occurrence of the same terms, παράκλησις (Isa 57:18; 66:11), ἀκαθαρσία (52:1, 11), δόλος (53:9), is found in the section where consolation is a dominant theme. Boring (2015:82-83) elaborates on this by stating that here Paul echoes Jeremiah 16:7, conveying the message of "God's eschatological comfort/consolation of Israel"; this theme could be a synonym for "eschatological salvation, the

---

39. Malherbe (2000:138) understands that this term can mean "exhortation" or "appeal." In the interpretation of the term παράκλησις, his unique contribution is to read it in the light of the tradition of Hellenistic moral philosophy that seeks to influence human behavior. He observes that this word belongs to the philosopher's vocabulary and corresponds with some Latin words, such as "*adhortatio, exhortatio, hortatio.*"

fulfilment of God's plan for history, the coming of the kingdom of God" through the Messiah. Noticeably, in 2:4, Paul also shows his own integrity by consistently employing scriptural languages. In so doing, he proves his pure motivation and integrity by appealing to God's qualification of him as a true prophet.[40] Paul presents God as the one who "examined him and found him worthy to be entrusted with the gospel (2:4a), also continues to examine him . . . and thus ensure that the apostle's motives are pure" (Weima 2007:873). In particular, Paul's passive stance with regard to the gospel ministry is emphasized. Consecutive divine passives (δεδοκιμάσμεθα ὑπὸ τοῦ θεοῦ πιστευθῆναι τὸ εὐαγγέλιον) denote that God plays a major role in approving of him and entrusting him with the gospel.

4.4.3 PAUL'S INNOCENT LOVE AND THE METAPHOR OF A NURSING MOTHER

Many commentators have ignored the fact that Paul's consistent use of antithetical statements is gradually developed to a climax. Paul articulates the Thessalonians' newly established identity based on God's calling of them into one family (1 Thess 2:1-12). McNeel (2014:148) observes that identifying the discursive function of kinship metaphors is a significant interpretative key to unlocking this pericope:

> [I]f the metaphor becomes part of the Thessalonians's thinking about themselves, it has a particularly powerful one for Paul as he sought to ground the Thessalonians's group identity in the new Christian community rather than in older kinship, business, and civic ties. The metaphor affects the social identity of the community through in-group/out-group differentiation and the use of kinship language.

Right before using kinship metaphors, a parenthetical statement in 2:7a, "δυνάμενοι ἐν βάρει εἶναι ὡς Χριστοῦ ἀπόστολοι" ("though we could have insisted on our reputation/authority as apostles of Christ") illustrates Paul's integrity in his repudiation of an assumed accusation (Weima 2014:144). It functions to shift our attention to his description of a unique role as a nursing mother in the positive half (ἀλλά . . .) in 2:7. In fact, as other letters defend his own apostolic authority (cf. Gal 1:1; 1 Cor 9:1-2; 2 Cor 10:1-18; 11:5), Paul could have appealed to his authority as the founder of the

---

40. In the Hebrew Scriptures the concept of "pleasing God" (e.g., Job 34:9; Ps 19:14; 69:31; 104:34; 1 Chr 29: 17; Prov 15:26; 16:7; Isa 59:15; Mal 3:4) and the idea of God testing human hearts (e.g., Ps 17:3 [16:3 LXX]; 26:2 [25:2 LXX]; 66:10 [65:10 LXX]; Jer 11:20; 17:20) frequently occur.

Thessalonian church.[41] In contrast to our expectation, it is remarkable to see that Paul, who stayed in Thessalonica for a short period of time, describes his role as a nursing mother.

4.4.3.1 INNOCENT (νήπιοι) OR GENTLE (ἤπιοι)?[42]

Particular attention must be paid to the transition from Paul's self-defense to his use of the nursing mother metaphor. Paul's employment of this metaphor conveys the innocence (νήπιοι) of himself and his coworkers through the articulation of their conduct and motives in contrast to the slanderers' flattery, greed, and seeking for their own glory (Fee 2009:73; McNeel 2014:55; Weima 2014:146). It is notoriously difficult to decide whether νήπιοι (infants) may have arisen by dittography or ἤπιοι (gentle) by haplography, since both textual variants have abundant transcriptional evidence (Frame 1912:100).[43] Wanamaker (1990:100) argues that ἤπιοι is a more reliable reading, since Paul never refers to himself or addresses his coworkers as "infants." Moreover, Sterner (1998:39) lists four reasons why ἤπιοι should be chosen: (1) This term fits better with the preceding idea, not creating a mixed metaphor in association with "nursing mother"; (2) A scribe's accidental or deliberate change to the more common term, νήπιοι; (3) The term ἤπιοι is more appropriate when it comes to comparison with a nursing mother's love; (4) Similarly, in agreement with Wanamaker, Sterner observes that Paul does not describe himself or the other apostles as νήπιοι anywhere else. Furthermore, this alternative reading of ἤπιοι is adopted by the majority of committees of English Bible translations (NRSV, NIV84, NASB, ESV) and commentators (Marshall 1983:70; Jewett 1986:152;

---

41. It is most likely that the present participle δυνάμενοι functions grammatically as a concessive in association with the series of the occurrences of the negative conjunction οὔτε in v. 6. And the term βάρος literally means "weight" and "burden." As BDAG suggests, this term indicates "influence that someone enjoys or claims, *claim of importance.*" Thus, this passage demonstrates that, even though Paul could have requested and demanded honor, respect, and glory as a church founder, he intentionally refrains from insisting on his authority. His attitude and behavior are distinct from the natural tendency of other authoritative figures who seek their own glory.

42. After completing my PhD dissertation, I have conducted extensive research on this topic and published it in a Korean academic journal. This specific section is updated by incorporating the content of my recent study. See Kiwoon Lee, "Textual-Critical Reading of 1 Thessalonians 2:7: νήπιοι or ἤπιοι?" *Korean Reformed Journal* Vol. 56 (2021): 303–36.

43. Νήπιοι is supported by 𝔓65 ℵ* B C* D* F G I Ψ* 104*. 326c it vgcl.ww sams bo and ἤπιοι is supported by ℵc A C2 D2 K L P Ψc 0278. 33. 81. 104c. 326*. 365. 630. 1241. 1505. 1739. 1881 𝔐 vgst (sy) samss; Cl. See NA28.

Johanson 1987:92; Bruce 1982:31; Malherbe 2000:145; Witherington III 2006:80; Richard [1995] 2007:82).

However, νήπιοι can be regarded as the original reading and can be supported by some external evidence (Fee 2009:70–71; McNeel 2014:38–43; Weima 2014:145). Firstly, the alternative reading, νήπιοι, is substantially based on the support of old witnesses (𝔓65 [third century], ℵ*[fourth century], C* [fifth century], D* [fourth century], I [fifth century]). Even the Codex Alexandrinus (A), which supports the reading of ἤπιοι, dates from fifth century. Other witnesses (C, D, K, L, P, Ψ) were scribed between th eighth and tenth centuries. Thus, most likely, when date of the oldest witnesses is considered, νήπιοι might have been changed to ἤπιοι by later scribes. Moreover, one must take into consideration of their geographical distribution and attestation among various text types (Alexandrian [𝔓65, ℵ*, B, I], Western [D, Old Latin], Byzantine [F, G, Ψ*], and Coptic [sahidic, bohairic]). This external evidence is sufficient to demonstrate that νήπιοι is attested to be original reading.

Bruce Metzger (1994:561) admits that it is difficult to make a decision between these two textual variants. Although he acknowledges that many significant and various external evidence support νήπιος, he considers ἤπιοι as original by pointing out that Paul never presents himself as νήπιος in his letters. Metzger (2005:330) articulates the reason for his decision: "By way of striking a balance in the arguments *pro et contra*, it appears that here internal considerations should be allowed to take precedence over external evidence." However, internal evidence cannot negate the significance and credibility of external evidence as Fee (2009:70) mentions:

> What is seldom noted, however, is a further significant historical factor: Since all the known early evidence—empire-wide—attests *nēpioi*, those who favor ēpioi need to offer good *historical* reasons as to how the (accidental) corruption of adding the *nu* happened so early (and so often) so that it came to be the only text known for several centuries, while the "original" reading escaped all the known early evidence only to emerge much later in the monolithic, but patently secondary, evidence of the Byzantine tradition. This is not thereby to deny that such could have happened; but one wonders why only the "accident" is universally known in the first four Christian centuries.

Secondly, in ancient Greek literature, νήπιος was mainly used in a negative sense as several dictionaries (e.g., LSJ, BDAG) do not show a full semantic range regarding this term. According to Sailors (2000:91), approximately 6.23 percent of all the usages of this word occurs in a positive sense. If νήπιος is original reading, its usage in verse 7 can belonged to this semantic category. In Pauline letters, the term νήπιοι implies a variety of meanings in the somewhat 'fluid' fashion (Weima 2014:145; cf. Fee 1992:177). These meanings include a pejorative connotation for immaturity, a basic reference to an infant or a very young child with a neutral connotation (cf. BDAG, νήπιος §1–2; Rom 2:20; 1 Cor 3:1; 13:11; Gal 4:3; Eph 4:14), and pure and innocent motivations (1 Cor 14:20). But to confirm a positive usage of this word, it is necessary to search for the specific examples in various Greek literature. Paul might be aware of some specific uses of νήπιος from Matt 11:25–26 (cf. Luke 10:21): "I thank you, Father, Lord of heaven and earth, that you have hidden these things from the wise and understanding and revealed them to little children [νηπίοις]; yes, Father, for such was your gracious will." Moreover, elsewhere in the LXX, νήπιοι is used when someone's motivations are pure and guileless (Gaventa 1990:196; e.g., Ps 19:7 [18:8 LXX]; 119:130 [118:130 LXX]; Wis 10:21). Most noticeable examples are found in some extrabiblical literature (see Weima 2014:183). This word is used in Dio Chrysostom's speech that establishes an analogy between the pure desire of humans to seek the gods and that of innocent children (νήπιοι, Or. 12.61). And Diodorus Siculus's *Library of History* describes the innocence and blamelessness of young children (νηπίους) who have no consciousness of an impending dangerous situation (*Hist.* 20.72.2). In addition, though in most cases Philo uses νήπιος negatively, sometimes it is employed to describe the innocence of an immature child (*Alleg. Interp* 2.53; *Jos.* 225.6; *Spec. Laws* 3.119; *Good Person* 160; *Flaccus* 68).

When it comes to the connotation of combining νήπιοι (infants) or ἤπιοι (gentle) and the metaphor τροφός (nurse or mother?), Malherbe (2000:146) reads 2:7b in the light of a philanthropic attitude reflected in Hellenistic philosophers' bold speech. Malherbe (1989:39–45) believes that the latter ἤπιοι fits well into the tradition of Hellenistic moral philosophers, in particular, Dio's contrast between the ideal philosopher and the charlatans (*Discourse* 77/78.38). While the nature of the genuine philosopher's harsh speech was accompanied by gentleness and a concern for the audience's needs, the Cynic charlatans "made up for the lack of content in their speeches by railing at the crowd, in this way hoping to secure its admiration" (Malherbe 1989:41). A number of philosophers' texts (Maximus of Tyre, Pseudo-Diogenes, Dio Chrysostom, Plutarch) customarily "contrast the harshness of a certain kind of παρρησία with gentle speech such as that of a nurse who knows her charges" (Malherbe 1970:211). However, it is problematic to merely accept that Paul alludes to Dio's use of the characteristic of the nurse. According to Gaventa (2007:22–23), the text Malherbe quotes firstly suggests the nurse as an example to elucidate what the speaker wants to emphasize, rather than comparing the metaphor to himself. Second, the nurse's concrete activity in Dio Chrysostom's description of the philosopher is not articulated. Third, the texts that Malherbe actually uses do not contain the term τροφὸς, but τίτθη (wet nurse). For these reasons, Gaventa (2007:23) concludes that whether or not "the behavior of the nurse has a fixed place in that topos" in Paul's day, Malherbe's suggestion is untenable.

4.4.3.2 PLAUSIBILITY OF A MIXED METAPHOR IN 2:7?

It is plausible that Paul employs the metaphor of the nursing mother (τροφὸς) to demonstrate his innocent motivation towards the newly established community. To understand the intent of his using this metaphor, it is required to consider its connection with νήπιοι in verse 7 and how individual phrase constitutes a single idea. Not a few scholars understand that since the οὐ ... ἀλλά construction in 2:5–8 is an independent literary unit, Paul can make a full stop after ἐν μέσῳ ὑμῶν in verse 7b (Weima 2000:556; Fee 2009:74; Shogren 2012:104; McNeel 2014:45; see NA 28). For them, the ὡς ἐάν phrase in verse 7c signals the beginning of the new sentence. Moreover, it has been regarded as improbable that Paul uses a mixed metaphor here because of the improbability of abrupt transition from infants to a nursing mother (Malherbe 2000:145; McNeel 2014:44). However, the ἀλλά clause and the ὡς ἐάν clause in verse 7 can be connected, making a single idea. Gaventa (1990:206) remarks that Paul uses a mixed metaphor to elucidate two aspects of his role, saying that "[t]he apostle is childlike, in contrast to the charlatan who constantly works to see how much benefit he can derive from his audience. Yet the apostle is also the responsible adult ... the nurse who approaches her charges with care and affection." Agreeing with this notion, I suggest that the ὡς ἐάν clause could be subordinated to the previous sentence so that Paul's comparison to a nursing mother in verse 7c can be related to the idea in verse 7b. The consecutive and abrupt occurrence of these two metaphors might be discursively designed to produce a fresh meaning. The continuity and correlation between Paul's mentioning that "we were innocent among you" in verse 7b and the ὡς ἐάν ... οὕτως construction in verses 7c–8 have been neglected:

2:5 Οὔτε γάρ ποτε ἐν λόγῳ κολακείας ἐγενήθημεν
(καθὼς οἴδατε)
οὔτε ἐν προφάσει πλεονεξίας
(θεὸς μάρτυς)
2:6 οὔτε ζητοῦντες
ἐξ ἀνθρώπων δόξαν

>   οὔτε ἀφ' ὑμῶν
>   οὔτε ἀπ' ἄλλων
> 2:7 δυνάμενοι ἐν βάρει
>   εἶναι ὡς Χριστοῦ ἀπόστολοι,
>   ἀλλὰ ἐγενήθημεν νήπιοι ἐν μέσῳ ὑμῶν.
>   ὡς ἐὰν τροφὸς θάλπῃ τὰ ἑαυτῆς τέκνα
> 2:8 οὕτως ὁμειρόμενοι ὑμῶν εὐδοκοῦμεν μεταδοῦναι ὑμῖν
>   οὐ μόνον τὸ εὐαγγέλιον τοῦ θεοῦ
>   ἀλλὰ καὶ τὰς ἑαυτῶν ψυχάς,
>   διότι ἀγαπητοὶ ἡμῖν ἐγενήθητε.

The ὡς ἐὰν ... οὕτως construction in verses 7c–8 represents the single idea that Paul compares his love for the Thessalonians with that of τροφός. In association with the ὡς ἐάν clause, the relative adverb οὕτως in verse 8 plays a role in completing Paul's comparing himself with a nursing mother's cares and love for her own children (Sterner 1998:39; Weima 2000:556). Furthermore, as Frame (1912:100) mentions, "[t]he change from νήπιοι to τροφός is due to a natural association of ideas." Moreover, the scholars' suggesting the potential existence of an implicit punctuation after ἐν μέσῳ ὑμῶν should be reconsidered. In Codex Sinaiticus (mid-4th century), the first letter in each verse tends to be outdented into margin as a visual aid for the readers' convenience. First Thessalonians 2:7 in this manuscript shows that the sentence ends at ἀπόστολοι and the next line begins with ἀλλά with the occurrence of outdentation again. Notably, there is no trace of making a full stop between ἀλλὰ ἐγενήθημεν νήπιοι ἐν μέσῳ ὑμῶν and ὡς ἐὰν τροφὸς θάλπῃ τὰ ἑαυτῆς τέκνα. This manuscript may reflect the early tradition of reading 1 Thess 2:7.

Despite Paul and the Thessalonians having sustained a relationship for a short period of time, the apostle's integrity in his relationship with these new converts is expressed through the former metaphor (νήπιοι), showing his innocence. If νήπιοι has a metaphorically positive connotation and combines with τροφός metaphor after ὡς ἐάν clause, Paul's mentioning of the term νήπιος refers to a nursing mother's *pure and innocent love* for her own children. Despite νήπιοι (infants) not referring to the nature of a nursing mother's love elsewhere in the New Testament, it is true that a mother's nurturing behavior has no intention or expectation of reward. Her behavior comes from her own innocent motivation to love and make sacrifices for her own baby. The adverb οὕτως (so, thus) in the beginning of verse 8 signifies how Paul's love for the community is concretely expressed in an act of preaching the gospel, deriving the logical inference from the preceding self-defense and the metaphor. Paul's preaching the gospel is not to distribute propaganda, but to share his own "inner life" just as "a lover wants to share his [or her] life with the beloved in an act of self-giving and union" (Marshall 1983:71). The participle ὁμειρόμενοι ("to have a strong yearning, *long for*" in BDAG) modifies the main verb εὐδοκοῦμεν ("consent, determine, resolve" in BDAG §1), presenting a greater sense of love towards the Thessalonian believers (Wanamaker 1990:102). The verb ὁμείρομαι does not occur elsewhere in the New Testament, but is found in a grave inscription that expresses the parents' longing for their dead children (Green 2002:128). But as Malherbe (2000:147) points out, an etymological explanation is not satisfactory. I remark that the literary context of Paul's using the mixed metaphor shows that his affection can be compared to a nursing mother's sacrificial love. With the imperfect verb εὐδοκοῦμεν, Paul emphasizes his continuous love in dedicating himself to this community (Malherbe 2000:147; Weima 2014:148). And in association with the infinitive μεταδοῦναι, this main verb concretely reveals the significant aspect of what the mixed metaphors ("infants" and "nursing mother") connotes, i.e., a supply of an indispensable thing (the gospel of God and Paul himself) with his innocent love. In addition, the conjunction διότι in verse 8 further elucidates that the cause of the apostle's missionary work in Thessalonica was attributed to love itself as opposed to any intent to pursue his own benefit and glory. In the connection to a central theme of Paul's metaphor, this conjunction reaffirms that Paul's pure motivation and integrity in the past mission work can be compared to *a nursing mother-like love*.

4.4.3.3 HELLENISTIC AND JEWISH BACKGROUND OF "WET NURSE"

Scholars have found that employing wet nurses, regardless of social standing, was a common practice in Hellenistic societies (Green 2002:128; Gaventa 2007:23; McNeel 2014:72; e.g., Homer, *Odyssey* 7.1–13; 15.437–453). Paul probably appealed to the audience's familiarity with the positive characteristics of wet nurses. Bonds of affinity, affection, and loyalty existed between wet nurses and nurslings in the activities of taking care of children and domestic affairs (Gaventa 2007:23). McNeel's remarkable research (2014:77–85) attempts to connect the broad perceptions of the roles of wet nurses to social identity theory, observing that family relationships play a decisive role in shaping social identity. Moreover, she (2014:80) derives the communal aspect of this metaphor from the custom of sharing the same wet nurses, saying that "[i]n households large and wealthy enough to designate a slave as the family wet nurse or retain the services of a free nurse for the long term, slave children and free children often shared the same wet nurse."[44]

44. One does not, however, necessarily apply this social background to this text by

In fact, it is hard to decide whether the meaning of a New Testament *hapax legomenon* τροφός is "nurse" or "mother" (BDAG). Many commentators understand that the New Testament *hapax legomenon* refers to "nursing mother," because the pronoun ἑαυτῆς contains a reflexive implication, portraying a mother's feeding her own children rather than a wet nurse taking charge of her duty (Marshall 1983:71; Richard [1995] 2007:82–83; Sterner 1998:40; Weima 2002b:221; 2014:147). Moreover, the picture of mother who cares for her own children seems to be appropriate in the light of Paul's using a series of family members' roles in 1 Thess 2. However, Paul's use the term τροφός is nonetheless remarkable, even though he could have articulated the love of a physical mother (μήτηρ) for her own children in his expression of love for the Thessalonians (Frame 1912:100–101). I think that Paul's using τροφός can be attributed to the common practice of employing wet nurses. Concurring with Bradley's remark, Gaventa (1998:27; see Bradley [1986] 1992:210) states that the wet nurse takes care of infants might have been natural, since in Paul's day the maternal death rate during childbirth was high and slave mother and infant fell apart by "transfer of slavery property from one household to another."

Whether the term τροφός indicates "nurse" or "biological mother," however, Paul's focus is not on a particular figure but rather on the affectionate behavior of women cherishing their own children in love.[45] His intentional use of the term τροφός might focus on her role of taking care of her own children. Specifically, the nursing metaphor elaborates the leader's nurturing role, which is comparable to a mother who feeds her own baby and provides sustaining nourishment. McNeel's research contributes to finding the implications of the communal identity in this text, based on a perceived *role* and its impression.

Furthermore, with regard to shaping group identity in the Christian community, one should not omit to mention that a nurse metaphor in Jewish traditions can also be a potential influence on Paul's notion of a leader's role as a nurse. First, Paul potentially echoes Num 11:12, in which Moses plays a role like that of a wet nurse (Bruce 1982:32; Gaventa 2007:23–24).

---

generalizing the relationship between wet nurses and nurslings in the Hellenistic world. In fact, it is difficult to confirm the point of Paul's analogy on the basis of various cases of wet nurse practices in his day; i.e., exactly what sort of perception (a general notion or a specific case?) does Paul share with his community through this metaphor?

45. I believe that Boring (2015:87) provides a balanced opinion on this controversy. He says that "[w]hile Paul's metaphor possibly pictures the mother herself, the image of the tenderness with which the *trophos* nurse cares for *her own* children most likely points to a nurse who also has her own children, one who not only is competent and responsible in her job, but also manifests authentic mother love to her biological children—and cares for them without being paid."

Although Num 11:12 does not use the term τροφός and the texts were written in a different context, both Moses and Paul commonly apply this female character to themselves and understand that God designates their role as leaders who should nurture God's chosen people with love (Gaventa 2007:341).[46] Secondly, in the Hodayot, 1QHa, the Teacher of Righteousness believes that God appointed him as a wet nurse: "You have appointed me as a father to the children of mercy and as a guardian to men of portent. They open the mouth wide like a nursing ch[ild . . .] and as a child delights in the embrace of its guardian" (1QHa 20:23–25).[47] Newsom (2004:299) comments that the Qumran community regularly read and recited these Hodayot: "[T]hey are themselves *acts* of leadership, verbal attempts to articulate a community through the self-presentation of the persona of the leader." In so doing, they function to shape the community ethos of the Qumranians. McNeel (2014:115; see Newsom 2004:287–8) agrees with Newsom's argument that these Hodayot represent "the persona of the current leader of the community" and the Qumranian leader identifies himself as the "I" of the hymns of the Teacher. She expands the idea that God's designation of the Teacher's role as a wet nurse would shape the leader's own identity and pertinent task. At the same time, as this psalm is meant to be overheard by the community members, the metaphor of the wet nurse functions to shape their identity and to strengthen the relationship with their leaders.

One should be careful not to over-interpret this metaphor in the light of its various usages in social and cultural contexts. But examining those clues can be useful inasmuch as considering the similarities and the dissimilarities between the metaphors might at least help us to construct Paul's emotion, his responsibility and his relationship with the Thessalonians (cf. McNeel 2014:121).

4.4.4 PAUL'S USE OF THE SIBLING METAPHOR

In 1 Thessalonians the metaphor "brothers and sisters" can be a significant discursive device, functioning to characterize the nature of their community, thereby reinforcing their solidarity. I argue that this sibling metaphor

---

46. In this passage, although the participle הָאֹמֵן (the nurse) is masculine, the act of carrying "a nursing child" (יֹנֵק) (הַיֹּנֵק, "*suck*, of infant at mother's breast" in BDB) indicates that the subject is "a female foster parent" (Budd 1998:128). McNeel (2014:114) well illustrates the reason for the participle, הָאֹמֵן in Num 11:12 being masculine, saying that "the participle is masculine not because the meaning is 'foster father,' but because the leader of the community, a man, is imagining himself in the role of a wet nurse."

47. See Wise, Abegg Jr and Cook (2005:190). I keep using their translation of the Qumran document in this study.

facilitates the Thessalonians' self-awareness and conviction that they adhere to the faith in Jesus Christ and loyalty to God's kingdom (cf. 2:12). This designation by the apostle is ascribed to a radical "break with the past and integration into the new community" by conversion (Meeks 1983a:88). Paul's use of the term ἀδελφός/ἀδελφοί (occurring nineteen times in 1 Thessalonians), alongside other terms that indicate brotherly and sisterly love (ἀγαπητοί and φιλαδελφία), is proportionally higher than the occurrences in Romans, the Corinthian correspondences, Galatians and Philippians (Burke 2003:166):

Letter	Frequency	Total No. of Verses	Ratio
Romans	13	432	1:33 vv.
1 Cor.	33	437	1:13.2
2 Cor.	9	256	1:28.4
Gal.	10	149	1:14.9
Phil	6	104	1:17.3
1 Thess.	19	89	1:4.6
2 Thess.	9	47	1:5.2
Phlm.	4	25	1:6.25

It has been questioned as to whether Paul adopted a particularly Hellenistic notion by using this fictive family metaphor. Meeks (1983a:87) claims that this sibling metaphor was not known "in pagan clubs and cult associations." However, recent studies have found crucial evidence for such an argument (Aasgaard 1997:178–80; Burke 2003:97–117; Paddock 2008:84–87). Harland (2005:496–512) provides further investigation into its usage in epigraphic and papyrological evidence from "Asia Minor, Greece, the Danube, the Bosporus and Egypt." According to him, the sibling metaphor occurs especially where membership of associations and cultic organizations is indicated.

Nevertheless, with a paucity of evidence in a confined geographical distribution, it is hard to affirm whether Paul adapted the sibling metaphor in the same way as other Greek associations or communities did. Even if those groups referred to their members as "brother," it merely indicated those who shared a common belief or religious community (NIDNTTE 1:149).[48] Rather, Paul's adoption of this sibling metaphor mainly originated

---

48. If one admits the Pauline authorship of 2 Thess, it can be seen that Paul uses ἀδελφοί 21 times (13 times in 1 Thess). Compared with other Pauline writings, a higher proportion of the occurrence of this word indicates that Paul expresses great intimacy towards the Thessalonian audience. Using a male-centered expression does not mean

from his Jewish practice. When Paul calls the Thessalonians ἀδελφοί, it is most likely he had in mind a religious title of the people of ancient Israel (Von Soden, TDNT 1:145; Beutler, EDNT 1:29; cf. Exod 2:11; Deut 3:18; 24:7; Lev 10:6; Ps 22:23 [21:23 LXX]; Jer 22:18; 31:34 [38:34 LXX]; Zech 7:9; 1 QS 6:10, 22; 1 QSa 1:18; CD 6:20; 1 QM 13:1; Josephus, *J.W.* 2.122). The early Christian community adopted it to recognize and acknowledge fellow Christians. The practices of the ancient Israelites are potentially integrated into Paul's theological reasoning in his adoption of this kinship metaphor. Just as other identity markers, such as their elected status and their calling to holiness, this sibling imagery assigns new moral/behavioral responsibility to them as befitted their newly established identity. Marshall (1983:52; cf. Weima 2014:89; Meeks 1983a:87) substantiates this notion by mentioning that Paul's deriving this metaphor from this Jewish practice corresponds to his belief that the gentiles are included into God's family as his children (Rom 8:14-23; Gal 3:26; 4:4-7). This can be observed by their addressing God as their father (Rom 8:15; Gal 4:6), and regarding the Son as their brother (Rom 8:29).[49] The term ἀδελφοί is a designation that refers to those who are united by their faith in Christ and became a part of God's family (NIDNTTE 1:150-1).

Accordingly, his metaphor purports to demonstrate the unity and solidarity of the community members, as Paul distinguishes them from the outside group. Esler (2000:170) notices this metaphor's function in the formation of the Thessalonian community in his explanation: "Paul was seeking to develop a group identity drawing on the most prominent model of harmonious intragroup relationships in the ambient culture." In the establishment of this new convert group, Paul's use of this sibling metaphor consequently imposes family members' responsibilities in maintaining their unity (Thompson 2014:44).

4.4.5 PAUL AS AN INSTRUCTING FATHER

As we read 1 Thess 2:1-12, a question could be raised as to whether the crux of this text is Paul's attempt to defend his own integrity or to provide

---

that Paul excludes the existence of women and children in that community (contra Ascough 2000:324).

49. Furthermore, it is not only Paul's appropriation. Other Jewish authors of the New Testament commonly address the believers as ἀδελφοί (see Acts 14:2; 15:23, 32, 33, 36, 40; 16:2, 40; 17:6, 10, 14; 18:18, 27; 21:7, 17, 20; 22:1, 5, 13; 23:1, 5, 6; 28:15, 17, 21; Heb 2:11, 12, 17; 3:1, 12; 10:19; 13:22; James 1:2, 9, 16, 19; 2:1, 5, 14, 15; 3:1, 10, 12; 4:11; 5:7, 9, 10, 19; 1 Pet 5:12; 2 Pet 3:15; 1 John 2:9, 10, 11; 3:10, 12-17; 4:20-21; 5:16; 3 John 5,10; Rev 1:9; 6:11; 12:10; 19:10; 22:9).

himself as an example of a moral life before the Thessalonians (see Malherbe 2000:134). I suggest instead that in this chapter we shift our focus to another question and aspect. Why does Paul employ a series of family metaphors and, more pertinently, why does he locate the father metaphor at the end of this pericope? Through using the father metaphor in 2:1-12, I contend that Paul reaches a climactic moment that manifests the major focus of this text. In the context of Paul's self-defense, as discussed (see 4.4.1), the family metaphors gradually draw our attention to Paul's pastoral devotion, integrity, accountability, affection and vision. Specifically, through the father metaphor, he probably attempts to re-socialize the community according to a "new belief," "way of life" and "new social world" (Burke 2000:69-71).

4.4.5.1 PATERNAL ROLE IN THE ANCIENT WORLD

The focal point shifts from the verbal qualifications in defending himself in comparison with other false teachers to expressing his pastoral vision. The combination of the three adverbial participles (παρακαλοῦντες, παραμυθούμενοι, and μαρτυρόμενοι) in verse 12 creates a literary unit. These participles denote Paul's concrete sense of his fatherly responsibility for instructing his own children. One should understand these participles in a collective sense rather than exploring their individual connotations (Fee 2009:82). In my estimation, these participles consistently point to Paul regarding himself as the one who plays "a didactic role" with regard to the community's moral formation (Burke 2003:143).

In fact, it is difficult to decide the meaning of the first verb παρακαλέω, since it has a wide range of meanings (BDAG). In my view, one does not need to opt for a single meaning, since both "command" ("implore" or "appeal") and "comfort" ("encourage" or "comfort" or "console") are not incompatible in the light of the textual context. But in the context of Hellenistic moral exhortations, this verb most likely has the meaning of "to exhort" someone to adopt a certain form of behavior (Green 2002:135).

The second verb, παραμυθέομαι ("console"), occurs twice in the Pauline letters, and only once in 1 Thessalonians (other occurrences in the New Testament are also found in John 11:19, 31). This verb's basic meaning is "to speak to someone in a friendly way" (Stählin, TDNT 5:821; Wolter, EDNT 3:32). More specifically, in the Hellenistic world this term "almost always has affective connotations, with the highly nuanced meaning of 'advise, encourage, console, comfort, speak calming words to, appease, soothe'" (Spicq 1994:3.30). Although the first and second verbs (παρακαλέω and παραμυθέομαι) are not synonymous, one cannot draw a clear distinction between admonition and providing comfort (Stählin, TDNT 5:821; cf. Malherbe 2000:151). In some cases, the latter could be the purpose of the former action (Green 2002:136).

The third verb μαρτύρομαι means "affirm," "insist" and "implore" in this context rather than its primary meanings of "testify" and "bear witness" (BDAG). It is particularly necessary to differentiate Paul's usage from the consolation of the secular world, which "often takes the form of moral exhortation." But through this verb his audience might have perceived Paul as taking a fatherly role in offering admonition with genuine comfort to the audience (Stählin, TDNT 5:821). Although paternal affection towards one's own children is a universal phenomenon, the notion of fatherly admonition in Hellenistic Judaism might have culminated in Paul's employment of this fatherly metaphor. In the Hellenistic world, one of a father's primary roles was to utilize "reason, exhortation, counsel, and praise of good conduct to instruct his children to follow virtue and shun vices" (Plutarch, [*Lib. ed.*]. 8F–9A, 13D, 14A, cited in Green 2002:134). Likewise, in Jewish contexts, according to Philo, teaching the Torah and God's saving act to his children was the primary responsibility of the father (Philo, *Spec.* 2.228, 232; NIDNTTE 3:679; e.g., Exod 12:26–27; 13:14–16; Deut 4:9–10; 6:7; 11:19; 30:19–20; 32:7, 46).

4.4.5.2 HIERARCHICAL CONNOTATION OF PATERNAL METAPHORS?

Many scholars assume that Paul's illustration of a fatherly relationship with the Thessalonians is intended to create an effect that calls attention to Paul's authoritative role in God's household (Best 1986b:16; Wanamaker 1990:106). Castelli (1991:109–10), for example, negates the potential implication of love in the father-child metaphor, saying that "the paternal metaphor does not necessarily evoke a sense of kindness or love." In addition, while Petersen (1985:128–31) does not refute that this metaphor can be associated with a sense of affection, he advocates that when Paul "does use father-child metaphors, he does so in the exercise of his loving yet superordinate position."

In response to the assumption that Paul's father-child metaphor implies a hierarchical position over the community, Burke (2000:61; see also Thompson 2014:226–8) provides a balanced argument based on extra-biblical sources. A wide spectrum of ancient documents indicates that a hierarchical relationship between fathers and their children and fathers' affection towards their children coexisted in Paul's day.⁵⁰ Paul's use of the father metaphor in 2:11–12 certainly implies a hierarchical relationship. However, Paul's emphasis on the father metaphor in 1 Thessalonians does not seem to highlight his authoritative position but rather his caring and mentoring role among them (cf. Moo 2014:62; contra Burke 2003:135–7). In the context of likening himself to a nursing mother, Paul expresses his integrity, accountability and affection to the Thessalonians. Moreover, he never appeals to the authority of his own apostleship. We note the parenthetical statement of the antithetical part in 2:5–6, which reads, "though we could have made demands as apostles of Christ." This reference indicates that Paul does not appeal to the glory that could be gained through his apostolic authority. Furthermore, it is difficult to derive the hierarchical relationship from this metaphor, since the paternal image in the Pauline letters focuses on his pivotal role in the formation of the gentile churches through preaching the gospel (1 Cor 4:15; Phil 2:22; Phlm 10). Furnish (2007:61–62) rightly perceives that the major concern of this metaphor is not Paul's authority as an apostle, but his fatherly devotion and affection towards the community (cf. 1:4; 2:8, 17; 3:5, 6):

> [I]n this context it is used more particularly to accent the seriousness with which he has taken his responsibility to provide instruction and guidance (v. 12). He is emphasizing his pastoral *devotion to* his Thessalonian "children" . . . not primarily his *authority over* them; note his remark that he has been attentive to the *individual* situations and needs of his converts ("we deal with each one of you," v. 11) (original emphasis).

Boring (2015:90) also points out that it is not necessary to comprehend this metaphor paternalistically, or in light of patriarchy in the first-century Mediterranean world. Rather, in this verse the father's affection to his own children is a crucial reason for Paul's sense of responsibility in instructing and educating the community.

As in shifting the metaphors from nursing mother to father in 2:9–10, the sentiment of Paul's taking care of the Thessalonians can continually be perceived in his self-defense. As the first evidence,⁵¹ Paul attempts to prove

---

50. Burke (2000:62–69) categorizes four patterns of paternal relationships in the ancient time: hierarchy/authority in Jewish evidence (e.g., Philo, *Dec.* 165–6; *Spec. Leg.* 2.228, 231; *Mut.* 217; Josephus, *Ag. Ap.* 2.199, 206); hierarchy/authority in Hellenistic evidence (e.g., Aristotle, *Pol.* 1.5.2; *Eth. nic.* 5.6.8; 8.11.2; Plutarch, *Frat. Amor.* 479F; [*Lib. ed.*]. 7E); affection in Jewish evidence (e.g., Philo, *Spec. Leg.* 1.137; 2.236, 240; *Jos.* 4; *Abr.* 196; Josephus, *Ant.* 2.184); affection in Hellenistic evidence (e.g., Aristotle, *Eth. nic.* 8.12.5; Plutarch, *Am. Prol.* 496C; Seneca, *De Pr.* 2.5).

51. The conjunction γάρ grammatically provides a ground or explanation for Paul's

his innocent motivation and affection by appealing to the Thessalonians' memory that he did not place any burden on them (v. 9). In order not to lead them to feel that they were responsible for supporting his ministry, Paul himself worked hard in his own manual labor and at the same time focused on preaching the gospel.[52] His toil and hardship for self-sufficiency substantiate how he cherishes the Thessalonians.[53] Second, in the consecutive occurrence of ὡς clauses (2:10–11), Paul tries to convince them of the impeccable nature of his own conduct in his relationship with the Thessalonians (Weima 2014:153; Boring 2015:89). Intriguingly, Paul sets out the three consecutive adverbs, ὁσίως (devoutly), καὶ δικαίως (uprightly), and ἀμέμπτως (blamelessly) in association with the main verb. In verse 10 one might expect that the main verb ἐγενήθημεν (more specifically, "to prove to be" or "to turn out to be." see BDAG) needs to be followed by predicate noun or adjectives. However, adverb can grammatically function as adjectives (BDF §434; cf. Acts 20:18). Using the consecutive adverbs emphasizes that his conduct in the previous missional work "points to the actions of the missionaries, what they actually did, not to a static quality" of Paul's character (Boring 2015:89; see also Wanamaker 1990:105). Immediately, after a discourse signal that reminds the Thessalonians of their previous memory (καθάπερ οἴδατε), the reader may confront some difficulties in understanding the sentence structure in verses 11–12 since there has been a controversy as to whether the main verb ἐγενήθημεν (v. 10) could continuously function as the main verb even in verses 11–12. Some scholars view that the sentence of verse 11 is grammatically dependent on the main clause of verse 10 (Burke 2000:69; see also Green 2002:133; Fee 2009:78–81). Fee understands the verb ἐγενήθημεν plays a role in carrying out the double task. First, this verb in verse 10 is expected to accompany such as predicate nominative or adjective in describing Paul and his co-workers' characteristics in

---

previous statement in 2:7–8 (Sterner 1998:40).

52. In v. 9 the present participle ἐργαζόμενοι modifies the main verb ἐκηρύξαμεν. Scholars agree that this grammatical construction might indicate that Paul's manual labor and his preaching the gospel of Christ took place contemporaneously (Malherbe 2000:149). Weima (2014:151; see also Hock 1979) substantiates this fact, saying that in the ancient times the workshop was "one of the conventional settings for intellectual discourse and instruction. During the long hours at his workbench, while cutting and sewing leather to make tents and other related goods, Paul was not only supporting himself, but also sharing the gospel with fellow workers and customers."

53. In v. 9 Paul unexpectedly sets the word order as "night and day" (not "day and night"); this word pair is also found in other Pauline letters (2 Thess 3:8; 1 Tim 5:5; 2 Tim 1:3). It is not possible from this work order per se to derive a concrete pattern of Paul's manual labor and preaching the gospel with regard to a time schedule (cf. Malherbe 2000:148; Green 2002:131). I agree with Sterner (1998:41) that this expression can be "an intensive marker" that emphasizes the long hours of work time.

relation to the Thessalonians. Second, this verb can be used to remind them of Paul's paternal role in verses 11–12, grammatically shaping periphrastic construction with three consecutive participles (Fee 2009:79). However, a grammatical understanding that ἐγενήθημεν and the three consecutive participles form a periphrastic construction is less likely due to the redundant use of objects, ἕνα ἕκαστον ὑμῶν and ὑμᾶς and somewhat remote distance between the main verb and the participles (Best 1986:106). For these reasons, it is likely that Paul intentionally drops the main verb of verse 11 and provides an opportunity for the audience to expect appropriate verb (Green 2002:133). Due to the nature of the father's role and affection in the next verses, as Weima (2014:153) suggests, it is more appropriate to consider that "a child-rearing verb like 'raised,' 'trained,' or 'brought up'" is implied than a somewhat more neutral meaning of, "deal with" (NEB, NIV, NRSV) or "treat" (Malherbe 2000:150; NET, NLT).

Nevertheless, readers should be cautious when selecting the omitted verb without a clear basis. Scholars' suggestions are varied, and their proposed solutions are often speculative while appearing reasonable. If the omission is deliberate, it could be because the verb's meaning aligns closely with that of the participles. Alternatively, it is worth noting that the participle can be regarded as an indicative verb within the context of "continuous style" in classical Greek (Green 2002:134; cf. *Ars Rhetorica* 3.9. 1–3). In any case, while it may be preferable to consider verses 10 and 11–12 as not being grammatically linked, this understanding should not lead to the conclusion that here Paul's argumentation is discontinuous.

4.4.5.3 DISCURSIVE FUNCTION OF THE FATHER METAPHOR

Ultimately, Paul took on a fatherly responsibility to instruct the community on a significant value based on his affection as can be seen in his admonition: "to walk in a manner worthy of God, who calls you into his own kingdom and glory" (2:12). The verb περιπατέω in verse 12, which corresponds to LXX's use of the Hebrew word, הָלַךְ, is occasionally used in a metaphorical sense (2 Kings 20:3; Eccl 11:9).[54] This term often occurs in Pauline letters to urge believers' towards adopting specific moral conduct (Seesemann, TDNT 5:943–4; e.g., Rom 6:4; 2 Cor 4:2; Gal 5:16; Eph 2:10; 4:1; 5:2, 8, 15; Phil 3:17; Col 4:5; 1 Thess 4:1; see 5.2).[55] The notion of living lives worthy

---

54. In fact, the LXX prefers to translate the Hebrew term, הָלַךְ as πορεύομαι (Exod 16:4; 18:20; Lev 18:3–4; 26:3; Deut 5:33; 19:9; 26:17; 28:9; 30:16; 3 Kgdm 3:14; 8:25; 2 Chr 6:14, 16; Isa 38:3; Ezek 36:27).

55. It is difficult to explain the reason for Paul's preference for the term περιπατέω.

of God is not Paul's own invention; rather, this idea appears in both Judaism (Wis 3:5; 7:15; Sir 14:11) and even in Jesus' teaching (Matt 10:37–38) (Green 2002:137). But it is most likely that the Thessalonians were familiar with the widespread notion of living worthily in relation to other deities and adopting certain standards required by the gods (e.g., Epictetus, *Ench.* 15). This expression was sufficient to remind the audience of the ethos of Greek religion that when the priests serve the gods, they were expected to live in a worthy of them (Marshall 1983:74–75). But for the Thessalonian believers, the object of worship was completely different from their previous participation in the pagan religious practices (1 Thess 1:9–10). Appropriating such a notion, Paul considers that required moral conduct should be in conformity with "the character and demands" of the true and living God (Weima 2014:157–8). This statement distinguishes the newly established identity and behavior of the Thessalonians from their surrounding social world. Furthermore, this concrete exhortation/calling enables the community members to recognize their *reoriented* social belonging as God's chosen people.

Paul's fatherly affection drove him to exhort the Thessalonian community to stand firm on the community's morality. The three adverbial participles in verse 12 (παρακαλουντες, παραμυθουμενοι, and μαρτυρομενοι) indicate that Paul's task can be compared with a father's responsibility of socializing and providing moral guidance for his own children (Boring 2015:90). As the construction of εἰς τό and infinitive clarifies, Paul's pastoral devotion with fatherly affection aims to infuse the eschatological vision for those who had suffered, so that they might have confidence in their newly established identity and lifestyle. Meeks (1983a:115) illustrates that one of the goals of this letter is "to shape the community's way of thinking and talking about itself that go to make a distinctive group ethos." Thompson (2011:64) pays attention to the fact that "Paul's moral instructions are neither arbitrary nor ad hoc responses to crises, but a concrete and coherent vision of the life that is worthy of the gospel" (Thompson 2011:64). This instruction, therefore, shaped the community ethos, reminding them of the nature of the community's calling. Although I do not agree with his hierarchical view of this metaphor, Burke (2000:70; cf. Wanamaker 1990:15) correctly observes the paternal role in ancient society: the fathers in the ancient world were involved in providing "the fundamental socialization of his offspring into the socio-economic and cultural way of life into which they were born and subsequently raised."

It is most likely that Paul might have avoided the use of πορεύομαι, since this term was used in the Hellenistic world in association with experiencing heavenly journeys in an ecstatic state (Holloway 1992:21, 24; cf. Rosner 2013:87).

As the climax of Paul's argumentation, the paternal imagery plays a pivotal role in drawing the audience's attention to those radical transformations in Christ and his kingdom. Through this metaphor, Paul provides for the development of their self-understanding, which is reshaped through the conversion to the living and true God. Not only that but he illustrates the nature of the world to which they now belong. Their conversion was accompanied by the re-socialization of their identity and morality, as Meeks (1993:30) illustrates:

> [C]onversion is described as the transformation both of a way of thinking and of a form of life, as a change of allegiance from many false gods to the one true God . . . as a radical resocialization, abandoning one's closest and most familiar ties and finding new ones, and as a fundamental reformation of morals.

Paul re-socializes the Thessalonians' identity into that of the members of God's kingdom, differentiating them from their surrounding pagan world. Their self-recognition should be transformed through the lens of the eschatological realization of God's kingdom.

4.5 CONCLUSION

In this chapter, I have argued that Paul's major concern in 1 Thessalonians is the formation of a new community through the theological and social redefinition of their identity and ethos. This purpose of redefining the community informs his identity- and ethos-building discourse. Its most crucial function was most likely to enable the audience not only to recognize their position in a pagan society, but also to take responsibility for their newly established identity as Christ's followers. Paul needed to remap and refashion the Thessalonians' symbolic universe, beliefs, and ethical standards according to "a completely new social-religious structure" as they went through radical changes in their lives after conversion (De Villiers 2006:338). In focusing on Paul's articulation of the gentiles' new identity, this chapter has taken into account the inseparable relationship between the theological and sociocultural dimensions of the first-century concept of Christian identity.

First, Paul does not explicitly cite the Hebrew Scriptures in this letter to describe the gentile inclusion into the people of God. Nonetheless, his theological rationale for the establishment of this gentile church is heavily rooted in the ancient Israelite tradition of election by God (cf. Thompson 2011:53–54). The notion of God's election could be a key concept inasmuch as it not only elucidates their distinct group identity as distinct from the rest of the world, but also the gentiles' inclusion into the people of God. Indeed, God's election and calling permeate the entire discourse, especially 1 Thess 1:1—2:12 (Thielman 2005:239; 1:4; 2:12; 3:3b; 4:7; 5:8; 5:24; cf. Deut 7:6–7; 14:2; Isa 41:8–9; 42:6; 48:12). Particularly, this concept is a major reason for thanksgiving in 1:2–10. Paul views God's election (ἐκλογή) of the Thessalonians being realized through his preaching of the gospel "not only in word, but also in power and in the Holy Spirit and with full conviction" (1:5). Their election was proven by their receiving the word in the midst of suffering with the joy of the Holy Spirit (1:6) and making it known to the region of Macedonia and Achaia (1:7). Neighboring believers' reports of their own conversion from idols to God and of faith in the Son concretely prove the firm foundation of their election (1:9–10).

While Paul reminds that the Thessalonians were called to be God's chosen people guiding them to adhere to his gospel, he wishes to maintain the affinity with the community and the communal solidarity among them. Paul's major goal in 1 Thess 2:1–12 is to defend his own integrity in his previous missionary work. Noticeably, family metaphors (mother, father, and siblings) are a major thrust throughout the whole part in achieving his purpose. The metaphors aim to shape an affinity between Paul and the Thessalonians, overcoming their abrupt and inevitable separation by their fellow citizens' social harassment. But his use of family metaphors did not merely envision the restoration of their relationship. Paul establishes fictive family relationships among the Thessalonians so as to locate this newly established community within God's family. In encouraging the community members' faith and solidarity, Paul's major and ultimate purpose in 2:1–12 was even extended to provide them with self-awareness in their social world and with alternative convictions, values and behavioral norms assigned to God's chosen people. In so doing, Paul urges that the Thessalonians as God's family in Christ would take a journey together for living a life in a manner worthy of God and participating in God's glorious kingdom.

5

Discursive Function of Scriptural Echoes in 1 Thess 4–5

THE PROCESS THROUGH WHICH Paul shaped a distinct identity and ethos among the Thessalonian believers was based on his appeal to God's election of Israel and various family-related metaphors in 1 Thess 1–2. This becomes even more pertinent in 1 Thess 4–5. Paul's discourse reaches its climax in the paraenetic section of the letter, in which echoes from Scripture seem to play a significant role in the shaping of their identity and ethos.[1] A remarkable characteristic of the paraenetic section is that Paul describes the Thessalonian believers as *God's eschatological people* who are called to embody specific virtues as they anticipate Christ's *parousia* (Weima 1996:99; cf. Goheen 2011:162).

1. It is difficult to determine the exact nuance of the phrase, λοιπὸν οὖν in 4:1, which occurs only once in the NT. BDAG provides a definition for the adjective λοιπός (finally): "as far as the rest is concerned, beyond that, in addition, finally." However, this adjective should be understood in an inferential sense and links the preceding content to the following exhortation (Marshall 1983:104; Boring 2015:133–4; e.g., 1 Cor 4:2; 7:29). Since it is associated with the particle, οὖν (therefore), which indicates the transition from indicative to imperative (e.g., Rom 12:1), this combination signals the beginning of Paul's exhortation (paraenesis). With regard to rendering the combination λοιπὸν οὖν, I do not offer an ideal translation of this phrase here, but interpreters should sense that this phrase functions to connect Paul's addresses earlier in chapters 1–3 and the paraenetic section in chapters 4–5. Marshall (1983:104) supports the NEB translation, "and now." And following Moule's translation (1960:161), Weima (2014:254) translates this phrase into "and so." More concretely, Boring (2015:133) translates that "[a]s for what remains to be said, then." In my view, through this combination of terms, Paul's identity-building discourse in 1 Thess 1–3 has reached the apex of his argumentation, entering a new phase where he highlights the moral characteristics befitting their new identity as God's elect.

This chapter of the study will concentrate on essential elements and motifs that probably constituted and undergirded Paul's paraenetic discourse, and on how these motifs were meant to function within it. According to various discourse markers that introduce different themes (τοῦτο ... ἐστιν in 4:3; περί ... in 4:9, 13, 5:1; δέ in 5:12), the paraenesis of 1 Thess 4–5 can be divided into five major parts with the exception of the introductory part (4:1–2) (see 4.3.1). In this division, I will selectively deal with the notions of *holiness* and *sanctification* (in view of sexual purity in the Holiness Code; 4:3–8), *fulfillment of the new covenant* (4:9–12), and *the day of the Lord* (5:1–11). These themes respectively summarize the main idea of each section of Paul's paraenesis.[2] In exploring possible echoes for these notions from the Hebrew Scriptures, I hypothesize that these concepts play a crucial role in reminding the believers of their shared story and communal ethos (Thompson 2014:20). As argued in chapter 4, tracing Paul's argument is a crucial step in establishing the thrust of his discourse. Based on the provided "tracings" as a reference guide, I discuss how scriptural concepts function within each part of the letter (see Appendix II).

5.1 APPROPRIATION OF SCRIPTURE IN 1 THESSALONIANS?

Scholars agree that no direct quotation from the Hebrew Scriptures occurs in 1 Thessalonians. For this reason, less attention has been paid to the functioning of scriptural echoes in the letter (Harnack [1928] 1995:29; Koch 1986:88–91; Schnelle 2005:110). Even where commentators consider various Hebrew texts as potential background to Paul's instruction, concrete comparisons among such texts have been sparsely attempted.[3] With regard to recognizing the nature and number of such occurrences, the majority of New Testament scholars are of the opinion that, due to a high degree of

---

2. It is probable that echoes from the Hebrew Scriptures occur also in 1 Thess 2:13–16, 2:17—3:10, 3:11–13, and 4:13–18. However, in my reading of 1 Thess, I focus on expressions such as ἁγιασμός (4:3), τὸν ... διδόντα τὸ πνεῦμα αὐτοῦ τὸ ἅγιον εἰς ὑμᾶς (4:8), and ἡμέρα κυρίου (5:2), which are explicitly related to identity- and ethos-building processes in the letter. A discussion of probable echoes in 1 Thess 4:13–18 will take us beyond the ambit of this study. Here Paul brings related OT imagery (such as "the sound of the trumpet of God" and "in the cloud," cf. Weima 2007:880) into play rather than appealing to specific concepts related to the identity and ethos of God's people.

3. Though Hays mainly discusses reflection of scriptural language in the letter to the Romans, he (1989:195; 1991:235–6; 2005:183) also suggests the possibility that 1 Thess may include a number of scriptural allusions or echoes. In addition, some recent scholars have researched allusions and echoes in 1 Thessalonians (see Steele 1984:12–17; Hester 2002:151–9; Weima 2007:871–83; Johnson 2012:143–62).

scriptural illiteracy in ancient times, Paul would probably not have expected his gentile audience to remember any particular texts of the Hebrew Scriptures (Stanley 2008:133-4).[4]

However, I argue that unfamiliarity with Scripture on the audience's side does not necessarily exclude the possibility of significant scriptural echoes in this letter. Even if direct quotations from Scripture do not appear in 1 Thessalonians, two motivations seem to allow us to detect scriptural influence on Paul's language, concepts, and ideas.

First, as Ciampa (2008:45) contends, Scripture potentially serves as noteworthy intertextual framework in Paul's writings. The theoretical ground of Ciampa's argument is that the degree of intertextual reference is extended from the notion of allusion and echo to more concrete concepts and ideas.[5] His presupposition is based on Keesmaat's understanding of the concept of scriptural influence:

> [T]exts occur not only in relation to other texts but also in dialogue with other aspects of the cultures in which they occur. Hence an intertextual reference may be to a ritual or a work of art, or indeed to a matrix of ideas which is informed by specific texts, but is not a text in itself . . . The writings of Paul also, I suggest, take place within certain 'cultural codes' which endow his writings with plausibility. Sometimes these can be traced to specific texts, but more commonly he is drawing on a matrix of ideas which cannot be linked to any specific text but which is shaped and formed by a number of texts (and traditions) within his culture (Keesmaat 1994:33).

Even in a text where no direct quotation occurs or the volume of echoes is only faintly heard, "all discourse depends upon, builds upon, modifies, and/or reacts to prior discourse and the prior use of words, concepts, and ideas" (Ciampa 2008:41).

Second, some scholars have a positive view with regard to establishing a conceptual connection to antecedent texts, merely from the general insight that allusion in poetry does not need to be articulated verbally (Miner 1993:39; Sommer 1998:14; Beetham 2008:29; Ciampa 2008:43). In this case,

---

4. I concur with Johnson's presumption that Paul shares with the Thessalonian audience "some fundamental notion that we recognize as biblical" (Johnson 2012:144). Though the historical relation between the book of Acts and Paul's letters may be contested among scholars (see footnote 13 in the introduction), I regard Acts 17:2 as significant evidence that the Thessalonian believers were familiar with the Hebrew Scriptures: "Paul went in, as was his custom, and on three Sabbath days he reasoned with them from the Scriptures."

5. For the difference between allusion and echo, see footnote 9 in the introduction.

to appreciate possible/probable links between texts, one has to identify a rare notion occurring in both texts (Beetham 2008:29).

With this presupposition in mind, I will postulate that Paul reconfigures major notions pertaining to *holiness/sanctification*, *new covenant*, and *the day of the Lord* from the Hebrew Scriptures in the paraenetic section of this letter (1 Thess 4:3–8; 4:9–12; 5:1–11).[6] Yet, the task of "finding" scriptural echoes entails more than merely identifying probable roots of the Hebrew Scriptures in a letter like this one. In this regard, Beetham (2008:22–24) articulates three potential benefits of identifying scriptural echoes, even if the original audience could not recognize them. It may help interpreters to grasp (1) "unstated correspondences," (2) the author's "unspoken *hermeneutical presuppositions*," and (3) his understanding of the Hebrew Scriptures' literary contexts. These benefits will be addressed in this chapter.

5.2 CHARACTERISTICS OF GOD'S CHOSEN PEOPLE (4:1–2): 'WALKING' AND PLEASING GOD

In Paul's diplomatic choice of words, particularly in the introduction, it is remarkable that he portrays the moral characteristics of God's eschatological people by using LXX-based terms (περιπατέω and ἀρέσκω). A presupposition underlying the introduction of the paraenetic section is that their new identity involved establishing "a new set of personal and social standards under the Lordship of Jesus" (Gupta 2016:78). The verb περιπατέω is a common metaphorical term found in the Hebrew Scriptures and rabbinic literature to denote the moral conduct of God's people (see 4.4.5.3). Moreover, the idea of pleasing God is often referred to as the supreme goal of human life in the Hebrew Scriptures (Num 23:27; Ps 68:32; Mal 3:4). Paul's employment of vocabulary from his Jewish tradition is probably not accidental.

---

6. My reference to the term "the Hebrew Scripture" implies that Paul was able to use both the LXX and the MT in his letters. To be more accurate, as Beetham (2008:37) mentions, Paul did know not only "the (proto-) LXX text-form family," but also "at least one witness from the proto-MT text-form family." Silva (1993:631) shows a chart of Paul's 107 citations of the Hebrew Scriptures (including the undisputed Pauline letters): 42 verses in Paul's letters agree with both the LXX and the MT; 7 verses agree with the MT, but disagree with the LXX; 17 verses agree with the LXX, but disagree with the MT; 31 verses disagree both the LXX and the MT; 10 verses have been debated among scholars. Such data indicate that Paul was also acquainted with the MT. Rosner (1999:20–21) assumes that Paul's Scripture "comprised those currently printed in the Hebrew Bible" based on E. Earl Ellis's argument. Ellis (1990:679) remarks that "in the first Christian century (Philo, Josephus) and even two centuries earlier (Ben Sira) Judaism possessed a defined and identifiable canon." For Paul's Jewish education, see 2.1.5.1 & 2.3.

He seems to deliberately portray the Thessalonians as elected and called, thereby indicating their incorporation into God's chosen people in Christ and their moral responsibility to please God (Boring 2015:136).

In his attempt to (trans)form the Thessalonian community's moral awareness ("how you ought to walk and to please God" in 4:1), Paul's exhortation appears to be strategic. He exhorts the audience with his apostolic authority in the Lord Jesus (2:1), as well as in a personal and friendly manner (Green 2002:183; Weima 2014:255). Remarkably, in 4:1-2, the majority of scholars find that Paul reflects the convention of Hellenistic letter writing. Bjerkelund (1967:43-50) finds that there are four common elements of the appeal formula widespread in Paul's day. Concretely, recent commentators of 1 Thessalonians agree with his observation that 4:1-2 reflects these four elements (Marshall 1983:104; Best 1986a:154-5; Green 2002:183; Weima 2014:254, 382). Specifically, this structure can be explained as: (1) the verb παρακαλέω or its synonym (here Paul adds ἐρωτάω) with the first person plural ("we");[7] (2) reference to the recipients (ἀδελφοί); (3) a prepositional phrase (ἐν κυρίῳ Ἰησοῦ in 4:1 and διὰ τοῦ κυρίου Ἰησοῦ in 4:2) that indicates an authoritative source; (4) an exhortation that occurs with a ἵνα clause or infinitive clause (Bjerkelund 1967:17, 188-9).

By appealing to this formula, Paul begins the paraenetic section with a friendly tone rather than forcing or rebuking the audience to follow his instruction in establishing a hierarchical relationship based on his apostleship. Weima (2014:255; cf. Marshall 1983:104) captures the nuance of this appeal formula well by explaining that, "[i]n situations where his authority is not questioned and he is confident that his exhortation will be obeyed, the apostle chooses, not in a heavy-handed manner, to 'command' his readers but rather in a more user-friendly way to 'appeal' to them." Moreover, when Paul illustrates what he asks for and urges, the conjunction καθώς (see 4.4.1) signals that his strategy is to remind his audience of the instructions that he passed on during his previous missionary work.[8] The second καθώς clause in 4:1 indicates that Paul acknowledges that the Thessalonian Christians were already living according to God's will and seeking to please God.[9] Some scholars claim that Paul uses discursive skills here by commending

---

7. Malherbe (2000:218) notices that the two verbs in 4:1, ἐρωτάω and παρακαλέω, give a more personal nuance to Paul's exhortation, particularly by using ἐρωτάω in association with the vocative, ἀδελφοί. Green (2002:183) also suggests that the characteristics of Paul's exhortation be regarded as "good advice" or "friendly suggestions."

8. The ἵνα clause in 4:1 is a direct object clause that provides the content of the main verbs, ἐρωτῶμεν (we ask) and παρακαλοῦμεν (we appeal) (Wallace 1996:475).

9. In some manuscripts the phrase καθὼς καὶ περιπατεῖτε is omitted (D2 K L Ψ 630. 1175. 1241. 2464.vid 𝔐 syp).

good behavior, thereby utilizing praise as a manner of implicit exhortation (Green 2002:184; cf. Lausberg [1960] 1998:§241).[10] As the function of the second ἵνα clause indicates, Paul aims to affirm what the audience was already doing in the progress of their journey of faith (Marshall 1983:105; cf. tracing 3, Appendix II). The conjunction γάρ in verse 2 makes Paul's previous statement more specific and explicit and gradually draws the audience's attention to his concrete exhortation in the next verse (see tracing 3, Appendix II).

Nevertheless, one cannot overlook the fact that the obligatory aspect of Paul's exhortation is paradoxically conducted with a friendly tone. First, Paul appeals to the authoritative source of his exhortation, ἐν κυρίῳ Ἰησοῦ, as this prepositional phrase denotes "the source of authority by which the letter sender issues the appeal" (Weima 2014:254; see Bjerkelund 1967:109–11).[11] Another prepositional phrase, διὰ τοῦ κυρίου Ἰησοῦ in 4:2, is used as parallel to the first one, ἐν κυρίῳ Ἰησοῦ in 4:1.[12] This prepositional clause indicates that Paul's commands during his first visit were based on the authority of Jesus (Moule 1960:57–58; Ellingworth & Nida 1976:76).[13] The

---

10. At the same time, his commendation is probably not merely a deliberate rhetorical scheme, but an actual response to Timothy's report that the new converts are on the right track, living by work of faith and labor of love (3:6; cf. 1:3). Richard ([1995] 2007:185) resolves the perceived tension between Paul's rhetorical approach and the actual situation as follows: "Paul's language, then, is both *diplomatic*, as he encourages renewed commitment to a God-inspired life, and *sincere*, as he expresses joy for the splendid news received from Thessalonica and renews pastoral encouragement to recent, beloved converts."

11. According to Marshall (1983:194), this prepositional phrase "conveys the thoughts both that Paul is issuing instructions which have the authority of the Lord behind them and also that the readers are people whose life is determined by their acceptance of Jesus as Lord and their entry into fellowship with him."

12. The combination of this prepositional phrase and the term παραγγελία might remind many scholars of a certain instruction of Jesus, reflecting his specific saying (Allison 1982:20–21). Admittedly, Paul might have had many opportunities to be informed about Jesus' life and his sayings from the disciples after his conversion. But, as Boring (2015:138) points out, "Paul has a different paradigm for understanding the gospel and the Christian faith than that represented by the (later!) Gospels and the traditions they include and interpret. Paul's faith and theology are profoundly oriented to Jesus Christ, but it is *theo*centric, focused on God's act in the Christ event, not on what the earthly Jesus said and did." Hence, one must be careful to think that the combination of this prepositional phrase and the term παραγγελία indicates a specific saying of Jesus. Except for 1 Thess 5:2, it seems that alleged parallels and citations do not occur.

13. In 4:2 Paul not only reiterates the idea of the previous verse, but also emphasizes what the Thessalonian believers necessarily follow. The conjunction γάρ, along with the term οἶδα (cf. 1:5; 2:1, 2, 5, 11; 3:3, 4), serves to clarify and reinforce what Paul had previously instructed the audience. The authoritative tone of 4:2 can be captured by Paul's use of the term παραγγελία. In the LXX the verbal form of this term, παραγγέλλω,

ἵνα clause in the appeal formula contains a central value, while the ultimate purpose of this paraenesis, which cannot be regarded as simply personal, seems to be light-hearted, or optional. Paul does not articulate what he taught as a specific accusative form of the noun (e.g., tradition or gospel). Rather, the neuter article τό in verse 1 introduces the concrete content of Paul's previous teaching. What the Thessalonians most likely received from the apostle seemed to be the gospel message of salvation (1:5, 10; 2:2, 4, 8–9; 3:2) and the kingdom of God (2:12). But instruction on what they should believe and the moral aspects cannot be separated in Paul's theological thinking. His focus on the necessity (δεῖ, it is necessary) of "walking" and pleasing God seems to indicate that moral exhortation had been an essential part of Paul's initial instruction during his earlier missions.

It is noticeable that he refers to their reception of his instruction by using the term παραλαμβάνω, that is "a technical work for the transmission of tradition" (Best 1986a:156; cf. 1 Cor 11:23; 15:1, 3; Gal 1:9, 12; Phil 4:9). Most likely, as a Jew, Paul imitates the Hebrew verb קָבַל("to receive") in the rabbinic tradition, in which instruction is transmitted from teacher to pupil according to the authoritative relationship between them (Delling, TDNT 4:13; Hodgson 1982:203; Davies [1948] 1955:249; Carras 1990:306; Green 2002:139; Weima 2007:876; 2014:257; cf. *Abot* 1.1). The tone of Paul's appeal formula seems to be friendly, based on the convention of Hellenistic letter writing. But here the relationship between Paul and his audience is not restrained by mere personal confidence. Rather, receiving the tradition in a religious context occurs "in a fellowship which has its sustaining basis, not in the person of the teacher, but in his office" (Delling, TDNT 4:13). In this respect the response of the Thessalonian believers to Paul's moral exhortation is not optional. Paul has passed on the gospel of God to them, and likewise now regards them as bearers of that gospel (1 Thess 2:2, 8, 9).

One may argue that Thessalonian believers would have understood both verbs in the light of the fact that such language also appeared in non-biblical Greek literature. The term περιπατέω, for instance, was used in connection with conducting a moral life in Philodemus of Gadara (*Lib.*

---

means "to summon, declare" (1 Sam 10:17) and is used in the context of kings' and commanders' military orders (Judg 4:10; 1 Sam 15:4; 23:8; 1 Kings 15:22; Jer [LXX] 27: 29; 28:27; 1 Macc 5:58; 9:63; 3 Macc 1:1) (Schmitz, TDNT 5:762–3; NIDNTTE 3:616). While the noun παραγγελία ("demand") is referred to in the works of Philo and Josephus in a secular context (Philo, *Flacc.* 141; Josephus, *A.J.* 16.241), the term παράγγελμα and the verbal form παραγγέλλω are noticeably often used to indicate God's commandments (e.g., Philo, *Decal.* 58, 65, 96, 106, 135). Paul's employment of this term might have been close to Philo's usage, i.e., announcement about something that needs to be done, *order, command, precept, advice,* and *exhortation* (BDAG, παραγγέλλω; Schmitz, TDNT 5:763).

23).[14] Yet it occurs less frequently than, and is synonymous with, the verb πορεύομαι (Weima 2014:257; NIDNTTE 3:674). Moreover, Malherbe (2000:220) argues that the second term ἀρέσκω could have been used by Paul in a moral sense, since Hellenistic moral philosophers regarded the notion of "pleasing God" as the goal of life (e.g., Epictetus, *Disc.* 4.4.48). However, this term seems to entail even more nuances. In 1 Thessalonians the term ἀρέσκω "characterizes man in a false or a valid attitude to life" (NIDNTTE 2:816; cf. G. Schneider, EDNT 1:151). Paul contrasts the status of Jews with that of the Thessalonian believers by mentioning that while the Jews did not please God (2:15), the gentile believers could now please God insofar as they had faith in Christ (4:1; Shogren 2012:156). Even if Paul might have selected these terms because of their familiarity to the audience, his employment of these specific verbs is most likely deliberate, since walking in accordance with God's will and pleasing God are significant characteristics of God's chosen people in Scripture. In fact, there is no difference in meaning between these two words as they are constructed as a *hendiadys* (Bruce 1982:79; Gaventa 1998:50; Shogren 2012:156). The LXX refrains from a literal translation of the notion of "walking." Intriguingly, a hitpael form of הלך in the Hebrew Scriptures is often rendered as εὐαρεστέω (please, be pleasing) in the LXX (Bertram, TDNT 5:943). While it is hard to trace whether Paul had the cognate verb εὐαρεστέω in mind (Louw & Nida 25.90, 93) or paraphrased it, he might have been acquainted with the idiomatic connotation of "walking" in the LXX as pleasing God. In using the term, furthermore, Paul might convey the "Torah ethos," since in the Hebrew Scriptures "walking" before God is often associated with observing God's commandments (Müller 2012:37–38; e.g., Deut 10:12; Josh 22:5). In this regard, Paul connects the notion of walking and pleasing God to a believer's life that is in accordance with the gospel and total dedication to God (Rosner 2013:92).

5.3 DISCURSIVE FUNCTION OF ECHOES FROM THE HOLINESS CODE IN 1 THESS 4:3–8?

In 1 Thess 4:3 the phrase "this is the will of God, your sanctification" can be viewed as a kind of thesis statement that runs through Paul's exhortation.[15]

---

14. This verb is used for describing the evildoer's form of walking: "[declaring failing] and other evils [with laughter or with an evil striding [swagger], he both treats those who are being admonished and . . . both toward someone he chances to know, [and] in the case of those he has chanced upon, and he does not conjecture about [evil people]. . ."

15. Regarding occurrences of the phrase "the will of God," it is not certain why the

This foundational statement in 4:3–8, which presents the life of sanctification (ἁγιασμός, 4:3, 4, 7) as God's will, echoes the phrase often referred to in Leviticus: "You shall be holy, for I the Lord your God am holy" (Lev 19:2; cf. 20:26).[16] The phrase [τ]οῦτο γάρ ἐστιν θέλημα τοῦ θεοῦ, ὁ ἁγιασμὸς ὑμῶν may be regarded as Paul's expository comment, and as a condensed summary of Leviticus' theology about holiness/sanctification.

More specifically, it may be argued that moral aspects of holiness have been integrated into Paul's use of the term ἁγιασμός.[17] Originally, the notion of holiness "was the defining characteristic and desired purpose for Israel, God's covenant people," according to the Hebrew Scriptures (Weima 2014:264). God's gracious election of Israel and conferment of the Torah at Mount Sinai were to distinguish the Israelites from other nations (Exod

---

phrase includes or lacks the definite article in the Pauline letters (Weima 2014:263). The definite article is attached to both nouns (in the undisputed letters [Rom 1:10; 12:2; Gal 1:4]; in the disputed letters [Eph 6:6]). The article does not occur in the phrase (in the undisputed letters [Rom 15:32; 1 Cor 1:1; 2 Cor 1:1; 8:5; 1 Thess 5:18]; in the disputed letters [Eph 1:1; Col 1:1; 2 Tim 1:1]). The phrase τοῦ θελήματος αὐτοῦ is found only in the disputed letters (Eph 1:5, 9, 11; Col 1:9). Elsewhere in the disputed letters some variant phrases appear: τὸ θέλημα τοῦ κυρίου (Eph 5:17); παντὶ θελήματι τοῦ θεοῦ (Col 4:12). 1 Thess 4:3 is the only place where Paul combines the anarthrous θέλημα and the arthrous θεοῦ. Some scholars explain that the anarthrous θέλημα indicates a broader sense of God's will (Lightfoot 1904:53; Marshall 1983:106). According to Bruce (1982:82), God's will cannot be broader than the sanctification of the Thessalonian believers. Most likely, the anarthrous θέλημα could be regarded as the predicate noun (contra Marshall 1983:106). The demonstrative pronoun οὗτος in 4:3 functions to emphasize that their sanctification is God's will (ἁγιασμός, 4:3, 4, 7).

16. In the NT the term ἁγιασμός occurs eight times in Paul's letters (Rom 6:9, 22; 1 Cor 1:30; 1 Thess 4:3, 4, 7; 2 Thess 2:13; 1 Tim 2:15).

17. Throughout the Church history, many scholars have recognized that the law in the Hebrew Scriptures is divided into moral, ceremonial, and civil law (Bayes [2005] 2017:3–6). It seems to be plausible and useful to make a distinction between ceremonial, civil, and moral law, but Paul never had this scheme in his mind. Consequently I do not intend to make a clear distinction between ceremonial and moral law here. In some cases the criteria of division are vague, as Dorsey (1991:330) points out: Even "[t]he Sabbath, the parapet law, the prohibition against muzzling of the treading ox—all the so-called 'ceremonial' and 'civic' laws embody or flesh out eternal moral and ethical principles." Even if concrete ceremonial regulations for holiness are no longer required under Christ's fulfillment of the law, the abrogation of the law does not negate "a revelatory and pedagogical" aspect of the law as well as the significance of holiness (Dorsey 1991:331; see also Schreiner 2010: 90). Schreiner (2010:94) well illustrates the reason that the moral law is authoritative: "What we typically call the moral norms of the law are fulfilled, at least in some measure, in the lives of believers. Nevertheless, they are not normative merely because they appear in the Mosaic covenant, for that covenant has passed away. It seems that they are normative because they express the character of God. We know that they still express God's will for believers because they are repeated as moral norms in the New Testament."

19:5–6; Deut 7:6–11; 14:2; 26:18–19; 28:9; Lev 11:44–45; 19:2; 20:7, 26; 22:32). Since terms related to ἅγιος occur countless times in the LXX, it is difficult to decide whether Paul has a specific notion of holiness in mind. Yet Paul's contrasting of the concepts of *impurity* and *sanctification* in 4:7 seems to be a noticeable clue to his echoing of the notion that "impure may never be brought into contact with what is holy" in Leviticus (Joosten 1996:124). Compared to other letters, the word appears intensively in 1 Thess 4, and its occurrence with the antithetic concept ἀκαθαρσίᾳ is remarkable. In addition, the antithetic relationship between "impurity" and "sanctification"—a central motif of Israel's distinctiveness as YHWH's elect people in Leviticus—occurs in 1 Thess 4:7 (cf. Rom 6:19). In considering comparisons between the Holiness Code in Leviticus (17–26) and 1 Thess 4:3–8, the code seems to permeate Paul's paraenetic exhortation to the Thessalonians with regard to sexual purity. In doing so, a particular aim of this exploration will be to consider the implied discursive effect of such echoes in Paul's paraenesis. By reconfiguring the Holiness Code, Paul assumes the gentile converts' incorporation into the people of God and gives guidelines as to what their new moral life in Christ could have entailed. Paul attempts to prevent converts in the Hellenistic world from assimilating "a very tolerant attitude toward sexual conduct, particularly sexual activity outside marriage" (Weima 1996:104; e.g., Demosthenes, Against Neaera 122; Plutarch, *Mor.* 144F).[18] Paul exhorts them to avoid sexual immorality, since it was associated with sensual characteristics of local gods (Weima 1996:105; Donfried 2002:22–30; see 3.2.3.4.2).

The potential source for Paul to persuade those who were in danger of regression to idol worship, exhorting them to avoid sexual immorality, was the Holiness Code of Leviticus, especially its clause on sexual purity (Lev 18:1–20; 20:7–21). Weima (1996:102) remarks that, for Paul, echoing the notion of holiness from the book of Leviticus was not unfamiliar to gentile believers:

---

18. Bruce (1982:82) argues that sexual intercourse outside marriage was a common phenomenon in Hellenistic societies: "Christianity from the outset has sanctified sexual union within marriage (as in Judaism); outside marriage, it was forbidden. This was a strange notion in the pagan society to which the gospel was first brought; various forms of an extramarital sexual union were tolerated and some were even encouraged. A man might have a mistress (ἑταίρα) who could provide him also with intellectual companionship; the institution of slavery made it easy for him to have a concubine (παλλακή), while casual gratification was readily available from a harlot (πόρνη). The function of his wife was to manage his household and be the mother of his legitimate children and heirs. There was no body of public opinion to discourage πορνεία, although someone who indulged in it to excess might be satirized on the same level as a notorious glutton or drunkard. Certain forms of public religion, indeed, involved ritual πορνεία."

> The holiness that previously has been the exclusive privilege and calling of Israel has now also become God's purpose for Gentiles at Thessalonica who have "turned from idols to serve the true and living God" (1:9). The holiness that has previously been the characteristic that distinguished Israel from the Gentile nations has now also become the boundary marker that separates the Thessalonian Gentile believers from "the Gentiles who do not know God" (4:5), those who are "outside" God's holy people (v. 12).

Paul illustrates that God's calling for holiness was not only applicable to God's chosen people in antiquity, but also to the new gentile converts.

Despite a lack of direct citations from the Hebrew Scriptures in 1 Thess 4:3–8, I will contend in this section that Paul's echoes of the Holiness Code, especially his exhortations regarding sexual purity, function to affirm and cultivate the gentile converts' new identity and ethos. In addition, Paul's reflecting the Holiness Code intends to demonstrate that believers who turned away from their idolatrous roots are now participating in a process of transformation, which began with their faith in Christ's death and resurrection. They are continually sanctified through the Holy Spirit's work—a process that will be completed with the restoration of God's whole creation for his glory (Schnelle 2005:390).

5.3.1 HODGSON'S RESEARCH ON 1 THESS 4:3–8

That the Holiness Code tradition (Lev 17–26) probably influenced Paul's exhortation to sexual purity in 1 Thess 4:3–7 can be substantiated by the occurrence of structural elements common in both texts. Hodgson (1982:199–215) suggests that the tradition of the Holiness Code was a potential *topos* in the period of Hellenistic Judaism (LXX and Pseudo-Phocylides) and the Qumranian community (CD). The pattern of moral exposition in the Holiness Code ("foundational statement," "concrete demands" and "motivations") is assumed to be widespread, and its arrangement is found in 1 Thess 4:1–12. Based on this hypothesis and Selwyn's comparison between the Holiness Code and 1 Pet 1:1—2:3, 11–12, Hodgson (1982:200-204) searched for similarities between this tradition and 1 Thess 4:1–12 by focusing on both internal and external evidence.

With regard to external evidence, foundational statements about God's holiness and ancient Israel's call to sanctification (Lev 19:2; 20:7, 26) are reiterated in Paul's statement that sanctification is God's will (1 Thess 4:3). Second, Hodgson (1982:200, 206) understands that Paul's concrete demands in 4:3b–6a are similar to a great number of exhortations in Leviticus, including: the prohibition of sexual intercourse (Lev 18:6–18; 20:19–23), denouncement of unjust business practices (19:13, 35; 25:13–17, 39–49), and the promotion of social justice (19:11, 15, 17–18; 25:43). Third, Hodgson (1982:206) finds common motivations for the exhortations in both Leviticus and 1 Thessalonians to be (1) God's judgment (Lev 26:14–22; 1 Thess 4:7), (2) comparison to the gentile's way of life (Lev 18:24–30; 20:22–26; 1 Thess 4:5), and (3) a concern for the sojourner (Lev 17:13, 15; 19:10, 33–34; 23:22; 24:22; 1 Thess 4:12a). When it comes to internal evidence and some modified elements (e.g., syntax, grammar) of the tradition in 1 Thess 4:1–12, Hodgson (1982:202–4) attempts to trace the tradition behind Paul's ethical discourse by comparing it to other occurrences of the tradition in the context of Hellenistic Judaism. By comparing the LXX (Lev 17–26), Pseudo-Phocylides and the Damascus Document, he attempts to substantiate the existence of an identifiable tradition of the Holiness Code behind the pericope. He concludes that Paul contains "the ethical exposition of the Holiness Code of Leviticus 17–26."

In spite of his fine observation, Hodgson's argument requires some minor improvements with regard to the issue of dividing 4:1–12 and maintaining thematic coherence. First, it is implausible to regard 4:1–12 as a coherent literary unit, since there are two separate themes: the Thessalonian Christians' sanctification with regard to sexual purity and brotherly/sisterly love (contra Hodgson 1982:200–201). Paul's first exhortation is demarcated by the discourse marker [π]ερὶ δὲ τῆς φιλαδελφίας in verse 9, which introduces the new theme of "brotherly love." Second, even in agreeing with Hodgson's discovery, it is far-fetched to fit the whole passage (4:1–12) into the pattern of the exhortation ("foundational statement," "concrete demands" and "motivations"). First Thessalonians 4:12 can reflect the motivation of Paul's demands, but strictly speaking it states the result, i.e., "so that you may walk properly before outsiders and be dependent on no one" (Ellingworth & Nida 1976:90).[19] Third, Hodgson (1982:200–201, 205) understands that Paul's exhortation in 4:3–6a contains two concrete demands: the prohibition of sexual immorality and "transgressing and defrauding one's brother in business." However, the fact that there is no transitional

---

19. In fact, it is difficult to decide whether the ἵνα clause indicates purpose or result. The majority of commentators understand that Paul wraps up his exhortation in this unit, illustrating the purpose of the Thessalonians' brotherly love (Hendriksen 1955:106; Marshall 1983:117; Wanamaker 1990:164; Malherbe 2000:250; Richard [1995] 2007:212; Weima 2014:299). Fee (2009:163) contends that the ἵνα clause can grammatically be both purpose and result. But he puts more emphasis on the latter, "since 'result' is the main thrust of the clause." Even if this clause can be rendered with the implication of purpose, one must differentiate a subtle nuance between motivation and purpose.

discourse marker to a new moral issue within 4:3b–6a leads us to conclude that Paul never digresses in his consistent exhortation to sexual purity. This controversial issue will be dealt with again later in the section for a brief comment on 4:3b–6a (see 5.3.2.1).

5.3.2 ECHOES OF THE HOLINESS CODE IN 1 THESS 4:3–8

Some similarities between 1 Thess 4:3–7 and Lev 10:10, 18:6–24, and 20:10–21 may corroborate the view that Paul might be echoing notions of sanctification. I concur with the view that Paul's utilization of the Holiness Code tradition generally has great potential. Nevertheless, as mentioned above, Hodgson's division of the texts and interpretations of the term πλεονεκτέω and the phrase ἐν τῷ πράγματι in 4:6a is problematic, since Paul's moral demand for sexual purity is a central theme throughout 4:3–8. This section will complement Hodgson's presupposition through an actual comparison of 1 Thessalonians with Leviticus with regard to the regulation of sexual purity and sanctification.

We do not find a definition for holiness/sanctification in the Pentateuch. But recognizing the contrast between holy (הַקֹּדֶשׁ) and common (הַחֹל), and between unclean (הַטָּמֵא) and clean (הַטָּהוֹר) in Leviticus 10:10, should be helpful in understanding the notion of sanctification in 1 Thess 4:3–7:

Lev 10:10 (MT)	Lev 10:10 (LXX)	1 Thessalonians 4:3, 4, 7
וּלֲהַבְדִּיל בֵּין הַקֹּדֶשׁ וּבֵין הַחֹל וּבֵין הַטָּמֵא וּבֵין הַטָּהוֹר׃	διαστεῖλαι ἀνὰ μέσον τῶν ἁγίων καὶ τῶν βεβήλων καὶ ἀνὰ μέσον τῶν ἀκαθάρτων καὶ τῶν καθαρῶν.	Τοῦτο γάρ ἐστιν θέλημα τοῦ θεοῦ, ὁ ἁγιασμὸς ὑμῶν. . . . . εἰδέναι ἕκαστον ὑμῶν τὸ ἑαυτοῦ σκεῦος κτᾶσθαι ἐν ἁγιασμῷ καὶ τιμῇ οὐ γὰρ ἐκάλεσεν ἡμᾶς ὁ θεὸς ἐπὶ ἀκαθαρσίᾳ ἀλλ' ἐν ἁγιασμῷ.

It is important to consider the notion of holiness within the ceremonial context as Lev 10:10 shows. Only God is inherently holy; nothing else on earth, such as people, objects, space or time, is holy but everything belongs to a common or profane sphere (Dumbrell 2002:45; Hartley 2003:420, 426). The holy and the unclean are contagious inasmuch as both influence the common and the clean respectively in certain cases, while the common and the clean are non-contagious (Joosten 1996:124). Hence, those who are involved in impure matters should ritually purify themselves, not only to maintain their identity as members of God's holy people but also to separate themselves from the gentile nations (cf. Sprinkle 2000:651). According to Lev 11–15, the concept of impurity is concretely illustrated with regard to edible animals, childbirth, skin diseases, and bodily discharges, and those who violate the regulation should be purified. With regard to the reason for issuing this law, recent scholars agree that purification leads Israel to "grasp the unity and perfection of God's creation, which in turn led to a shared worldview and common sense of purpose that set them apart from their neighbors" (House 1998:136; cf. Douglas 1966:54–57; Hartley 2003:429).

It is generally regarded that the word group that contains the Hebrew root קדשׁ carries the notion of separation or division, even if there is room for debate (NIDNTTE 1:124–5; cf. Procksch, TDNT 1:89). Since the etymological meaning of "holiness" is difficult to define in the Hebrew Scriptures, this word should be examined in consideration of its use in particular contexts. In many cases this word group is used in cultic contexts; everything that has to do with sacrifice to YHWH should be consecrated (e.g., temple, instruments for sacrifice, priests' garments; see Num 5:17; Exod 28:2–4, 36). Yet the cultic notion of holiness cannot be separated from its moral values: for instance, "sexual intercourse is in no way unethical or immoral, but in the context of the sacred cult it is regarded as ceremonially impure, preventing a person from coming into contact with the holy" (NIDNTTE 1:125). In this sense, the (cultic) regulation of separation between the unclean and the clean implies a "moral force" to make a distinction between Israel and all other nations (Hartley 2003:429; NIDNTTE 1:125). Although the word of YHWH in Lev 10:10 was given to the priests in a cultic sense, the core value of separation between the unclean and the clean permeates the rest of the book of Leviticus, extending its relevance to all Israelites (House 1998:135). In the relationship with the holy God, the covenantal people must take heed of the exhortation, "You shall be holy, for I the Lord your God am holy" (Lev 19:2). The Israelites' calling to holiness required them to conform to YHWH's holy characteristic, i.e., to participate in the process of "sanctification" (Dumbrell 2002:47). Recently, scholars increasingly come to the view of an inseparable association between cultic and ethical requirements in Leviticus. Cothey (2005:144) remarks that Leviticus' ritual preoccupations "serve straightforward ethical purposes by teaching ethical values and by providing a training in recognized ethical virtues." Moreover, Meyer (2013:3) notices that in the first half of Leviticus (e.g., Lev 11:44–45,), "holiness becomes a quality not only reserved for the cult, its officials and materials, but indeed the congregations of Israel and Yahweh."

Specifically, the priest's role in teaching Israel to discern between the clean and unclean, the common and holy, was specifically articulated in YHWH's prohibition of sexual immorality in Lev 18:6–24 and 20:10–21. Leviticus 18:6–24 sets out four prohibited sexual practices found among the Egyptians and the Canaanites (incestuous sexual relations, adultery, homosexuality, and bestiality) that end up defiling those who violate the regulations and even the promised land. Leviticus 20:10–21 instructs the leader of the community to encourage its members to avoid sexual transgression with a statement of the penalties. The reason for the regulation of sexual purity has to do with Israel's prosperity through sexual fertility. In contrast to the gentiles, who regard sex as the means to satisfy human sexual desire, Israel was supposed to have a different perspective on and morality for sexuality (NIDOTTE 4:921; House 1998:143). According to Leviticus, a distinct way of life from gentile practices had to accompany their response to God's grace in bringing them into the land. In this sense, House (1998:144) states "[v]igilance will be needed for Israel to remain distinctly Yahweh's when the people enter the new land and are confronted with new worldviews and value systems that are more like those in Egypt than those revealed at Sinai."

To summarize, the notion of separation between clean and unclean in Lev 10:10 consistently permeates regulations to remind Israel of their distinctive identity. The text encourages this by means of exhortations such as: "Consecrate yourselves, therefore, and be holy, for I am the Lord your God" (Lev 20:7) and "You shall be holy to me, for I the Lord am holy and have separated you from the peoples, that you should be mine" (Lev 20:26).

Paul seems to be well-acquainted with the inseparable relationship between ceremonial and moral laws in the book of Leviticus. Since Christ has fulfilled the law, Paul regards those who are in Christ as no longer being under the influence of the ceremonial law, while the moral law is still effective as normative guidance for Christian life. The moral force of God's calling for holiness in the Hebrew Scriptures is now applicable to the new gentile converts, as Wanamaker (1990:150) explains:

> Paul understood God to be the holy God of the OT who was set apart from every form of sin and impurity and who demanded similar holiness from the people of Israel through separation (Lv. 11:44f.; 19:2; 21:8). God had not changed, so the same requirement was laid on the new people of God, the Christians.

The term ἁγιασμός (sanctification) in 1 Thess 4:3 reflects the differentiated lifestyle of God's covenant people. With regard to the meaning of "holiness" in the Pauline letters, Paul does not seem to use the term in a cultic or ritualistic context. Rather, as Porter (1993a:397) illustrates, "he democratizes the concept by removing it from the domain of the cult and making it the spiritual responsibility of every believer." Specifically, Paul seems to have in mind that the term ἁγιωσύνη in 3:13 connotes the Thessalonian believers' "status of being holy" (Porter 1993a:398). Holiness pertains to an essential attribute of God. Yet at the same time their calling to holiness requires God's chosen people to behave in response to God's will. Here Paul may have had in mind aspects of holiness in Deuteronomy which present Israel as God's holy people as distinguished from other nations by observing the Torah (NIDNTTE 1:126). For Paul, the believers are called to participate in a process of sanctification, which God will bring to perfection on the last day (1 Thess 3:13). Israel's calling to actualize holiness was a significant aspect of the life of God's covenant people (Exod 19:5–6; Lev 11:44; Deut 26:18–19). This is now appropriated in Paul's exhortation to the Thessalonian believers. Scholars tend to differentiate holiness from sanctification, since the latter implies "the process of making holy" (Porter 1993a:398; cf. Marshall 1983:106). According to Bruce (1982:82), the notion of sanctification has a "strong ethical sense" in the New Testament and early Christian documents. To sum up, Paul's use of the term ἁγιασμός (sanctification in 4:3, 4, 7) seems to imbue the audience with Israel's distinct ethos, encouraging them to live likewise, namely as God's chosen people in the midst of a pagan society.

5.3.2.1 A MAJOR THEME OF 1 THESS 4:3–8: SEXUAL PURITY

In 4:3b–6a, as Paul elaborates on what sanctification is through five consecutive infinitives in three clauses, he specifically indicates that the Thessalonians' sanctification (ὁ ἁγιασμὸς ὑμῶν) entails self-restraint from sexual immorality:

4:3b	ἀπέχεσθαι ὑμᾶς
	ἀπὸ τῆς πορνείας,
4:4	εἰδέναι ἕκαστον ὑμῶν
	κτᾶσθαι τὸ ἑαυτοῦ σκεῦος
	ἐν ἁγιασμῷ καὶ τιμῇ
4:5	μὴ ἐν πάθει ἐπιθυμίας
	καθάπερ καὶ τὰ ἔθνη τὰ μὴ εἰδότα τὸν θεόν
4:6a	τὸ μὴ ὑπερβαίνειν
	καὶ τὸν ἀδελφὸν αὐτοῦ ἐν τῷ πράγματι
	πλεονεκτεῖν

The infinitives (ἀπέχεσθαι, εἰδέναι and τὸ μὴ ὑπερβαίνειν καὶ πλεονεκτεῖν) are explanatory (Sterner 1998:91; Weima 2014:266) or appositional (Wallace 1996:606). Hodgson (1982:203–4; see also MHT 4:89) postulates that the Hebrew infinitive construction in the Torah (e.g., Exod 20:8; Deut 5:12) influences Paul's use of infinitives in 1 Thess 4:3b-6a. While one cannot be certain of reflection of Semitic usage in the paraenetic section, Paul's use of infinitives most likely implies imperatival force (Wanamaker 1990:151; Marshall 1983:106; Weima 2014:266). I regard the series of infinitives in this pericope as being interrelated, consistently pointing to the Thessalonians' moral responsibility to avoid sexual immorality (cf. tracing 3, Appendix II).

A major thrust of this section is the exhortation to sexual purity. First, in 4:3b Paul focuses on the sexual ethics of the Thessalonian community abstaining from sexual immorality.[20] An abrupt transition from referring to sanctification to advocating sexual purity does not mean that sanctification itself can be merely identified as the mere avoidance of sexual sins. This exhortation reflects the actual situation of the complex religious web in Thessalonica, in which sexual immorality was an essential feature of the local pagan gods (see 3.2.3.4.2). In this milieu, for Paul, the typical Jewish idiomatic expression ἀπέχεσθαι ... ἀπό is most suitable for reminding the Thessalonians of their conversion from paganism to becoming God's chosen people. The combination of the first infinitive, ἀπέχεσθαι ("*keep away, abstain, refrain from*" [BDAG]) and the preposition ἀπό often occurs in both Hellenistic and Jewish moral instruction with regard to various forms of vices (for a list of examples, see Green 2002:190).[21] Although a different verb, προσέχω, in an imperative form, and the extended description (from the spirit of sexual immorality) are referred to in these texts, the occurrence of a similar construction of Paul's exhortation in 4:3b is significant.

Second, there has been some debate about the interpretation of 1 Thess 4:4 because of the enigmatic combination of σκεῦος and κτᾶσθαι.[22] In the

---

20. Most scholars agree that the arthrous singular form of πορνεία ("unlawful sexual intercourse, *prostitution, unchastity, fornication*" [BDAG]) does not indicate a specific sexual immoral act, but any sort of sexual sin in a general sense (Ellingworth & Nida 1976:78; Jensen 1978:179-83; Witherington III 2006:112; Boring 2015: 143).

21.. The most noticeable echoes of 4:3b in the intertestamental documents may be found in Tobit 4:12 (πρόσεχε σεαυτῷ, παιδίον, ἀπὸ πάσης πορνείας) and the Testament of Leviticus 9:9 (πρόσεχε, τέκνον, ἀπὸ τοῦ πνεύματος τῆς πορνείας).

22. The reason for the difficulty in the interpretation of the terms σκεῦος and κτᾶσθαι can be attributed to the fact that various meanings are equally possible. There are three major options in the interpretation of this verse (to review the full discussion of the options, see Weima 2014:268-74). First, this combination can mean "to acquire his own wife," denoting that believers should not remain in single but be married to avoid sexual immorality (Frame 1912:149-50; Hendriksen 1955:102; Collins 1983:424; Yarbrough 1985:68-76; Malherbe 2000:227-8; cf. Sir 36:29). Second, in employing a durative sense of the verb, the meaning "to live with his own wife" is possible (Maurer, TDNT 7:365; Best 1986a:162). In this case, as Witherington III (2006:116) well illustrates, Paul had in mind that "[e]ach man should have his own wife and have sexual relationships with his

second infinitive construction Paul most likely exhorts the Thessalonian believers to *control their bodies*—an exhortation with sexual connotations (ESV, NIV 2011, NRSV, NLT, etc.; Chrysostom, NPNF 1.13:344; Whitton 1982:142–3; Richard [1995] 2007:198; Green 2002:191–4; Beale 2003:117; Shogren 2012:161–4; Boring 2015:143–4; Gupta 2016:81). More specifically, the term σκεῦος can be used in a figurative sense, most likely indicating one's genitalia (BDAG; LSJ; Ellingworth & Nida 1976:79; Bruce 1982:83; Marshall 1983:108–9; Wanamaker 1990:152–3; Elgvin 1997:604–19; Fee 2009:149; Weima 2014:270–4).[23] And the verb κτάομαι (this is the only occurrence in Paul's letters) has the meanings of "to gain possession of, *procure for oneself, acquire, get*" and "*possess*" in a durative sense (BDAG). This meaning is more natural than other translations such as "acquire" or "possess" in a transient sense (MM 4:362). Hence, Paul most likely exhorts the believers to preserve sexual purity by controlling their bodies (concretely, genitalia) in accordance with God's calling for sanctification.

With regard to the third infinitive construction, I argue that Paul continues to exhort the Thessalonians to "abstain from sexual immorality" (4:3). Richard ([1995] 2007:200–202) contends that Paul moves on to a new ethical issue with regard to justice in business based on three pieces of evidence. First, he notes the absence of the connotation of sexual immorality in the light of 2 Cor 12:17–18, in which the term πλεονεκτέω indicates one's taking advantage of others' financial profits in the context of earning some money. Second, in classical Greek the plural form of the term πρᾶγμα could be translated in verse 6a as "fortunes," "cause," "circumstances" and "law business" (LSJ). Third, in the occurrence of five consecutive infinitives, the fact that the last two infinitives are anarthrous with the negative particle, μὴ "underscore[s] the verb's resumptive function as it alludes back to *hagiasmos* of verse 3a and further explicates another characteristics of what a pure life must be" (Richard [1995] 2007:202). However, I claim that this ambiguous phrase, "in this matter," should be clarified in the light of the consistent flow of the moral discourse on sexual purity rather than surveying the usages of πρᾶγμα in non-biblical literature.

---

own wife and not invade someone else's marriage, but also should treat his own wife with honor and respect, not merely as a sex object." The third option is "to control one's body" combining the meaning of "one's body" and the durative sense of "possess."

23. Scholars agree that the Hebrew term בְּלִי ("vessel"), which corresponds to σκεῦος, is mentioned to indicate the male genitalia of David's young men in 1 Sam 21:5. Elgvin (1997:604–19) provides more evidence from Qumranian documents to clarify the sexual connotation of the term σκεῦος in 1 Thess 4:4. According to him, Paul's reference to σκεῦος as a euphemistic expression of the sexual organ can be substantiated by the expression כלי [ח]קבהי ("the vessel of your bosom") in 4Q416.

It could be suggested to read this part in the light of the larger discursive context of the letter. First, one must pay attention to the structure of this unit as *a single sentence*, containing one cohesive idea. Introducing a new issue about justice in business is somewhat unusual, since it interrupts this consistency. Even after this sentence ends, verses 7-8 function as the ground for Paul's exhortation to sexual purity in 4:3b-6. In the transition from the anarthrous infinitives to the arthrous infinitives, Paul shifts his focus "from the consequences of sexual conduct on one's own life to that of *others*" (Weima 2014:275).

Second, in identifying the meaning of the phrase ἐν τῷ πράγματι in verse 6a, the singular definite article indicates the matter that is related to the consistent issue of sexual immorality. Moreover, one should not exclude the two infinitives' reference to any sort of sexual immorality (cf. NIDNTTE 3:781). Here, Paul has in mind the term ὑπερβαίνω (literally, "go beyond") in a moral sense as BDAG defines it: "to transgress by going beyond proper limits in behavior, *trespass, sin*." Therefore, this term connotes "crossing a forbidden boundary, and hence trespassing (sexually) on territory which is not one's own" (Bruce 1982:84). The second verb, πλεονεκτέω, in this context can indicate cheating or deceiving someone for the purpose of satisfying one's sexual desire. While Paul focuses in verse 4 on controlling the body for the sake of sexual purity, in verse 6 he is concerned with the awful result of sexual intercourse outside of marriage. An improper sexual relationship will consequently deceive and harm his or her spouse who is a brother or sister in Christ. Gupta (2016:83) substantiates that the terms are used in this sense by noting the relevance of this text to Josephus's recounting the story of Joseph and Potiphar's wife (*Ant.* 2.42; cf. Gen 39:1-19). Joseph rejects the seduction of Potiphar's wife in accordance with his beliefs. Another reason for abstaining from sexual sin is that the immorality would result in deceiving, damaging and mistreating Potiphar, who had purchased him as a slave. Moreover, πρᾶγμα can be a euphemistic term used to indicate a sexual affair in the community (BDAG; MM:532; Marshall 1983:111; Green 2002; Fee 2009:150-1; Weima 2014:276; Furnish 2007:91).

Paul's exhortation for sexual purity is encompassed by sanctification and holiness, which thematically form *inclusio*. Sexual purity in one's marriage life and concern for others (though it was expressed as not harming others in a passive sense) is significant evidence to demonstrate one's genuine identity as God's chosen people. Exhortation for sanctification definitely imbues the Thessalonians with the communal ethos of the ancient Israelites who were called to pursue holiness. Trespassing a forbidden boundary by cheating on one's spouse is not only a violation of the seventh clause in the Ten Commandments but also a critical ignorance of brotherly/sisterly love (φιλαδελφία).

5.3.2.2 THE THESSALONIANS' DISTINCT IDENTITY AND ETHOS IN 4:3–8

In 1 Thess 4:4c–5 the implied meaning of exhortations to sexual purity is clarified by the contrast between holiness/honor (ἐν ἁγιασμῷ καὶ τιμῇ) and the passion of lust (ἐν πάθει ἐπιθυμίας). I regard this contrast between the Thessalonians' calling for holiness and the pagan way of life as Paul's discursive strategy to notify the Thessalonians of their differentiated identity and ensuing moral responsibility as God's chosen people. Paul's echo that ancient Israel was called to be a holy nation among the nations primarily functions as the community ethos that draws the boundary between insiders and outsiders (cf. Wanamaker 2002:138). But, more concretely, Paul highlights their distinct identity and differentiated morality from their pagan neighbors through (1) the various appropriations of the code of honor and shame, (2) Jewish notion of sexual immorality, and (3) establishing divine authority.

5.3.2.2.1 CODE OF HONOUR AND SHAME

Paul appropriates the cultural code of "honor and shame" that was prevalent in the ancient Mediterranean world in his estimation of one's moral life within the believers' community. As DeSilva (2000:281) remarks, in the early church the notions of purity, defilement, and holiness continued to be referred to as an important standard in Christian moral teaching. Honor was not granted by their pagan neighbors but derived from the community of believers. He adds that certain behaviors are considered as dangerous to the sanctified believer in Christ and "a condition of communal wholeness and abstinence from destructive vices" are encouraged as the most suitable for them. The virtue that one can receive honor in the community is not simply good in a moral sense, but is sanctification. Eventually, God alone can determine who deserves to receive honor in terms of sanctification (cf. Green 2002:194). In reflecting the honor code, Paul shapes a communal ethos of differentiation that promotes the moral formation of the newly established community. This notion is strengthened in verse 5 by describing in negative terms the characteristics of the gentiles who do not know God. Paul juxtaposes two contrasting qualities of life: gentiles' lustful passion (ἐν πάθει ἐπιθυμίας) and the distinct mark of God's chosen people (ἐν ἁγιασμῷ καὶ τιμῇ). Such a contrast is part of a significant ethos that encourages God's new covenant people to control their bodies in accordance with God's will.[24] Before the Thessalonian community was converted, it lived

---

24. See also Rom 1:26 and Col 3:5. In contrast with Col 3:5, in which the terms

in a world where the association between sexual immorality and worshiping gods was not abnormal (cf. Green 2002:35–36). According to DeSilva (1996:65), through the exhortation not to emulate the gentiles' lustful passion, Paul attempts to distinguish the "values served by the two groups, and the incompatibility and inferiority of the unbelievers' values with the enlightened ethos of the Christian group." In so doing, Paul establishes a proper behavioral norm by setting the boundaries between the Christian community and the pagan world.

5.3.2.2.2 JEWISH NOTIONS OF SEXUAL IMMORALITY

In his exhortation Paul appeals to Jewish notions of sexual immorality to remind the Thessalonians of their distinct identity as God's holy people. As in some parts of the Holiness Code (Lev 17–26), the notion of holiness has to do with distinctiveness from other nations' sexual immorality. In addition, the Prophets often referred to sexual immorality (πορνεία) figuratively to indicate ancient Israel's unfaithfulness to God (Jer 13:27; Ezek 16:41; 23:29; Hos 1:2; 2:6; 4:12; 5:4; Mic 1:7; Nah 3:4). A majority of Jewish documents also show that sexual immorality is associated with idolatry, indicating that sexual purity represents what distinguishes God's people from unbelieving pagans (Wis 14:12, 26–27; *Sib. Or.* 3:591–9; *T. Sim.* 5:3).[25] In calling for abstaining from sexual immorality in his letters, Paul sets the boundaries between the groups and imbues the Thessalonian believers with ideals of Jewish ethics (Carras 1990:314).[26] Paul reflects the common Jewish sentiment that sexual transgression is a typical moral characteristic of gentiles who do not know God. In doing so, he attempts "to distinguish these converts from the morals of their non-Christian contemporaries in a similar way that Jewish ethics marked out Jews from pagans" (Carras 1990:314). Particularly, in the expression "not . . . like the Gentiles who do not know God" (1 Thess 4:5; see also 1 Cor 1:21; Gal 4:8; 2 Thess 1:8), Paul also echoes "the OT concept

---

πάθος and ἐπιθυμία are individually referred to in a list of vices, the combination of these words in 1 Thess 4:5 emphatically refers to the gentiles' unbridled sexual passion.

25. Most likely, Paul borrows this term from the Hebrew, גּוֹי; this word's first meaning is "the gentile," but in the texts that Paul has in mind it can be translated as "heathen" (BDB; NIDNTTE 2:89). While the term ἔθνος is often used in a neutral sense to imply the target of Paul's mission (Rom 11:13; 16:4, 25–27; Gal 2:12), this verse indicates the gentile non-believers in Thessalonica.

26. In 1 Thess 4:1–7, the term ἀκαθαρσία is used as a synonym for πορνεία. While the term, ἀκαθαρσία has a broader range of meanings than πορνεία, elsewhere in the Pauline letters it indicates sexual impurity (Rom 1:24; 6:19; 2 Cor 12:21; Gal 5:19; Eph 5:3; Col 3:5).

of a culpable ignorance of God" (Seesemann, TDNT 5:117) and this notion affects the Thessalonians' identity and moral recognition, for example:

Jeremiah 10:25a (MT)	Jeremiah 10:25a (LXX)	1 Thessalonians 4:5
שְׁפֹךְ חֲמָתְךָ עַל־הַגּוֹיִם אֲשֶׁר לֹא־יְדָעוּךָ וְעַל מִשְׁפָּחוֹת אֲשֶׁר בְּשִׁמְךָ לֹא קָרָאוּ	ἔκχεον τὸν θυμόν σου ἐπὶ ἔθνη τὰ μὴ εἰδότα σε καὶ ἐπὶ γενεὰς αἳ τὸ ὄνομά σου οὐκ ἐπεκαλέσαντο	μὴ ἐν πάθει ἐπιθυμίας καθάπερ καὶ τὰ ἔθνη τὰ μὴ εἰδότα τὸν θεόν
Psalms 79:6 (MT)	Psalms 78:6 (LXX)	
שְׁפֹךְ חֲמָתְךָ אֶל־הַגּוֹיִם אֲשֶׁר לֹא־יְדָעוּךָ וְעַל מַמְלָכוֹת אֲשֶׁר בְּשִׁמְךָ לֹא קָרָא	ἔκχεον τὴν ὀργήν σου ἐπὶ ἔθνη τὰ μὴ γινώσκοντά σε καὶ ἐπὶ βασιλείας, αἳ τὸ ὄνομά σου οὐκ ἐπεκαλέσαντο	

The LXX's translations of both Hebrew texts are quite straightforward, demonstrating the idea of ignoring YHWH as a typical characteristic of the gentiles. The Hebrew definite article ה was, however, not reflected in both LXX translations and each book differently renders יָדַע ("to know") as οἶδα and γινώσκω respectively.[27] In 1 Thess 4:5 Paul inserts the definite article τὰ before ἔθνη and employs οἶδα rather than γινώσκω. Except for replacing "you" with "God," the similarities seem to indicate his reliance on the MT version of Jer 10:25a or possibly Ps 79:6. Through these echoes, Paul illustrates the preconversion mindset of the gentiles that sexual immorality had nothing to do with the obedience to the divine will and morality.[28] However, as the converts accepted this new concept that moral transformation cannot be separated from "knowing God," they came to belong to a new group that serves the holy God alone. A comparison between each corresponding word and phrase in verses 4–5 also emphasizes a sharp distinction between God's chosen people and the gentiles:

27. In Hebrew the definite article can be used generically (Arnold & Choi [2003] 2009:31). Thus, omission of the article ה in the LXX may be regarded as natural, since attaching the definite article in the MT indicates a class of gentiles. Particularly when it is associated with a plural noun, as in the case of Jer 10:25a and Ps 79:6 (MT), biblical authors typically include all gentiles.

28. In these texts the contrast between God's people and the gentiles is referred to in the context of the authors' pleading for the coming of God's righteous wrath/anger upon those who are ignorant of God. In the context of the Israelites facing imminent exile (Jer 10), the prophet solemnly warned them against practicing other nations' customs or following foreign gods. The prophet pointed out the futility of worshiping idols and then prayed that God's wrath would fall upon the gentiles. The narrator in Ps 79 also pleaded for the pouring out of God's anger upon the nations and expected God to cease his anger towards the Israelites and to seek their deliverance.

1 Thess 4:4		1 Thess 4:5
ἕκαστον ὑμῶν (each one of you)	↔	τὰ ἔθνη (the gentiles)
εἰδέναι ... τὸ ἑαυτοῦ σκεῦος κτᾶσθαι (know ... how to control one's own body)	↔	μὴ εἰδότα τὸν θεόν (do not know God)
ἐν ἁγιασμῷ καὶ τιμῇ (in holiness and honour)	↔	ἐν πάθει ἐπιθυμίας (in lustful passion)

In the Hebrew Scriptures "to know God" can be regarded as a technical reference to being in a covenant relationship with God (Deidun [1981] 2006:19; Weima 2014:274). The gentiles generally pursued knowledge of moral goodness in the Hellenistic philosophical milieu (Boring 2015:140-1). However, gaining a new identity in Christ through conversion led the converts to move on to totally different sphere of life in which knowing God corresponded to participation in his supreme attributes (i.e., holiness) (cf. Boring 2015:140-1).

5.3.2.2.3 ESTABLISHING DIVINE AUTHORITY

The third motivation for reinforcing the community's identity and morality in verses 4-6 is more explicitly substantiated through the conjunction διότι, which marks a causal connection to the previous sentence.

First, Paul mentions that one should not mistreat brothers and sisters sexually *because* the Lord Jesus is an avenger whose role is that of an agent of divine wrath/anger (Watson 1999:72; Wanamaker 2002:138). In verse 6b Paul may be describing the final judgment at the eschaton through the key concept ἔκδικος ("the one who punishes" or "an avenger"; see BDAG). This term does not indicate personal revenge with hostility, but has "the positive sense of bringing about justice (the root δικ-) by rightly punishing the wicked for their sins against God and others" (Weima 2014:277). The notion that God is an avenger who vindicates the chosen people comes from the Hebrew Scriptures and its Semitic influence on Paul's use of the term ἔκδικος is crucial. The most probable echo of Scripture in 1 Thess 4:6b is Ps 94:1: "Ὁ θεὸς ἐκδικήσεων κύριος, ὁ θεὸς ἐκδικήσεων ἐπαρρησιάσατο" (see also Deut 32:35; Ps 18:47; 99:8; Jer 11:20; Amos 3:2; Mic 5:15; Nah 1:2; Wis 12:12). The psalmist similarly calls YHWH the God of vengeance (אֵל־נְקָמוֹת), and beseeches him to judge the wicked and to vindicate the suffering of God's people.

Noticeably, in interpreting YHWH's judgment upon the wicked from the Hebrew texts in a Christological sense, Paul may have envisaged that the Lord Jesus' vengeance and vindication will take place on the day of the judgment (Morris [1984] 2009:82; Beale 2003:122; Furnish 2007:92; Fee 2009:47). That the Lord is ἔκδικος ("avenger" or "the one who punishes," LSJ; BDAG; Louw & Nida 38.9) in verse 6b indicates that Jesus takes on his role as the agent of God's final judgment. The διότι clause, "because the Lord is an avenger in all these things," lends weight to Paul's exhortation for abstaining from sexual immorality (cf. tracing 3, Appendix II). According to Watson (1999:72), the concept that Jesus is an avenger provides Paul with divine authority: "He is like the person in apocalyptic literature who is selected to bring the hidden mysteries to the righteous people to help them live through the coming distress. His ethical instruction had come through the Lord Jesus and carried his divine authority" (v. 2). Paul declares that, on the one hand, when believers stand at the judgment seat of God at the eschaton (Rom 14:10; 2 Cor 5:1), those who are obedient to God's will through a life of sanctification will be delivered from the wrath of God (1 Thess 1:9; 5:9; cf. Alsup 1978:43). On the other hand, those who disobey God's will, regarding themselves as believers but acting like non-believers, will not escape from God's eschatological judgment (Wanamaker 2002:138; Beale 2003:122). This newly formulated contrast thus seems to create a significant ground for solidifying the believers' distinct identity and ethos in their surrounding world.

Second, in 1 Thess 4:8, through the notion of God's new covenant, he imbues his own exhortation for the Thessalonians' sanctification with divine authority (Ezek 36:25–27; 37:6, 14). In the antithetical construction (οὐκ . . . ἀλλά), Paul emphasizes that spurning the exhortation to sanctification denotes ignoring or rejecting God himself.[29] The conjunction γάρ in verse 7 seems to function as a connection to Paul's thesis-like statement, "this is the will of God, your sanctification: that you abstain from sexual immorality" (4:3), and to specify his major exhortation, forming an inclusio with verse 3 (see tracing 3, Appendix II). This idea is extended more through an addendum in the sentence that begins with the definite article ὁ. This article functions as a relative pronoun explaining God as the one "who gives his Holy Spirit" to the Thessalonians. In the illustration of what God has done for the believers, Paul implies that the community's sanctification links to the work of the Holy Spirit that "inspire[s] them inwardly toward holiness [hagiasmos] and to accomplish in them the great aim of desiring to please him [God]" (Beale 2003:123). Based on the inferential

---

29. In the NT the word ἀθετέω is often referred to in order to denote the attitude or act of disobedience to God (Mark 7:9; Luke 7:30; 10:16; Heb 10:28; cf. Isa 1:2; Jer 5:11; Ezek 22:26; John 12:28). Best (1986a:169) argues that it is uncertain whether Paul appoints himself as an authoritative instructor or has a specific person in mind, since a definite article does not occur before ἄνθρωπον in v. 7. However, since the omission emphasises "the qualitative aspect of the noun, namely, the 'humanness' of the one giving the instructions," it can be an implicit reference to Paul himself (Wanamaker 1990:158; see also Marshall 1983:113; Green 2002:200; Weima 2014: 281).

force of the particle τοιγαροῦν, not listening to Paul's exhortation in 4:3–8 may be linked to disregarding the Holy Spirit's involvement in the Thessalonians' journey to sanctification (see tracing 3, Appendix II).[30] Furthermore, I maintain that in the light of Ezekiel 36:35–36 and 37:6, 14 the rejection of God's Spirit can be extended to indicate a disavowal of their newly gained identity as God's covenant people. What Paul demonstrates in echoing Scripture is the elucidation of God pouring out the Holy Spirit on the Thessalonian believers "as part of the covenant blessings to be enjoyed in the messianic era" (Weima 2014:282).

As many recent commentators agree, it is highly possible and plausible that Paul echoes the promise of the gift of the Holy Spirit in Ezek 36:35–36 and 37:14 in 1 Thess 4:8:

Ezek 36:26 (MT)	Ezek 36:26 (LXX)	1 Thes 4:8
וְנָתַתִּי לָכֶם לֵב חָדָשׁ וְרוּחַ חֲדָשָׁה אֶתֵּן בְּקִרְבְּכֶם וַהֲסִרֹתִי אֶת־לֵב הָאֶבֶן מִבְּשַׂרְכֶם וְנָתַתִּי לָכֶם לֵב בָּשָׂר׃	καὶ δώσω ὑμῖν καρδίαν καινὴν καὶ πνεῦμα καινὸν δώσω ἐν ὑμῖν καὶ ἀφελῶ τὴν καρδίαν τὴν λιθίνην ἐκ τῆς σαρκὸς ὑμῶν καὶ δώσω ὑμῖν καρδίαν σαρκίνην.	τοιγαροῦν ὁ ἀθετῶν οὐκ ἄνθρωπον ἀθετεῖ ἀλλὰ τὸν θεὸν τὸν [καὶ] διδόντα τὸ πνεῦμα αὐτοῦ τὸ ἅγιον εἰς ὑμᾶς.
Ezek 37:6 (MT)	Ezek 37:6 (LXX)	
וְנָתַתִּי עֲלֵיכֶם גִּדִים וְהַעֲלֵתִי עֲלֵיכֶם בָּשָׂר וְקָרַמְתִּי עֲלֵיכֶם עוֹר וְנָתַתִּי בָכֶם רוּחַ וִחְיִיתֶם וִידַעְתֶּם כִּי־אֲנִי יְהוָה׃	καὶ δώσω ἐφ' ὑμᾶς νεῦρα καὶ ἀνάξω ἐφ' ὑμᾶς σάρκας καὶ ἐκτενῶ ἐφ' ὑμᾶς δέρμα καὶ δώσω πνεῦμά μου εἰς ὑμᾶς, καὶ ζήσεσθε, καὶ γνώσεσθε ὅτι ἐγώ εἰμι κύριος.	
Ezek 37:14 (MT)	Ezek 37:14 (LXX)	
וְנָתַתִּי רוּחִי בָכֶם וִחְיִיתֶם וְהִנַּחְתִּי אֶתְכֶם עַל־אַדְמַתְכֶם וִידַעְתֶּם כִּי־אֲנִי יְהוָה דִּבַּרְתִּי וְעָשִׂיתִי נְאֻם־יְהוָה׃	καὶ δώσω τὸ πνεῦμά μου εἰς ὑμᾶς, καὶ ζήσεσθε, καὶ θήσομαι ὑμᾶς ἐπὶ τὴν γῆν ὑμῶν, καὶ γνώσεσθε ὅτι ἐγὼ κύριος λελάληκα καὶ ποιήσω, λέγει κύριος.	

Before Ezekiel prophesies Israel's restoration from Babylonian exile in 36:25–28, he points out the Israelites' failure to maintain their differentiated identity by defiling themselves (Ezek 36:17–20). Ezekiel's main task is to

---

30. The compound and emphatic inferential particle τοιγαροῦν ("so for that reason," Shogren 2012:166–7) is used to indicate an inference from a previous statement (Wolter, EDNT 3:364). This term occurs only twice in the NT (1 Thess 4:8; Heb 12:1) and in some extra-biblical sources, and it is sometimes referred to in the context of exhortation (BDAG, τοιγαροῦν; see Josephus, *C. Ap.* 2.201; *Bar.* 4:16).

lead the Israelites not only to recognize their sins as the foundational cause of their being in exile but also to repent of their sins (Ezek 1–33). He ultimately proclaims that the restoration of Israel's true identity as God's chosen people will take place (Ezek 34–48) (cf. Renz 2002:112). Specifically, Ezekiel concretely points out that what Israel transgressed was the Holiness Code through idolatry, sexual immorality (cf. Lev 19:4), oppression, robbery (cf. Lev 19:13), and adultery (cf. Lev 20:10) (Thielman 1994:56). In Leviticus the issue of whether the Israelites could live in the promised land was uncertain and relative to whether their obedience to God's law is maintained. Ezekiel 36–37 illustrates Israel's failure to observe God's law and the subsequent punishment, reflecting the doom-laden predictions indicated in Lev 26:14–39 (disease, fever, famines, invasion, punishment, and banishment from the land). The prophet also envisages that Israel will be restored based on God's covenant with them in Lev 26:40–45.

It can be argued that 1 Thess 4:8 contains the Ezekielian tradition inasmuch as both texts indicate that the gift of God's Spirit is connected to the internal renewal of chosen people's hearts and minds. The sequence in 1 Thess 4:8 explains that the Thessalonians are called to be clean and that God gives the Holy Spirit, which is noticeably similar to Ezek 36:25–26. God's purification of Israel from all their defilement (טֻמְאָה/ἀκαθαρσία; 1 Thess 4:7) and idols (גִּלּוּל/εἴδωλον; 1 Thess 1:9) is articulated in the language of the priest's cleansing and blood-sprinkling rituals; this notion further indicates the internal renewal of God's chosen people's hearts and minds (Block 1998:354–5). By giving a new heart and putting the new spirit within Israel, God will remove their obstinacy and cause them to keep the Torah and to walk in the statutes (36:26–27). Paul echoes this Ezekiel prophesy in an eschatological sense in conveying that the outpouring of the Holy Spirit upon the believers is now actualized in Christ (Thielman 1994:77; Weima 2007:878; cf. Marshall 1983:114). Israel's covenantal identity in relationship with God would be renewed and should accompany their allegiance to God in obedience to God's will (i.e., sanctification in 1 Thess 4:3). In 1 Thesss 4:8 Paul's echo adds the nuance of the fulfillment of Ezekiel's prophesy in the eschatological era, and he applies the new covenant language to this gentile community (Weima 2014:282). First, Paul's scriptural echo with the present participle form of δίδωμι denotes God's fulfillment of the prophecy from the perspective of the present time and its constant influence on the believers' lives. Second, the phrase τὸ πνεῦμα αὐτοῦ τὸ ἅγιον is prominent here in comparison to other descriptions of the Spirit in Paul's writings (e.g., πνεύματος ἁγίου [Rom 5:5; 15:13; 1 Cor 6:19; 1 Thess 1:6]). The accusative in simple apposition to τὸ πνεῦμα occurs with a genitive form of the pronoun αὐτοῦ, and is modified by τὸ ἅγιον. This word order emphasizes an attribute of the Spirit (cf. Eph 4:30), indicating that the Spirit comes from God and is characterized as "holy" (Fee 2009:153). In Paul's view, the Spirit is involved in the believers' sanctification, guiding them in fulfilling God's will while producing holiness within their lives (Deidun [1981] 2006:56-57; Fee 2009:153-4).[31] Third, with regard to using the preposition in verse 8, Paul seems to rely on Ezek 37:6, 14 inasmuch as the LXX version translates the Hebrew preposition, בְּ, as εἰς. This awkward use of the preposition εἰς rather than ἐν is intentional to emphasize God's action of continuous interiorization (Deidum [1981] 2006:56). Fee (2009:154) remarks that the notion of interiorization in Paul's reference to the preposition "reflects a Pauline understanding of the gift of the Spirit as the fulfillment of Old Testament promises that God's own Spirit will come to indwell his people."

Paul's reference to that God gives the Holy Spirit may intend to remind God's chosen people of their internal renewal in Christ. For Paul, the Holy Spirit is not only the essential mark that represents one's belonging to Christ but also the eschatological power that "breaks into the old age . . . so as to enable the believer to live in the old age with the power and the light of the new" (NIDNTTE 3:815; cf. Rom 7:14-25; 8:9-11, 12, 23; 1 Cor 15:44-46; 2 Cor 3:17-18; 5:1-5). God's redemptive history began with the Holy Spirit's initiative of transformation when the gospel of God was preached to the Thessalonians (1 Thess 1:6). The Spirit plays a role in the believers' sanctification in the between times (1 Thess 4:3). Finally, God's work in the salvation history is completed "when the Spirit takes full control over the whole person in the resurrection of the body" (NIDNTTE 3:816).

Specifically, the Spirit has power in the process of internal renewal of the believer (NIDNTTE 3:816). Paul notes that the eschatological fulfillment of the believers' internal renewal subsequently leads them to their distinctive morality in the midst of the religiously pluralistic environment. Deidun ([1981] 2006:54) points out the occurrence of the common theme of interior communication of YHWH's Spirit in those texts:

> It is important to insist on the ethical perspective in which these Old Testament passages place the promise of God's future intervention, for it is this that determines the peculiarity of Paul's interpretation of the New Covenant and explains the particular emphasis that he puts on the ethical role of the Spirit.

In addition, Allen (1998:180) remarks on the moral implication of God giving a new heart and new spirit, saying that "[e]ven now, that ideal creates a moral challenge to live up to the grace of inaugurated eschatology."

---

31. I do not agree with Deidun's understanding of τὸ ἅγιον as merely "a sanctifying energy."

Fee (2009:155) also considers the gift of the Spirit "as the constant divine companion, by whose power one lives out holiness, that is, a truly Christian ethic."

5.4 DISCURSIVE FUNCTION OF ΘΕΟΔΙΔΑΚΤΟΙ IN 1 THESS 4:9–12

Paul introduces a second theme, "brotherly/sisterly love" (φιλαδελφία), in 4:9 with the discursive signal περὶ δὲ. Paul's echo of new covenant prophecy in 4:8 seems to continue to function as a central concept in 4:9–12.

Paul's referring to the neologism θεοδίδακτοί draws our attention since it occurs only once throughout ancient Greek documents.[32] With regard to the interpretation of the neologism θεοδίδακτοί several scholars have tried to establish what it means. The difficulty in identifying its meaning can be attributed not only to its rarity, but also to its association with the theme "love of brother and sister" as the purpose clause in verse 9 indicates (cf. tracing 4, Appendix II). In this section identifying scriptural echoes will shed light on our understanding of the neologism in this text. I argue that Paul's creation of this new term could be traced back to Isaiah 54:13, and perhaps Jeremiah 31:33–34 (38:31–34 [LXX]). A further important consideration is that, as this chapter has kept asserting, scriptural echoes embedded in Paul's neologism θεοδίδακτοί seem to play an indispensable role in his paraenetic discourse.

5.4.1 αὐτοδίδακτος IN THE HELLENISTIC PHILOSOPHICAL TRADITION?

Some scholars attempt to clarify Paul's neologism in light of the Hellenistic philosophers' use of certain words that are compounded with διδακτός. Koester (1979:39) observes that in the light of the term αὐτοδίδακτος (self-taught), Paul's neologism occurs both in the Hellenistic philosophical paraenesis and Philo, and so concludes that both words connote "independence of moral action." Moreover, Malherbe (2000:244) suggests that Paul contrasts God's teaching of love with the Hellenistic philosophers' tradition (especially, Epicureans) of αὐτοδίδακτος (self-taught) by which certain knowledge was acquired through practice or ἀδίδακτοι ("untaught," see LSJ).

---

32. In his saying οὐ χρείαν ἔχετε γράφειν ὑμῖν (literally, "you do not need to write to you"), a rhetorical device, *paralipsis* (*praeteritio*) is employed (Gaventa 1998:56). This rhetorical feature is used when "the orator pretends to pass over something which he in fact mentions" (BDF §495.1).

This notion indicates possession of innate knowledge. Malherbe (1983:253) argues that Paul's employment of θεοδίδακτοί can be "a conscious rejection of something that is αὐτοδίδακτος, self-taught, or ἀδίδακτος, untaught, or of someone who is αὐτουργὸς τῆς φιλοσοφίας, a self-made philosopher." However, Paul never intends the Thessalonians' independence or self-reliance to be the focus; rather, he emphasizes his own involvement in their lives as an instructor (2:13; 4:1–2; cf. Witmer 2006:241). There is no clue in his exhortation for the antithetical relation between "God's teaching" and "self-teaching" being implied.

Rotzel (1986:328) further develops Koester's understanding of αὐτοδίδακτος, establishing the main background of this neologism from Philo's usage. He remarks that Philo employs the term αὐτοδίδακτος when he lists the persons who do not need a human teacher because they are directly instructed by God (e.g., Adam [*Creation* 148], Melchizedek [*Prelim. Studies* 99], Abraham [*Rewards* 27]; cf. Moses [*Moses* 1 80]). Although Rotzel's argument is well researched with regard to the Hellenistic-Jewish usage of the word, I argue that in addition to Philo's use, a more in-depth comparative study should be undertaken in order to determine if there are other occurrences in other Hellenistic Jewish circles. To substantiate his contention, Rotzel needs to further investigate the word's relevance to Paul's neologism. It is still an open question as to why Paul did not adopt the same term that Philo had used?

5.4.2 θεοδίδακτοί ECHOING BROTHERLY LOVE IN THE DIOSCURI CULT?

Kloppenborg (1993:265–89) takes a step further in the scholarly discussion of Paul's coinage of this new term in 4:9. He utilizes both rhetorical and social-historical approaches to clarify its meaning. In the light of the fact that the rhetoricians of Paul's time were careful about coining words (e.g., Quintilian, *Inst.* 8.3.30–37), Kloppenborg (1993:282) suggests that Paul's neologism in 4:9 is "given the degree of rhetorical self-consciousness present in chaps. 1–2." In refuting the suggestions of Koester and Malherbe, he provides another explanation based on "the actual shape of Paul's rhetoric." According to Kloppenborg (1993:282–3), the implication of Paul's neologism θεοδίδακτος could be clarified by its connection with the term φιλαδελφία. For Kloppenborg, the audience was familiar with the brotherly love of the twin gods, the Dioscuri (i.e., Castor and Polydeuces). Kloppenborg (1993:284) presents significant evidence that ancient people around the first-century Mediterranean world recognized that the twins were represented as "examples of self-sacrifice and in particular as paradigms of those who share tears and pain and who reject insinuations and calumnies." In this sense he (1993:287) concludes that Paul aimed to advance the community's solidarity and sacrificial sharing by reminding them of the examples of Dioscuri. However, his argument is open to some criticism. First, even if the cult of the Dioscuri had been well known to the Thessalonian audience, it does not make sense that Paul exhorted the audience to take the pagan gods' brotherly love as a moral example (Witmer 2006:240; Weima 2014:287). Kloppenborg comments (1993:288) that Paul's neologism, rather than citing διδακτοὺς θεοῦ in Isa 54:13, is "a measured rhetorical strategy" to prevent the audience from being confused by Paul's statement about θεός in 1 Thessalonians. But in my view it is questionable that the widespread notion of the example of the Dioscuri per se can be a potential reason for establishing the background of 4:9. Is there any other plausible source (e.g., the Hebrew Scriptures) that may include a combined notion of divine instruction and the community members' sacrificial love of one another? Second, Paul did not need to provide a specific model of loving one another, since elsewhere he mentions that the Thessalonian believers had already practiced the "labor of love" (cf. 1:2; 4:10).

5.4.3 θεοδίδακτοί AS PAUL'S NEWLY COINED TERM FROM THE LXX

As a significant alternative view, I wish to posit that the arguments of Witmer (2006:245–9; see also Weima 2007:249) are credible and helpful in understanding Paul's recasting of the phrase διδακτοὺς θεοῦ. Gaventa (1998:57; cf. Kloppenborg 1993:278) does not give much credit to scriptural echoes in this text because of the differences between the LXX and Paul's neologism. However, Witmer (2006:245–9) notices that Paul's neologism θεοδίδακτοί indeed reflects the pattern of the LXX translation of the Masoretic Text. Witmer's argument is based on Emanuel Tov's analysis, which showed that two or three Hebrew words tend to be translated into one Greek compound word in the LXX (2006:248; see Tov 1977:189–212). Witmer confirms that the phrase לִמּוּדֵי יְהוָה, in Isaiah 54:13 can be translated θεοδίδακτοί. He further states that:

> There are significant similarities between Paul's word-creation and the translation patterns discussed in Tov's article. The Hebrew of Isa 54.13 contains two words (adjective and noun) closely linked in the construct state, thus making it a prime candidate for translation with a compound word ... Paul might

naturally have used the 'reverse and combine' pattern of word creation so frequently noted in the LXX itself.

If Paul's neologism is equivalent to the phrase לִמּוּדֵי יְהוָה in Isa 54:13, Paul here echoes the prophet's anticipation of a time when God's covenant people "will no longer need to be taught by human intermediaries but will instead be 'taught of God'" (Weima 2014:288).[33]

Not only that, but the thematic echo of Jer 31:33–34 (38:31–34 [LXX]) permeates 1 Thess 4:9 in the sense that the internalization of God's teaching is fulfilled through the gift of the Spirit in the heart of God's people (see 5.4.1).[34] Specifically, the Thessalonian believers' love for their brothers and sisters could be equivalent to God's internalization of the law (especially, Lev 19:18, "you shall love your neighbor as yourself") in their hearts as the new covenantal people. God's teaching of the love of brothers and sisters in Christ is an unprecedented concept. The term φιλαδελφία, which is used only for brothers and sisters who share the same biological origin, is now applicable to non-familial relationships amongst the Thessalonian believers (see also Rom 12:10; Heb 13:1; 1 Pet 1:22; 2 Pet 1:7).[35] Being taught by God to love those unrelated to one as a family suggests that the eschatological dimension of the divine teaching envisaged by the prophets has been realized

---

33. For the notion that God's teaching is an eschatological blessing in the OT, see also Isa 2:2–4, Mic 4:1–3, and *Ps. Sol* 17:32 (Weima 2007:879). Cf. John 6:45. The apostle, John quotes Isa 54:13: "ἔστιν γεγραμμένον ἐν τοῖς προφήταις· καὶ ἔσονται πάντες διδακτοὶ θεοῦ· πᾶς ὁ ἀκούσας παρὰ τοῦ πατρὸς καὶ μαθὼν ἔρχεται πρὸς ἐμέ" (John 6:45; italics and emphasis are mine).

34. Although there is no specific connection between giving the Holy Spirit to the believers and God's teachings of brotherly/sisterly love, one can regard the notion of the "inward and transformative work" in 1 Thess 4:8 as being continuously implied inasmuch as the Spirit inwardly teaches them to practice brotherly/sisterly love (Gupta 2016:85; see also Hendriksen 1955:103; Calvin 1960:361; Marshall 1983:115; cf. Weima 2014:289).

35. Plutarch's use of the term φιλαδελφία informs a widespread ancient notion of brotherly/sisterly love. As he begins *On Brotherly Love (De Fraterno Amore)*, Plutarch refers to this term in the context of considering the crisis of fraternal relationships in his day (Plutarch, *Frat. amor.* 478 C) by explaining that "[b]rotherly love is as rare in our day as brotherly hatred was among the men of old." He conveys that brotherly/sisterly love is superior to any kind of love, appealing to the same biological origin (Burke 2003:99) in saying that "[f]or most friendships are in reality shadows and imitations and images of that first friendship which nature implanted in children toward parents and in brothers toward brothers" (Plutarch, *Frat. amor.* 479 C–D). Moreover, he mentions his brother, Timon, whose fraternal love is described as having "always transcended and still transcends all the rest" (487E). The paradigm of brotherly/sisterly in the Hellenistic world might have brought into Paul's mind that the view the Thessalonians' fellow Christians should practice brotherly/sisterly love for "collaboration, solidarity, and harmony or concord" (Green 2002:204).

among the new converts (cf. Boring 2015:151). Moreover, practicing "love of brother and sister" and regarding one another as God's family in Christ is the essential mark of God's eschatological people (cf. Weima 2014:289). Paul does not need to instruct the Thessalonian believers about brotherly/sisterly love since they had already "experienced an inward, divine compulsion to love one another" and were practicing God's teaching to the believers in the region of Macedonia (Marshall 1983:115).

Noticeably, Witmer (2006:249) remarks that in the process of shaping Christian identity, Paul used the neologism in an attempt to shape Christian identity of the early Christian community:

> Paul's neologism in 4.9 may be part of his larger epistolary strategy of strengthening the identity and cohesiveness of the Thessalonian community . . . Paul's neologism provided a unique descriptor for the Thessalonian Christians as those who were receiving the fulfilment of the eschatology prophecy.

5.4.4 φιλαδελφία AND RESPECT FOR NON-BELIEVERS

Paul does not have to write about the subject of "brotherly/sisterly love" since the Thessalonian believers have been taught by God, loved one another in accordance with God's teaching, and even extended their love towards neighboring believers in Macedonia. The logic of Paul's argument becomes clearer as he begins his exhortation with δέ in verse 10b (see tracing 4, Appendix II). Paul probably has in mind that φιλαδελφία entails respect for non-believers (outsiders), as the resultative clause (ἵνα . . .) in verse 12 indicates in saying "so that you may walk properly before outsiders."

In verse 10b the conjunction δέ can be regarded as adversative (Malherbe 2000:245). However, it signals Paul's diplomatic (rhetorical) strategy to supplement something that the Thessalonians' practice of love in relation to both insiders and outsiders seems to have lacked. The conjunction functions to draw the audience's attention to a new set of exhortations (introduced by the consecutive infinitives in v. 11) so as to intensify the previous exhortations (e.g., to sanctification [4:1] and to brotherly/sisterly love [4:10b]). In shaping Christian identity and enhancing the Thessalonians' moral attitudes, Paul did not intend for this new group of converts to be characterized as being a community totally segregated from their fellow citizens. They were branded as a subversive group against the Roman Empire and no longer wanting anything to do with their local associations and pagan cults. In this respect, Paul expected his audience to maintain a low profile in their city (Weima 2014:295; Boring 2015:153).

Paul's exhortations to brotherly/sisterly love are concretely expressed through the consecutive infinitive constructions (φιλοτιμεῖσθαι ἡσυχάζειν, πράσσειν τὰ ἴδια, ἐργάζεσθαι ταῖς [ἰδίαις] χερσὶν ὑμῶν). The term φιλοτιμέομαι originally meant "to love or seek after honor" (LSJ). Malherbe (2000:246) suggests that this term can most likely be understood based on its usage in the Hellenistic world. This verb implies a negative ambition for reputation, success in political life, involvement in public affairs (e.g., Philo, *Rewards* 11), but it also more generally means to "*strive eagerly to* do a thing" in a positive sense during that period (e.g., Plato, *Phaedr.* 231a in LSJ, φιλοτιμέομαι). Here, a controversial issue arises as to whether the infinitive φιλοτιμεῖσθαι can be linked with the first or with the first and second or with all three infinitives (Weima 2014:291). I argue that these three infinitives cannot be understood separately, since they express some progression with regard to the idea (Malherbe 2000:246). Thus, I regard the infinitive φιλοτιμεῖσθαι takes all three infinitives (ἡσυχάζειν, πράσσειν, and ἐργάζεσθαι) as its objects (Malherbe 2000:246; Green 2002:209-12; Shogren 2012:170-1).

The notion of "living quietly" (ἡσυχάζειν)[36] and "minding your own affairs" (πράσσειν τὰ ἴδια) as stated by Paul can be clarified in the light of the often-used combination of these two words and phrases in some ancient documents (Malherbe 2000:248-9; Green 2002:210; Weima 2014:296; e.g., Plato, *Rep.* 4.441D-E; 6.496D; Dio Cassius 60.27.4; Plutarch, *Mor.* 798E-F).[37] According to Malherbe (2000:247), Paul employs the Hellenistic rhetorical device *oxymoron*.[38] This rhetorical device expresses an idea that seems to be self-contradictory, but it paradoxically evokes a rhetorical effect. The combination of these two terms occurs in the context of the exhortation to refrain from a public activity in order to avoid creating trouble in relationships with non-believers. For those who are socially marginalized, the most efficient means of demonstrating an exemplary attitude is working hard and living quietly (Witherington III 2006:124).

In addition, Paul reminds his audience that they should work with their own hands, as he referred to the Thessalonians' "labor of love" in 1 Thess 1:3. Chances are that two hypotheses can be identified as the potential

---

36. I suggest that the expression "living quietly" in this verse does not mean merely "be quiet" in a literal sense (cf. Luke 14:4), but is the antithetical concept to that of busybody activities characterized by meddling in the affairs of other (Philo, *Abraham* 20, cited in Weima 2014:293).

37. Plato particularly illustrates the attitude of the philosopher: "ἡσυχίαν ἔχων καὶ τὰ αὑτοῦ πράττων." He views "remaining quietly" and "minding one's own affairs" as justice.

38. Lausberg ([1960] 1998:§807) defines this figure of speech as "the closely tightened syntactic linking of contradictory terms into a unity which, as a result, acquires a strong contradictive tension."

foundation of Paul's exhortation, "work with your hands." First, misunderstanding of the imminence of parousia seemed to lead some converts to take extreme decisions such as quitting their jobs (Best 1986a:175; Bruce 1982:91; Jewett 1986:172–5; Gaventa 1998:59). As a result, their ignoring of the life on this earth led them to become idlers (τοὺς ἀτάκτους) who took advantage of other members of their community (1 Thess 5:14; cf. 2 Thess 3:6–13). Second, scholars who adopt a sociological perspective argue that Paul had in mind the patron-client relationship in the political context of his day (Green 2002:208–13). The clients in a lower social stratum received some benefits from their wealthy patrons from the upper classes and expressed their gratitude toward them through political participation in support of their patrons (e.g., voting for them). Paul urges the urban poor not to depend on such sources of income from their patrons and instead calls them to earn money through manual labor, and this exhortation might have been regarded as extraordinary by the Thessalonians (Green 2002:211).

Even if these hypotheses fit the historical context of Paul's exhortation, one must be careful not to rely too exclusively on them, since there are not many evidential clues to substantiate them (Weima 2014:295). The point here is that brotherly/sisterly love is concretely demonstrated by the community's taking responsibility for and mutually supporting one another. Significantly, this exhortation can be attributed to the fact that manual labor and loving one's neighbors were not separated in the Jewish tradition. Thompson (2011:83) suggests *The Testament of Issachar* 5:2–3 as significant evidence of the interrelatedness between labor and love: "Love the Lord and your neighbor; be compassionate toward poverty and sickness. Bend your back in farming, perform the tasks of the soil in every kind of agriculture, offering gifts gratefully to the Lord."[39] For the Thessalonians, the loss of identity in their society might have been accompanied by economic hardships because of the alienation from their associations and society. In the midst of this suffering the believers were encouraged not to take advantage of other's profits. Rather, Paul's exhortation was supposed to lead them not only to "walk properly before outsiders" but also to pursue self-sufficiency through their manual labor (see tracing 4, Appendix II). In so doing, the community's solidarity would be strengthened through affirming mutual responsibility. At the same time, he encouraged the Thessalonians not to lose their minds even in the midst of suffering but rather to be models that the society could imitate in the practice of love and labor. Therefore, their behavior would be approved by non-believers, since even though the

---

39. See *Old Testament Pseudepigrapha* volume I (Charlesworth [1983] 2011:803–4).

Thessalonians were alienated from their society, they did not neglect the values that the society esteemed highly (cf. Thompson 2011:83).

5.5 DISCURSIVE FUNCTION OF "THE DAY OF THE LORD" IN 1 THESS 5:1-11

I contend that Paul's focus on the implication of the imminent coming of the day of the Lord, for both outsiders and insiders, characterizes his exhortation as a climactic attempt to shape both the identity and morality of the new converts. Similar to the περὶ δέ construction that introduces a new theme as in 4:9, Paul's employing the signal phrase in 5:1 indicates that he moved from the issue of believers' participation in parousia (4:13-18) to the new theme of χρόνος and καιρός.[40] One cannot rule out the possibility that Paul was responding to the Thessalonian community's question about when the parousia would take place. But this pair is a fixed phrase for the time of God's eschatological judgment (Weima 2014:344; e.g., Acts 1:7). The audience's prior knowledge of "the day of the Lord" is affirmed by Paul's use of the adverb ἀκριβῶς (accurately, carefully, well, BDAG) in association with a pronoun αὐτοί.[41]

---

40. With regard to the meaning, the distinction could be made that "χρόνος designates a 'period of time' in a linear sense, while καιρός frequently refers to 'eschatologically filled time, time for decision'" (Baumgarten, EDNT 2:233). Although the individual meaning is maintained, these two words are synonyms, i.e., hendiadys (Hübner, EDNT 3:488; Malherbe 2000:288; Bruce 1982:108-9; Marshall 1983:132; Smith 2000:726; Weima 2014:344). In the NT, while χρόνος indicates a duration of time, it can also have an eschatological sense when its context is related to eschatology and the apocalyptic expectation of Christ's coming (NIDNTTE 4:705-6; Acts 3:21; 1 Pet 1:20). The term καιρός often denotes a specific time of judgment and parousia in the New Testament (Matt 8:29; Mark 13:33; Luke 19:44; Act 3:20; Rom 13:11; 1 Cor 4:5; 1 Tim 6:14-15; 1 Pet 1:5; Rev 1:3; 22:10).

41. Malbon's discourse analysis (1983) provides a paradigmatic (or 'logical') structure for the text in order to answer the question as to why Paul repeats familiar topics to the audience. She (1983:70) proposes that Paul's purpose in 1 Thessalonians is to satisfy their need to know. She explains that "the very writing of Paul's letter to the Thessalonians suggests another need: the need for (subjective) knowing Action, i.e.,, the need to express and strengthen the personal knowing of one another and of God (and the Lord) in action, including the action of letter-writing!" According to Malbon (1983:62-63), 1 Thess 5:2-8 is another assertion of "knowing" as mentioned in 5:1, including metaphorical demonstration or explanation of "knowing" of "the day of the Lord." She rightly notices the inseparable relationship between knowing and action as well as the dynamic correlation between the syntagmatic and paradigmatic dimensions of this letter. Nevertheless, she could have specified a concrete paraenetic purpose for why Paul introduces something that the Thessalonians already knew.

Noticeably, the contrast between outsiders and insiders is a major thrust in this pericope, listed as follows: "the implied subject (they) of λέγωσιν" vs. "brothers and sisters" in verses 3–4; "darkness/night" vs. "day" in verses 4, 7–8; "the children of light/day" vs. "the sons of night/darkness" in verse 5; "others" vs. "the implied subject (we) of γρηγορῶμεν καὶ νήφωμεν" in verse 6; "those who sleep, get drunk" vs. "let us be sober (νήφωμεν)" in verses 7–8; "for wrath (εἰς ὀργὴν)" vs. "for salvation (εἰς περιποίησιν σωτηρίας)" in verse 9 (cf. tracing 5, Appendix II). In this series of antithetical pairs, one should note the discursive function of the repeated opposite fates between outsiders and insiders in 5:1–11. As Wanamaker (2002:140) notes, the reference to the crisis that is attributed to God's imminent judgment aims to enable the new converts to recognize their distinct identity vis-à-vis the society. He contrasts the audience's knowledge about the imminence of the day of judgment to the outsiders' ignorance and their reliance on false security. Paul integrates the imagery of a destructive and negative image of the day of the Lord into his paraenesis to reverse it in a positive direction; for the insiders the day of the Lord is not a disaster (Luckensmeyer 2009: 299). As DeSilva (1996:66–67) views the concept, the deliberate contrasts between outsiders and insiders not only reinforce the group boundaries and distinct identity, but also clarify their opposite fates at the eschaton.

Contrasting the fate of outsiders and insiders based on apocalyptic dualism discursively functions to build up the fledging community as is evident from the words (see 1.3.3; 3.1): "[T]herefore, encourage one another and build one another up" (5:11). Meeks (1993:180) provides a good illustration of what Paul's appropriation of the apocalyptic dualism aims at. He argues that "[t]he apocalyptic language of separation, of the moral opposition between the children of light and the children of darkness, is here pressed into an assurance of the ultimate unity of those who are 'in Christ.'" This logical consequence is substantiated by Paul's use of the inferential conjunction διό in 5:11, which plays a role as the logical link to the previous statements (cf. tracing 5, Appendix II).[42] Moreover, Pauline usage of the term οἰκοδομέω includes two aspects of the apostle's ministry with regard to specific apostolic activity for the sake of community formation (2 Cor 10:8; 12:19; 13:10) and spiritual growth (Michel, TDNT 5:140–1). Paul perceives his calling for the formation of the community's identity and morality to be in continuity with the prophets' anticipation that God would rebuild/restore Israel (Jer 24:6; 49:10 [LXX]) (Furnish 2007:112; Weima 2014:372). These two aspects cannot be separated inasmuch as Paul was

---

42. Contra Wanamaker (1990:189): "The conjunction διό is inferential, but v. 11 is certainly not a necessary or even obviously logical inference from what immediately precedes it."

directly or indirectly involved in the formation and edification of the Thessalonian community. He ultimately takes on "not only his own apostolic responsibility to build up the church ... but also ... the responsibility of all members of the church to build each other up" (Weima 2014:372).

In the series of the contrasting fates of outsiders and insiders, the thematic echoes of the phrase "the day of the Lord," which often occurs in the Prophets and Minor Prophets, can readily be seen as permeating this pericope (e.g., Isa 13:6; Jer 46:10; Ezek 13:5; 30:3; Joel 1:15; 2:1; Amos 5:18–20; Obad 15; Zeph 1:7, 14; Mal 4:5). Paul's reference to "the day of the Lord" does not merely declare God's judgment upon the outsiders but intentionally reflects Jewish apocalyptic dualism. He appropriates the apocalyptic dualism to describe the contrast between God's ideal world and this world dominated by sins and evil. Paul demonstrates that while God's creation is under the curse of sin, God is sovereign over creation and would break into the history of this age to transform this present reality and order in a moral and physical sense (ISBE Vol. 1:153).

This section suggests the most probable texts that could correspond to Paul's notion of "the day of the Lord" in 1 Thess 5:1–11. In search of echoes in Paul's letter, exploring both the similarities and dissimilarities between some texts may be helpful to estimate the possibility of his echoing Scripture or particular Jewish usage. I will argue that Paul's reference to the "day of the Lord" most likely echoes Amos 5:18–20.[43] The contrast darkness (σκότος) versus light (φῶς), in association with the expression the "day of

---

43. Luckensmeyer (2012:99) also finds thematic echoes of Obadiah in Paul's employment of the notion of "the day of the Lord" in 1 Thess 5. He accepts Aichele, Miscall, and Walsh's presupposition that the readers play a significant role in making connections between the texts: "Meaning is not located in the single text, planted there perhaps by an originating author, but instead meaning is only found between texts, as they are brought together in the insight (and corresponding blindness) of their various readers" (2009:399). He demonstrates abundant verbal and thematic similarities. For instance, the term ὄλεθρος (destruction) in 1 Thess 5:4 is verbally related to the various similar descriptions of the day of the Lord (ἀπόλλυμι in Obad 8; ἀπώλεια [ruin] in vv. 12–13; πτοέομαι [terrified] in v. 9; ἐξαίρω [remove] in vv. 9–10; αἰχμαλωτεύω [take captive] in v. 11). He suggests more probable verbal parallels (e.g., coming of thieves at night, κλέπται in Obad 5; 1 Thess 5:2, 4; νυκτός in Obad 5; 1 Thess 5:2, 5, 7). Nevertheless, the occurrences of similar ideas are not a guarantee of the certainty of verbal parallels. The metaphor of thieves in Obadiah is different from Paul's usage in 1 Thess 5, since the former is related to the idea that "thieves can only take what they can carry away" (Stuart 2002:417) and the latter indicates the suddenness and unexpectedness of thieves' coming. But his proposal of thematic similarities between Obadiah and 1 Thess is still convincing (e.g., inescapable and inevitable affliction on the day of the Lord in Obad 14–15 and 1 Thess 5:3; drunkenness in Obad 16 and 1 Thess 5:7; opposite fates of insiders and outsiders in Obad 7, 15, 17, 18, 20, 21 and 1 Thess 5:4–8, 9; the paradigmatic language of "separation" from outsiders in Obad 16, 17, 18, 20 and 1 Thess 2:10; 3:13; 4:3, 4, 7; 5:23).

the Lord," is found in a remarkably analogous way in both 1 Thess 5:5 and Amos 5:18-20. It seems necessary to discuss Hebrew notions of "darkness" and "light" in order to understand Paul's use of the "day of the Lord" in verse 5: "For you are all children of light, children of the day. We are not of the night or of the darkness."

In addition, it is possible that Paul appropriates the contrasting notion of light/darkness from the Dead Sea Scrolls as distinction between outsiders and insiders. Below I will discuss the antithetical pairs (particularly, "children of light" vs. "children of darkness") in 1 Thess 5:1-11 to indicate that they are the reflection of *cosmological, eschatological,* and *ethical* dualisms. In so doing, I will attempt to figure out the discursive function of these echoes in 5:1-11.

5.5.1 IDENTITY OF OUTSIDERS AND THEIR FATE ON THE DAY OF THE LORD

Paul describes the coming of the Lord in association with his shaping of the identity-awareness and ethos of the Thessalonian community, since this eschatology as the future event "serves to call the Thessalonians to a holy lifestyle in the present" (De Villiers 2011:305). His response is more than replying to the enquiry about the "times and seasons."

Essentially, the day of the Lord in the Hebrew Scriptures is frequently mentioned in a negative sense, being identified with God's fierce judgment upon the disobedient (e.g., Isa 13:6-22; Lam 2:22; Joel 2:1-11; 3:14-21; Zeph 2:2-3). Here Paul's referring to "the day of the Lord" (יום יהוה) is the earliest occurrence in the Pauline letters. In other letters Paul interchangeably uses this eschatological expression with "the day of our Lord Jesus" (1 Cor 1:8; 2 Cor 1:14), "the day of Jesus Christ" (Phil 1:6), "the day of Christ" (Phil 1:10; 2:16). In regarding παρουσία (1 Thess 2:19, 3:13, 4:15, and 5:23) as the coming of "the day of the Lord" Paul echoes the prophets' envisaging that God's wrath would fall on the wicked. He (re)interprets the Day of YHWH as the time of God's eschatological salvation accomplished through Christ's second coming (Fee 2007:46-47; cf. Shogren 2012:202). In so doing, Paul's echo of "the day of the Lord" noticeably represents its ambivalent characteristics: *a positive event for the believers* and *a negative event for non-believers.*

A distinct feature in 1 Thess 5:2 is that Paul's use of this scriptural notion occurs in association with the imagery of a thief. The thief imagery also occurs in LXX (Job 24:14; Jer 2:26; 30:4; Joel 2:9), but it never occurs in conjunction with the concept of "the day of the Lord." Some scholars argue that the combination of these two concepts in other New Testament texts (2

Pet 3:10; Rev 3:3; 16:15) might have originated from Jesus' teaching (Matt 24:42–44; Luke 12:39–40).⁴⁴ In this context, the primary focus should be on how this imagery functions within the specific situation of the sudden and unexpected eschatological destruction of non-believers (1 Thess 5:3). In verse 3 the comparative particle ὡς combined with οὕτως highlights the *vulnerability* of the non-believers/outsiders as the Day of Judgment ineluctably comes. In the ὡς . . . οὕτως construction of verse 2, Paul does not use the future tense of ἔρχομαι. Scholars agree that Paul's employing the present tense denotes the certainty of the coming of ἡμέρα κυρίου (Eadie 1877:176; Lünemann 1880:146; Malherbe 2000:290; Weima 2014:346). Paul compares the essential feature of the day with a thief's unexpected invasion in the night. In addition, the ὡς . . . οὕτως construction functions to enhance the irony: "what you accurately know is that you cannot know what you seek to know" (Malherbe 2000:290).

In noting the features of the day's coming, Paul relates that the outsiders who pursued "peace and security" would nevertheless inevitably be led to confront a devastating fate, accompanying birth pains, through God's judgment. In the ὅταν . . . τότε construction, the present subjunctive of λέγω with the temporal particle ὅταν presents iterative and indefinite action; at the same time it can be contemporaneous with the verb in the main clause (MHT 3:112; BDAG, ὅταν §1; Best 1986a:207). But, specifically, the present verb ἐφίσταται with the correlative particle τότε introduces the subsequent devastating event (see tracing 5, Appendix II). This verb not merely communicates a "customary or gnomic present" but indicates "a somewhat broader time frame," implying the progression of the present time towards the future event (Wallace 1996:518–19; BDAG, ἐφίστημι §2; cf. Luckensmeyer 2009:279).⁴⁵ Paul demonstrates that the outsiders' satisfaction with their political status quo of "peace and security" would be abruptly and unexpectedly disrupted, since sudden destruction through the Lord's coming would befall them.⁴⁶ The ὥσπερ clause in verse 3 elaborates

---

44. Tuckett (1990:168–76) finds the parallels between 1 Thess 5 and Synoptic traditions: 1 Thess 5:1 (Matt 24:36), 5:2 (Matt 24:43–44; Luke 12:39–40), 5:3a (cf. Matt 24:37–39; Luke 17:26–30), 5:3b (Luke 21:34–36), 5: 5–6 (cf. Matt 24:42; Mark 13:34–36; Luke 12:36–38), and 5:6–7 (cf. Matt 24:45–51; Luke 12:42–46; Luke 21:34).

45. If NA28's view of the textual variations is right, v. 3, which has no conjunction (i.e., *asyndeton*), can be structurally connected either to the previous and the subsequent verse. On the one hand, in the connection to v. 2, v. 3 amplifies Paul's previous statement that the day of the Lord will come unexpectedly like a thief in the night; on the other hand, in the connection to the next verse (5:4), Paul makes a contrast between the fates of unbelievers and believers (Sterner 1998:117; Weima 2014:347–8).

46. The term, ὄλεθρος in LXX is used to indicate eschatological destruction (Jer 31:3; Wis 1:12; 4 Macc 10: 15; cf. J. Schneider, TDNT 5:169).

what the sudden destruction would be like. Gempf (1994:119–35) provides a well-researched conclusion that the metaphor of birth pain(s) denotes "productive," "intense," "helpless" and "cyclical" pains. But even if his suggestions are plausible, ὠδίν most likely indicates a sudden and inevitable agony in one's childbirth (NIDNTTE 4:740).⁴⁷ Certainly, the successive ideas in verses 2–3 (e.g., "the day of the Lord will come like a thief in the night" and "sudden destruction" and "they will not escape") emphasize the "certainty," "unexpectedness" or "unpredictability," and "inevitability" of the divine judgment upon non-believers (Best 1986a:203; Weima 2014:352).⁴⁸

Concretely, Paul points out the fragility and insecurity of Roman imperial propaganda by envisaging the failure and futility of the slogan about "peace and security" when the day of the Lord comes. Here he warns against those who rely on the political power of Rome (Oakes 2005:317–18; Furnish 2007:108; Weima 2014:351; see 3.2.2.3). Recent scholars have increasingly noted that Paul cites the Roman imperial propaganda that was used for consolidating the *Pax Romana* (Wengst 1987:19–21; Still 1999:262–6; Green 2002:233–4; Witherington III 2006:147; Furnish 2007:108; Weima 2012:331–3; 2014:349–50). Traditionally, scholars have argued that the phrase "peace and security" alludes to the prophetic condemnation of false visions of peace (see Beale 2003:142–3; Fee 2009:189). However, the words "peace and security" never occur together in the Prophets (see Jer 6:14; 8:11; Ezek 13:10, 16). Hendrix (1991:111), moreover, notes the nuance of the discourse formula ὅταν . . . τότε in 1 Thess 5:3; it temporally and causally links the declaration of "peace and security" and the destruction of those who involved in that slogan. He maintains that the formula denotes a specific temporal and causal event that was expected to destroy Rome's false promise of peace and security. Hence, he concludes that "Such specificity seems to engender more precision than a prediction of judgment directed generally against all non-Christians on prophetic analogy with 'the nations' (Isa 13:8) or a recalcitrant Israel (Jer 6:24; Hos 13:13)." Moreover, many scholars regard the combination of these two terms as Roman imperial propaganda and offer various forms of evidence. Hendrix (1991:113) offers the

---

47. The term ὠδίν might correspond to the Hebrew words חִיל (Exod 15:14; Deut 2:25) or חֵבֶל (Isa 13:8; Jer 13:21).

48. Here Paul does not have in mind that God discarded the non-believers, excluding the opportunity for evangelism. Barclay (1993:518) argues that this apocalyptic dualism does not exclude the potential conversion of those who are regarded as "children of darkness" in the future. Rather, he mentions that the function of the dualistic view is to "establish clear boundaries and mark outsiders as alien unless, and until, they come 'inside.'"

argument that before Augustus ruled, the Greeks applauded Roman peace and security:

> The decree of those of Pergamus: "When Cratippus was prytanis, on the first day of the month Desius, the decree of the praetors was this: Since the Romans, following the conduct of their ancestors, undertake dangers for the common *safety* of all mankind, and are ambitious to settle their confederates and friends in happiness, and in firm *peace*, and since the nation of the Jews, and their high priest Hyrcanus, sent as ambassadors to them" (Josephus, *Ant*. 14. 10. 22; italics mine).

Furthermore, it is remarkable that some monuments contain exactly the same phrase, "peace and security," which occurs in 1 Thess 5:3. First, an inscription on the monument was discovered in Ilium, which was the ancient city of Troy. It shows that the citizens expressed their appreciation to Pompey, since his protection of them from the danger of wars and freebooters restored peace and security: "ἀποκαθεστάκοτα δὲ *[τὴν εἰρ]ήνην καὶ τὴν ἀσφάλειαν καὶ κατὰ γῆν καὶ κατὰ θάλασσαν*" (SEG XLVI 1565 cited in Weima 2012:341-2; italics added). Second, the local senate and the citizens erected twin altars of Securitas and Pax in Praeneste (modern Palestrina in Italy) to give thanks to Augustus for the peace and security following their civil war (Zanker 1990:307; Weima 2012:345-6).

However, some scholars argue that the word pair "peace" and "security" does not necessarily imply Roman imperial propaganda. White (2013:382-95) raised a question as to whether "peace" and "security" carry the same connotation. He (2013:393-5) argues that the ideology of *securitas* was introduced in the later period of Nero's rule since Roman upper classes were vulnerable to insecurity. According to him, this ideology seems to have been prevalent at least 15 years after Paul wrote 1 Thessalonians. The common occurrence of the phrase "peace and security" in the above-mentioned resources cannot be regarded as proof for the existence of Roman imperial propaganda in Paul's day (White 2013:394; Boring 2015:180).

Contrary to this, Tellbe (2001:125) argues that the prophetic witness from the Hebrew Scriptures and Roman monumental inscriptions should not necessarily be regarded as incompatible. According to him, the phrase "peace and security" in 5:3 should be understood against the background of both the Hebrew Scriptures and Roman political propaganda. He regards this reference as Paul's adaptation of the prophecies in Jer 6:14 and Ezek 13:10 "*that aim[s] to call into question the idea of* pax et securitas *in imperial propaganda.*" However, in terms of the plausibility of the double connotation, Tellbe's argument suffers from a lack of evidence.

Even if one accepts that Paul was aware of Roman political propaganda, it is difficult to identify what the concepts "peace and security" exactly referred to. First Thessalonians only alludes to this slogan once. Paul's discourse cannot merely be located in "anti-Roman polemic" (Boring 2015:180). Boring (2015:180) argues that Paul's use of the phrase "peace and security" indicates a "common mind-set in Thessalonica," which was probably related to the benefits of Roman rulership during the decades after the civil war of 42 BCE. Paul might have warned those who found comfort in the peace and safety brought about by Rome as social-political salvation (cf. Tellbe 2001:125).

Then, to whom does the saying "peace and security" apply? According to Green (2002:232), "[t]he implied subject of the declaration that there is *peace and safety* is the unconverted who persecute the Thessalonians (2:14)." There is little reason to regard those who trust Roman "peace and security" as believers, since Paul continues to contrast the fate of outsiders and insiders in the context (cf. Horrell 2005:135; Witherington III 2006:148; Kucicki 2014:178). By referring to those non-believing opponents' false peace and safety, he argues that they will not escape from future destruction and God's wrath.

5.5.2 THESSALONIAN CHRISTIANS AS CHILDREN OF THE LIGHT/DAY

Paul begins to describe the opposite destiny of God's elect to that of the outsiders. In the beginning of verse 4 the adversative δέ functions to categorize their consequential fates into two opposite realms (i.e., darkness and light/day). The third person in the previous verse changed into the second personal pronoun ὑμεῖς with the vocative ἀδελφοί. The emphatic pronoun ὑμεῖς signals the transition of the author's focus from the negative description of those who promote the false vision of "peace and security" to the positive illustration of believers' ontological realm (cf. Boring 2015:181). Paul explains that the Thessalonian believers are not in darkness so that the day of the Lord would not surprise them just as a thief in the night; thus they do not need to fear divine judgment (see BDAG, ἵνα §3; Wallace 1996:473).[49] In so doing, a discursive goal of this contrast is not only to affirm the community's belief by locating them in the realm of light/

---

49. Most commentators argue that the ἵνα clause in 5:4 should be understood in a resultative sense, understanding that the negation particle, οὐκ in 4a, also governs the ἵνα clause in 4b (BDF § 391[5]; Bruce 1982:110; Wanamaker 1991:181; Sterner 1998:120; Weima 2014:355; cf. Zerwick 1963:122).

day but also to consolidate their newly established identity and community solidarity. According to Wanamaker (1990:181; cf. Meeks 1983a:94-96), these antithetical pairs are a reflection of apocalyptic dualism: they "serve to divide humanity and even the cosmos itself into simplistic categories. At the same time, they strengthen group identity and the group boundaries of those who employ the antitheses to create their own positive self-image." Meeks (1993:180) also understands that the function of this dualism is to maintain unity in the community: "The apocalyptic language of separation, of the moral opposition between the children of light and the children of darkness, is here pressed into an assurance of the ultimate unity of those who are 'in Christ.'"[50] In summary, for Paul, this apocalyptic dualism, with a modification based on his own Christological view, is a significant concept to reassure them of their genuine identity and belonging (Malherbe 2000:293).

With regard to the implied meaning of these pairs, scholars understand that Paul's figurative use of light/day and darkness/night indicates the dualism of the *human condition*, particularly widespread in ancient Israel's belief system and Second Temple Judaism (Malherbe 2000:293; Weima 2014:354). "Darkness" can connote an unrighteous deed in view of the antithetical idea of "light," which is connected to righteous behavior in a moral sense (Bruce 1982:111; Marshall 1983:135).[51] More specifically, Wanamaker (1990:181) regards the metaphor of darkness as possibly having two meanings: (1) the *status* of being distant from and rejecting God; (2) *ignorance* of the imminence of the day of the Lord. Sterner (1998:119) contends that the phrase "in darkness" should be interpreted in the light of Rom 2:19 as the manifestation of those who are in spiritual ignorance. In fact, because of the fluid nature of the term "darkness" (and its antithetical concept "light"), one cannot easily decide what Paul intends here in mentioning the antithetical pairs, even if one surveys the various range of their meaning.[52] Unfortu-

---

50. The juxtaposition of "light" and "darkness" also occurs elsewhere in the Pauline letters (Rom 13:12; 2 Cor 6:14; Eph 5:8).

51. But in the NT the notion of being in the darkness does not merely indicate the status of transgressor; rather, it often denotes the totality of the unrepentant person who abides in the dominion of sin (John 3:19; Rom 13:12; 2 Cor 6:14; Eph 5:11 cited in Green 2002:235).

52. In the LXX "darkness" has various ranges of meanings, including human situation (Jer 13:16), blindness (Deut 28:29; Isa 42:7; Tob 5:10), sorrow (Lam 5:17), disaster (Ps 69:23), captivity (Ps 107:10), evil (Ps 44:19; Job 19:8; 22:11; 30:26), wickedness (Ps 11:2; 74:20; 82:5), and death (Job 10:20-22) (Conzelmann, TDNT 7:428). On the other hand, "light" connotes YHWH's divine nature/attribute (Dan 2:22; Isa 60:19-20) and theophany (Exod 13:21-22). Only YHWH is the source of light (Ps 4:6; 44:3; 89:15). A notable usage is that "light" represents YHWH's deliverance/salvation (Ps 27:1).

nately, most of these scholars seem to neglect the point that this metaphor is used in association with the preposition ἐν, thereby having a *locative sense*. As Gaventa (1998:71) remarks, "the darkness of night as the realm in which a thief operates has become the realm of darkness that stands over against God's realm and God's rule." The antithesis between light and darkness emphasizes two different ontological realms, according to one's belief and status (Shogren 2012:205–6). Paul's employing the antithetical pairs reflects a correlation between light and salvation in some texts. In Isa 60: 1 the prophet declares, "[a]rise, shine, for your light has come, and the glory of the Lord has risen upon you. For behold, darkness shall cover the earth, and thick darkness the peoples." Having entered into the realm of salvation, believers are guided on their path of life by the light of YHWH's word (Ps 119:105). In addition, Isa 9:2 describes the characteristics of the life of God's chosen people: "[t]he people who walked in darkness have seen a great light; those who dwelt in a land of deep darkness, on them has light shone."

The expressions, "the children of light/the day" and "the children of night/darkness" in the next verse can shed light in more concrete terms on how the terms, darkness and light/day are used figuratively. The conjunction γάρ in verse 5 elaborates on the previous statement, "you are not in darkness" and specifies the Thessalonians' identity by providing a series of genitive nouns (υἱοὶ φωτός, υἱοὶ ἡμέρας, Οὐκ ἐσμὲν [υἱοὶ] νυκτὸς οὐδὲ [υἱοὶ] σκότους).⁵³ This genitive construction has several implications: one who shares in something, who is worthy of something, who has a relationship with other (BDAG, υἱός §2.c.β). Grammatically, the consecutive genitive nouns can be categorized as descriptive, indicating a certain quality of the community members (e.g., enlightened sons; MHT 3:207–8; Wallace 1996:81; Malherbe 2000:294; Weima 2014:356).⁵⁴ But to appreci-

---

53. Paul himself formulates the expression "children of the day" in this verse. Some scholars argue that the day in the phrase "children of the day" contains an eschatological implication of "the day of the Lord" (Malherbe 2000:294). Bruce (1982:111) argues that "[t]he day had not yet arrived, but believers in Christ were children of the day already, by a form of 'realized eschatology.'" Moreover, Weima (2014:356) understands that the term "day" has double connotations, which are that "day" is not only an interchangeable use of "light" in a metaphorical sense, but also indicates the day of the Lord. But the phrases "children of light" and "children of the day" construct a figurative doublet (Sterner 1998:121). A chiastic structure of 1 Thess 5:5 shows that "light" and "day" can be used synonymously:

A πάντες γὰρ ὑμεῖς υἱοὶ φωτός ἐστε
   B καὶ υἱοὶ ἡμέρας.
   B' Οὐκ ἐσμὲν νυκτὸς
A' οὐδὲ σκότους

54. Many scholars agree that the genitive construction ("sons of") is most likely Semitic rather than typically Greek (Moule 1960:175; MHT 3:207–8; Morris [1984]

ate the discursive function of these metaphors in this pericope, I think that identifying certain qualitative features in a grammatical sense is not sufficient. First, it is crucial to consider another usage of the metaphors "light" and "darkness" in the Hebrew Scriptures, which likely influenced on Paul's use of these metaphors. Second, it is noteworthy to recognize that the usage of "children of light" and "children of darkness" in specific Dead Sea Scrolls play a significant role in enhancing our understanding of the metaphors of "darkness" and "light."

5.5.2.1 AMOS 5:18-20 ECHOED IN 1 THESS 5:4-5?

Paul's use of this antithetical pair in 1 Thess 5:4-5 can be further clarified by a specific notion of "darkness" in the Hebrew Scriptures. This metaphor often denotes God's ultimate destruction of those who are ungodly and disobedient (Joel 2:2, 10; Amos 8:9), while "light" connotes God's theophany and the coming of salvation. Unfortunately, many commentators have neglected the similarities between Amos 5:18-20 and 1 Thess 5: 5-6, merely putting the former into the category of texts where the notion of divine judgment on that day occurs. However, as I briefly mentioned earlier (see 5.5), chances are that Paul had in mind the usage of this antithetical pair from Amos 5:18-20, since the contrasting ideas between "darkness" (σκότος) and "light" (φῶς) in relation to the day of the Lord appear commonly. The rarity of this combination in Scripture might increase the possibility that Paul had kept Amos 5:18-20 in his mind. In addition, Paul might be acquainted with the trajectory of the development of this concept; it is a good point of departure to take Amos 5:18-20 into account, since the expression יוֹם יהוה is one of the earliest occurrences in the Prophets (Hoffmann 1981:38-39; Andersen & Freedman 1989:521).

I wish to postulate a probable correlation between Amos 5:18-20 and 1 Thess 5:4-5. Paul's statement that "you are not in darkness" in verse 4 means that the sudden and inevitable destruction will never affect the believers. Paul's reference to the two contrasting fates on "the day of the Lord" could be elucidated in the light of Amos' representing the destructive portent of the Day as "darkness." In fact, with regard to the word arrangement, there is no specific match between the texts. But I posit that the metaphors Amos employed are most likely brought into Paul's wording in 1 Thess 5:4-5:

2009:95; Richard [1995] 2007:252; Weima 2014:356).

Amos 5:18–20 (MT)	Amos 5:18–20 (LXX)	1 Thess 5:4–5
הוֹי הַמִּתְאַוִּים אֶת־יוֹם יְהוָה לָמָּה־זֶּה לָכֶם יוֹם יְהוָה הוּא־חֹשֶׁךְ וְלֹא־אוֹר׃ כַּאֲשֶׁר יָנוּס אִישׁ מִפְּנֵי הָאֲרִי וּפְגָעוֹ הַדֹּב וּבָא הַבַּיִת וְסָמַךְ יָדוֹ עַל־הַקִּיר וּנְשָׁכוֹ הַנָּחָשׁ׃ הֲלֹא־חֹשֶׁךְ יוֹם יְהוָה וְלֹא־אוֹר וְאָפֵל וְלֹא־נֹגַהּ לוֹ׃	Οὐαὶ οἱ ἐπιθυμοῦντες τὴν ἡμέραν κυρίου, ἵνα τί αὕτη ὑμῖν ἡ ἡμέρα τοῦ κυρίου; καὶ αὐτή ἐστιν σκότος καὶ οὐ φῶς, ὃν τρόπον ὅταν φύγῃ ἄνθρωπος ἐκ προσώπου τοῦ λέοντος καὶ ἐμπέσῃ αὐτῷ ἡ ἄρκος, καὶ εἰσπηδήσῃ εἰς τὸν οἶκον αὐτοῦ καὶ ἀπερείσηται τὰς χεῖρας αὐτοῦ ἐπὶ τὸν τοῖχον καὶ δάκῃ αὐτὸν ὁ ὄφις. οὐχὶ σκότος ἡ ἡμέρα τοῦ κυρίου καὶ οὐ φῶς; καὶ γνόφος οὐκ ἔχων φέγγος αὐτῇ.	ὑμεῖς δέ, ἀδελφοί, οὐκ ἐστὲ ἐν σκότει, ἵνα ἡ ἡμέρα ὑμᾶς ὡς κλέπτης καταλάβῃ· πάντες γὰρ ὑμεῖς υἱοὶ φωτός ἐστε καὶ υἱοὶ ἡμέρας. Οὐκ ἐσμὲν νυκτὸς οὐδὲ σκότους·

First, the implication of YHWH's theophany in Amos 5:18–20 may have been integrated into Paul's understanding of the *parousia*. Paul reinterprets "the day of the Lord" from a Christ-centered eschatological perspective. Hoffmann (1981:45) argues that "the day of the Lord" was a somewhat ambiguous notion in Amos's time, representing the idea of the appearance of YHWH's power. In fact, some scholars raise the question of whether an eschatological implication may be indicated in this text.[55] However, I contend that "the day of the Lord" most likely indicates YHWH's appearance and epiphany for Israel's salvation. The complementary statement "gloom with no brightness in it" (5:20) provides us with a significant clue to the potential of its eschatological implication. Andersen and Freedman (1989:521) regard the other interchangeable terms אֹפֶל (groom) and נֹגַהּ (brightness) as theophanic language that can be applied to the nature of imminent apocalyptic events (see Ps 17:10 [LXX]; Hab 3:4, 11). They also elucidate that "Amos' interpretation of the 'Day' . . . marks an important moment in the reinterpretation of *Urzeit* terminology for *Endzeit* phenomena." Amos's prophecy most likely indicates the destruction of Israel by an external military attack

---

55. In terms of the implication of "the day of the Lord," it is difficult to identify the historical background of Amos's reference to it. But according to Smith (1998:239–42), the scholarly views are largely divided into five alternatives: (1) the day of cosmic catastrophes in an eschatological sense; (2) the great autumn New Year's festival (the day of YHWH's enthronement as King); (3) a holy war against the enemies; (4) a developed notion of holy war in association with tradition of blessing and curse, revolving around the covenant; and (5) YHWH's theophany.

in a historical sense (i.e., the context of the exile). Nevertheless, a variety of traditions of YHWH's theophany that have to do with "war, blood, cosmic upheaval and judgment of the evil" may have developed extended meanings throughout the historical development of its usages (Hoffman 1981:45).

Intriguingly, Aalen (TDOT 1:165-6) finds that the notion of YHWH's theophany in the Hebrew Scriptures is deeply associated with "the light symbolism of salvation." He remarks that Isa 60:1-3 is a significant case for indicating that the notions of YHWH's glory and the term זָרַח ("dawning or shining") are used together. The combined occurrence can represent the notion that the theophany would lead to the transformation of the old age, characterized by darkness, into the dawning age of deliverance. If Paul introduces the implication of "light" from this tradition and (re)appropriates it based on his Christological belief, he might describe the daylight of YHWH's theophany, which had long been anticipated, as now shining in darkness through the fulfillment of Christ's death and resurrection. With a modified Jewish eschatological perspective through the lens of the Christ event, Paul might render the "light" or "day" metaphor as indicating the believers' ontological reality that now comes to participate in Christ's salvation.

For Paul, furthermore, the salvation could have been illustrated more cosmologically, with the idea of light breaking into the darkness. Beale (2003:146) thinks that Paul's contrast between "light" and "darkness" is intended to describe "the inauguration of the in-breaking latter-day new creation through Christ (Jn 1:1-5) and his followers (Eph 4:22-24; 5:8-13; Col. 1:12-13)." He illustrates that Paul understands Christ is the light of God's creation that breaks into the dark and chaotic world (Gen 1:15) and the light of the eschatological new creation that will shine upon the earth (Is 60:1-3, 19-20). Boring (2015:182) similarly argues that though the present age is characterized by darkness, light is not only dawning in the darkness of this world, but it is also anchored in Christ's parousia.

Second, for both Amos and Paul, the metaphorical usage of "light" and "darkness" commonly represents the opposite fates of those who seek the Lord on that day and those who do not. Admittedly, Amos does not explicitly depict the fates of insiders and outsiders as Paul does in 1 Thess 5:1-11. Essentially, YHWH's theophany is regarded as a negative event for the enemies of Israel, while it is positive for Israel. However, an unexpected reversal of Israel's fate could occur since, from the perspective of Amos, widespread syncretism and Israel's oppression of the marginalized cannot be differentiated from the attitude and behavior of God's enemies (Hoffmann 1981:44). The metaphors of "darkness" and "light" represent the destructive and advantageous aspects of "the day of the Lord" respectively; Israel's fate would be decided according to whether they respond faithfully to YHWH's commandment. This contrast reveals the discrepancy between Amos's understanding of the election tradition and the Israelites' false belief. Israel misunderstood that its election would be eternally guaranteed to all the physical descendants of Abraham. Smith (1991:39) states that "Amos believed that the eternal promises were conditionally available to those who maintained their covenant relationship with God . . . Amos' view is consistent with the nation's covenantal traditions, which his audience has ignored or perverted." The prophet appealed to the election tradition in using the metaphors so as to reveal the Israelites' misconception of their status. Ignorance of social justice and the failure to meet God's requirements would lead some unidentified audiences, who had desired the day of the Lord, to be confronted with severe calamity and destruction. The contrast between insiders and outsiders may be implied in the text, since it is described in the discrepant views between Amos and those who perverted the election tradition, as well as between the two antithetical fates of salvation and destruction.

Third, a series of similes in Amos 5:19 shares the ideas of *inescapability* and *unexpectedness* with the notion of the day of YHWH in 1 Thess 5:2–4. The nature of the day can be compared with an unexpected incident of a man fleeing from a lion only to encounter a bear. In the second simile a man enters his house and leans his hands on the wall with a sense of relief at his safety, but he ends up being bitten by a serpent.[56] These similes illustrate that Israel cannot escape the divine judgment, even if they try to find their own ways to survive. They failed to maintain their identity as God's elect and instead chose disobedience and betrayal. Attempting to flee dangers ultimately proves to be fruitless, and nothing can guarantee safety and security any longer. The unfaithful are exposed to divine wrath and their over-confidence that their peace and safety is guaranteed would be turned into full-scale terror because the day would come as a disaster for them. Similarly, Paul compares "the day of the Lord" to the inescapable nature of birth pains (1 Thess 5:3) as well as to the unexpected coming of a thief at night (5:2, 4). Paul might have brought the critical situation of Israel mentioned in Amos into his paraenetic discourse. His echo functions to remind his audience that the day of the Lord would not surprise the Thessalonian believers, since their status and belonging are grounded in the firm foundation of salvation through Christ.

---

56. Though the definite article ה occurs before the Hebrew words for the animals in Amos 5:19, I translated these terms in an indefinite sense.

5.5.2.2 "THE CHILDREN OF LIGHT" FROM QUMRAN?

In order to further elucidate the implications of Paul's use of these two contrasting metaphors, light/day and night/darkness, in 1 Thess 5:5, one cannot neglect the possibility of echoes from the Qumran literature. Recently there have been discussions on how Qumranian ideas and expressions in 1 Thess may be understood (Luckensmeyer 2009:298; Donfried 2010:509; Kucicki 2014:51–93).[57] In this section I especially devote attention to the dualistic perspective of the Qumran communities to shed light on how Paul analogously appropriates these metaphors into his discourse: "children of light" (בני אור, 1 QS col. 1:9; 2:16; 3:13, 24–25; 1 QM col. 1:1, 3, 9, 11, 13; 8:16; 4Q177 frags. 10—11:7; frags. 12–13. col. 1:7; 4Q280 frag. 2:1; 4Q510 frag. 1:7; 11Q13 col. 2:8); "children of darkness" (בני חושך, 1 QS 1:10; 1 QM 1:1, 7, 10, 16; 3:6, 9; 13:16; 14:17; 16:11).

In fact, the Qumran community leader's understanding of "children of light" is definitely not the same as Paul's. But I consider that in the use of the two contrasting metaphors (light/day and night/darkness in v. 5), there are remarkable similarities between Paul and the Qumran documents. Community members' elected status by God is a major thrust of many of the instructions in both the Qumranian literature and in Paul. Specifically, the Qumran community's instructor encouraged his communities to perceive their own elected status by God. His teaching can be compared with Paul's intention inasmuch as the leader constitutes the community ethos, shaping their identity and morality as God's covenant people. I specifically argue that dualisms referred to in the Qumranian community's identity and ethos formation are beneficial in clarifying connotations of "children of the light" (5:5). To be specific, the cosmological (God/Christ vs. Satan), eschatological (final or eternal salvation vs. punishment), and moral dualisms are respectively embedded in Paul's usage of the antithetical pair (light/day and night/darkness) (cf. Frey 2014:290; Murphy 2012:9; Kucicki 2014: 54).

57. Donfried (2010:509) sets out seven similarities between some Qumran documents and 1 Thessalonians, which include: (a) the eschatological/apocalyptic expectation of the end of the world; (b) the concepts of God's election and calling (1:4); (c) holiness and sanctification (4:3); (d) the dualism of "the light and night" and "day and darkness" and the expression "children of light" (5:5); (e) the antithetical fate of wrath and salvation (5:9); (f) the parallel between the phrase "church of God" in 2:14 and the Qumran term קָהָל; and (g) the similar connection of "ἄτακτος and the ethical order" in 5:14 and the Community Rule (1QS). Donfried (2002:221–31) translates ἄτακτος in 5:14 as "who are out of order" with regard to the instructions of the Lord Jesus, the life of holiness, and preparation for spiritual warfare in the light of three usages of סרך ("rule" or "order") in the Dead Sea Scrolls (1QS 5.1; 6.22; 1QM 5.3–4). His suggestion is that the ἄτακτοι in 1 Thess 5:14 probably describes those who do not follow the community rules in 1 Thess 4:1–12.

5.5.2.2.1 COSMOLOGICAL AND ESCHATOLOGICAL IMPLICATIONS OF "CHILDREN OF LIGHT" AND "CHILDREN OF DARKNESS"

Apocalyptic dualism in the Qumranian description of "children of light" and "children of darkness" is a comprehensive concept that combines cosmology and eschatology (cf. Heger 2010:70–71). According to 1QS (col. 3, 13—4, 26), the Qumran community believed that there are two spirits of "truth and falsehood." Those who belong to truth are governed by "the Prince of Light" and walk in "the paths of light." But those who belong to falsehood are ruled over by "the Angel of Darkness" and walk in "the paths of darkness." This document shows that their respective moral characteristics, way of life and final destiny are the opposite. May (1963:5) has discovered that a significant characteristic of the Qumranian community's cosmology is dualism:

> The dualistic, cosmic reference of the Qumran two spirits doctrine is evident not only from the association of the two spirits with the prince of light [1 QM col. 13, 10] and the angel of darkness [1 QM col. 13, 11–12], but also from the references to these two at other points in the Qumran literature, the former to be identified with Michael and the latter with Belial.

In addition, according to the so-called "War Scroll," eschatological warfare between "the sons of light" and "the sons of darkness" (i.e., "the army of Belial") will break out (1QM col. 1, 1–15). In the Qumranian world perspective, the conflict of these two opposite forces involves an inseparable relationship between cosmological and eschatological dimensions. Elgvin (2000:34, 36) observes that the conflict of these two opposite forces involves an inseparable relationship between cosmological and eschatological dimensions. He remarks that their perception of the world is framed by apocalyptic dualism:

> [S]ectarian authors drew upon a number of dualistic-apocalyptic works when they described the cosmic realities that encounter their 'community of latter days saints'. From their predecessors (or: from literary works they held in high esteem) they had learned about the cosmic struggle between light and darkness and the spiritual forces that oppose the sons of light. The present as well as the future were interpreted in light of this apocalyptic dualism.

Ultimately, the cosmological conflict between these two groups will be completed through the intervention of "the Prince of Light" for God's chosen people. The Qumran community envisaged that in the last days God will intervene in the battle and bolster the children of light to enable them to defeat the children of darkness, saying that:

> The Sons of Light and the forces of Darkness shall fight together to show the strength of God with the roar of a great multitude and the shout of gods and men; a day of disaster. It is a time of distress fo[r all] people who are redeemed by God. In all their afflictions none exists that is like it, hastening to its completion as an eternal redemption ... In three lots the Sons of Light shall stand firm so as to strike a blow at wickedness, and in three the army of Belial shall strengthen themselves so as to force the retreat of the forces [of Light. And when the] banners of the infantry cause their hearts to melt, then the might of God will strengthen the he[arts of the Sons of Light.] In the seventh lot the great hand of God shall overcome [Belial and al]l the angel of his dominion, and all the men of [his forces shall be destroyed forever] (1 QM col. 1, 11–15)

For the children of light, the day of victory will be "a time of salvation" (1 QM col. 1, 5).

Admittedly, in 1 Thess 5 there is no indication of a cosmic war between the two opposite powers.[58] But Paul's exhortation to be alert in 1 Thess 5:6–7 and a military metaphor in 5:8 could represent the ongoing inferred conflict between two antagonistic groups. If Paul was acquainted with this Qumranian tradition, it is not merely coincidental that the fusion of a military metaphor and light/darkness imagery occurs naturally (see also Rom 13:12; cf. Eph 6:11–12; Weima 2014:363). Paul's exhortation to put "on the breastplate of faith and love, and for a helmet the hope of salvation" reminds the believers of the need for vigilance in the preparation for a certain struggle. In fact, the conflict between outsiders and insiders does not appear in the form of physical combat. But the Thessalonians as "the children of light" are called to participate in the struggle to actualize their distinctive beliefs and lifestyle. In the meanwhile, they are indeed confronted with a huge challenge in their social, cultural, and religious environments. In that struggle Paul describes the believers as sentries who are armed in readiness and are

---

58. There is no connotation of cosmic war, at least except for 1 Thess 2:18. The warfare imagery of "Satan" is adopted to describe his opponents hampering Paul's pastoral ministry. Through this imagery, Paul might have sought to illustrate the reality of the politarchs' interruption as being manipulated by Satan (Ramsay 1907:230–1; Bruce 1982:55; Witherington III 2006:90).

alert and will not be surprised by the sudden arrival of the day of the Lord (Best 1986a:215). On that day the Lord will be ultimately involved in the conflict between the two contrasting groups and finally vindicate "the children of the light."

5.5.2.2.2 MORAL IMPLICATIONS OF "CHILDREN OF LIGHT" AND "CHILDREN OF DARKNESS"

Moral aspects of dualism are also found in the Qumran documents, revolving around the issue of how one observes the requirements of Torah. For the Qumranian community, one's morality, commitment to Torah, and the relationship with God are intertwined with one another. The author defines those who are faithful to the Community Rules as "the children of light" and God's election is a foundational notion in defining one's spiritual and behavioral status in an exclusive sense. In 1 QS col. 1, 1-3, while the expression "the children of light" occurs in the context of establishing the boundary in relation to the unfaithful, the instructor is responsible for teaching the community members "to seek God with all their heart and with all their soul, to do that which is good and upright before Him, just as He commanded through Moses and all his servants the prophets." The extent of showing their love should be confined only to those who evince good behavior (practicing truth, justice, and righteousness), maintain the status of covenantal relationship with God, and observe the standard rules of the community. On the other hand, the children of darkness are the objects of hatred. In contrasting these two opposite groups, a major strategy to establish the community's ethos is the building of a differentiated identity and separation from outsiders.[59] Jokiranta (2013:63-69) investigates the similarities of the Qumranian communities' self-perception of their identity and sociological position within their surrounding environment. With regard to the opposite camps of "the children of light" and "the children of darkness," he remarks that the *Damascus Document* (4Q266) and the *Community Rule* (1QS) show *antagonism* towards unqualified members or outsiders. The Community Rule is concerned with one's membership and the Damascus Document draws a boundary to distinguish between the covenant people and those who are ruled by Belial. Jokiranta (2013:65) notes that articulating one's

---

59. Another Qumranian document, 4Q397 frags. 14-21 shows their self-recognition of separate identity: "[But you know that] we have separated from the majority of the peo[ple and from all their uncleanness] [and] from being party to these matters or going along w[ith them] in these things."

distinctive identity is more than providing a contrast to the outsider; it is seen as an "ethically oriented way of expressing particularistic beliefs."

I suggest that the moral implication of these metaphors in the Qumran documents might have been integrated into Paul's paraenesis (1 Thess 5:6–11). The metaphors foster the audience's self-recognition of their distinctive identity in Christ and establish the moral values of this new fledging Christian community. The metaphors of light and darkness appeal to the community ethos so that the drawing of the boundary between oneself and the others (οἱ λοιποί in 1 Thess 5:6) expresses a sense of separation from the surrounding world. In so doing, Paul attempts to affect the new converts' perception of "who a genuine community member of Christ is." In addition, he affirms the behavioral norms required of those who belong to the realm of salvation through Christ. For the Qumranian, a moral response has to do with observing the Torah as a significant identity marker. But Paul indicates that the basis for the realization of the newly established community's values is rooted in God's act of salvation through Christ who died for the believers (5:9–10). Paul's precepts to preserve their moral distinctiveness from their surrounding environment revolve around the notion of the audience's salvation through Christ. The combined conjunction ἄρα οὖν strongly marks a typical Pauline transition from "the indicative" to the "imperative" and articulates "the behavioral result" of their new identity (Weima 2014:357). As instruction and admonition are necessary in this ongoing situation of suffering and persecution, the occurrences of the series of hortatory subjunctives ("let us not sleep," "let us keep awake and be sober" in 1 Thess 5:6) highlight the expected morality of the Christian community in accordance with their ontological status in Christ.[60]

Moreover, Paul develops the imagery of night into two potentially related activities that could occur at night. The acts of sleeping and being drunk could metaphorically describe one's insensibility and unpreparedness with regard to preparation for Christ's parousia. In drawing our attention to the first person plural pronoun ἡμεῖς, and the adversative δέ, Paul highlights that the audience must be *vigilant* and *self-controlled*. Many scholars and commentators have recognized the distinctive meaning of the verbs γρηγορέω and νήφω in verse 6. The former contains a sense of being "in constant readiness" (BDAG, γρηγορέω §2). Specifically, it means "to be spiritually and morally *alert and vigilant* in eschatological context" (Green 2002:238; Matt 24:42–44; Mark 13:34–37; Luke 12:37; Rev. 3:2–3). The second verb νήφω denotes the status of being "free from every form of

---

60. It is remarkable that in this letter, except for παρακαλεῖτε in 4:18, imperative forms of the verb appear intensively in 5:11–26.

mental and spiritual 'drunkenness,'" so it most likely means the condition of being "self-controlled" (BDAG). While each term has its own independent meaning, one should avoid separating these two words (Best 1986a:212; Malherbe 2000:295); rather, both should be counted as one unit regarding the notion that largely contrasts with the stance and status of night people (sleeping and being drunken). Elsewhere in the NT the fact that these words occur together can substantiate their inseparable relationship of being sober-minded and being watchful (νήψατε, γρηγορήσατε)" (1 Pet 1:13; 5:8). Malherbe (2000:296) understands that Paul combines these two words to provide a special sense of the latter, γρηγορέω. While Paul uses only the second word, νήφω in verse 8, a remarkable point is that his repetition of the verb shows the development of his argument with a military metaphor, shifting the meaning of νήφω "slightly from being 'clear-headed' to being vigilant" (Best 1986a:213).

This idea in made more specific in Paul's using military imagery, which he used to advance faith, love, and hope as essential Christian values in this letter (cf. 1 Thess 1:3).[61] Metaphorically, these virtues are described as "defensive armor that will insure that the Christians are prepared for the 'day of the Lord,' whenever it comes" (Green 2002:241).[62] Through these metaphors Paul encourages the Thessalonian believers to have confidence in anticipating Christ's parousia, since they belong to the realm of light/day, i.e., the salvation of God. By equipping them with vigilance and

---

61. In v. 8 one should not necessarily render the aorist participle ἐνδυσάμενοι as past tense (BDF §339). According to Porter (1989:381), in this case the aorist participle is used with the main verb, and the participle functions to illustrate an action concurrent with the main verb. Weima (2014:362) illustrates the nature of Paul's use of this aorist participle based on Porter's view in saying that: "the 'putting on' of the armor occurs simultaneously with the action of being self-controlled and therefore provides the means by which believers exercise self-control." But it is debatable here whether this participle's grammatical function is "cause" or "means." I understand that this aorist participle can simply specify the action of being self-controlled.

62. According to Seifrid (1999:60), one should not overlook the fact that this triad is a central theme of the gospel as Paul presents in the whole letter of 1 Thessalonians. As it forms an inclusio of this letter (1:3; 5:8), Paul provides a coherent gospel message to this congregation. He summarizes the inseparable relationships within the triad, saying: "The living hope of Christ's coming, which sprang forth from faith in Christ and his saving work, meant not only deliverance from death, but also from the tribulations into which the Thessalonian believers had been thrust on account of their faith in Christ. They, with all believers, were placed in the great struggle between the fallen world and its Creator, which shall come to an end only with the arrival of the day of judgment. In the community of 'the sons of light and the day,' the eschaton has entered the world already. Among them, the age to come is present in the reality of love. If we are to teach the Thessalonian letters properly, we must remember that Paul's eschatology is hope, which is inseparable from faith and love."

admonishing them to be self-controlled (spiritual and moral sobriety), Paul ultimately shapes the *ethos* and *moral solidarity* of God's chosen community.

5.6 CONCLUSION

This chapter has explored the discursive function of scriptural echoes in the paraenetic section of Paul's first letter to the Thessalonians (particularly 4:1–12; 5:1–11; see Appendix II). A significant feature I observed was that Paul seems to have integrated particular echoes into a framework of dualism (e.g., by contrasting outsiders and insiders). In this way his appeal to the audience regarding their identity and moral responsibility seems to be strengthened. Based on these beliefs, Paul thought that, according to faith in the Son (1:9; 5:5), there are only two kinds of people—believers and non-believers. Yet this distinction was not meant merely to articulate their opposite fates and thus to denigrate or demonize non-believers. By contrasting the two groups, he does not instigate a sense of superiority over the other, but shapes the new fledging community's identity and ethos through known images from their surrounding world.

Above all, in the midst of the audience's crisis of identity (see 3.2.3.4.2), Paul needed to furnish them with a theological foundation to affirm their newly obtained status in Christ and their corresponding moral responsibility. He proclaimed that the Thessalonians have become the renewed Israel, since their status is to be viewed in continuity with the election tradition of ancient Israel and within God's larger redemptive history. At the same time, they are reaching forward to the climactic moment of Christ's parousia. In this way, Paul established the conceptual foundations of their identity and moral uprightness in continuity with God's calling to the Israelites as "a light for the nations" (Isa 49:6). In Paul's paraenetic discourse, various scriptural echoes—sanctification in the Holiness Code, new covenant, and the day of the Lord—function to imbue the audience with an identity and ethos clearly distinguished from those of the pagan world. In Christ, they were to recognize themselves as God's eschatological people, forsaking the transient belief systems of their social world. Paul's contrast between outsiders and insiders ultimately encourages the Thessalonians to embark on and continue their new journey together, while embodying sanctification, representing God's new covenant and loving one another. Finally, the believers' journey of God's calling was supposed to proceed in joy and anticipation of the eschatological hope that Christ would complete God's salvation history at his parousia.

6

Conclusion

Transformative Power of 1 Thessalonians for Present-Day Readers/Audiences

As a conclusion to this study, this chapter revisits the title, research motivation, problem statement, methodology, and main results that my exploration of 1 Thessalonians has brought to light. The chapter will conclude with a brief engagement between the ways in which Paul constituted a distinct identity and ethos in early (gentile) believing communities and the perceived moral crisis in our days.

In chapter 1, I questioned the benefits of current research that delves into the probable social-cultural setting of Paul's ethical exhortations in 1 Thessalonians. I pointed out that approaches based (only) on Hellenistic rhetorical theory tend to confine the wide range of Paul's complex conceptual map to the single social-cultural context of the ancient Greek and Roman world. Admittedly, previous research introduced a new phase in Pauline studies under the premise that Paul could have used widely known letter-writing styles, forms, genres and *topoi* familiar to audiences in the first-century Hellenistic world. However, in spite of their usefulness, I raised the question as to whether such generic formal conventions would be adequate for understanding the thrust of Paul's discourse.

Rather than simply investigating established patterns of Hellenistic rhetorical conventions, the study has been concerned with utilizing significant tenets of modern discourse analysis to examine the full scope of the 1 Thessalonians text. I argued that accounting for the multidimensional nature of the letter might enable present-day readers to appreciate Paul's discourse as a dynamic, potentially transformative, communicative act (see 1.3; 1.4.1; 1.4.2). First, words and phrases were analyzed in light of the probable interaction between the author's use of notions from the Hebrew Scriptures and the audience's social, cultural, political, and religious contexts. Second, the thrust and purpose of Paul's discourse in 1 Thessalonians was explored through examining each literary unit and its correlation with other units. In so doing, the rich yet complex cohesion of the text could be established (tentatively), and the development of the author's argumentation as a whole be recognized (cf. Green 1995: 177). Third, through analyzing communicative processes represented by Paul's discourse, its possible appropriation by subsequent believers in different contexts, including the 21st century, became clearer (cf. Green 1995:176).

The final chapter of this study does not conduct a contextual analysis of the perceived concrete ethical dilemma, but wishes to highlight how the text of 1 Thessalonians continues to invite subsequent readers to (re)appropriate its implied transformative potential. In order to describe this process, I will first summarize my discussions of Paul's discourse in the letter (cf. Hays 1996:3). In continuation with his strategy of re-serializing the newly established communities of Thessalonica, later readers who live in totally different social, cultural and historical contexts may be informed and inspired to do likewise (cf. Mouton 2002:178).

6.1 SUMMARY: DISCURSIVE FUNCTION OF ECHOES FROM THE HEBREW SCRIPTURES IN 1 THESSALONIANS

A major concern of this project has been to shed light on the nature of the communication between Paul and the Thessalonians. I devoted attention to the dynamic interaction between the author's conceptual and scriptural world and the (entextualized but also broader) social circumstances of the Thessalonians (see 1.3.1; 1.4.2). I have indicated how Paul, under the circumstances of social harassment from their fellow citizens, established his discursive strategy, primarily providing a resolution for the identity and moral crisis of the newly established Christian community at Thessalonica. As an anomalous diaspora Jew and apostle of Christ, Paul creatively appropriated scriptural language (themes and echoes from his but also their inherited tradition) within a reconfigured apocalyptic framework, thereby providing an alternative perspective on their dire circumstances. It appears that Paul intentionally integrated his knowledge of the Hebrew Scriptures into his discourse with a (mainly) gentile audience. By elucidating (the logic of) their new identity and ethos as God's chosen people in the end-time, he attempted to resolve the perceived crisis in the early Christian community at Thessalonica.

6.1.1 CONSTRUCTING PAUL'S SCRIPTURAL/CONCEPTUAL WORLD

For diaspora Jews in the first-century world of Hellenistic Judaism (such as Paul), the notion of being God's chosen people was not negotiable. This fundamental identity awareness determined not only who they were but also how they lived their concrete everyday lives. Based on this notion, I explored the presupposition that Paul's conceptual world, shaped by the Hebrew Scriptures (both the MT and LXX), was substantially reflected in processes of identity and moral formation among early Christian communities. Opposed to the tendency among recent scholars strictly to divide the so-called "Hellenistic" and "Jewish" Paul, chapter 2 examined Paul's complex and wide-ranging conceptual world as an anomalous diaspora Jew and apostle of Christ.

I focused here on two recent types of academic pursuit based on assumptions that Paul breathed mainly Hellenistic sociocultural air. Accordingly, Paul has been understood in the light of (1) a Hellenistic social setting and (2) its literary/rhetorical environment (see 1.3.1; 2.1.3). However, I raised a question about the limited interpretive payoff when Paul's letters are examined only in the light of this milieu. In my view, various scholars investigated the extent to which Paul was familiar with, or influenced by, Hellenistic social and rhetorical environments insufficiently.

I pointed out that it is impossible to dissociate Paul and Judaism in the light of his education, the influence of Jewish apocalyptic thinking, and the integration of the halakhic tradition into his discourse. However, this needs to be nuanced further. One has to be careful not to fall into another kind of one-sidedness by overlooking the *discontinuity* between Paul and Judaism. To avoid oversimplifying Paul's conceptual world, it is necessary to consider the context of first-century Hellenistic Judaism. This entails determining the extent to which Paul assimilated, acculturated, accommodated to the influences of Hellenization. I concluded that, even if Paul was familiar with the (broad) Hellenistic social and literary/rhetorical environment, he probably grew up in a diaspora Jewish family that considered maintaining their identity as God's chosen people as the foundation for their daily ethos. For Paul, this foundation was recalibrated and renewed through the lens of his faith in Christ's death and resurrection. This would *inter alia* lead to his profound strategy of defining gentile believers as the new Israel of God.

6.1.2 CONSTRUCTING A DISCURSIVE EXIGENCY IN THE THESSALONIAN COMMUNITY?

In chapter 3, I constructed the Thessalonian Christian community's existential crisis by examining a potential conflict between them and their fellow citizens from political and religious perspectives. Paul's discursive themes and argumentation did not emerge in a vacuum, nor was his discourse unilaterally communicated. Rather, its occasion was (tentatively) described as a specific identity crisis which both speakers and audience experienced and recognized. Paul seems to have (re)interpreted the existential circumstances of social harassment and persecution that they faced from an apocalyptic perspective. In so doing, he portrayed the faith community as the eschatological people of God's (alternative) kingdom, situated amidst political and religious conflicts with their fellow citizens.

Specifically, I argued that in order to construct the discursive exigency within the Thessalonian community, it is necessary to consider three potential threats: Jewish agitators, Roman imperial ideology, and local religious cults.

First, I regarded Acts 17:1–9 as a significant secondary resource for constructing a potential conflict between Paul's (mainly gentile) converts and some Jews in Thessalonica. Paul and his coworkers preached the crucified and resurrected Jesus of Nazareth as Messiah to them. As some synagogue attenders joined the believing community, some Jews became jealous of the apostles and their message and finally led to a commotion associated with a mob against the new converts.

The second cause of conflict may be attributed to the new converts' violation of "the decrees of Caesar," proclaiming Jesus as another king (Acts 17:7). I discussed the point that, if Christ's parousia was a major part of his initial preaching at Thessalonica, his message might have been regarded as a violation of the "decrees of Caesar." In Paul's day, predictions of the emperor's health and death were prohibited, since that was closely tied to issues of succession to the throne. Paul's apocalyptic message of Christ's coming might have been considered as a prediction of the usurpation of the emperor's throne. Paul's message would be considered as endangering Thessalonian citizens' status and their relationship with the emperor as benefactor. Those who turned to the living God and awaited Christ's parousia were probably also branded as potentially subversive and would therefore have been socially and politically isolated from society.

Third, the Thessalonians' religious sentiments and customs cannot be fully described because of a lack of textual evidence. Some archaeological evidence may, however, help to substantiate that the religiously pluralistic environment of first-century Thessalonica was not compatible with the Christian community's beliefs and required morality. Around Paul's time, Thessalonian voluntary associations used to gather under the name of Dionysus and Egyptian gods in expectation of the local gods' goodwill for economic well-being and protection of their businesses. This was the nature of converted Thessalonians' former life in which their religious sentiments and social identity were closely intertwined. Furthermore, after their conversion, the Dionysus and Cabirus (or Cabiri) cults—characterized by Bacchic frenzy, ecstasy and phallus worship—would no longer be compatible with their calling to holiness. Consequently, the Thessalonians' abandoning of idols and turning to God (1 Thess 1:9) would be viewed by the local population as atheism, which could provoke the gods' anger and even endanger the Roman *pax deorum*.

In sum, these conflicts might have been the reason why Thessalonian believers were socially discriminated against and ostracized by their fellow citizens. Such social harassment could have been sufficient motivation for Paul to situate the audience in an eschatological timeline.

6.1.3 PAUL'S IDENTITY- AND ETHOS-BUILDING DISCOURSE IN 1 THESS 1:1—2:12

Chapter 4 illustrated how eager Paul was to resolve the identity and moral crisis of the Christian community in Thessalonica. This chapter analyzed 1 Thess 1:1—2:12, concentrating on the implied formative effect of some identity markers on these early believers' self-awareness and lifestyle (see Appendix I). This chapter concluded that 1 Thessalonians is fundamentally characterized as identity- and ethos-building discourse. This identification was substantiated by taking theological and social aspects of the text into account.

First, at a theological level, the author defines the newly established community's identity as rooted in Scripture's narrative world. Although Paul uses ἐκλογή only once in the letter (1:4), it seems to be a crucial concept for him. This term, which probably originates from the election tradition of Deuteronomy (4:37; 10:15; 33:12), permeates the letter. Furthermore, this notion is related to the terms μιμητής in 1:6 and τύπος in 1:7 in so far as the Thessalonians' imitating of Paul and Jesus, as well as their influence over the surrounding regions of Greece, was meant to be a chain reaction stemming from God's election. Paul reminds his audience that ancient Israel's distinctive responsibility to represent YHWH among the nations has now been expanded to gentile believers. Through a dynamic process of reinterpretation and reconfiguration, Paul integrated and contextualized them within the symbolic framework of Jewish Scripture.

Second, at a sociological level, Paul consolidates communal aspects of the election tradition by emphasizing the image of God's larger family gathered around God's kingdom and glory (1 Thess 2:12). It seems that conflicts between Paul, Thessalonian believers, and other citizens led to Paul's sudden departure from the city. In accounting for his role among them, Paul's self-defensive mood is deeply associated with his use of a series of family metaphors (see 4.4.3; 4.4.4; 4.4.5). Family metaphors in 2:7–12 (nursing mother, brother and sister, father) denote that Paul's self-defense was an expression of his affection and devotion to shaping the community's unprecedented identity awareness and ethos as distinguished from the rest of society. Ultimately, these family metaphors present Paul's affection, pastoral vision, and re-socialization of the believers to align their lives with God's kingdom and glory. In so doing, Paul emphasizes the new community's participation in God's ongoing redemptive history.

6.1.4 DISCURSIVE FUNCTIONING OF SCRIPTURAL ECHOES IN 1 THESS 4:1—5:11

Chapter 5, as the climax of my analysis of Paul's identity and ethos-building discourse in 1 Thessalonians, explored the discursive function of scriptural echoes in a substantial portion of the paraenetic section (see Appendix II). I argued that many scholars have overlooked the pivotal role that Paul's Jewish tradition plays in the letter's paraenetic discourse. The chapter focused on Paul's probable echoing of "holiness/sanctification" in the Holiness Code of the Hebrew Scriptures, God's "new covenant," and "the day of the Lord." These echoes seem to reinforce the community's distinct identity and ethos from that of their surrounding world.

First, I argued that Paul's foundational statement, "this is the will of God, your sanctification" (4:3), has to be seen as his expository commentary and illustration of Leviticus' theology of holiness. The prohibition of sexual immorality (Lev 18:6–24; 20:10–21), for example, rejects sexual practices in Egypt and Canaan in accordance with YHWH and Israel's core value of holiness. For Israel, holy living was their response to God's bringing them into the promised land. Based on this observation, I concluded that Paul's use of the term ἁγιασμός (sanctification) in 4:3–4 probably echoes ancient Israel's calling to holiness. In addition, the shared root of ἅγιος as well as a rare combination of impurity and sanctification occur in both 1 Thess 4:7 and the Holiness Code (e.g., Lev 10:10). I argued that God's calling to holiness is meant to be embodied through a practical lifestyle of sanctification and love, as Leviticus indicates. According to Paul, the Thessalonian believers are likewise called to participate in God's holiness by practicing an ethos of love and respect. The series of infinitives in 4:3b–6a functions to remind the community that they are God's chosen people who carry out God's will, i.e., sanctification.

Second, I noted that Paul's neologism θεοδίδακτοί (being "taught by God") in 4:9 primarily echoes Isa 54:13, based on the principle that when a Hebrew phrase is translated into LXX Greek, translators tend to reverse and combine phrases. Following the arguments of Emanuel Tov and Witmer, I suggested that Paul might have recast the phrase לִמּוּדֵי יְהוָה (διδακτοὺς θεοῦ in the LXX) in Isa 54:13 into θεοδίδακτοί. In the transition from a first echo of holiness/sanctification in 4:3–4 to a second one in 4:7–8, Paul seems to link the gift of God's Spirit to the internal renewal of God's covenant people in the Ezekielian tradition (Ezek 36:26, 37:6, 14). By using this neologism, Paul implies that God's gift of the Holy Spirit is an essential mark of the fulfillment of new covenant prophecies that envisaged the internalization of God's teaching in the hearts of God's people (Jer 31:33–34). Paul remarkably (re)appropriates the language of the new covenant to emphasize the importance of loving one's neighbor (1 Thess 4:9–10), drawing parallels to the principles articulated in the Holiness Code and specifically Lev 19. The term φιλαδελφία was originally used within the Hellenistic world to describe the bond between siblings who share a biological origin. Yet, this term undergoes an unprecedented transformation in Paul's usage, symbolizing the inclusive bond among members of God's new covenant community. In the advent of God's eschatological era, believers experience the guidance of the Holy Spirit who enables them to extend love and care beyond biological kinship. Notably, their love and respect transcend the boundaries of the insider community, encompassing outsiders as well (4:11–12).

Third, as the climax of Paul's paraenetic discourse, 1 Thess 5:1–11 deals with the opposite fate of outsiders and insiders on the day of God's judgment. A recurrence here of the thematic echo of "the day of the Lord" (יוֹם יהוה) in the Prophets makes it most likely that 1 Thessalonians employs apocalyptic discourse. This echo is probably associated with Paul's apocalyptic dualism of outsiders and insiders. Particularly, through the contrasts of light/darkness and day/night, Paul represents the existence of two different realms with regard to the believers' ontological status, namely social belonging and morality. I argued in this section that Paul's expressions "you are not in darkness" and "we are not of the night or of the darkness" in 5:4–5 remarkably echo "day of the Lord" imagery in Amos 5:18–20. Furthermore, the expressions "children of light" and "children of the day" in 1 Thess 5:5 seem to echo the contrast between "the children of light" and "the children of darkness" in Qumranian traditions.

To conclude, it seems most likely that Paul includes echoes from the Hebrew Scriptures in his paraenesis to the Thessalonian believers. In this way he provides them with a reinterpreted Christian identity and ethos, distinguishing them from pagan thinking and customs. They are God's elected people who participate in and continue God's redemptive history in the world. At the same time, they are God's eschatological people, exhorted to live holy lives in the hope of Christ's parousia (1 Thess 3:13; 4:3, 4, 7, 5:23).

6.2 RESOLVING A MORAL CRISIS?: REVISITING RESEARCH MOTIVATION AND PROBLEM STATEMENT

Confronted with concrete moral dilemma all over the world, I wish to invite subsequent readers/audiences of 1 Thessalonians to consider the implications of my research. Thessalonian believers of the first century were exhorted to live in accordance with their calling and moral responsibility in the midst of a crisis. Through Paul's discursive strategy of reinterpreted scripture, he encouraged his audience to remain truthful to their identity as God's elect people amidst imperial realities. The text of 1 Thessalonians, and particularly the dynamic processes of (re)interpretation and (re)conceptualization embedded in it, encourage present-day believers to (re)interpret their scriptural traditions likewise.

Beyond identifying constituent sociocultural layers behind Paul's discourse, this study aimed to explore multidimensional textual layers in 1 Thessalonians (see 1.3; 1.4.1). I highlighted methodological limitations in utilizing rhetorical criticism based *only* on Hellenistic rhetorical genres and speech. Such interpretations seem to confine Paul's argumentation and strategy of persuasion to his immediate rhetorical environment. This means that readers are restricted to establishing the meaning of a text only in accordance with designated rhetorical functions and arrangements. In my view, such a narrow emphasis would not be able to help today's audiences to understand either the flow of Paul's discourse, or the discursive functioning of key concepts he used in resolving the crisis in Thessalonica. Instead, this study explored the dynamic interrelatedness of syntactic, semantic, and pragmatic elements in the letter in an attempt to establish the coherent thrust of Paul's argument. In light of my analysis of the text, I concluded that Paul's discursive strategy is mainly established through his use of scriptural concepts and echoes. By emphasizing the Thessalonian community's distinct identity and ethos in continuation with that of Israel, he seems to locate them in the continuing story of God's salvation.

In continuation with Paul's interpretive strategy, how can modern readers/audiences of 1 Thessalonians appropriate this text in different circumstances today? With our days' moral crisis in mind, I briefly account for the authority and potential (trans)formative functioning of this letter in a modern context. Can this letter be appropriated to recover Christian moral consciousness and to make specific ethical decisions? And if yes, how is that anticipated to happen? (cf. Mouton 2002:252)?

6.2.1 AUTHORITY OF THE BIBLE AND READERS' RESPONSIBILITY

In order to consider the validity of Paul's discourse in 1 Thessalonians for today, it is important to account for the life-giving authority of Scripture. Throughout Christian history, the Bible has been considered as the primary resource for the formation of Christian character and morality. According to Hays (1996:8), the Bible is referred to "as a word *extra nos*, a voice that can correct or even challenge tradition." The transformative power of this voice should not be underestimated, even in postmodern contexts where the (often biased) role of readers is increasingly emphasized and questioned (Verhey 2007:24). To allow the Bible to continue to speak "authoritatively" in processes of ethical decision-making would require rigorous exegetical work and creative hermeneutical choices. If faith communities today are not open to the multidimensional nature and intentions of Scripture, as argued in this study, it could easily be abused merely to support personal or communal interests and ideologies (cf. Smit 1991:62). Where this happens, God's redemptive story loses its credibility in society (Smit 1991:64–65).

Present-day readers of 1 Thessalonians are first of all responsible for respecting the thrust and potential of the text in shaping the identity and character of a specific community. People often attempt to find answers to the question of how a biblical foundation for ethics could be established in positing some systematic or comprehensive code of conduct. Smit (1991:52) argues that scholarly discussions on ethical decision-making should be differentiated from factors that affect people's "moral world," i.e., ethos. According to him, ethicists are often interested in how biblical principles and norms may be applied to ethical decisions in specific sociopolitical contexts. However, he points out that their own "ethics" often merely reflects and rationalizes the "ethos" or habits of the groups to which they belong. He argues that, while ethics does not necessarily change a group's ethos, their ethos typically influences their ethical decision-making. Contemporary readers should thus go beyond merely establishing a biblical foundation for their ethics, and rather focus on (trans)formative processes embedded in biblical texts, through which Christian believers' self-awareness and ethos were supposed to be challenged and renewed. I, therefore, believe that Paul's identity- and ethos-building discourse in 1 Thessalonians has the potential to play a significant role in (trans)forming the character, ethos and moral identity of contemporary readers.

6.2.2 FUNCTIONING OF THE BIBLE IN ETHICAL DECISION-MAKING

Many scholars have raised questions of how contemporary audiences may overcome the epochal and cultural gap between "antiquity and modernity (or postmodernity)" (Cosgrove [2011] 2013:31). In search of methodological validity, they seriously consider how the Bible can be regarded as "necessary affirmation for those who would construe their moral reflection as part of the continuing life of the Christian community" (Verhey 1984:232).

In this regard, Richard Hays (1996:216–90) introduces various processes and modes of ethical decision-making.[1] He discusses the pros and cons of utilizing hermeneutical strategies suggested by Reinhold Niebuhr, Karl Barth, John Howard Yoder, Stanley Hauerwas, and Schüssler Fiorenza. With regard to Christian's moral judgment, Hays (1996:293) especially endorses the validity and authority of four modes of ethical decision-making—"*principles* of love, justice, and equity" (Niebuhr), "specific *rules* and commandments" (Barth), the *paradigm* of Jesus' redemptive story (Yoder & Hauerwas), "an open-ended *paradigm* . . . that encourages imaginative elaboration and transformation" (Fiorenza). Through various modes of moral discourse, he argues, biblical texts (may) still appeal to modern audiences. Communities whose ethos is shaped by Scripture learn how to live as

---

1. Presupposing that NT ethics is a "normative theological discipline," Hays sets out a fourfold task for New Testament ethics in his book *The Moral Vision of the New Testament*. It provides important guidelines for contemporary discussions on the relation between Scripture and ethics (Hays 1996:3). This fourfold task of NT ethics—the descriptive, synthetic, hermeneutical and pragmatic tasks—were designed to establish theological grounds for NT ethics as "a normative theological discipline:" (1) the nature of the *descriptive* task is exegetical practice that reads each biblical writing carefully; (2) the nature of the *synthetic* task is to establish coherency amongst the canonical books; (3) the *hermeneutical* task plays a role in bridging the interpretative differences between antiquity and modernity; (4) the purpose of the *pragmatic* task is to embody "Scripture's imperatives in the life of the Christian community" (Hays 1996:7). Hays' major concern in carrying out these tasks is to manifest "how the church can read Scripture in a faithful and disciplined manner so that Scripture might come to shape the life of the church."

followers of Christ, responding to a spectrum of authoritative modes communicated through it. Hence, Hays (1996:294) remarks that people should be careful of merely utilizing *"one mode of appeal to Scripture to override the witness of the New Testament in another mode."* Hays concludes by stating that various ethical modes in the New Testament (such as rules, principles, paradigms and symbolic worlds) are to be considered as equally authoritative and necessary for shaping Christian ethos in different contexts (cf. Hays 1996:310).

When reading 1 Thessalonians today, it seems that all these modes may be potentially appropriate for ethical decision-making, depending on the particular context and exigency of the situation. Examples of each mode are found throughout the letter, providing modern readers with important clues towards (re)appropriating these modes:

- "Principle of love" (1 Thess 1:3; 3:6, 12; 5:8, 13; see 5.4)
- "Specific commandments" (see the paraenetic section and 5.3; 5.4; 5.5)
- "The paradigm of Jesus' redemptive story" (1:4–5, 10, 2:16; 3:13; 5:8–10; see 4.3.3; 4.3.6)
- "An open-ended paradigm for imaginative reading" (5:27)

Therefore, to (re)appropriate a text such as 1 Thessalonians in present-day contexts, it is crucial to approach it with respect and sensitivity, recognizing its rich yet complex multidimensional nature, purpose, and its diverse intersecting modes of ethical discourse. Unfortunately, however, the complexity of biblical (re)interpretation has often been underestimated in the past. Old and New Testament Scriptures have often been regarded as prescriptive laws, codes or regulations, without (adequately) accounting for the networks of relations in which such discourses are embedded. A serious consequence is that such perspectives merely disclose and/or control moral insufficiency rather than shaping morality.

In this final section of the study, I wish to indicate that the Bible eventually influences the ethos of Christian communities inasmuch as it "represent[s] metaphorical processes in narrative form" and thereby "redescribe[s] and reshape[s] reality, present[s] alternative worlds, and open[s] new ways of seeing and being" (Mouton 2002:168). Hays (1996:295) explains that, since the New Testament was communicated primarily based on the form of Jesus' redemptive story, "a Christian community . . . will find itself drawn repeatedly to the paradigmatic mode of using the New Testament in ethics, seeking to shape analogies between the story told there and the life of the community." He (Hays 1996:299) reiterates that, since the New

Testament consists of culturally and temporally conditioned documents, it is not possible to derive timeless truths from it to be applied to every situation. In processes of ethical decision-making, therefore, modern audiences are responsible for engaging "in metaphor-making [processes], placing our community's life imaginatively within the world articulated by the texts." In doing so, the story can provide a concrete and practical framework in rationalizing these modes and is the essential content of the Christian communities' faith and way of life.

In this regard, the story enlivens the participants' moral figuration in both ancient and modern times (cf. Mouton 2002:172). The story exerts a profound influence on shaping the worldview, beliefs, and moral characteristics of the Christian community (cf. Smit 1991:56; Hauerwas 1981:9–52; Mouton 2002:168). Narratives of what the triune God of the Bible has done throughout history play a (trans)formative role in Christian communities' discernment about how their lives should be characterized, and how they should respond to and participate in Jesus Christ's redemptive history (Hays 1996:298). As Calvin compared the Bible to spectacles, communities of believers have to learn to see the world differently, and to understand the realities of life (cf. Smit 1991:59; Mouton 1997:245;). In this way the Bible enables readers/audiences to adopt biblical perspectives and to experience its potential of (re)shaping Christ-like characters (cf. Mouton 2002:172). Birch and Rasmussen (1989:106–7) argue that the pragmatic effect of Jesus' redemptive story is to "mold people's identities and their sense of the world and reality . . . [and to] create a basic orientation for those who are drawn into them . . . They create and shape virtue, value, vision, and obligation . . . All this creates a certain framework for decision making."

6.2.3 HOLINESS/SANCTIFICATION IN THE CONTINUING SALVATION STORY OF GOD

According to 1 Thessalonians, Paul's affirmation of the newly established community's identity-awareness and his shaping of their new ethos are largely framed by God's salvation story. This narrative formed the core of early Christian communities' self-understanding. It was based on God's initiative of electing them, their conversion, and their future-oriented hope for Christ's parousia. Through its textual analyses, the study showed how Paul tried to persuade early gentile believers of their new identity by including them in Israel's story of God's election. Throughout the Hebrew Scriptures YHWH called Israel to be his chosen people. The covenantal relationship between them emphasized not only God's initiative but also

Israel's responsibility to hold fast to God's promises and to present him to the nations. Through the salvation story of Jesus Christ (culminating in his death and resurrection), and by echoing election traditions and key concepts from the Hebrew Scriptures, Paul established continuity between the faith/identity-awareness of ancient Israel and that of the new converts in Thessalonica. By receiving this gospel, the Thessalonians were incorporated into God's chosen people and experienced the blessings of the fulfillment of God's new covenant prophecies.

As the new converts were separated from their associations and former social networks, their turning from idols to the God of Israel (1:9) might have given rise to concrete issues of withdrawal of faith, an identity crisis and a moral dilemma, and even to having their livelihood endangered. After their conversion, these gentile believers were characterized by enduring such inexorable circumstances and standing firm (3:3, 8) in the tension of "already, but not yet" until Christ's parousia would be fulfilled. Paul reminded them that Christ's second coming would be the final and decisive moment of God's vindication for those who were persecuted, bringing ultimate salvation. For early Christian communities Christ was the beginning and the end, and his second coming would be the climactic moment of God's salvation history. In the times between beginning and end, Paul referred to this new convert group as God's eschatological people. His description of the Thessalonians' identity denotes that they were brought into a new covenantal relationship with God. Through establishing the foundation and direction of their faith, they are encouraged to hold fast to their primary calling to live *holy and sanctified lives* (see 5.3.2), that is, to love one another, and to keep their eschatological hope alive. According to the letter, Paul's ultimate hope is the Thessalonians' holiness on the day of parousia (1 Thess 3:13; 5:23). In the final analysis, Christ's parousia is the culminating moment of the eschatological hope of Christian communities—ancient and modern. Contemporary Christian believers are—like their predecessors—called to be holy in filling out their communal story in the between times. The (trans)formative power of God's Word forms "our character," to affirm "our vision of God," and to accept "responsibility for our decisions and actions" (cf. Mouton 2002:172).

6.3. TRANSFORMATIVE POTENTIAL OF 1 THESSALONIANS

Present-day Christian believers are invited by the New Testament writings continuously to adopt the perspective of these texts, to affirm their calling as God's elected people, and to enliven their eschatological hope in Christ. This implies an ongoing interaction between texts, readers, and their contexts, as Mouton (2002:254) remarks:

> Consequently, moral identity and ethos are shaped by these ongoing 'moments of interaction' between texts and readers—a process which involves Christ's healing presence on the one hand, and the readers' moral choices—whether large or trivial in scope and consequence—and imaginative responses to what God is doing on the other ... in a way similar to the identity and moral formation of the early Christians.

In 1 Thessalonians, Paul's discourse does not guide his readers simply to be future-oriented at the expense of their present reality. Rather, it invites them to share the perspective that the present is located within "the climaxing context of redemptive history" (Beale 2011:18). Paul's description of the end-time ultimately purports to represent what the readers' present lives should be like, and consequently guides them to appreciate the (trans)formative force of his discourse. Early Christian communities are thus depicted as participants in the drama of God's redemption, still awaiting its culmination at Christ's parousia. In recognizing this urgency, their apocalyptic anticipation was/is meanwhile meant to be embodied in their sanctification by the Spirit as God's chosen, eschatological people. In the temporal gap and creative tension between present and future, faith communities were and still are called to remember their identity in Christ, and to resolve their moral issues from this orientation.

In searching for concrete solutions to the crisis, this study helped me identify basic steps involved in complex processes of moral and social transformation, namely the internal logic of 1 Thessalonians that also responded to a moral crisis. I have discovered that Paul's strategy of strengthening the Thessalonian community's identity and ethos in their particular context holds the potential to motivate believers in their (different) context today. Particularly, Paul's creative reinterpretation of scriptural echoes (such as election, holiness and love) seems to provide modern readers with an important clue to the restoration of morality. Believers all over the world are invited and encouraged by this text to deeply engage with its narrative world, and likewise to (re)appropriate its vision and perspectives on God and humanity to their own lives. In this way they will continue God's story of love and grace, embodying their primary calling as God's elected, sanctified people among the nations in the end-time.

Appendix I[1]

---

1. In Appendix I and II, I use Schreiner's abbreviations in tracing and establishing possible relations among phrases (see Schreiner [1990] 2008:97–126).

APPENDIX I

Tracing 1 (1 Thess 1:1–10)

Sender: Παῦλος καὶ Σιλουανὸς καὶ Τιμόθεος

Recipient: τῇ ἐκκλησίᾳ Θεσσαλονικέων

      ἐν θεῷ πατρὶ καὶ κυρίῳ Ἰησοῦ Χριστῷ,

Greeting: χάρις ὑμῖν καὶ εἰρήνη.

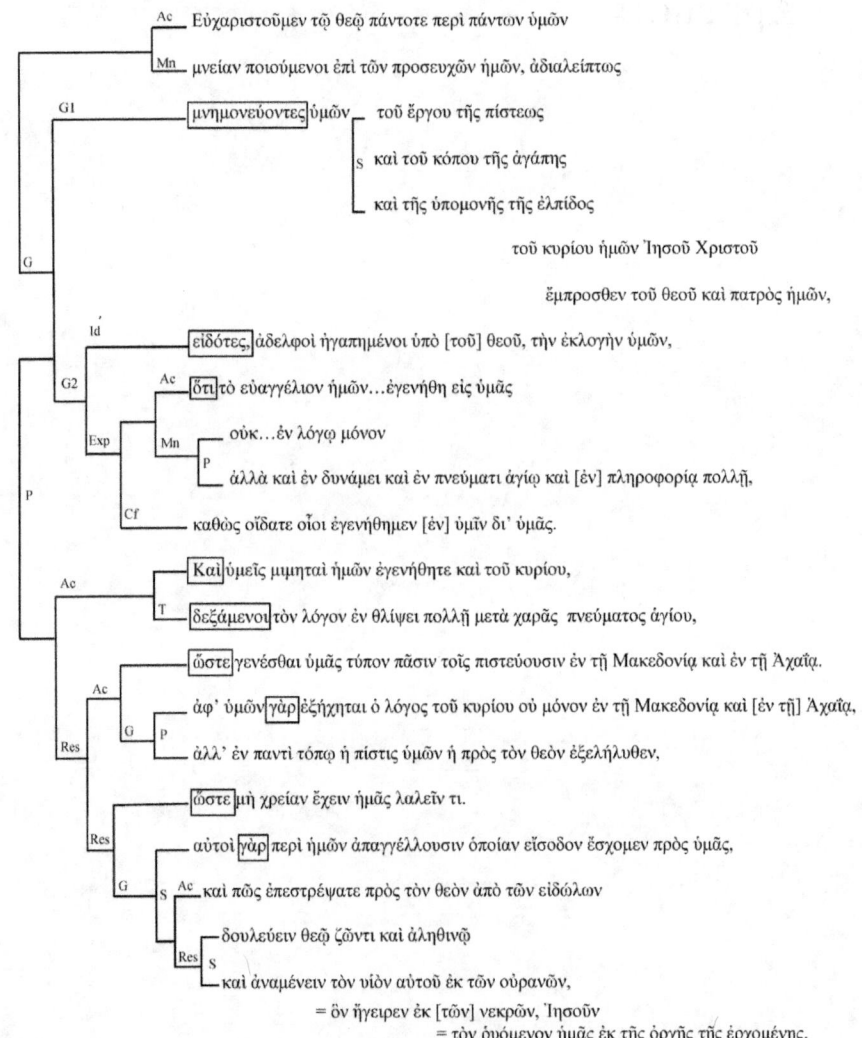

APPENDIX I

Tracing 2 (1 Thess 2:1–12)

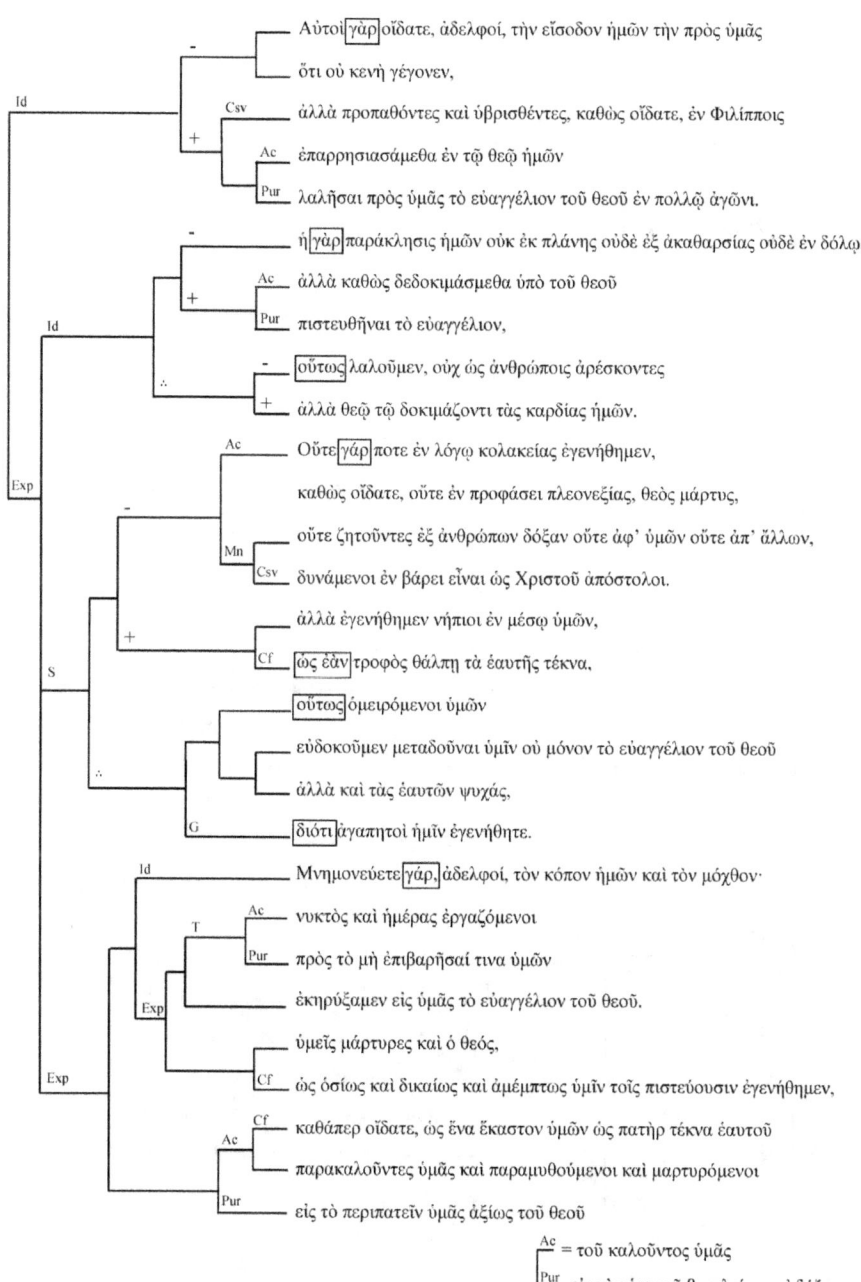

Appendix II

Tracing 3 (1 Thess 4:1–8)

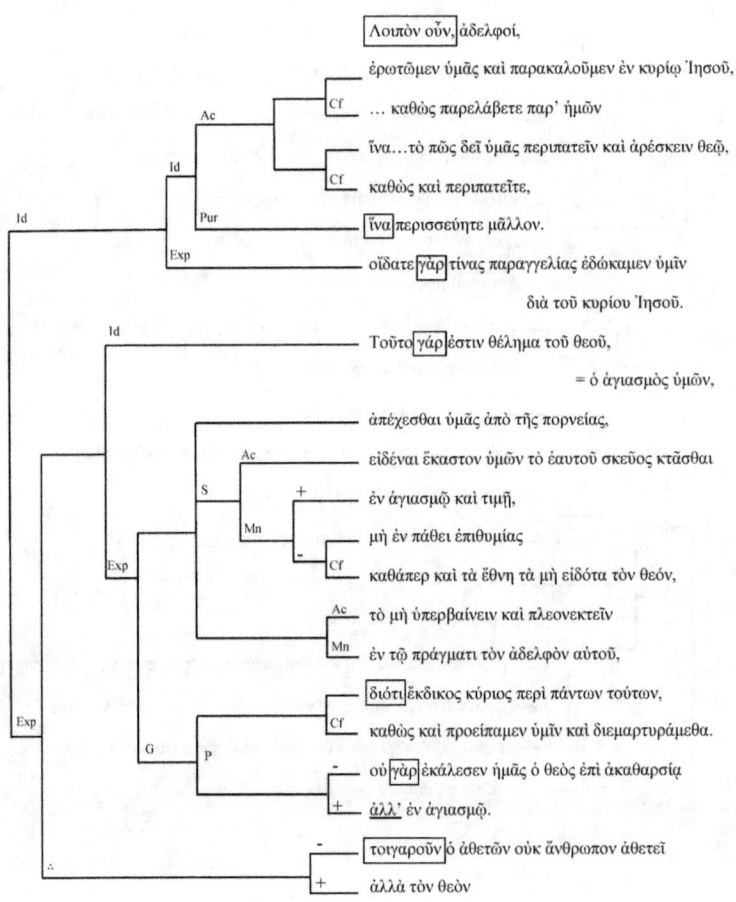

Tracing 4 (1 Thess 4:9-12)

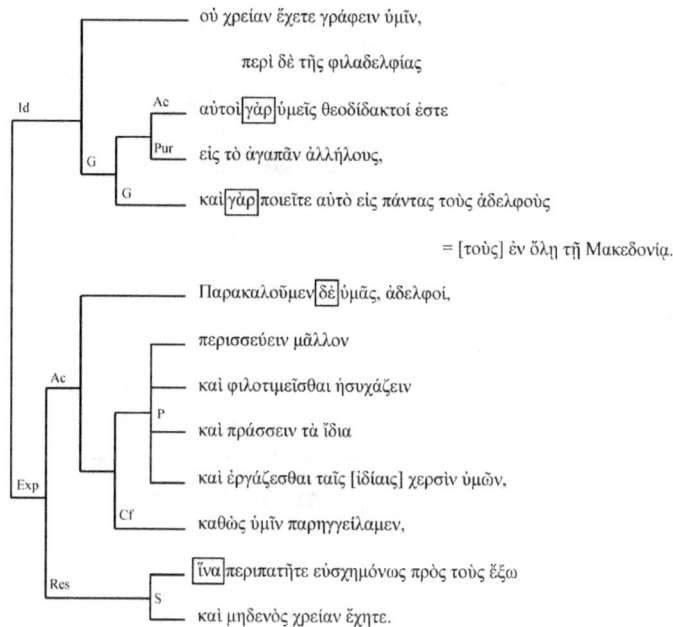

APPENDIX II

Tracing 5 (1 Thess 5:1–11)

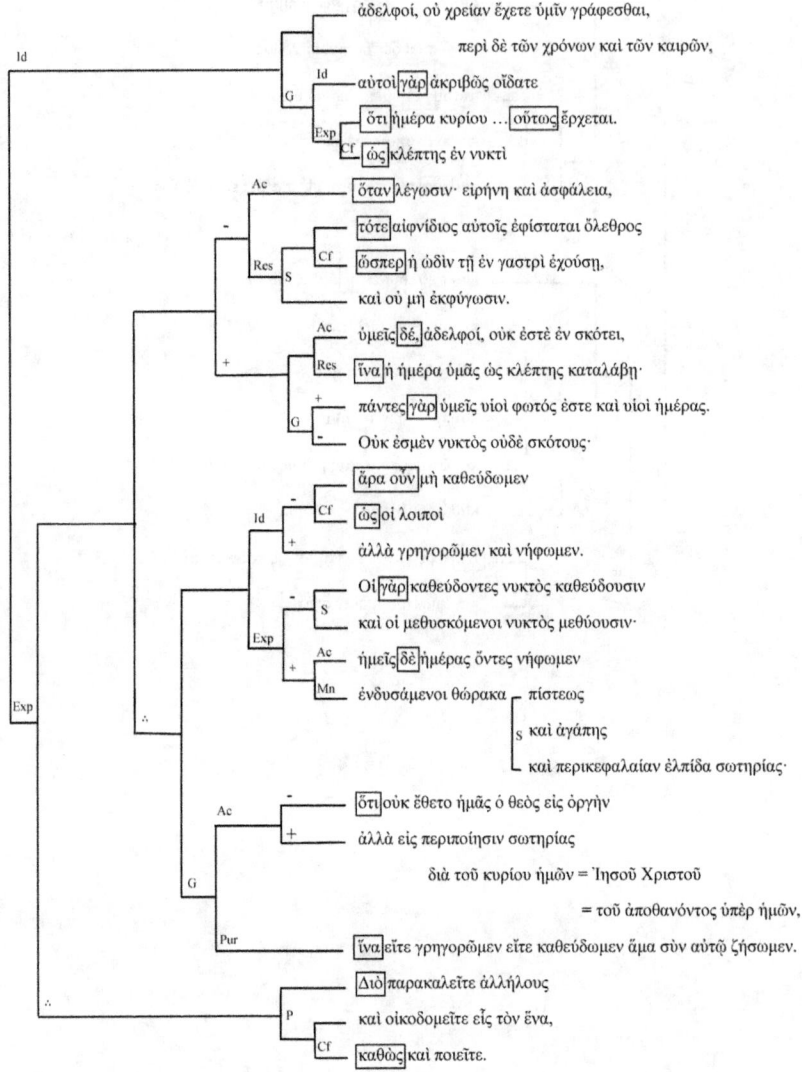

Bibliography

Aalen. "God and Light in Theophanic Texts." *TDOT* 1:164–7.
Aasgaard, R. 1997. Brotherhood in Plutarch and Paul, in H. Moxnes (ed.), 1997:166–182.
———. 2004. *'My Beloved Brothers and Sisters!': Christian Siblingship in Paul*. London: T & T Clark.
Adams, D. J. (ed.) 1997. *From East to West: Essays in Honor of Donald G. Bloesch*. Lanham, MD: University Press of America.
Aernie, M. D. 2011. *Forensic Language and the Day of the Lord Motif in Second Thessalonians 1 and the Effects on the Meaning of the Text*. Eugene, OR: Wipf & Stock.
Aichele, G. & Miscall, P. & Walsh, R. 2009. An Elephant in the Room: Historical-Critical and Postmodern Interpretation of the Bible. *JBL* 128, 383–404.
Alexander, T. E. & Baker, D. W. (eds.) 2003. *Dictionary of the Old Testament Pentateuch*. Downers Grove: IVP.
Allamani-Souri, V. 2003. Imperial Cult, in D. V. Grammenos (ed.), 2003:98–119.
Allen, L. C. 1998. *Ezekiel 20–48*: Word Biblical Commentary. Dallas: Word.
———. 2008. *Jeremiah*: The Old Testament Library. Louisville: Westminster John Knox.
Allison, D. C. J. 1982. The Pauline Epistles and the Synoptic Gospels: the Pattern of the Parallels. *NTS* 28, 1–32.
Alsup, J. E. 1978. Eschatology and Ethics in Paul. *Austin Seminary Bulletin* 94, 40–52.
Andersen, F. I. & Freedman, D. N. 1989. *Amos*: The Anchor Bible. New York: Doubleday.
Apuleius. 1947. *The Golden Ass: Being the Metamorphoses of Lucius Apuleius*. Translated by W. Adlington. Loeb Classical Library. Cambridge, MA: Harvard University Press.
Aristotle. 2004. *Nicomachean Ethics*. Translated by R. Crisp. Cambridge, UK: Cambridge University Press.
———. 1959. *Politics*. Translated by H. Rackham. Loeb Classical Library. Cambridge, MA: Harvard University Press.
———. 1967. *The Art of Rhetoric*. Translated by J. H. Freese. Loeb Classical Library. Cambridge: Harvard University Press.
Arnold, B. T. & Choi, J. H. [2003] 2009. *A Guide to Biblical Hebrew Syntax*. Cambridge, UK: Cambridge University.
Arzt, P. 1994. The "Epistolary Introductory Thanksgiving" in the Papyri and in Paul. *NovT* 36 (1), 29–46.
Ascough, R. S. 2014. *1 and 2 Thessalonians: Encountering the Christ Group at Thessalonike*. Phoenix Guides to the New Testament. Sheffield: Sheffield Phoenix.

———. 2011. Paul's 'Apocalypticism' and the Jesus Associations at Thessalonica and Corinth, in R. Cameron & M.P. Miller (eds.), 2011:151–86.

———. 2004. A Question of Death: Paul's Community-Building Language in 1 Thessalonians 4:13–18. *JBL* 123/3, 509–30.

———. 2000. The Thessalonian Christian Community as a Professional Voluntary Association. *JBL* 119, 311–28.

Ascough, R. S. & Harland, P. A. & Kloppenborg, J. S. (eds.) 2012. *Associations in the Greco-Roman World: A Source Book*. Waco: Baylor University Press.

Aune, D. E. 1993. Apocalypticism, in G. F. Hawthorne & R. P. Martin & D. G. Reid (eds.), 1993:25–35.

———. (ed.) 2010. *The Blackwell Companion to the New Testament*. Chichester: Blackwell.

———. 1987. *The New Testament in Its Literary Environment*. Philadelphia: Westminster John Knox.

———. 2000. Religion, Greco-Roman, in C. A. Evans & S. E. Porter (eds.), 2000:917–26.

———. 2003. *The Westminster Dictionary of New Testament and Early Christian Literature and Rhetoric*. Louisville: Westminster John Knox.

Aune, D. E. & Geddert, T. J. & Evans, C. A. 2000. Apocalypticism, in C. A. Evans & S. E. Porter (eds.), 2000:45–58.

Bagnall, R. S. & Brodersen, K. & Champion, C. B. & Erskine, A. & Huebner, S. R. (eds.) 2013. *The Encyclopedia of Ancient History*. Vol. IX. Chichester: Blackwell.

Balch, D. L. & Ferguson, E. & Meeks, W.A. (eds.). 1990. *Greeks, Romans, and Christians: Essays in Honor of Abraham J. Malherbe*. Minneapolis: Fortress.

Balch, D. L. & Osiek, C. (eds.) 2003. *Early Christian Families in Context: An Interdisciplinary Dialogue*. Grand Rapids: Eerdmans.

Balz, H. R. & Schneider, G. (eds.) 1990. *Exegetical Dictionary of the New Testament*. 3 vols. Grand Rapids: Eerdmans.

Barclay, J. M. G. 1993. Conflict in Thessalonica. *CBQ* 55 (3), 512–30.

———. 1996. *Jews in the Mediterranean Diaspora: From Alexander to Trajan (323 BCE–117 CE)*. Edinburgh: T & T Clark.

———. 1987. Mirror-Reading a Polemical Letter: Galatians as a Test Case. *JSNT* 31, 73–93.

———. 1995. Paul among Diaspora Jews : Anomaly or Apostate? *JSNT* 60, 89–120.

———. 2016. *Pauline Churches and Diaspora Jews*. Grand Rapids: Eerdmans.

———. 1992. Thessalonica and Corinth: Social Contrasts in Pauline Christianity. *JSNT* 47, 49–74.

Bassler J. M. 1993. Paul's Theology: Whence and Whither?, in D. M. Hay (ed.), 1993:3–17.

———. (ed.) 1991. *Pauline Theology Vol. I: Thessalonians, Philippians, Galatians, Philemon*. Minneapolis: Fortress.

Bauckham, R. 2003. *Bible and Mission*. Grand Rapids: Baker.

Bauer, W. [1957] 2000. *A Greek-English Lexicon of the New Testament and Other Early Christian Literature*, rev. by F. W. Danker, W. F. Arndt, & F. W. Gingrich. 3rd edition. Chicago: University of Chicago.

Baumgarten J. "χαιρός." In *EDNT* 2:232–6.

Baur, F. C. 1873. *Paul: The Apostle of Jesus Christ : His Life and Works, His Epistles and Teachings: a Contribution to a Critical History of Primitive Christianity*. Translated by E. Zeller. Edinburgh: Williams and Norgate.

Bayes, J. F. [2005] 2017. *The Threefold Division of the Law*. Newcastle-upon-Tyne: The Christian Institute.
Beale, G. K. 2003. *1–2 Thessalonians*. The IVP New Testament Commentary Series. Downers Grove: IVP.
———. 2011. *A New Testament Biblical Theology: The Unfolding of the Old Testament in the New*. Grand Rapids: Baker.
Beale, G. K. & Carson, D. A. (eds.) 2007. *Commentary on the New Testament Use of the Old Testament*. Grand Rapids: Baker.
Beetham, C. A. 2008. *Echoes of Scripture in the Letter of Paul to the Colossians*. Leiden: SBL.
Beker, J. C. 1980. *Paul the Apostle: The Triumph of God in Life and Thought*. Philadelphia: Fortress.
Bell, G. I. (ed.) 1924. *Jews and Christians in Egypt: The Jewish Troubles in Alexandria and the Athanasian Controversy*. Oxford: Oxford University.
Berding, K. 2003. The Hermeneutical Framework of Social-Scientific Criticism: How Much Can Evangelicals Get Involved? *EvQ* 75, 3–22.
Bertram, G. "The Paideia Concept in the New Testament." In *TDNT* 5:619–25.
———. "πατέω and Compounds in the LXX." In *TDNT* 5:941–43.
Best, E. 1986a. *First and Second Epistles to the Thessalonians*. Black's New Testament Commentary. London: Continuum.
———. 1986b. Paul's Apostolic Authority—? *JSNT* 27, 3–25.
Betz, H. D. 1975. The Literary Composition and Function of Paul's Letter to the Galatians. *NTS* 21, 353–79.
———. [1979] 1989. *Galatians*: Hermeneia. Philadelphia: Fortress.
Beutler J, "ἀδελφός." In *EDNT* 1:28–30.
Birch, B. C. & Rasmussen, L. L. 1989. *Bible and Ethics in the Christian Life*. Minneapolis: Augsburg.
Bird, M. F. 2016. *An Anomalous Jew: Paul among Jews, Greeks, and Romans*. Grand Rapids: Eerdmans.
———. 2008. Reassessing a Rhetorical Approach to Paul's Letters. *ExpTim* 119 (8), 374–79.
Bjerkelund, C. J. 1967. *Parakalô: Form, Funktion und Sinn der Parakalô-Sätze in den Paulinischen Briefen*. Oslo: Universitetsforlaget.
Black, C. C. & Watson, D. F. (eds.) 2008. *Words Well Spoken: George Kennedy's Rhetoric of the New Testament*. Waco: Baylor University.
Black, D. A. & Dockery, D. S. 2001. *Interpreting the New Testament: Essays on Methods and Issues*. Nashville: B&H.
Blasi, A. J. & Duhaime, J. & Turcotte, P. (eds.) 2002. *Handbook of Early Christianity*. Walnut Creek, CA: Altamira.
Blass, F. & Debrunner, A. 1961. *A Greek Grammar of the New Testament and Other Early Christian Literature*. Translated and edited by R. W. Funk. Chicago: University of Chicago.
Block, D. I. 1998. *The Book of Ezekiel, Chapters 25–48*: The New International Commentary on the Old Testament. Grand Rapids: Eerdmans.
Bockmuehl, M. 2008. Jewish and Christian Public Ethics in the Early Roman Empire, in G. N. Stanton & G. G. Stroumsa (eds.), 2008:342–55.
———. 2000. *Jewish Law in Gentile Churches*. Grand Rapids: Baker.

———. 2005. The Noachide Commandments and New Testament Ethics: With Special Reference to Acts 15 and Pauline Halakah. *RB* 102 (1), 72–101.

Boers, H. 1976. Form Critical Study of Paul's Letters : I Thessalonians as a Case Study. *NTS* 22, 140–58.

Botterweck, G. J & Ringgren, H. & Fabry, H. (eds.) 1977–2012. *Theological Dictionary of the Old Testament*. 15 vols. Translated and edited by J. T. Willis, G. W. Bromiley, D. E. Green, and D. W. Stott. Grand Rapids: Eerdmans.

Boring, M. E. 2015. *I & II Thessalonians*. The New Testament Library. Louisville: Westminster John Knox.

Bousset, W. [1913] 1970. *Kyrios Christos*. Translated by J. E. Steely. Nashville: Abingdon.

Bradley, K. R. [1986] 1992. Wet-Nursing at Rome: a Study in Social Relations, in B. Rawson (ed.), 1986: 201–29.

Brawley, R. L. (ed.) 2007. *Character Ethics and the New Testament: Moral Dimensions of Scripture*. Louisville: Westminster John Knox.

Bromiley, G. W. 1988. *The International Standard Bible Encyclopedia*. Vol 4. Grand Rapids: Eerdmans.

Brown, F. & Driver, S. & Briggs, C. [1906] 2005. *Brown-Driver-Briggs Hebrew and English Lexicon*. 9th ed. Peabody: Hendrickson.

Brown, G. & Yule, G. 1983. *Discourse Analysis*. Cambridge, UK: Cambridge University Press.

Brown, R. E. 1997. *An Introduction to the New Testament*. New York: Doubleday.

Bruce, F. F. 1962. Christianity Under Claudius. *BJRL* 44, 309–26.

———. 1982. *1 and 2 Thessalonians*: World Biblical Commentary. Waco: Word Books.

———. 1976. Is the Paul of Acts the Real Paul? *BJRL* 58, 282–305.

———. 1977. *Paul, Apostle of the Heart Set Free*. Grand Rapids: Eerdmans.

Brunner, E. 1947. *The Divine Imperative*. Translated by O. Wyon. Philadelphia: Westminster.

Budd, P. J. 1998. *Numbers*: Word Biblical Commentary. Dallas: Word.

Burke, T. J. 2003. *Family Matters: A Socio-Historical Study of Kinship Metaphors in 1 Thessalonians*. London & New York: T & T Clark.

———. 2000. Pauline Paternity in 1 Thessalonians. *TynBul* 51 (1), 59–80.

Cahill, L. S. & Mieth, D. (eds.) 1995. *The Family*. Maryknoll, NY: Orbis.

Calvin, J. 1960. *The Epistles of Paul the Apostle to the Romans and to the Thessalonians*. Translated by R. Mackenzie. Grands Rapids: Eerdmans.

Cancik, H. 2000. The End of the World, of History, and of the Individual in Greek and Roman Antiquity in J. J. Collins (ed.), 2000:84–125.

Canoy, R. W. 1999. Teaching Eschatology and Ethics in the Thessalonian Letters. *RevExp* 96, 249–61.

Cameron, R. & Miller, M. P. (eds.) 2011. *Redescribing Paul and the Corinthians*. Atlanta: SBL.

Campbell, W. S. 2008. *Paul and the Creation of Christian Identity*. London: T & T Clark.

Carey, G. 1998. How to Do Things with (Apocalyptic) Words: Rhetorical Dimensions of Apocalyptic Discourse. *LTQ* 33 (2), 85–101.

———. 1999. Introduction: Apocalyptic Discourse, Apocalyptic Rhetoric, in G. Carey & L. G. Bloomquist (eds.), 1999:1–17.

Carey, G. & Bloomquist, L. G. (eds.) 1999. *Vision and Persuasion: Rhetorical Dimensions of Apocalyptic Discourse*. St. Louis: Chalice.

Carras, G. P. 1990. Jewish Ethics and Gentile Converts Remarks on 1 Thess 4:3-8 in Collins, R. F. (ed.), 1990:306-15.
Carroll, J. T. & Cosgrove, C. H. & Johnson, E. E. (eds.) 1990. *Faith and History: Essays in Honor of Paul W. Meyer*. Eugene, OR: Wipf & Stock.
Carson, D. A. & Moo, D. J. 2005. *An Introduction to the New Testament*. 2nd ed. Grand Rapids: Zondervan.
Carson, D. A. 2014. Mirror-Reading with Paul and against Paul: Galatians 2:11-14 as a Test Case, in M. S. Harmon & J. E. Smith (eds.), 2014:99-112.
Cassius Dio. 1924. *Dio's Roman History*. Vol. VII. Translated by E. Cary. Loeb Classical Library. New York: G. P. Putnam's Sons.
Castelli, E. A. 1991. *Imitating Paul: A Discourse of Power*. Louisville: Westminster/John Knox.
Charlesworth, J. H. (ed.) [1983] 2011. *The Old Testament Pseudepigrapha Vol. 1: Apocalyptic Literature and Testaments*. Peabody, MA: Hendrickson.
———. (ed.) [1983] 2011. *The Old Testament Pseudepigrapha Vol. 2: Expansions of the "Old Testament" and Legends, Wisdom and Philosophical Literature, Prayers, Psalms, and Odes, Fragments of Lost Judeo-Hellenistic Works*. Peabody, MA: Hendrickson.
Church, F. F. & George, T. (eds.) 1979. *Continuity and Discontinuity in Church History*. Leiden: Brill.
Ciampa, R. E. 2008. Scriptural Language and Ideas, in S. E. Porter & C. D. Stanley (eds.), 2008:41-57.
Cicero. 1956. *De Natura Deorum Academica*. Translated by H. Rackham. Loeb Classical Library. Cambridge, MA: Harvard University Press.
Classen, C. J. 1993. St Paul's Epistles and Ancient Greek and Roman Rhetoric, in S. E. Porter & T. H. Olbricht (eds.), 1993:265-91.
Clauss, M. [1999] 2001. *Kaiser und Gott: Herrscherkult im Römischen Reich*. München & Leipzig: K. G. Saur.
Collins, J. J. 1986. *Between Athens and Jerusalem*. New York: Crossroad.
———. (ed.) 2000. *The Encyclopedia of Apocalypticism Vol. 1: The Origins of Apocalypticism in Judaism and Christianity*. London: The Continuum.
———. 1979. Introduction: Towards the Morphology of a Genre. *Semeia* 14, 1-20.
———. (ed.) 2014. *The Oxford Handbook of Apocalyptic Literature*. Oxford: Oxford University Press.
Collins, J. J. & Daniel, C. H. (eds.) 2010. *The Eerdmans Dictionary of Early Judaism*. Grand Rapids: Eerdmans.
Collins, R. F. 1993. *The Birth of the New Testament*. New York: Crossroad.
———. 2000. "I Command that This Letter Be Read": Writing as a Manner of Speaking, in K. P. Donfried & J. Beutler (eds.), 2000:319-39.
———. (ed.) 1990. *The Thessalonian Correspondence*. Louvain: Peeters.
———. 1983. The Unity of Paul's Paraenesis in 1 Thess 4:3-8; 1 Cor 7:1-7, A Significant Parallel. *NTS* 29 (3), 420-29.
Conzelmann, H. [1963] 1987. *Acts of the Apostles: A Commentary on the Acts of the Apostles*. Philadelphia: Fortress.
Cosgrove, C. H. [2011] 2013. Scripture in Christian Ethics, in J. B. Green (ed.), [2011] 2013:10-31.
Cothey A. 2005. "Ethics and Holiness in the Theology of Leviticus." *JSOT* 30 (2): 131-51.

Crim, K. (ed.) 1976. *The Interpreter's Dictionary of the Bible, Supplementary Volume*. Nashville: Abingdon.

Curran, C. E. & McCormick, R. A. (eds.) 1984. *Reading in Moral Theology No. 4: The Use of Scripture in Moral Theology*. New York: Paulist.

Davies, W. D. [1948] 1955. *Paul and Rabbinic Judaism*. London: SPCK.

De Beaugrande, R. & Dressler, W. 1981. *Introduction to Text Linguistics*. London & New York: Longman.

De Boer, M. C. 2000. Paul and Apocalyptic Eschatology, in J. J. Collins (ed.), 2000:345–83.

Deidun, T. J. [1981] 2006. *New Covenant Morality in Paul*. Rome: Editrice Pontificio Istituto Biblico.

Deissmann, A. 1908. *Light from the Ancient East: The New Testament Illustrated by Recently Discovered Texts of the Graeco-Roman World*. Translated by Lionel, R. M. & Strachan, M. A. London: Hodder and Stoughton.

———. 1926. *Paul: A Study in Social and Religious History*. Translated by W. E. Wilson. London: Hodder and Stoughton.

DeLamater, J. & Ward, A. 2013. *Handbook of Social Psychology*. 2nd ed. New York: Springer.

Delling. "The Question of Tradition in Judaism." In *TDNT* 4:12–13.

———. "πληροφορία." In *TDNT* 6:310–1.

Demetrius. 1902. *Demetrius on Style: The Greek Text of Demetrius De Elocutione with Introduction, Translation, Facsimiles, Etc.* Translated by W. R. Roberts. Cambridge, UK: Cambridge University Press.

Demosthenes. 1964. *Private Orations L-LVIII*. Translated by A. T. Murray. Loeb Classical Library. London: William Heinemann; Cambridge, MA: Harvard University Press.

Denis, A. M. 1957. L'Apôtre Paul, Prophète "Messianique" des Gentils: Étude Thématique de I Thess 2:1–6. *ETL* 33, 245–318.

DeSilva, D. A. 2000. *Honor, Patronage, Kinship & Purity: Unlocking New Testament Culture*. Downers Grove: InterVarsity.

———. 1995. Paul and The Stoa: A Comparison. *JETS* 38 (4), 547–64.

———. 1996. "Worthy of His Kingdom": Honor Discourse and Social Engineering in 1 Thessalonians. *JSNT* 64, 49–79.

De Ste. Croix, G. E. M. 1963. Why Were the Early Christians Persecuted? *The Past and Present Society* 26, 6–38.

De Villiers, P. 2006. Identity and Ethics in the Thessalonian Correspondence, in J. G. Van der Watt (ed.), 2006:335–55.

———. 2011. In the Presence of God: the Eschatology of 1 Thessalonians, in J. G. Van der Watt (ed.), 2011:302–32.

De Vos, C. S. 1999. *Church and Community Conflicts: The Relationships of the Thessalonian, Corinthian, and Philippian Churches with Their Wider Civic Communities*. Atlanta: Scholars.

Dio Chrysostom. 1940. *Oration III*. Translated by J. W. Cohoon & H. L. Crosby. Loeb Classical Library. Cambridge, MA: Harvard University Press.

———. 1946–1951. *Oration IV-V*. Translated by L. Crosby. Loeb Classical Library. Cambridge, MA: Harvard University Press.

Dodd, C. H. 1951. *Gospel and Law: The Relation of Faith and Ethics in Early Christianity*. New York: Columbia University.

Donaldson, T. L. 1997. *Paul and the Gentiles: Remapping the Apostle's Convictional World*. Minneapolis: Fortress.
Donfried, K. P. 1985. The Cults of Thessalonica and the Thessalonian Correspondence. *NTS* 31:336–56.
———. 2010. 1 Thessalonians, in D. E. Aune (ed.), 2010:504–14.
———. 1987. The Kingdom of God in Paul, in W. L. Willis (ed.), 1987:175–90.
———. 2002. *Paul, Thessalonica, and Early Christianity*. Grand Rapids: Eerdmans.
Donfried, K. P. & Beutler, J. (eds.) 2000. *The Thessalonians Debate*. Grand Rapids: Eerdmans.
Dorsey, D. A. 1991. The Law of Moses and the Christian: A Compromise. *JETS* 34 (3), 319–34.
Doty, W. G. 1973. *Letters in Primitive Christianity*. Philadelphia: Fortress.
Douglas, M. 1972. Deciphering a Meal. *Daedalus* 101 (1), 61–81.
———. 1966. *Purity and Danger: an Analysis of Concepts of Pollution and Taboo*. London: Routledge & Kegan Paul.
Dumbrell, W. J. 2002. *The Faith of Israel: A Theological Survey of the Old Testament*. Grand Rapids: Baker.
Dunn, J. D. G. 1996. *The Acts of the Apostles*: Narrative Commentaries. Valley Forge, PA: Trinity Press International.
Du Toit, P. G. 2015. "Was Paul Torah Observant Perspectives on 1 Corinthians 7:19," presented at the New Testament Seminar, Stellenbosch University, 18 March 2015.
Eadie, J. 1877. *A Commentary on the Greek Text of the Epistles of Paul to the Thessalonians*. Edited by W. Young. London: Macmillan.
Edson, C. 1948. Cults of Thessalonica (Macedonica III). *HTR* 41, 153–204.
———. (ed.) 1972. *Inscriptiones Graecae. Vol. 10: Inscriptiones Thessalonicae et Viciniae*. Berlin: de Gruyter.
Elgvin, T. 1997. 'To Master His Own Vessel'. 1 Thess 4.4 in Light of New Qumran Evidence, *NTS* (43), 604–19.
———. 2000. Wisdom With and Without Apocalyptic, in D. K. Falk & F. G. Martínez & E. M. Schuller (eds.), 2000:15–38.
Ellingworth, P. & Nida, E. A. 1976. *A Handbook on Paul's Letters to the Thessalonians*: UBS Handbook Series. New York: United Bible Societies, 1976.
Ellis, E. E. 1990. The Old Testament Canon in the Early Church, in M. J. Mulder & H. Sysling (eds.), 1990:653–90.
———. 1970. The Role of the Christian Prophet in Acts, in W. W. Gasque & R. P. Martin (eds.), 1970:55–67.
Elwell, W.A. 1993. Election and Predestination, in G. F. Hawthorne & R. P. Martin & D. G. Reid (eds.), 1993:225–9.
Engberg-Pedersen, T. 1995. Introduction, in T. Engberg-Pedersen (ed.), 1995:xiii–xxiv.
———. (ed.) 2001. *Paul beyond the Judaism/Hellenism Divide*. Louisville: Westminster John Knox.
———. (ed.) 1995. *Paul in His Hellenistic Context*. Minneapolis: Fortress.
Epictetus. 1926. *The Discourses as Reported by Arrian, the Manual, and Fragments*. Vol. I. Translated by W. A. Oldfather. Loeb Classical Library. New York: G. P. Putnam's Sons.
———. 1959. *The Discourses as Reported by Arrian, the Manual, and Fragments*. Vol. II. Translated by W. A. Oldfather. Loeb Classical Library. London: William Heinemann.

Eriksson, A. & Olbricht, T. H. & Übelacker, W. (eds.) 2002. *Rhetorical Argumentation in Biblical Texts: Essays from the Lund 2000 Conference*. Harrisburg: Trinity Press International.

Esler, P. F. 2000. "Keeping It in the Family": Culture, Kinship and Identity in 1 Thessalonians and Galatians, in J. W. van Henten & A. Brenner (eds.), 2000:145–84.

Eusebius. 1953. *The Ecclesiastical History*. Vol. II. Translated by J. E. L. Oulton. Loeb Classical Library. Cambridge, MA: Harvard University Press.

Evans, C. A & Porter, S. E. (eds.) 2000. *Dictionary of New Testament Background*. Downers Grove: IVP.

Evans, C. A. & Zacharias, H. D. 2012. *'What Does the Scripture Say?' Studies in the Function of Scripture in Early Judaism and Christianity Vol. 2: The Letters and Liturgical Traditions*. London: T & T Clark.

Fairclough, N. 1992. *Discourse and Social Change*. Cambridge; Malde: Polity.

Falk, D. K & Martínez, F. G. & Schuller, E. M. (eds.) 2000. *Sapiential, Liturgical, and Poetical Texts from Qumran: Proceedings of the Third Meeting of the International Organization for Qumran Studies, Oslo, 1998: Published in Memory of Maurice Baillet*. Leiden: Brill.

Fee, G. D. 2009. *The First and Second Letters to the Thessalonians*: New International Commentary on the New Testament. Grand Rapids: Eerdmans.

———. 1994. *God's Empowering Presence: the Holy Spirit in the Letters of Paul*. Peabody: Hendrickson.

———. 1992. On Text and Commentary on 1 and 2 Thessalonians. *SBL Seminar Papers* 31, 165–83.

———. 2007. *Pauline Christology: An Exegetical-Theological Study*. Peabody, MA: Hendrickson.

Ferguson, E. 1993. *Backgrounds of Early Christianity*. Grand Rapids: Eerdmans.

Fiorenza, E. S. 1987. Rhetorical Situation and Historical Reconstruction in 1 Corinthians. *NTS* (33), 386–403.

Firmicus. 1970. *The Error of the Pagan Religions: Ancient Christian Writers*. Translated by C. A. Forbes. New York: Newman.

Fishwick, D. 2012. *Cult, Ritual, Divinity and Belief in the Roman World*. Burlington, VT: Ashgate.

Fitzgerald, J. T. & Olbricht, T. H. & White, L. M. (eds.) 2003. *Early Christianity and Classical Culture: Comparative Studies in Honor of Abraham J. Malherbe*. Leiden: Brill.

Frame, J. E. 1912. *A Critical and Exegetical Commentary on the Epistles of St. Paul to the Thessalonians*. The International Critical Commentary. Edinburgh: T & T Clark.

France, R. T. 1986. *The Evidence for Jesus*. London: Hodder & Stoughton.

Freedman, D. N. (ed.) [1992] 2008. *Anchor Bible Dictionary*. 6 vols. New Haven: Yale University Press.

Frey, J. 2014. Apocalyptic Dualism, in J. J. Collins (ed.), 2014:271–94.

———. 2007. Paul's Jewish Identity, in J. Frey & D. R. Schwartz & S Gripentrog (eds.), 2007:285–321.

Frey, J. & Schwartz, D. R. & Gripentrog, S. (eds.) 2007. *Jewish Identity in the Greco-Roman World (Jüdische Identität in der griechisch-römischen Welt)*. Leiden: Brill.

Furnish, V. P. 2007. *1 & 2 Thessalonians*: Abingdon New Testament Commentaries. Nashville: Abingdon.

———. 1968. *Theology and Ethics in Paul*. Nashville: Abingdon.
Gager, J. G. 1975. *Kingdom and Community: The Social World of Early Christianity*. Englewood Cliffs: Prentice-Hall.
Garnsey, P. & Saller, R. [1987] 1990. *The Roman Empire: Economy, Society and Culture*. London: Duckworth.
Gasque, W. W. & Martin, R. P. (eds.) 1970. *Apostolic History and the Gospel: Biblical and Historical Essays Presented to F. F. Bruce on his 60th Birthday*. Grand Rapids: Eerdmans.
Gaventa, B. R. 1990. Apostle as Babes and Nurses in 1 Thessalonians 2:7, in J. T. Carroll & C. H. Cosgrove & E. E. Johnson (eds.), 1990:193–207.
———. 1998. *First and Second Thessalonians*: Interpretation. Louisville: Westminster John Knox.
———. 2007. *Our Mother Saint Paul*. Louisville: Westminster John Knox.
Gempf, C. 1994. The Imagery of Labor Pangs in the New Testament. *TynBul* 45, 119–35.
Goheen, M. W. 2011. *A Light to the Nations: the Missional Church and the Biblical Story*. Grand Rapids: Baker.
Goppelt. "τύπος, ἀντίτυπος, τυπικός, ὑποτύπωσις." In *TDNT* 8:246–59.
Gordon, R. 2011. The Roman Imperial Cult and the Question of Power, J. A. North & S. R. F. Price (eds.), 2011:37–70.
Gow, A. S. F. & Page, D. L. (ed.) 1968a. *The Greek Anthology: The Garland of Philip and Some Contemporary Epigrams. Vol. 1: Text and Translation*. Cambridge, UK: Cambridge University.
———. (ed.) 1968b. *The Greek Anthology: The Garland of Philip and Some Contemporary Epigrams. Vol. 2: Commentary and Indexes*. Cambridge, UK: Cambridge University.
Gradel, I. 2002. *Emperor Worship and Roman Religion*. Oxford: Clarendon.
Grammenos, D. V. (ed.) 2003. *Roman Thessaloniki*. Translated by D. Hardy. Thessaloniki: Thessaloniki Archaeological Museum.
Grant, R. M. 1961. Hellenistic Elements in 1 Corinthians, in A. P. Wikgren (ed.), 1961:60–66.
———. 1952. Hellenistic Elements in Galatians. *AThR* 34, 223–6.
———. 1949. Irenaeus and Hellenistic Culture. *HTR* 42 (1), 41–51.
Green, G. L. 2002. *The Letters to the Thessalonians*. The Pillar New Testament Commentary. Grand Rapids: Eerdmans.
Green, J. B. 1995. "Discourse Analysis and New Testament Interpretation," in J. B. Green (ed.), 1995:175–96.
———. (ed.) 1995. *Hearing the New Testament*. Grand Rapids: Eerdmans.
———. (ed.) [2011] 2013. *The New Testament and Ethics*. Grand Rapids: Baker.
Grindheim, S. 2005. *The Crux of Election: Paul's Critique of the Jewish Confidence in the Election of Israel*. Tübingen: Mohr Siebeck.
Gruen, E. S. 2004. *Diaspora: Jews amidst Greeks and Romans*. Cambridge, MA: Harvard University Press.
Gupta, N. K. 2016. *1–2 Thessalonians*: New Covenant Commentary Series. Eugene, OR: Cascade Books.
———. 2010. *Worship that Makes Sense to Paul: A New Approach to the Theology and Ethics of Paul's Cultic Metaphors*. Berlin: Walter de Gruyter.
Gustafson, J. M. 1984. The Place of Scripture in Christian Ethics: A Methodological Study, in C. E. Curran & R. A. McCormick (eds.), 1984:151–77.

Guthrie, G. 2001. Discourse Analysis, in D. A. Black & D. S. Dockery (eds.), 2001:253–71.
Haenchen, E. 1971. *The Acts of the Apostles: A Commentary*. Oxford: Blackwell.
Hagner, D. A. 2012. *The New Testament: A Historical and Theological Introduction*. Grand Rapids: Baker.
Halliday, M. A. K. 1973. *Explorations in the Functions of Language*. London: Edward Arnold.
Hanson, P. D. 1976. Apocalypticism, in K, Crim (ed.), 1976:28–34.
———. [1992] 2008. Introductory Overview in Apocalypses and Apocalypticism, in D. N. Freedman (ed.), Vol. 1. [1992] 2008:280–2.
Harland, P. A. 2002. Connections with Elites in the World of the Early Christians, in A. J. Blasi & J. Duhaime & P. Turcotte (eds.), 2002:385–408.
———. 2005. Familial Dimensions of Group Identity: "Brothers" (αδελφοι) in Associations of the Greek East. *JBL* 124, 491–513.
Harmerton-Kelly, R. 1990. Sacred Violence and "Works of Law." "Is Christ Then an Agent of Sin?" (Galatians 2:17). *CBQ* 52, 55–75.
Harmon, M. S. & Smith, J. E. (eds.) 2014. *Studies in the Pauline Epistles: Essay in Honor of Douglas J. Moo*. Grand Rapids: Zondervan.
Harnack A. [1928] 1995. The Old Testament in the Pauline Letters and in the Pauline Churches, in B. S. Rosner (ed.), 1995:27–49.
———. [1901] 1904. *What is Christianity?* 3rd ed. Translated by T. B. Saunders. New York: G. P. Putnam's Sons.
Harrington, D. J. 2010. Ethics, in J. J. Collins & C. H. Daniel (eds.), 2010:605–9.
Harrison, J. R. 2011. *Paul and the Imperial Authorities at Thessalonica & Rome: A Study in the Conflict of Ideology*. Tübingen: Mohr Siebeck.
Hartley, J. E. 2003. Holy and Holiness, Clean and Unclean, in T. E. Alexander & D. W. Baker (eds.), 2003:420–31.
Hauerwas, S. 1981. *A Community of Character: Toward a Constructive Christian Social Ethic*. Notre Dame: University of Notre Dame.
Hawthorne, G. F. 2004. *Philippians*: World Biblical Commentary. Dallas: Word.
Hawthorne, G. F. & Martin, R. P. & Reid, D. G. (eds.) 1993. *Dictionary of Paul and His Letters*. Downers Grove: IVP.
Hays, R. B. 2005. *The Conversion of the Imagination: Paul as Interpreter of Israel's Scripture*. Grand Rapids: Eerdmans.
———. 1991. Crucified with Christ: A Synthesis of the Theology of 1 and 2 Thessalonians, Philemon, Philippians, and Galatians, in J. M. Bassler (ed.), 1991:227–46.
———. 1989. *Echoes of Scripture in the Letters of Paul*. New Haven: Yale University. Press
———. 1996. *The Moral Vision of the New Testament: Community, Cross, New Creation, A Contemporary Introduction to New Testament Ethics*. San Francisco: Harper Collins.
Heger, P. 2010. Another Look at Dualism in Qumran Writings, in G. G. Xeravits, 2010:39–101.
Hellholm, D. (ed.) 1983. *Apocalypticism in the Mediterranean World and the Near East*. Tübingen: Mohr Siebeck.
———. 1980. *Das Visionenbuch des Hermas als Apokalypse: Formgeschichtliche und Texttheoretische Studien zu einer literarischen Gattung. I. Methodologische Vorüberlegungen und Makrostrukturelle Textanalyse*. Lund: Gleerup.
Hemberg, B. 1950. *Die Kabiren*. Uppsala: Almqvist & Wiksells.

Hendriksen, W. 1955. *I and II Thessalonians*: New Testament Commentary. Grand Rapids: Baker.
Hendrix, H. L. 1991. Archaeology and Eschatology, in B. A. Pearson (ed.), 1991:107–18.
———. 1987. Thessalonica. in H. Koester and H. L. Hendrix (eds.), 1987:1–49.
———. 1984. Thessalonians Honor Romans. ThD dissertation. Harvard University Press.
Hengel, M. 1989. *The 'Hellenization' of Judea in the First Century after Christ*. Translated by J. Bowden. Philadelphia: Trinity Press International.
———. 1980. *Jews, Greeks, and Barbarians: Aspects of the Hellenization of Judaism in the Pre-Christian Period*. Philadelphia: Fortress.
———. 1974. *Judaism and Hellenism: Studies in their Encounter in Palestine during the Early Hellenistic Period*. Vol. 1. Philadelphia: Fortress.
———. 1991. *The Pre-Christian Paul*. London: SCM.
Herodotus. 1966. *Herodotus I*. Translated by A. D. Godley. Loeb Classical Library. Cambridge: Harvard University Press.
Hester, J. D. 2002. Apocalyptic Discourse in 1 Thessalonians, in D. F. Watson (ed.), 2002:137–63.
Hester, J. D. & Hester, J. D. (Amador) (eds.) 2004. *Rhetorics and Hermeneutics: Wilhelm Wuellner and His influence*: Emory Studies in Early Christianity. New York: T & T Clark.
Hock, R. F. 1979. The Workshop as a Social Setting for Paul's Missionary Preaching. *CBQ* 41, 438–50.
Hodgson, R. 1982. 1 Thess 4:1–12 and The Holiness Tradition (HT). *SBL* Seminar Papers.
Hoffmann, Y. 1981. The Day of the Lord as a Concept and a Term in the Prophetic Literature. *ZAW* 93 (1), 37–50.
Holloway, J. O. 1992. *Peripateō as a Thematic Marker for Pauline Ethics*. San Francisco: Mellen Research University.
Holmes, M. W. 1998. *1 & 2 Thessalonians*: The NIV Application Commentary. Grand Rapids: Zondervan.
Holtz, T. 2000. On the Background of 1 Thessalonians 2:1–12, in K. P. Donfried & J. Beutler (eds.), 2000:69–80.
———. 1966. Zum Selbstverständnis des Apostels Paulus. *TLZ* 91, 322–30.
Homer. 1917. *The Iliad*. Vol. II. Translated by A. T. Murray. Loeb Classical Library. Cambridge: Harvard University Press.
Hopper, P. (ed.) 1982. *Tense-Aspect: Between Semantics & Pragmatics*. Amsterdam: John Benjamins.
Hornblower, S. & Spawforth, A. & Eidinow, E. (eds.) 2012. *The Oxford Classical Dictionary*, 4th ed. Oxford: Oxford University.
Horrell, D. G. 2005. *Solidarity and Difference: A Contemporary Reading of Paul's Ethics*. London: T & T Clark.
Horsley, G. H. R. 2007. Deissmann, Gustav Adolf (1866–1937), in S. E. Porter (ed.), 2007:72–73.
———. 1994. The Politarchs in Macedonia, and Beyond. *Mediterranean Archaeology* 7, 99–126.
House, P. R. 1998. *Old Testament Theology*. Downers Grove: IVP.
Hughes, F. W. 1990. The Rhetoric of 1 Thessalonians in R. F. Collins (ed.), 1990:94–116.
Jenkins, R 1996. *Social Identity*. London: Routledge.

Jensen, J. 1978. Does Porneia Mean Fornication?: A Critique of Bruce Malina. *NovT* 20 (3), 161–84.

Jewett, R. (ed.) 1986. *The Thessalonian Correspondence*. Philadelphia: Fortress.

Johanson, B. C. 1987. *To All the Brethren: A Text-Linguistic & Rhetorical Approach to I Thessalonians*. Stockholm: Almqvist and Wiksell.

Johnson-DeBaufre, M. 2010. "Gazing Upon the Invisible": Archaeology, Historiography, and the Elusive Wo/men of 1 Thessalonians" in L. Nasrallah & C. Bakirtzis & S. J. Friesen (eds.), 2010:73–108.

Johnson, E. E. 2012. Paul's Reliance on Scripture in 1 Thessalonians, in C. D. Stanley (ed.), 2012:143–62.

Johnson, L. T. 2009. *Among the Gentiles: Greco-Roman Religion and Christianity*. New Haven: Yale University.

Johnson, M. 2013. Pax Deorum, in R. S. Bagnall *et al* (eds.), 2013:5116–7.

Jokiranta, J. 2013. *Social Identity and Sectarianism in the Qumran Movement*. Leiden: Brill.

Joosten, J. 1996. *People & Land in the Holiness Code: An Exegetical Study of the Ideational Framework of the Law in Leviticus 17–26*. Leiden: Brill.

Josephus, T. F. [1987] 1993. *The Works of Josephus*. Translated by W. Whiston. Peabody, MA: Hendrickson.

Joubert, S. J. 1995. Managing the Household: Paul as Paterfamilias of the Christian Household Group in Corinth, in P. F. Esler (ed.), 1995:208–18.

Judge, E. A. 1971. Decrees of Caesar at Thessalonica. *RTR* 30, 1–7.

Kamesar, A. (ed.) 2009. *The Cambridge Companion to Philo*. Cambridge, UK: Cambridge University Press.

Kasch. "ῥύομαι." In *TDNT* 6:998–1003.

Keener, C. S. 2014. *Acts: An Exegetical Commentary*. Vol. 3: 15:1—23:35. Grand Rapids: Baker.

Keesmaat, S. C. 1994. Exodus and the Intertextual Transformation of Tradition in Romans 8:14–30. *JSNT* 54, 29–56.

Kennedy, G. A. 1984. *New Testament Interpretation through Rhetorical Criticism*. Chapel Hill: University of North Carolina Press.

Kim, S. 2005. Paul's Entry (εἴσοδος) and the Thessalonians' Faith (1 Thessalonians 1—3). *NTS* 51, 519–42.

Kittel, G. & Friedrich, G. 1964–1976. *Theological Dictionary of the New Testament*. 10 vols. Translated and edited by G. W. Bromiley. Grand Rapids: Eerdmans.

Kittredge, C. B. 1998. *Community and Authority: The Rhetoric of Obedience in the Pauline Tradition*. Harrisburg: Trinity Press International.

Kloppenborg, J. S. 1993. ΦΙΛΑΔΕΛΦΙΑ, ΘΕΟΔΙΔΑΚΤΟΣ and the Dioscuri: Rhetorical Engagement in 1 Thessalonians 4.9–12. *NTS* 39, 265–89.

Knopf, R. 1914. Paul and Hellenism. *AJT* 18 (4), 497–520.

Koch, D. A. 1986. *Die Schrift als Zeuge des Evangeliums*. Tübingen: J. C. B. Mohr (Paul Siebeck).

Koester, H. 1979. 1 Thessalonians—Experiment in Christian Writing, in F. F. Church and T. George (eds.), 1979:33–44.

Koester, H. & Hendrix, H. L. 1987. *Archaeological Resources for New Testament Studies: A Collection of Slides on Culture and Religion in Antiquity*, Vol. 1. Philadelphia: Fortress.

Kraabel, A. T. 1992. Unity and Diversity among Diaspora Synagogue, in J. A. Overman & R. S. MacLennan (eds.), 1992:21–31.
Kraus, W. 1996. *Das Volk Gottes: zur Grundlegung der Ekklesiologie bei Paulus*. Tübingen: Mohr Siebeck.
Kremer, J. "ἀνατρέφω." In *EDNT* 1:94.
Krentz, E. 2000. 1 Thessalonians: Rhetorical Flourishes and Formal Constraints, in K. P. Donfried & J. Beutler (eds.), 2000:287–318.
Kucicki, J. 2014. *Eschatology of the Thessalonian Correspondence: A Comparative Study of 1 Thess 4,13—5, 11 and 2 Thess 2, 1-12 to the Dead Sea Scrolls and the Old Testament*. Bern: Peter Lang.
Lambrecht, J. 1994. A Call to Witness by All Evangelisation in 1 Thessalonians, in J. Lambrecht. 1994:343–61.
———. 1994. *Pauline Studies: Collected Essays*. Leuven: Leuven University Press.
———. 2000. A Structural Analysis of 1 Thessalonians 4-5, in K. P. Donfried & J. Beutler (eds.), 2000:163–78.
Larsson E. "μιμητής." In *EDNT* 2:428–30.
Lategan, B. 1993. Textual Space as Rhetorical Device, in S. E. Porter & T. H. Olbricht (eds.), 1993:397–408.
Lau, P. H. W. 2011. *Identity and Ethics in the Book of Ruth a Social Identity Approach*. Berlin: De Gruyter.
Lausberg, H. 1998. *Handbook of Literary Rhetoric: A Foundation for Literary Study*. Translated by M. T. Bliss & A. Jansen & D. E. Orton; edited by D. E. Orton & R.D. Anderson. Leiden: Brill.
Levick, B. 1990. *Claudius*. London: Routledge.
Lichtenberger, H. "ῥύομαι." In *EDNT* 2:214–5.
Liddell, H. G. & Scott, R. & Jones, H. S. & Mckenzie, R. [1843] 1996. *A Greek-English Lexicon with New Supplement*. 9th ed. Oxford: Clarendon.
Lieu, J. M. 2004. *Christian Identity in the Jewish and Graeco-Roman World*. Oxford: Oxford University Press.
Lightfoot, J. B. 1904. *Notes on Epistles of St. Paul from Unpublished Commentaries*. London: Macmillan.
———. 1913. *Saint Paul's Epistle to the Philippians*. London: Macmillan.
Litfin, D. 1994. *St. Paul's Theology of Proclamation: 1 Corinthians 1—4 and Greco-Roman Rhetoric*. Cambridge: Cambridge University.
Livy. 1952-1960. *Livy*. Vols. I–III. Translated by B. O. Foster. Loeb Classical Library. London: Harvard University Press.
Long, F. J. 2005. From Epicheiremes to Exhortation: A Pauline Method for Moral Persuasion in 1 Thessalonians, in T. H. Olbricht & A. Eriksson (eds.), 2005:179–95.
Longenecker, R. N. (ed.) 1996. *Patterns of Discipleship in the New Testament*. Grand Rapids: Eerdmans.
———. 1964. *Paul, Apostle of Liberty*. Grand Rapids: Baker.
Louw, J. P. & Nida, E. A. (eds.) 1989. *Greek-English Lexicon of the New Testament Based on Semantic Domains 2 vols*. 2nd ed. New York: United Bible Societies.
Luckensmeyer, D. 2009. *The Eschatology of First Thessalonians*. Göttingen: Vandenhoeck & Ruprecht.
———. 2012. Intertextuality Between Obadiah and First Thessalonians, in C. A. Evans & H. D. Zacharias (eds.), 2012:98–120.

Lucretius. [1924] 1992. *De Rerum Natura*. Translated by W. H. D. Rouse. Loeb Classical Library. Cambridge, MA: Harvard University Press.

Lüdemann, H. 1872. *Die Anthropologie des Apostels Paulus*. Kiel: Universitäts Buchhandlung.

Lünemann, G. 1880. *Critical and Exegetical Handbook to the Epistles of St. Paul to the Thessalonians*. Translated by P. J. Gloag. Edinburgh: T & T Clark.

Malbon, E. S. 1983. No Need to Have Any One Write: A Structural Exegesis of 1 Thessalonians. *Semeia* 26, 57–83.

Malherbe, A. J. 1988. *Ancient Epistolary Theorists*. Atlanta: Scholars Press.

———. 1983. Exhortation in First Thessalonians. *NovT* 25, 238–56.

———. 1970. "Gentle as a Nurse": The Cynic Background to I Thess II. *NovT* 12, 203–17.

———. 1992. Hellenistic Moralist and the New Testament. *ANRW* 2.26.1, 267–333.

———. 2000. *The Letters to the Thessalonians*. The Anchor Bible: Doubleday.

———. 1986. *Moral Exhortation, A Greco-Roman Sourcebook*. Philadelphia: The Westminster Press.

———. 1989. *Paul and the Popular Philosophers*, Minneapolis: Fortress.

———. 1987. *Paul and the Thessalonians: The Philosophic Tradition of Pastoral Care*. Philadelphia: Fortress.

———. 1985. Paul: Hellenistic Philosopher or Christian Pastor? *AThR* 68 (1), 3–13.

———. [1977] 1983. *Social Aspects of Early Christianity*. Philadelphia: Fortress.

Marcus, J. & Soards, M. L. (eds.) 1989. *Apocalyptic and the New Testament*. Sheffield: Sheffield Academic.

Marshall, I. H. 1980. *The Acts of the Apostles*: Tyndale New Testament Commentaries. Grand Rapids: Eerdmans.

———. 1990. Election and Calling to Salvation in 1 and 2 Thessalonians, in R. F. Collins (ed.), 1990:259–76.

———. 1983. *1 and 2 Thessalonians*. The New Century Bible Commentary. Grand Rapids: Eerdmans.

Martin, D. B. 2001. Paul and the Judaism/Hellenism Dichotomy: Toward a Social History of the Question, in T. Engberg-Pedersen (ed.), 2001:29–61.

———. 2003. Slave Families and Slaves in Families, in D. L. Balch & C. Osiek (eds.), 2003:207–30.

Martin, D. M. 1995. *1, 2 Thessalonians*. The New American Commentary. Nashville: B&H.

Martin, T. W. 2010. Invention and Arrangement in Recent Pauline Rhetorical Studies: A Survey of the Practices and the Problems, in J. P. Sampley & P. Lampe (eds.), 2010:48–118.

Matera, F. J. 2007. *New Testament Theology: Exploring Diversity and Unity*. Louisville: Westminster John Knox.

Maurer. "σκεῦος." In *TDNT* 7:358–67.

May, D. M. 1991. *Social Scientific Criticism of the New Testament: A Bibliography*. Macon Mercer University Press.

May, H. D. 1963. Cosmological Reference in the Qumran Doctrine of the Two Spirits and in Old Testament Imagery. *JBL* 82 (1), 1–14.

McDonald, L. M. & Porter, S. E. 2000. *Early Christianity and Its Sacred Literature*. Peabody, MA: Hendrickson.

McNeel, J. H. 2014. *Paul as Infant and Nursing Mother: Metaphor, Rhetoric, and Identity in 1 Thessalonians 2:5–8*. Atlanta: SBL.

Meeks, W. A. 1983a. *The First Urban Christians: The Social World of the Apostle Paul.* New Haven: Yale University.

———. 2001. Judaism, Hellenism, and the Birth of Christianity, in T. Engberg-Pedersen (ed.), 2001:17–27.

———. 1986. *The Moral World of the First Christians.* Philadelphia: The Westminster.

———. 1993. *The Origins of Christian Morality: The First Two Centuries.* New Haven and London: Yale University Press.

———. 1983b. Social Functions of Apocalyptic Language, in D. Hellholm (ed.), 1983:687–705.

———. 1972. *The Writings of St. Paul.* New York: Norton.

Meiser, M. (ed.) 2012. *Torah in the Ethics of Paul.* Edinburgh: T & T Clark.

Metzger, B. M. 1994. *A Textual Commentary on the Greek New Testament. 2nd ed.: A Companion Volume to the United Bible Societies' Greek New Testament. 4th ed.* New York: United Bible Societies.

Metzger, B. M. & Ehrman, B. D. 2005. *The Text of the New Testament: Its Transmission, Corruption, and Restoration.* 4th ed. New York; Oxford: Oxford University.

Meyer, E. E. 2013. "From cult to community: The two halves of Leviticus." *Verbum et Ecclesia* 34 (2): 1–7.

Michaelis. "σκηνοποιός." In *TDNT* 5:393–4.

Michel. "οἰκοδομέω in the NT." In *TDNT* 5:138–42.

Míguez, N. O. 2012. *The Practice of Hope: Ideology and Intention in 1 Thessalonians.* Minneapolis: Fortress.

Milligan, G. 1908. *St. Paul's Epistles to the Thessalonians.* Classic Commentaries on the Greek New Testament. London: Macmillan and Co.

Miner, E. 1993. Allusion, in A. Preminger & T. V. F. Brogan (eds.), 1993:38–40.

Moo, D. J. 2013. *Galatians.* Baker Exegetical Commentary on the New Testament. Grand Rapids: Baker.

———. 2007. Paul's Universalizing Hermeneutic in Romans. *SBJT* 11 (3), 62–90.

Moo, J. A. 2014. Of Parents and Children: 1 Corinthians 4:15–16 and Life in the Family of God, in M. S. Harmon & J. E. Smith (eds.), 2014:57–73.

Moore, G. F. [1927] 1955. *Judaism in the First Centuries of the Christian Era: the Age of the Tannaim.* Vol. 1. Cambridge: Harvard University Press.

Morris, C. [1938] 1955. Foundations of the Theory of Signs, in O. Neurath & R. Carnap & C. Morris (eds.), [1938] 1955:78–137.

Morris, L. [1984] 2009. *1 and 2 Thessalonians*: Tyndale New Testament Commentaries. Downers Grove: IVP.

Moule, C. F. D. 1960. *An Idiom Book of New Testament Greek.* Cambridge: Cambridge University Press.

Moulton, J. H. & Howard, W. F. & Turner, N. [1906] 1976. *A Grammar of New Testament Greek.* Vol. 3. Edinburgh: T. & T. Clark.

Mouton, E. 1996. The Communicative Power of Ephesians, in S. E. Porter & T. H. Olbricht (eds.), 1996:280–307.

———. 2002. *Reading a New Testament Document Ethically.* Atlanta: SBL.

———. 1997. The (Trans)formative Potential of the Bible as Resource for Christian Ethos and Ethics. *Scriptura* 62, 245–57.

Moxnes, H. (ed.) 1997. *Constructing Early Christian Families: Family as Social Reality and Metaphor.* London: Routledge.

———. 1997. What is Family? Problems in Constructing Early Christian Families, in H. Moxnes (ed.), 1997:13–41.
Mulder, M. J. & Sysling, H. (eds.) 1990. *Mikra: Text, Translation, Reading and Interpretation of the Hebrew Bible in Ancient Judaism and Early Christianity*. Assen: Van Gorcum.
Müller, M. 2012. Torah Ethics in First Thessalonians, in M. Meiser (ed.), 2012:31–40.
Munck, J. 1967. *The Acts of the Apostles*. The Anchor Bible. Garden City: Doubleday.
Munro, W. 1983. *Authority in Paul and Peter: the Identification of a Pastoral Stratum in the Pauline Corpus and 1 Peter*. Cambridge, UK: Cambridge University Press.
Murphy, F. J. 2012. *Apocalypticism in the Bible and Its World*. Grand Rapids: Baker.
Murphy-O'Connor, J. 1996. *Paul: A Critical Life*. Oxford; New York: Oxford University.
Myers, J. M. & Freed, E. D. 1966. Is Paul also Among the Prophets? *Interpretation* 20, 40–53.
Nanos, M. D. 2009. The Myth of the 'Law-Free' Paul Standing Between Christians and Jews. *Studies in Christian-Jewish Relations* 4, 1–21.
Nasrallah, L. & Bakirtzis, C. & Friesen, S. J. (eds.) 2010. *From Roman to Early Christian Thessalonikē: Studies in Religion and Archaeology*. Cambridge, MA: Harvard University Press.
Neurath, O. & Carnap, R. & Morris, C. (eds.) [1938] 1955. *International Encyclopedia of Unified Science* Vol. I, Nos. 1–5. Chicago: University of Chicago Press.
Neusner, J. [1973] 1979. *From Politics to Piety: The Emergence of Pharisaic Judaism*. New York: KTAV.
———. 1982. Two Pictures of the Pharisees: Philosophical Circle or Eating Club. *AThR* 64, 525–38.
Newsom, C. A. 2004. *The Self as Symbolic Space: Constructing Identity and Community at Qumran*. Leiden: Brill.
Nicholl, C. R. 2004. *From Hope to Despair in Thessalonica*. Cambridge, UK: Cambridge University Press.
Nida, E. A. & Louw, J. P. & Snyman, A. H. & Cronje J. v. W. 1983. *Style and Discourse: With Special Reference to the Text of the Greek New Testament*. Cape Town: Bible Society.
Nigdelis, P. M. 1994. Synagoge(n) und Gemeinde der Juden in Thessaloniki: Fragen auf grund einer neuen jüdischen Grabinschrift der Kaiserzeit, *ZPE* 102, 297–306.
———. 2010. Voluntary Associations in Roman Thessalonikē : In Search of Identity and Support in a Cosmopolitan Society, in L. Nasrallah & C. Bakirtzis & S. J. Friesen (eds.), 2010:13–47.
Norden, E. 1898. *Die Antike Kunstprosa: vom VI. Jahrhundert v. Chr. Bis in Die Zeit der Renaissance*. Leipzig: Teubner.
North, J. A. & Price, S. R. F. (eds.) 2011. *The Religious History of the Roman Empire: Pagans, Jews, and Christians*. Oxford: Oxford University Press.
Oakes, P. 2005. Re-mapping the Universe: Paul and the Emperor in 1 Thessalonians and Philippians. *JSNT* 27 (3), 301–22.
O'Brien, P. T. 1991. *The Epistle to the Philippians*: The New International Greek Testament Commentary. Grand Rapids: Eerdmans.
Olbricht, T. H. 1990. An Aristotelian Rhetorical Analysis of 1 Thessalonians, in D. L. Balch & E. Ferguson & W. A. Meeks (eds.), 1990:216–36.
Olbricht, T. H. & Eriksson, A. (eds.) 2005. *Rhetoric, Ethic, and Moral Persuasion in Biblical Discourse*. London: T & T Clark.

Osborne, G. R. 2006. *The Hermeneutical Spiral: A Comprehensive Introduction to Biblical Interpretation*. Downers Grove: IVP.

Osiek, C. 1995. "The New Testament and the Family," in L. S. Cahill & D. Mieth (eds.), 1995:1–9.

Otto, W. F. 1965. *Dionysus: Myth and Cult*. Translated with an Introduction by R. B. Palmer. Bloomington: Indiana University.

Overman, J. A. & MacLennan, R. S. (eds.) 1992. *Diaspora Jews and Judaism: Essays in Honor of, and in Dialogue with, A. Thomas Kraabel*. Atlanta: Scholars Press.

Owens, T. J. & Samblanet, S. 2013. Self and Self-Concept, in J. DeLamater & A. Ward (ed.), 2013:225–50.

Paddock, A, 2008. Putting Family Language Back into the Family of God. *Stone-Campbell Journal* 11, 83–91.

Peacock, J. L. [1986] 2004. *The Anthropological Lens: Harsh Light, Soft Focus*. 2nd ed. Cambridge: Cambridge University.

Pearson, B. A. 1971. 1 Thessalonians 2:13–16: a Deutero-Pauline Interpolation. *HTR* 64, 79–94.

———. (ed.) 1991. *The Future of Early Christianity*. Minneapolis: Fortress.

Perelman, C. & Olbrechts-Tyteca, L. 1969. *The New Rhetoric*. Translated by J. Wilkinson & P. Weaver. Notre Dame: University of Notre Dame.

Petersen, N. R. 1985. *Rediscovering Paul: Philemon and the Sociology of Paul's Narrative World*. Philadelphia: Fortress.

Pfleiderer, O. 1906. *Primitive Christianity: Its Writings and Teachings in Their Historical Connections*. 4 vols. Translated by W. Montgomery. New York: G. P. Putnam's Sons.

Philo. 1995. *The Works of Philo*. Translated by C. D. Yonge. Peabody, MA: Hendrickson.

Philodemus. 1998. *On Frank Criticism*. Introduction, Translation, and Notes by D. Konstan. & D. Clay. & C. E. Glad & J. C. Thom. & J. Ware. Atlanta: *SBL*.

Plato. 1937–1942. *The Republic*. Vol. I-II. Translated by P. Shorey. Loeb Classical Library. Cambridge, MA: Harvard University Press.

Pliny. 1969–1975. *Letters and Panegyricus*. Vol. I–II. Translated by B. Radice. Loeb Classical Library. Cambridge, MA: Harvard University Press.

Plummer, R. L. 2006. *Paul's Understanding of the Church's Mission: Did the Apostle Paul Expect the Early Christian Communities to Evangelize?* Waynesboro, GA: Paternoster.

Plutarch. 1970. *De Iside Et Osiride*. Translated by J. G. Griffiths. Cardiff: University of Wales.

———. 1949–1956. *Moralia*. Vol. I–II. Translated by F. C. Babbitt. Loeb Classical Library. Cambridge: Harvard University Press.

———. 1939. *Moralia*. Vol. VI. Translated by W. C. Helmbold. Loeb Classical Library. Cambridge: Harvard University Press.

———. 1959. *Moralia*. Vol. VII. Translated by P. H. Lacy. & B. Einarson. Loeb Classical Library. Cambridge, Harvard University Press.

———. 1936. *Moralia*. Vol. X. Translated by H. N. Fowler. Loeb Classical Library. Cambridge: Harvard University Press.

Pobee, J. S. 1985. *Persecution and Martyrdom in the Theology of Paul*. Sheffield: JSOT.

Polhill, J. B. 1992. *Acts*: The New American Commentary. Nashville: Broadman & Holman.

Popkes W. "ζηλόω." In *TDNT* 5:100–101.

Porter, S. E. (ed.) 2007. *Dictionary of Biblical Criticism and Interpretation*. London: Routledge.

———. 1995. Discourse Analysis and New Testament Studies: An Introductory Survey, in S. E. Porter & D. A. Carson (eds.), 1995:14–35.

———. 2010. A Functional Letter Perspective: Towards a Grammar of Epistolary Form, in S. E. Porter & S. A. Adams (eds), 2010:9–31.

———. 1993a. Holiness, Sanctification, in G. F. Hawthorne & R. P. Martin & D. G. Reid (eds.), 1993:397–402.

———. 2015. *Linguistic Analysis of the Greek New Testament: Studies in Tools, Methods, and Practice*. Grand Rapids: Baker Academic.

———. 1997. Rhetorical Analysis and Discourse Analysis, in S. E. Porter & T. H. Olbricht (eds.), 1997:249–74.

———. 1993b. Theoretical Justification for Application of Rhetorical Categories to Pauline Epistolary Literature, in S. E. Porter & T. H. Olbricht (eds.), 1993:100–122.

———. 1989. *Verbal Aspect in the Greek of the New Testament, with Reference to Tense and Mood*. New York: Peter Lang.

Porter, S. E. & Adams, S. A. (eds) 2010. *Paul and the Ancient Letter Form*. Leiden: Brill.

Porter, S. E. & Carson, D. A. (eds.) 1995. *Discourse Analysis and Other Topics in Biblical Greek*. Sheffield: Sheffield Academic.

Porter, S. E. & Olbricht, T. E. (eds.) 1993. *Rhetoric and the New Testament: Essays from the 1992 Heidelberg Conference*. Sheffield: JSOT.

———. (eds.) 1996. *Rhetoric, Scripture & Theology: Essays from the 1994 Pretoria Conference*. Sheffield: Sheffield Academic.

———. (eds.) 1997. *The Rhetorical Analysis of Scripture: Essays from the 1995 London Conference*. Sheffield: Sheffield Academic.

Porter, S. E. & Stanley, C. D. (eds.) 2008. *As It Is Written: Studying Paul's Use of Scripture*. Atlanta: *SBL*.

Porter, S. E. & Tombs, D. (eds.) 1995. *Approaches to New Testament Studies*. Sheffield: Sheffield Academic.

Preminger, A. & Brogan, T. V. F. (eds.) 1993. *The New Princeton Encyclopedia of Poetry and Poetics*. Princeton: Princeton University.

Price, S. R. F. 1984a. Gods and Emperors: The Greek Language of the Roman Imperial Cult. *JHS* 104, 79–95.

———. 1984b. *Rituals and Power: The Roman Imperial Cult in Asia Minor*. Cambridge, UK: Cambridge University Press.

Procksch. "The Use of the Term Holiness in the OT." In *TDNT* 1:89–91.

Punt, J. 2011. Hermeneutics in Identity Formation: Paul's Use of Genesis in Galatians 4. *HvTSt* 67 (1), 1–9.

Purvis, J. D. 1976. The Paleography of the Samaritan Inscription from Thessalonica. *BASOR* 221, 121–3.

Quintilian. 2001. *The Orator's Education II, III, V*. Translated by D. A. Russell. Loeb Classical Library. Cambridge, MA: Harvard University Press.

Ramsay, W. M. 1907. *St. Paul the Traveller and the Roman Citizen*. London: Stoughton.

Rawson, B. (ed.) [1986] 1992. *The Family in Ancient Rome: New Perspectives*. London: Routledge.

Reed, J. T. 1996. Discourse Analysis as New Testament Hemeneutic: A Retrospective and Prospective Appraisal. *JETS* 39 (2), 223–40.

———. 1997. *A Discourse Analysis of Philippians: Method and Rhetoric in the Debate over Literary Integrity*. Sheffield: Sheffield Academic.

———. 1993. Using Ancient Rhetorical Categories to Interpret Paul's Letters: A Question of Genre, in S. E. Porter & T. H. Olbricht (eds.), 1993:292–324.

Renz, T. 2002. *The Rhetorical Function of the Book of Ezekiel*. Leiden: Brill.

Rice, D. G. & Stambaugh, J. E. 1979. *Sources for the Study of Greek Religion*. Missoula: SBL.

Richard, E. J. [1995] 2007. *First and Second Thessalonians*: Sacra Pagina. Collegeville, MN: The Liturgical.

Richards, I. A. [1936] 1965. *The Philosophy of Rhetoric*. New York: Oxford University Press.

Riches, J. K. 1993. *A Century of New Testament Study*. Cambridge, UK: Lutterworth.

Ricoeur, P. 1990. *Time and Narrative*. Vol. 3. Translated by K. Blamey & D. Pellauer. Chicago: University of Chicago.

Riesner, R. 1998. *Paul's Early Period: Chronology, Mission Strategy, Theology*. Translated by D. Stott. Grand Rapids: Eerdmans.

Robbins, V. K. 1996. *Exploring the Texture of Texts: A Guide to Socio-Rhetorical Interpretation*. Valley Forge: Trinity Press International.

———. 2002. The Intertexture of Apocalyptic Discourse in the Gospel of Mark, in D. E. Watson (ed.), 2002:11–44.

———. 2004. Where is Wuellner's Anti-Hermeneutical Hermeneutic Taking Us?: From Schleiermacher to Thistleton and Beyond, in J. D. Hester & J. D. Hester (Amador) (eds.), 2004:105–25.

Roberts, A. & Donaldson, J. & Coxe, A. C. (eds.) 1951. *The Ante-Nicene Fathers*. Vol. 1–3. Grand Rapids: Eerdmans.

Roetzel, C. J. [1975] 1982. *The Letters of Paul: Conversations in Context*. London: SCM.

———. 1999. *Paul: The Man and the Myth*. Edinburgh: T & T Clark.

———. 1986. Theodidaktoi and Handwork in Philo and 1 Thessalonians, in A. Vanhoye (ed.), 1986:324–31.

Roloff J. "ἐκκλησία." In *EDNT* 1:410-5.

Rosner, B. S. 2013. *Paul and the Law*: New Studies in Biblical Theology. Downers Grove: IVP.

———. 1999. *Paul, Scripture, and Ethics: A Study of 1 Corinthians 5–7*. Grand Rapids: Baker.

———. (ed.) 1995. *Understanding Paul's Ethics*. Grand Rapids: Eerdmans.

Rousseau, J. 1986. *A Multidimensional Approach toward the Communication of an Ancient Canonised Text: Towards Determining the Thrust, Perspective and Strategy of 1 Peter*. D.D. thesis. University of Pretoria.

Rowland, C. 2010. Apocalypticism, in J. J. Collins & D. C. Harlow (eds.), 2010:345–8.

Runge, S. E. 2010. *Discourse Grammar of the Greek New Testament: A Practical Introduction for Teaching and Exegesis*. Peabody, MA: Hendrickson.

Safrai, S. & Stern M. 1976. *The Jewish People in the First Century Vol. 2: Historical Geography, Political History, Social, Cultural and Religious Life and Institutions*. Amsterdam: Van Gorcum.

Sailors, T. B. 2000. Wedding Textual and Rhetorical Criticism to Understand the Text of 1 Thessalonians 2.7. *JSNT* 80, 81–98.

Sanders, J. T. "The Transition from Opening Epistolary Thanksgiving to Body in the Letters of the Pauline Corpus." *JBL* 81:348–62.

Sandnes, K. O. 1994. *A New Family: Conversion and Ecclesiology in the Early Church with Cross-Cultural Comparisons*. Berne: Peter Lang.

Schenk, W. 1984. *Die Philipper Briefe des Paulus*. Stuttgart: Kohlhammer.

Schlueter, C. J. 1994. *Filling up the Measure: Polemical Hyperbole in 1 Thessalonians 2:14–16*. Sheffield: Sheffield Academic.

Schneider G. "ἀρέσκω." In *EDNT* 1:151.

———. "παιδεία." In *EDNT* 3:3.

Schneider J. "ὄλεθρος." In *TDNT* 5:168–9.

Schnelle, U. 2005. *Apostle Paul: His Life and Theology*. Translated by Eugene Boring. Grand Rapids: Baker.

Schmitz. "παραγγέλλω, παραγγελία: The Hellenistic Jewish Usage." In *TDNT* 5:762–3.

Schoedel, W. R. & Wilken, R. L. (eds.) 1979. *Early Christian Literature and the Classical Intellectual Tradition: In Honorem Robert M. Grant*. Paris: Beauchesne.

Schreiner, T. R. [1990] 2008. *Interpreting the Pauline Epistles*. Grand Rapids: Baker.

———. 2010. *40 Questions about Christians and Biblical Law*. Grand Rapids: Kregel.

Schrenk. "ἐκλογή in the New Testament." In *TDNT* 4:179–80.

Schuler, C. 1960. The Macedonian Politarchs. *CP* 55 (2), 90–100.

Schweitzer A. 1931. *The Mysticism of Paul the Apostle*. London: A & C Black.

———. [1933] 1949. *Out of My Life and Thought*. Translated by E. Skillings. New York: Henry Hold and Company.

Seesemann. "πατέω and Compounds in the NT." In *TDNT* 5:943–5.

Segal, A. F. 1992. *Paul the Convert: The Apostolate and Apostasy of Saul the Pharisee*. New Haven: Yale University Press.

Seifrid, M. A. 1999. Faith, Hope, and Love: Paul's Message to the Church at Thessalonica. *SBJT* 3 (3): 58–64.

———. 1992. *Justification by Faith: The Origin and Development of a Central Pauline Theme*. Leiden: Brill.

Seneca. 1967. *Ad Lucilium Epistulae Morales*. Vol. I. Translated by R. M. Gummere. Loeb Classical Library. Cambridge, MA: Harvard University Press.

———. 1958. *Moral Essays*. Vol. I. Translated by J. W. Basore. Loeb Classical Library. Cambridge, MA: Harvard University Press.

Sherk, R. K. (ed.) 1988. *The Roman Empire: Augustus to Hadrian*. Cambridge, UK: Cambridge University Press.

Shogren, G. S. 2012. *1 & 2 Thessalonians*: Exegetical Commentary on the New Testament. Grand Rapids: Zondervan.

Silva, M. (ed.) 2014. *New International Dictionary of New Testament Theology and Exegesis*. 4 vols. Grand Rapids: Zondervan.

———. 1993. Old Testament in Paul. in G. F. Hawthorne *et al* (eds.), 1993:630–42.

———. 2005. *Philippians*: Baker Exegetical Commentary on the New Testament. Grand Rapids: Baker Academic.

Sissa, G. & Detienne, M. 2000. *The Daily Life of the Greek Gods*. Translated by J. Lloyd. Stanford: Stanford University Press.

Smit, D. J. 1991. The Bible and Ethos in a New South Africa. *Scriptura* 37, 51–67.

———. 1990. The Ethics of Interpretation—New Voices from the USA. *Scriptura* 33, 16–28.

Smith, A. 1995. *Comfort One Another: Reconstructing the Rhetoric and Audience of 1 Thessalonians*. Louisville: Westminster John Knox.

―――. 2000. *The First Letter to the Thessalonians*: The New Interpreter's Bible Vol. XI: 673–737. Nashville: Abingdon.
Smith, D. E. [1992] 2008. Table Fellowship, in D. N. Freedman (ed.), Vol. 6. [1992] 2008:302–4.
Smith, G. V. 1998. *Amos*: Mentor Commentary. Fearn, Ross-shire: Mentor.
―――. 1991. Continuity and Discontinuity in Amos' Use of Tradition. *JETS* 34, 33–42.
Sommer, B. D. 1998. *A Prophet Reads Scripture: Allusion in Isaiah 40-66*. Stanford: Stanford University Press.
Spicq, C. 1994. *Theological Lexicon of the New Testament*. Vol. 3. Translated by J. D. Ernest. Peabody, MA: Hendrickson.
Sprinkle, J. M. 2000. The Rationale of the Laws of Clean and Unclean in the Old Testament, *JETS* 43 (4), 637–57.
Stählin. "παραμυθέομαι, παραμυθία, παραμύθιον." In *TDNT* 5:816–23.
Stamps, D. L. 1993. Rethinking the Rhetorical Situation, in S. E. Porter & T. H. Olbricht (eds.), 1993:193–210.
―――. 1995. Rhetorical Criticism of the New Testament: Ancient and Modern Evaluations of Argumentation, in S. E. Porter & D. Tombs (eds.), 1995:129–69.
Stanley, C. D. 1992. *Paul and the Language of Scripture: Citation Technique in the Pauline Epistles and Contemporary Literature*. Cambridge, UK: Cambridge University.
―――. (ed.) 2012. *Paul and Scripture*. Atlanta: SBL.
―――. 2008. Paul's "Use" of Scripture: Why the Audience Matters, in S. E. Porter & C. D. Stanley (eds.), 2008:125–55.
―――. 1990. 'Under a Curse': A Fresh Reading of Galatians 3.10–14. *NTS* (36), 481–511.
Stanton, G. N. & Stroumsa, G. G (eds.). 2008. *Tolerance and Intolerance in Early Judaism and Christianity*, Cambridge, UK: Cambridge University Press.
Steele, E. S. 1984. The Use of Jewish Scriptures in 1 Thessalonians. *BTB* 14 (1), 12–17.
Stegner, W. R. 1993a. Diaspora, in G. F. Hawthorne *et al* (eds.), 1993:211–3.
―――. 1993b. Jew, Paul the, in G. F. Hawthorne *et al* (eds.), 1993:503–11.
Sterner, R. H. 1998. *A Semantic and Structural Analysis of 1 Thessalonians*. Dallas: Summer Institute of Linguistics.
Still, T. D. 1999. *Conflict at Thessalonica: A Pauline Church and Its Neighbours*. Sheffield: Sheffield University.
Stock, B. 1983. *The Implications of Literacy: Written Language and Models of Interpretation in the Eleventh and Twelfth Centuries*. Princeton: Princeton University Press.
Stowers, S. K. 1986. *Letter Writing in Greco-Roman Antiquity*. Philadelphia: Westminster.
Stuart, D. 2002. *Hosea-Jonah*: Word Biblical Commentary. Dallas: Word.
Suetonius. [1914] 1997. *Suetonius*. Vol. II. Translated by J. C. Rolfe. Loeb Classical Library. London: William Heinemann; New York: G. P. Putnam's Sons.
Tajfel, H. 1978. *Differentiation between Social Groups: Studies in the Social Psychology of Intergroup Relations*. London: Academic Press.
Tajra, H. W. 1989. *The Trial of St. Paul: A Juridical Exegesis of the Second Half of the Acts of the Apostles*. Tübingen: J. C. B. Mohr (Paul Siebeck).
Tellbe, M. 2001. *Paul between Synagogue and State: Christian, Jews, and Civic Authorities in 1 Thessalonians, Romans, and Philippians*. Stockholm: Almqvist & Wiksell International.
Termini, C. 2009. Philo's Thought within the Context of Middle Judaism, in A. Kamesar (ed.), 2009:95–123.

Thielman, F. 1994. *Paul and the Law: A Contextual Approach*. Downers Grove: IVP.
———. 2005. *Theology of the New Testament*. Grand Rapids: Zondervan.
Thom, J. C. 2003. "The Mind is Its Own Place": Defining the Topos, in J. T. Fitzgerald & T. H. Olbricht & L. M. White (eds.), 2003:555–73.
Thomas, J. "παράκλησις." In *EDNT* 5:23–27.
Thompson, J. W. 2014. *The Church According to Paul: Rediscovering the Community Conformed to Christ*. Grand Rapids: Baker.
———. 2011. *Moral Formation According to Paul*. Grand Rapids: Baker.
Thurén, L. 2002. Is There Biblical Argumentation? in A. Eriksson, & T. H. Olbricht, & W. Übelacker (eds.), 2002:77–92.
Tomson, P. J. 1990. *Paul and the Jewish Law*. Leiden: Brill.
Tov, E. 1977. Compound Words in the LXX Representing Two or More Hebrew Words. *Bib* 58 (2), 189–212.
Trebilco, P. 2011. Why Did the Early Christians Call Themselves ἡ ἐκκλησία? *NTS* 57 (3), 440–60.
Tuckett, C. M. 1990. Synoptic Tradition in 1 Thessalonians?, in R. F. Collins (ed.), 1990:160–82.
Tzanavari, K. 2003. The Worship of Gods and Heroes in Thessaloniki, in D. V. Grammenos (ed.), 2003:177–262.
Van der Merwe, D. G. 2006. Ethics in the Johannine Epistles, in J. G. van der Watt (ed.), 2006:167–97.
Van der Watt, J. G. (ed.) 2011. *Eschatology of the New Testament and Some Related Documents*. Tübingen: Mohr Siebeck.
———. (ed.) 2006. *Identity, Ethic, and Ethos in the New Testament*. Berlin; New York: Walter de Gruyter.
VanGemeran, W. A (ed.) 2012. *New International Dictionary of Old Testament Theology and Exegesis*. 5 vols. Grand Rapids: Zondervan.
Van Henten, J. W. & Brenner, A. (eds.) 2000. *Families and Family Relations*. Leiden: Deo.
Vanhoye, A. (ed.) 1986. *L'Apôtre Paul: Personnalité, Style et Conception du Ministère*. Leuven: Leuven University Press.
Van Kooten, G. H. 2012. ἐκκλησία τοῦ θεοῦ: The 'Church of God' and the Civic Assemblies (ἐκκλησίαι) of the Greek Cities in the Roman Empire: A Response to Paul Trebilco and Richard A. Horsley. *NTS* 58 (4), 522–48.
Van Unnik, W. C. 1962. *Tarsus or Jerusalem, the City of Paul's Youth*. London: Epworth.
Van Voorst, R. 2000. *Jesus Outside the New Testament: An Introduction to the Ancient Evidence*. Grand Rapids: Eerdmans.
Várhelyi, Z. 2010. *The Religion of Senators in the Roman Empire*. Cambridge, UK: Cambridge University Press.
Verhey, A. 1984. *The Great Reversal*. Grand Rapids: Eerdmans.
———. 2007. Scripture as Script and as Scripted: The Beatitudes, in R. L. Brawley (ed.), 2007:19–34.
Von Soden. " ἀδελφός, ἀδελφή, ἀδελφότης, φιλάδελφος, φιλαδελφία, ψευδάδελφος." In *TDNT* 1:144–6.
Wallace, D. B. 1996. *Greek Grammar beyond the Basics: An Exegetical Syntax of the New Testament*. Grand Rapids: Zondervan.
Wallace, S. 1982. Figure and Ground: The Interrelationships of Linguistic Categories, in P. Hopper (ed.), 1982:201–23.

Walton, S. 1995. What Has Aristotle to Do with Paul?: Rhetorical Criticism and 1 Thessalonians. *TynBul* 46 (2), 229-50.
Wanamaker, C. A. 2002. Apocalyptic Discourse, Paraenesis and Identity Maintenance in 1 Thessalonians. *Neot* 36, 131-45.
———. 1987. Apocalypticism at Thessalonica. *Neot* 21, 1-10.
———. 1990. *The Epistle to the Thessalonians*: New International Greek Testament Commentary. Grand Rapids: Eerdmans.
———. 2000. Epistolary vs. Rhetorical Analysis: Is a Synthesis Possible? in K. P. Donfried & J. Beutler (eds.), 2000:255-86.
Ware, J. P. 1992. The Thessalonians as a Missionary Congregation: 1 Thessalonians 1,5-8. *ZNW* 83, 126-31.
Watson, D. E. 2008. The Influence of George Kennedy on Rhetorical Criticism of the New Testament, in C. C. Black & D. F. Watson (eds.), 2008:41-61.
———. 1997. Integration of Epistolary and Rhetorical Analysis of Philippians, in S. E. Porter & T. H. Olbricht (eds.), 1997:398-426.
——— (ed). 2002. *The Intertexture of Apocalyptic Discourse in the New Testament*. Atlanta: SBL.
———. 1999. Paul's Appropriation of Apocalyptic Discourse: The Rhetorical Strategy of 1 Thessalonians, in G. Carey & L. G. Bloomquist (eds.), 1999:61-80.
Watson, F. [2004] 2016. *Paul and the Hermeneutics of Faith*. 2nd ed. Bloomsbury: T & T Clark.
Weima, J. A. D. 1997a. An Apology for the Apologetic Function of I Thessalonians 2:1-12. *JSNT* 68, 73-99.
———. 2000. "But We Became Infants Among You": The Case for NHPIOI in 1 Thess 2.7. *NTS* 46 (4), 547-64.
———. 2014. *1-2 Thessalonians*: Baker Exegetical Commentary on the New Testament. Grand Rapids: Baker.
———. 2007. 1 and 2 Thessalonians, in G. K. Beale & D. A. Carson (eds.), 2007:871-83.
———. 2002a. *1 Thessalonians*: Zondervan Illustrated Bible Backgrounds Commentary. Grand Rapids: Zondervan.
———. 1996. "How You Must Walk to Please God": Holiness and Discipleship in 1 Thessalonians," in R. N. Longenecker (ed.), 1996:98-119.
———. 2002b. Infants, Nursing Mother, and Father: Paul's Portrayal of a Pastor. *CTJ* 37, 209-29.
———. 1994. *Neglected Endings: The Significance of the Pauline Letter Closings*. Sheffield: JSOT.
———. 2012. "Peace and Security"(1 Thess 5.3): Prophetic Warning or Political Propaganda? *NTS* 58, 331-59.
———. 1997b. What Does Aristotle Have to Do With Paul?: An Evaluation of Rhetorical Criticism. *CTJ* 32, 458-68.
Wengst, K. 1987. *Pax Romana and the Peace of Jesus Christ*. Translated by J. Bowden. London: SCM.
Westfall, C. L. 2005. *A Discourse Analysis of the Letter to the Hebrews: the Relationship between Form and Meaning*. London; New York: T & T Clark.
White, J. L. 1971. Introductory Formulae in the Body of the Pauline Letter. *JBL* 90, 91-97.
White, J. R. 2013. "Peace and Security" (1 Thessalonians 5.3): Is It Really a Roman Slogan? *NTS* 59, 382-95.

White, L. M. 1988. Ancient Greek Letters, in D. E. Aune (ed.), 1988:85–105.
Whitton, J. 1982. A Neglected Meaning for *Skeuos* in 1 Thessalonians 4:4. *NTS* 28, 142–3.
Wikgren, A. P. (ed.) 1961. *Early Christian Origins: Studies in Honor of Harold R. Willoughby*. Chicago: Quadrangle.
Wilken, R. L. 1984. *The Christians as the Romans Saw Them*. New Haven: Yale University Press.
Willis, W. L. (ed.) 1987. *The Kingdom of God in 20th-century Interpretation*. Peabody, MA: Hendrickson.
Wilson, T. A. 2007. *The Curse of the Law and the Crisis in Galatia: Reassessing the Purpose of Galatians*. Tübingen: Mohr Siebeck.
Wilson, W. T. 2000. Hellenistic Judaism, C. A. Evans and S. E. Porter (eds.), 2000:477–82.
Wise, M. & Abegg, M. Jr. & Cook, E. (trans.) 2005. *The Dead Sea Scrolls: A New Translation*. NY: HarperSanFrancisco.
Witherington III, B. 2006. *1 and 2 Thessalonians: A Socio-Rhetorical Commentary*. Grand Rapids: Eerdmans.
Witmer, S. E. 2006. θεοδίδακτοι in 1 Thessalonians 4.9: A Pauline Neologism. *NTS* 52, 239–50.
Wolfson, H. A. 1948. *Philo: Foundations of Religious Philosophy in Judaism, Christianity, and Islam*. Vol. 1. Cambridge, MA: Harvard University Press.
Wolter, M. "παραμυθέομαι." In *EDNT* 3:32.
Wright, N. T. 1992. *The New Testament and the People of God*. Minneapolis: Fortress.
Wuellner, W. 1990. The Argumentative Structure of 1 Thessalonians as Paradoxical Encomium, in R.F. Collins (ed.), 1990:117–36.
———. 1979. Greek Rhetoric and Pauline Argumentation, in W. R. Schoedel & R. L. Wilken (eds.), 1979:177–88.
———. 1987. Where is Rhetorical Criticism Taking Us? *CBQ* 49, 448–63.
Xenophon. [1923] 1997. *Memorabilia and Oeconomicus*. Translated by E. C. Marchant. Loeb Classical Library. Cambridge: Harvard University Press.
Xeravits, G. G. (ed.) 2010. *Dualism in Qumran*. London: T & T Clark.
Yamauchi, E. M. 1993. Hellenism, in G. F. Hawthorne *et al* (eds.), 1993:383–88.
Yarbrough, O. L. 1985. *Not Like the Gentiles: Marriage Rules in the Letters of Paul*. Atlanta: SBL.
Yee, T. N. 2005. *Jews, Gentiles and Ethnic Reconciliation: Paul's Jewish Identity and Ephesians*. Cambridge, UK: Cambridge University Press.
Zanker, P. 1990. *The Power of Images in the Age of Augustus*. Translated by A. Shapiro. Ann Arbor: The University of Michigan.
Zerwick, M. 1963. *Biblical Greek Illustrated by Examples*. Rome: Pontificio Istituto Biblico.
———. [1974] 1996. *A Grammatical Analysis of the Greek New Testament*, 5th Revised ed. Roma: Biblical Institute.

Author Index

Aalen, 191
Aasgaard, R., 94, 94n2, 135
Abegg, M. Jr., 134n47
Aernie, M. D., 40
Aichele, 181n43
Allamani-Souri, V., 72
Allen, L. C., 171
Allison, D. C., 150n12
Alsup, J. E., 168
Andersen, F. I., 189, 190
Arzt, P., 99n6
Ascough, R. S., 14n12, 77n21, 78, 81, 87, 87n30, 89, 136n48
Aune, D. E., 34, 34n7, 42, 46, 67, 81, 89n33

Barclay, J. M. G. (John), 10, 13, 15, 52, 53, 54, 55, 56–57, 58, 59, 65, 66, 84n27, 86, 87, 89, 89n32, 124, 184n48
Barth, Karl, 209
Bassler, J. M., 105
Bauckham, R., 115
Baumgarten, 179n40
Baur, F. C. (Ferdinand Christian), 26–27, 27
Beale, G. K., 18, 100, 106n14, 108, 118, 162, 168, 184, 191, 213
Beetham, C. A., 10n9, 147, 148, 148n6
Beker, 42
Bell, G. I., 72
Berding, K., 49n15
Bertram, 40n12, 152

Best, E., 64, 66, 87, 103, 106n13, 109, 109n21, 138, 141, 149, 151, 161n22, 168n29, 178, 184, 196, 198
Betz, H. D., 33, 33n6, 35
Beutler, 136
Beutler, J., 3n4
Birch, B. C., 2n2, 211
Bird, M. F., 5, 11, 13, 61
Bjerklund, C. J., 149, 150
Block, D. I. (Daniel), 7n6, 170
Bockmuehl, M., 49, 50
Boers, H., 33, 100
Boring, M. E., 70, 84, 90, 100, 105, 108, 111, 113, 116, 125, 133n45, 139, 140, 142, 145n1, 149, 150n12, 161n20, 162, 167, 176, 185, 186, 191
Bousset, W. (Wilhelm), 28, 43
Bradley, K. R., 133
Brown, G., 19
Brown, R. E., 69
Bruce, F. F., 16n13, 40, 72, 73, 73n13, 86, 106n12, 121n33, 123n36, 128, 133, 152, 154n18, 160, 162, 163, 178, 179n40, 186n49, 187, 188n53, 195n58
Budd, P. J., 134n46
Bultmann, Rudolf, 16n13
Burke, T. J., 120, 135, 137, 138, 139, 139n50, 140, 142, 175n35

Calvin, J., 175n34, 211
Campbell, W. S., 95, 96, 98, 104

Cancik, H., 14n12
Carey, G., 14n10, 48
Carras, G. P., 151, 165
Carson, D. A., 39, 40, 48n15, 101n8, 124
Castelli, E. A., 138
Charlesworth, J. H., 56n17
Ciampa, R. E., 147
Classen, C. J., 4n5, 5
Clauss, M., 71
Collins, 52, 53, 54
Collins, J. J., 97, 100
Collins, R. F., 43, 84, 161n22
Conzelmann, H., 16n13, 40n11, 187n52
Cook, E., 134n47
Cosgrove, 209
Cothey, 158

Davies, W. D., 42, 43, 44, 49, 50, 151
De Beaugrande, R., 18n15
De Boer, M. C., 15n12, 42
De Ste. Croix, G. E. M., 89
De Villiers, P., 143, 182
De Vos, C. S., 73n14, 77, 85, 85n28, 89, 89n31
Deidun, T. J., 167, 171, 171n31
Deissmann, A. (Adolf), 28, 29n3
Delling, 110n21, 151
Denis, A. M., 125
DeSilva, D. A., 26, 94, 164, 165, 180
Detienne, M., 80
Dibelius, 16n13
Dodd, C. H., 42
Donfried, K. P., 3n4, 15, 16n13, 67, 70, 71, 77, 80, 81n24, 82, 84, 85, 88, 100, 103, 124, 125, 154, 193, 193n57
Dorsey, D. A., 153n17
Doty, W. G., 99, 100
Douglas, M., 60, 158
Du Toit, P. G., 50
Dumbrell, W. J., 157, 158
Dunn, J. D. G., 90

Eadie, J., 183
Edson, C., 79, 81, 82, 82n24
Elgvin, T., 162, 162n23, 194

Ellingworth, P., 99, 103, 124n38, 150, 156, 161n20, 162
Ellis, E. E., 125
Ellis, E. Earl, 148n6
Elwell, W. A., 104n10
Engberg-Pedersen, T., 29
Esler, P. F., 92, 93, 136

Fairclough, N., 20, 22
Fee, G. D., 103, 105, 106n12, 107, 108, 109, 109nn20-21, 110, 110nn22-23, 111, 115, 116, 121n33, 123n36, 125, 127, 128, 129, 130, 137, 140, 141, 156n19, 162, 163, 168, 171, 172, 182, 184
Ferguson, E., 71
Fiorenza, E. S., 63, 209
Fishwick, D., 71
Frame, J. E., 127, 131, 161n22
France, R. T., 73n13
Freed, E. D., 125
Freedman, D. N., 189, 190
Frey, J., 57, 59, 193
Furnish, V. P., 2n2, 7, 25, 73n14, 100, 101n8, 103, 105, 106n14, 113, 116, 116n29, 123n36, 139, 163, 168, 180, 184

Gager, J. G., 45
Garnsey, P., 94n2
Gaventa, B. R. (Beverly), 3, 106n14, 129, 130, 132, 133, 152, 172n32, 174, 178, 188
Gempf, C., 184
Goheen, M. W., 145
Goppelt, 113, 114
Gordon, R., 71
Gow, A. S. F., 78
Gradel, I., 71, 72
Grant, R. M. (Robert M.), 29-30
Green, G. L., 3n4, 4, 5, 15, 64, 69, 70, 71, 73n14, 75, 78, 79n23, 80, 84, 87, 99, 100, 106n14, 109n20, 110n22, 111, 117, 123n36, 125, 132, 137, 138, 140, 140n53, 141, 142, 149, 149n7, 150, 151,

AUTHOR INDEX

161, 162, 163, 164, 165, 168n29, 175n35, 177, 178, 184, 186, 198
Green, J. B. (Joel), 18, 19, 21, 22, 201
Griffiths, 80
Grindheim, S., 91, 91n1, 104, 109
Gruen, E. S., 53
Gupta, N. K., 14n10, 117, 148, 163, 175n34
Gustafson, J. M., 17
Guthrie, G., 18n15

Haenchen, E., 16n13, 40, 40n10
Hagner, D. A., 97, 100
Halliday, M. A. K., 21n17
Hanson, P. D., 14, 14n11, 14n12
Harland, P. A., 94, 135
Harmerton-Kelly, R., 38
Harnack, A. (Adolf von), 13, 38, 146
Harrington, D. J., 56
Harrison, J. R., 71, 72n11, 76, 76n20
Hartley, J. E., 157, 158
Hauerwas, Stanley, 209, 211
Hawthorne, G. F., 41, 41n13, 42
Hays, R. B. (Richard), 2, 7, 10n9, 11n9, 96, 146n3, 201, 208, 209, 209n1, 210, 211
Heger, P., 194
Hellholm, D., 20
Hemberg, B., 82n24
Hendriksen, W., 64, 106n14, 123n36, 156n19, 161n22, 175n34
Hendrix, H. L., 70, 70n8, 82, 83n25, 184
Hengel, M. (Martin), 26, 26n2, 41, 54, 55, 56, 57, 58, 59
Hester, J. D., 62, 146n3
Hock, R. F., 86n30, 140n52
Hodgson, R., 151, 155, 156, 157, 160
Hoffmann, Y., 189, 190, 191
Holloway, J. O., 142n55
Holmes, M. W., 106, 109n20
Holtz, T., 67, 121n33, 125
Hornblower, S., 79
Horrell, D. G., 51, 93, 95, 186
Horsley, G. H. R., 28, 74n17, 75, 75nn18–19
House, P. R., 158, 159
Hübner, 179n40

Hughes, F. W., 34n7

Jarvie, 45
Jensen, J., 161n20
Jewett, R. (Robert), 33, 34–36, 34n7, 35, 73n14, 87, 88, 100, 127, 178
Johanson, B. C. (Bruce), 6, 18n14, 36, 36n8, 37, 97, 99, 100, 128
Johnson, E. E., 146n3, 147n4
Johnson, L. T., 41
Johnson, M., 89n33
Johnson-DeBaufre, M., 88
Jokiranta, J., 196
Joosten, J., 154, 158
Judge, E. A., 73n14, 74n16, 75

Kamesar, A., 54
Kasch, 118n31
Keener, C. S., 69
Keesmaat, S. C., 147
Kennedy, G. A. (George A.), 33–34, 35
Kim, S., 121n33, 122, 122n35
Kittredge, C. B., 63
Kloppenborg, J. S., 173–74
Knopf, R. (Rudolf), 29
Koch, D. A., 146
Koester, H., 33, 172, 173
Kraabel, A. T., 52, 53
Kraus, W., 102
Kremer, 40n12
Krentz, E., 5, 11
Kucicki, J., 186, 193

Lambrecht, J., 100, 111, 114
Larsson, 110
Lategan, B., 11
Lau, P. H., 24n1
Lausberg, H., 150, 177n38
Levick, B., 73n13
Lichtenberger, 118n31
Lieu, J. M. (Judith), 96, 96nn3–4, 97
Lightfoot, J. B., 41, 69, 123n36
Litfin, D., 58
Longenecker, R. N., 52
Louw, J. P., 152, 168
Luckensmeyer, D., 3n4, 47, 86, 86n29, 100, 181n43, 183, 193
Lüdemann, H., 27

Lünemann, G., 183

Malbon, E. S., 179n41
Malherbe, A. J. (Abraham J.), 13, 16n13, 30–33, 31n4, 32n5, 34n7, 36, 38, 44, 79n23, 100, 101n8, 102n9, 103, 106nn13–14, 107, 109, 109n20, 117n30, 118, 119, 120, 121, 122, 123n36, 124, 125n39, 128, 129, 130, 132, 137, 138, 140n52, 140n53, 141, 149n7, 152, 156n19, 161n22, 172, 173, 176, 177, 179n40, 183, 187, 188, 188n53, 198
Marshall, I. H., 16n13, 40n10, 64, 85, 99, 100, 104, 106, 107, 109n21, 114, 117, 121n33, 123n36, 124n38, 125, 127, 132, 133, 136, 142, 145n1, 149, 150, 150n11, 153n15, 156n19, 160, 160n13, 161, 162, 163, 168n29, 170, 175n34, 176, 179n40, 187
Martin, D. B., 27, 94
Martin, D. M., 4, 114
Martin, T. W., 63n1
Matera, F. J., 107
Maurer, 161n22
May, H. D., 194
McDonald, L. M., 99
McNeel, J. H., 83, 94, 120, 126, 127, 128, 130, 132, 133, 134, 134n46
Meeks, W. A. (Wayne), 2, 2n3, 3, 27, 43, 44, 46, 87, 95, 96, 102, 120, 135, 136, 142, 143, 180, 187
Metzger, B. M. (Bruce), 128
Meyer, 158
Michaelis, 86n30
Michel, 180
Míguez, N. O., 105, 110, 112, 113
Milligan, G., 85n28
Miscall, P., 181n43
Moo, D. J. (Douglas), 7n6, 39, 40, 48n15, 59, 60, 101n8, 139
Morris, C., 20, 100, 103, 109n20, 110n21, 123n36, 160n13, 168, 188n54
Moule, C. F. D., 145n1, 150, 188n54

Mouton, E., 2n2, 2n3, 12, 16, 17, 20, 20n16, 92, 95, 201, 208, 210, 211, 212, 213
Moxnes, H., 94
Müller, M., 91n1, 152
Munck, J., 40n10
Murphy, F. J., 14n10, 14n12, 46, 193
Murphy-O'Connor, J., 41
Myers, J. M., 125

Nanos, M. D., 49
Neusner, J., 59n20, 60n20
Newsom, C. A., 134
Nicholl, C. R., 85
Nida, E. A., 21, 99, 103, 124n38, 150, 152, 156, 161n20, 162, 168
Niebuhr, Reinhold, 209
Nigdelis, P. M., 69, 77, 77n21, 79, 81, 87
Norden, E., 58n19

Oakes, P., 75, 76, 184
O'Brien, P. T., 41
Olbrechts-Tyteca, L., 8
Olbricht, T. H., 32, 33, 36n8
Osborne, G. R., 18, 20
Osiek, C., 94
Otto, W. F., 80
Owens, T.J., 1n1

Paddock, A., 94n2, 135
Page, D. L., 78
Peacock, J. L., 48
Pearson, B. A., 67
Perelman, C., 8
Petersen, N. R. (Normar), 12, 138
Pfleiderer, O. (Otto), 27
Plett, 20n16
Plummer, R. L., 115, 117
Pobee, J. S., 84, 85
Polhill, J. B., 40, 69
Popkes, 69
Porter, S. E., 5, 6, 8n7, 17, 18, 20, 21, 35, 99, 101n7, 159, 160, 198n61
Price, S. R. F., 72, 72n11
Procksch, 158
Punt, J., 25
Purvis, J. D., 69

Ramsay, W. M., 195n58
Rasmussen, L. L., 2n2, 211
Reed, J. T. (Jeffrey), 4, 4n5, 5, 11, 18,
    18n15, 19, 20, 21, 22, 101n7
Reitzenstein, 43
Renz, 170
Rice, D. G., 79
Richard, E. J., 114, 118n31, 125, 128,
    133, 150n10, 162, 189n54
Richards, I. A., 34
Riches, J. K., 27, 43
Ricoeur, P., 24n1
Riesner, R., 68, 73n14, 73n15, 74, 75, 84
Robbins, V. K., 31n4, 48, 92
Roetzel, C. J., 13, 100
Roloff, 102n9
Rosner, B. S., 2, 38, 38n9, 142n55,
    148n6, 152
Rotzel, C. J., 173
Rousseau, J., 20n16
Rowland, C., 46
Runge, S. E., 21

Safrai, S., 52, 54, 55
Sailors, T. B., 128
Saller, R., 94n2
Stambaugh, J. E., 79
Samblanet, S., 1n1
Sanders, 99
Sandnes, K. O., 94
Schenk, W., 20
Schmitz, 124n38, 151n13
Schneider, G., 40n12, 152
Schneider, J, 183n46
Schnelle, U., 13, 146, 155
Schoedel, W. R., 30
Schreiner, T. R., 9n8, 153n17
Schrenk, 110n21
Schuler, C., 74, 75, 75nn18–19
Schweitzer, A. (Albert), 29, 39, 43
Seesemann, 141, 166
Segal, A. F., 49, 50
Seifrid, M. A., 26, 64, 198n62
Selwyn, 155
Sherk, R. K., 70n8
Shogren, G. S., 100, 106nn12–14, 108,
    114, 123n36, 130, 152, 162,
    169n30, 177, 182, 188

Silva, M., 41
Sissa, G., 80
Smit, D. J., 208, 211
Smith, D. E., 60, 179n40, 190n55, 192
Sommer, B. D., 147
Spicq, C. D., 138
Sprinkle, J. M., 158
Stählin, 137, 138
Stamps, D. L., 5, 12, 63n1
Stanley, C. D. (Christopher), 63n1,
    65n2, 104, 147
Steele, E. S., 146n3
Stegner, W. R., 41, 52, 57
Stern, M., 52, 54, 55
Sterner, R. H., 18n14, 114, 127, 131,
    133, 140n53, 160, 183n45,
    186n49, 187, 188n53
Still, T. D., 70, 85n28, 86, 88, 89, 120,
    121n33, 184
Stock, B., 96n4
Stowers, S. K., 34n7
Stuart, D., 181n43

Tajfel, H. (Henri), 93
Tellbe, M., 68, 68n4, 69, 70, 71, 75,
    75n19, 104, 125, 185, 186
Termini, C., 55
Thielman, F., 104, 107, 144, 170
Thomas, 124n38
Thompson, J. W., 2n3, 52, 54, 60, 65n2,
    91, 94, 95, 96, 97n5, 102, 102n9,
    103, 104n10, 107, 108, 119, 125,
    136, 138, 142, 143, 146
Thompson J. W., 178, 179
Thurén, L., 35
Tomson, P. J., 49, 50
Tov, Emanuel, 174, 206
Trebilco, P., 102, 102n9
Tuckett, C. M., 183n44
Tzanavari, K., 80, 82, 83

Van der Merwe, D. G., 92
Van Kooten, G. H., 101n9, 102n9
Van Unnik, W. C., 40
Van Voorst, R., 73n13
Várhelyi, Z., 71, 71n10
Verhey, A., 208, 209

von Harnack, A. (Adolf). *See* Harnack, A. (Adolf von)
Von Soden, 136

Wallace, D. B., 17, 149n8, 160, 183, 186, 188
Wallace, S. (Stephen), 21n17, 160n13
Walsh, R., 181n43
Walton, S., 33, 122
Wanamaker, C. A. (Charles), 3n4, 16n13, 44, 45, 47–49, 48, 49n15, 64, 67, 85n28, 100, 106nn13–14, 109n20, 111, 127, 132, 138, 140, 142, 156n19, 159, 161, 162, 164, 168, 168n29, 180, 180n42, 186n49, 187
Ware, J. P., 114
Watson, D. E. (Duane), 3n4, 34, 44, 46–47, 167, 168
Watson, F., 10
Weima, J. A. D., 5, 10, 11, 15, 16, 49, 50, 57n18, 66, 67, 68n5, 69, 70, 73n14, 79, 80, 81, 82, 83n26, 85, 85n28, 86, 87, 90, 98, 99, 100, 101n8, 102, 103, 106nn12–14, 107, 109, 109nn20–21, 110, 111n26, 114, 115, 116n29, 117, 117n30, 120, 121n33, 122, 124, 124n38, 125, 126, 127, 128, 129, 130, 131, 132, 133, 136, 140, 140n52, 141, 142, 145, 145n1, 146nn2–3, 149, 150, 151, 152, 153, 153n15, 154, 156n19, 160, 161, 161n22, 162, 163, 167, 168n29, 169, 170, 174, 175, 175n33, 175n34, 176, 177, 178, 179, 179n40, 180, 181, 183, 183n45, 184, 185, 186n49, 187, 188, 188n53, 189n54, 195, 197, 198n61
Wengst, K., 184
Westfall, C. L., 21n17
White, J. L., 99
White, J. R., 185
White, L. M., 97, 99n6
Whitton, J., 162
Wilken, R. L., 30, 88
Wilson, T. A., 26n2, 50
Winter, 122
Wise, M., 134n47
Witherington III, B., 73n14, 84, 128, 161n20, 161n22, 177, 184, 186, 195n58
Witmer, S. E., 173, 174, 176, 206
Wolfson, H. A., 54, 54n16, 55
Wolter, 137, 169n30
Wright, N. T., 119, 119n32
Wuellner, W., 7, 8, 62, 67

Yamauchi, E. M., 58
Yarbrough, O. L., 161n22
Yee, T. N., 96
Yoder, John Howard, 209
Yonge, 69n6
Yule, G., 19

Zanker, P., 185
Zerwick, M., 41n14, 186n49

Scripture Index

OLD TESTAMENT

Genesis

	50
1:15	191
17:12	41
39:1–19	163

Exodus

2:11	107n15, 136
3:9	111n28
4:31	111n28
9:16	115
12:26–27	138
13:14–16	138
13:21–22	187n52
15:14	184n47
16:4	141n54
18:20	141n54
19:4–6	115
19:5–6	153–54, 160
20:8	161
28:2–4	158
28:36	158
32:12	51
32:25	51
34:6	118

Leviticus

	154, 155, 156, 158, 159, 205
4:3–4	205
4:3b–6a	206
4:9	206
10:6	136
10:10	157, 158, 159, 205
10:10 LXX	157
10:10 MT	157
11–15	158
11:44	160
11:44–45	154, 158
11:44f	159
12:3	41
17:13	156
17:15	156
17–26	50, 154, 155, 156, 165
18:1–20	154
18:3–4	141n54
18:6–18	156
18:6–24	157, 159, 205
18:24–30	156
19:2	153, 154, 155, 158, 159
19:4	170
19:10	156
19:11	156
19:13	156, 170
19:15	156
19:17–18	156
19:18	175
19:33–34	156
19:35	156
20:7	154, 155, 159
20:7–21	154
20:10	170
20:10–21	157, 159, 205

Leviticus (continued)

20:19–23	156
20:22–26	156
20:26	153, 154, 155, 159
21:8	159
22:32	154
23:22	156
24:22	156
25:13–17	156
25:39–49	156
25:43	156
26:3	141n54
26:14–22	156
26:14–39	170
26:40–45	170

Numbers

5:17	158
11:12	133, 134, 134n46
14:14–16	51
14:21	118
14:28	118
23:27	148

Deuteronomy

	7n6, 160
2:4	107n15
2:25	184n47
3:18	136
4:3	160
4:4	160
4:7	160
4:9–10	138
4:29	111n28
4:37	104n11, 204
5:12	161
5:33	141n54
6:7	138
7:6–7	144
7:6–11	91n1, 154
7:7–11	108n18
9:25–29	51
10:12	152
10:15	104n11, 204
11:19	138
12:5	108n18
12:11	108n18
12:18	108n18
12:21	108n18
14:2	91n1, 144, 154
15:3	107n15
15:12	107n15
16:6	108n18
16:7	108n18
16:11	108n18
16:15	108n18
16:16	108n18
17:8	108n18
17:10	108n18
17:15	108n18
19:9	141n54
24:7	136
26:17	141n54
26:18–19	154, 160
28:9	141n54, 154
28:29	187n52
30:2	116
30:8	116
30:10	116
30:12–14	7n6
30:16	141n54
30:19–20	138
32:7	138
32:35	167
32:40	118
32:46	138
33:12	104n11, 107n17, 204

Joshua

4:24	115
22:5	152

Judges

2:7	117
4:10	151n13
8:17	118

1 Samuel

10:17	151n13
12:14	117
15:4	151n13
17:26	118

17:36	118	34:9	126n40
21:5	162n23		
23:8	151n13	**Psalms**	
		2:11	117
1 Samuel (1 Kingdoms)		4:6	187n52
10:18	111n28	11:2	187n52
		16:3 LXX	126n40
1 Kings		17:3	126n40
12:21	41	17:10 LXX	190
15:22	151n13	18:8 LXX	129
20:28	51	18:47	167
		19:7	129
		19:14	126n40
1 Kings (3 Kingdoms)		21:23 LXX	107n15, 136
3:14	141n54	22:22	107n15
8:25	141n54	22:23	136
		25:2 LXX	126n40
2 Kings		26:2	126n40
20:3	141	27:1	187n52
		30:2	118
		33:20 LXX	66n3
2 Kings (4 Kingdoms)		34:19	66n3
19:3 LXX	111n28	44:3	187n52
		44:19	187n52
1 Chronicles		60:5	104n11, 107n17
		65:10 LXX	126n40
29:17	126n40	66:10	126n40
		67:1–3	115
2 Chronicles		68:32	148
6:14	141n54	69:23	187n52
6:16	141n54	69:31	126n40
15:3	118	74:20	187n52
30:6	116	78:6 LXX	166
30:8	117	79	166n28
30:9	116	79:6 MT	166, 166n27
		82:5	187n52
Nehemiah		86:15	118
13:1	102n9	89:15	187n52
		94:1	167
Job		99:8	167
		104:34	126n40
10:20–22	187n52	106:8	115
19:8	187n52	107:10	187n52
22:11	187n52	118:130 LXX	129
24:14	182	119:105	188
30:26	187n52	119:130	129

Proverbs

15:26	126n40
16:7	126n40

Ecclesiastes

11:9	141

Isaiah

1:2	168n29
2:2–4	175n33
4:3–4	206
4:7–8	206
9:2	188
13:6	181
13:6–22	182
13:8	184, 184n47
14:1	108n18
38:3	141n54
41:8	104n11
41:8–9	108n18, 144
42:1	108n18
42:6	144
42:7	187n52
43:6b–7	115
43:10	108n18
43:20	108n18
44:1–2	108n18
44:2	104n11, 107n17
45:4	108n18
45:22	116
48:12	144
49:6	199
49:7	108n18
52:1	125
52:11	125
53:9	125
54:13	174, 175, 175n33, 206
57:18	125
59:11	118
59:15	126n40
59:19 LXX	118
59:19–20	118
60:1	188
60:1–3	191
60:19–20	187n52, 191
65:9	108n18
65:16	118
66:11	125

Jeremiah

2:26	182
5:11	168n29
6:14	184, 185
6:24	184
8:11	184
10	166n28
10:10	118
10:25a	166n27
10:25a LXX	166
10:25a MT	166
11:15	107n17
11:20	126n40, 167
13:1	118
13:16	187n52
13:21	184n47
13:27	165
17:20	126n40
22:18	107n15, 136
23:56	118
24:6	180
24:7	116
27:29 LXX	151n13
28:27 LXX	151n13
30:4	182
31:3	183n46
31:33–34	172, 175, 206
31:34	107n15, 136
38:31–34 LXX	172, 175
38:34 LXX	107n15, 136
46:10	181
49:10 LXX	180

Lamentations

2:22	182
5:17	187n52

Ezekiel

1–33	170
13:5	181
13:10	184, 185
13:16	184
16:41	165

22:26	168n29	3:14–21	182
23:29	165		
30:3	181	## Amos	
34–48	170		
36:17–20	169		191
36:25–26	170	3:2	167
36:25–27	168	3:2a	91n1
36:25–28	169	5:7	91n1
36:26	206	5:11a	91n1
36:26 LXX	169	5:18–20	181, 182, 189, 190, 206
36:26 MT	169	5:18–20 LXX	190
36:26–27	170	5:18–20 MT	190
36:27	141n54	5:19	192, 192n56
36:35–36	169	8:9	189
36–37	170		
37:6	168, 169, 171, 206	## Obadiah	
37:6 LXX	169		181n43
37:6 MT	169	1:5	181n43
37:14	168, 169, 171, 206	1:7	181n43
37:14 LXX	169	1:8	181n43
37:14 MT	169	1:14–15	181n43
		1:15	181, 181n43
## Daniel		1:16	181n43
2:22	187n52	1:17	181n43
12:1	66n3	1:18	181n43
		1:20	181n43
## Hosea		1:21	181n43
1:2	165	## Micah	
2:1	118		
2:6	165	1:7	165
3:5	116	4:1–3	175n33
4:12	165	5:15	167
5:4	165		
6:1	116	## Nahum	
11:1	104n11	1:2	167
13:13	184	3:4	165
## Joel		## Habakkuk	
1:15	181	3:4	190
2:1	181	3:11	190
2:1–11	182		
2:2	189	## Zephaniah	
2:9	182		
2:10	189	1:7	181
2:12–13	116	1:14	181
2:28–32	115	2:2–3	182

Zechariah

7:9	107n15, 136

Malachi

3:4	126n40, 148
4:5	181

DEUTEROCANONICAL BOOKS

1 Maccabees

5:58	151n13
9:63	151n13

2 Maccabees

	56
4:13	41

3 Maccabees

1:1	151n13

4 Maccabees

	58
1:1	56
5:18	56
5:31	56
6:21	56
7:15	56
7:21	56
7:21–23	56
10:15	183n46

Baruch

4:16	169n30

Book of Judith

5:19	116

Psalms of Solomon

17:32	175n33

Sirach

2:6–8	118
14:11	142
36:29	161n22

Tobit

4:12	161n21
5:10	187n52

Wisdom of Solomon

1:12	183n46
3:5	142
7:15	142
10:21	129
12:12	167
14:12	165
14:26–27	165

PSEUDEPIGRAPHA (OLD TESTAMENT)

Letter Aristeas

	58
16	54

Testament of Issachar

5:2–3	178

Testament of Leviticus

9:9	161n21

Testament of Simeon

5:3	165

DEAD SEA SCROLLS

	29

1 QM

1:1	193
1:7	193
1:10	193
1:16	193

3:6	193	66 (Damascus Document)	
3:9	193		196
5:3–4	193n57	4Q2	80
13:1	136	frag. 2:1	193
13:16	193	4Q3	97
14:17	193	frags. 14–21	196n59
16:11	193	4Q4	16162n23
col. 1	194, 195	4Q5	10
col. 1:1	193	frag. 1:7	193
col. 1:3	193		
col. 1:9	193	**11Q13**	
col. 1:11	193	col. 2:8	193
col. 1:13	193		
col. 1–15	194	**CD**	
col. 5	195	6:20	136
col. 8:16	193	6.20–21	107n15
col. 10	194		
col. 11–12	194	**Hodayot**	
col. 11–15	195	1QHa	134
col. 13	194	20:23–25	134
		"War Scroll"	194

1 QS (Community Rule)

	193n57, 196
1:10	193
5:1	193n57
6:10	136
6:22	136, 193n57
6.10	107n15
6.22	107n15
col. 1	196
col. 1–3	196
col. 1:9	193
col. 2:16	193
col. 3	194
col. 3:13	193
col. 3:24–25	193
col. 13—4	194
col. 26	194

1 QSa

1:18	136
4Q1	77
frags. 10—11:7	193
frags. 12–13	
col. 1:7	193
4Q2	

ANCIENT JEWISH WRITERS

Aristobulus of Alexandria

	58
4:3–4	54
4:7–8	54

Josephus   148n6, 151n13

Antiquities of the Jews

2.184	139n50
2.42	163
11.55	118
14.10.22	185
16.241	151n13

Against Apion (Conta Apionem)

2.199	139n50
2.201	169n30
2.206	139n50
12.11	107n15
13.1	107n15

Jewish War

2.122	107n15, 136

Philo of Alexandria

54, 54n16, 55–56, 58, 138, 148n6, 151n13, 173

On Abraham
20	177n36
196	139n50

Allegorical Interpretation
2.53	129

De Mutatione Nominum
217	139n50

On the Decalogue
58	151n13
65	151n13
96	151n13
106	151n13
135	151n13
165–166	139n50

Every Good Person Is Free
160	129

Against Flaccus
68	129
141	151n13

On Joseph
4	139n50
225.6	129

Moses
2.12	56
14–15	56
17	56
25–27	56
43–44	56

On Rewards and Punishments
11	177

Special Laws
1	107n15
1.137	139n50
2.228	138, 139n50
2.231	139n50
2.236	139n50
2.240	139n50
3.119	129
52	107n15
232	138

Virtues
103–4	107n15
179	107n15

RABBINIC WORKS

Talmud

Mishna
Abot (Pirkei Avot)   151
Demai	44
Pirke Aboth	44

Tractates
Derek Eretz Rabba   44

NEW TESTAMENT

Matthew
8:29	179n40
10:37–38	142
11:25–26	129
24:9	111
24:25–51	183n44
24:36	183n44
24:37–39	183n44
24:42	183n44
24:42–44	183, 197
24:43–44	183n44
27:32	76

Mark
4:17	111
7:9	168n29
13:33	179n40
13:34–36	183n44
13:34–37	197

Luke
4:16	40n12
7:30	168n29
10:16	168n29
10:21	129
12:36–38	183n44
12:37	197
12:39–40	183, 183n44
12:42–46	183n44
14:4	177n36
17:26–30	183n44

19:44	179n40	17:6–9	75
21:34	183n44	17:7	73, 74, 203
21:34–36	183n44	17:7–8	75
		17:10	136n49
John		17:13	69n7
		17:14	136n49
1:1–5	191	18:3	86n30
3:19	187n51	18:18	136n49
6:45	175n33	18:27	136n49
11:19	137	20:18	140
11:31	137	21:7	136n49
12:28	168n29	21:17	136n49
16:33	111	21:20	136n49
		21:27	69n7
Acts		21:40	42
		22:1	136n49
1:4	106	22:2	42
3:20	179n40	22:3	39, 40, 42, 51
3:21	179n40	22:5	136n49
7:20	40n12	22:13	136n49
7:21	40n12	23:1	136n49
7:60	84	23:5	136n49
10:34–48	108	23:6	39, 42, 136n49
11:15–18	108	26:4	39
13:36	85	26:4–5	42
13:50	69n7	28:15	76, 136n49
14:2	69n7, 136n49	28:17	136n49
14:5	69n7	28:21	136n49
14:19	69n7		
14:22	111	**Romans**	
15:23	136n49		
15:32	136n49		7n6, 135, 146n3
15:33	136n49	1:10	153n15
15:36	136n49	1:16	59
15:40	136n49	1:18–32	50
16:2	136n49	1:24	165n26
16:16–24	123	1:26	164n24
16:40	136n49	2:17	51
17	68	2:19	187
17:1–2	16	2:20	129
17:1–9	203	3:9	51
17:2	11, 147n4	3:22	51
17:5	68, 69n7	4	60
17:5–6	68, 106	5:3	111
17:5–7	16	5:5	170
17:5–10	69	5:20	38
17:6	74n17, 136n49	6:4	141
17:6–8	72, 74	6:9	153n16

Romans (continued)

6:19	154, 165n26
6:22	153n16
7:14–25	171
7:24	118n31
8:9–11	171
8:12	171
8:14–23	136
8:15	136
8:17	111
8:23	171
8:29	136
8:30	64
9:3–5	39
9–11	104n10
9:11	104n10
10:4	7n6
10:5–8	7n6
10:12	51
11:1	39, 41
11:6	104n10
11:7	104n10
11:13	165n25
11:26	118n31
11:28	104n10
12:1	145n1
12:2	153n15
12:10	175
12:12	111
13:11	179n40
13:12	187n50, 187n51, 195
14:10	168
14:14	59
15:13	170
15:32	153n15
16:3	51
16:3–15	73n15
16:4	165n25
16:7	51
16:11	51
16:25–27	165n25

1 Corinthians

	135
1:1	101, 153n15
1:2	103
1:8	182
1:9	64
1:21	165
1:22–24	59
1:24	51
1:30	153n16
3:1	129
4:2	145n1
4:5	179n40
4:15	139
5:9–11	57
6:12–20	57
6:19	108, 170
7:29	145n1
7:39	85
8–10	70
9:1–2	126
9:20	51
9:21	7n6
10:14	57
11:23	151
11:30	85
12:3	108
12:13	1, 51
13:11	129
14:20	129
15:1	151
15:3	151
15:33	2n2
15:44–46	171
15:51	85

2 Corinthians

	135
1:1	101, 103, 153n15
1:1–14	101n8
1:4–5	111
1:14	182
1:18	101n8
1:24	101n8
3:17–18	171
4:2	141
5:1	168
5:1–5	171
6:14	187n50, 187n51
7:4	111
7:5–7	101n8
7:12—8:8	101n8

8:2	111	4:1	141
8:5	153n15	4:22–24	191
10:1–18	126	4:30	171
10:8	180	5:2	141
11:5	126	5:3	165n26
11:21–22	39	5:8	141, 187n50
12:17–18	162	5:8–13	191
12:19	180	5:11	187n51
12:21	165n26	5:15	141
13:10	180	5:17	153n15
		6:6	153n15
		6:11–12	195

Galatians

	135	## Philippians	
1:1	126		
1:2	101		135
1:4	153n15	1:1	103
1:6	64	1:6	182
1:9	151	1:10	182
1:12	151	2:16	182
1:14	39	2:22	139
2:12	165n25	3:4–6	39
2:14	59	3:5	41, 51
2:18	59	3:17	141
3	60	4:9	151
3:1	30	4:14	111
3:1–6	116		
3:26	136	## Colossians	
3:28	1, 51		
4:3	129	1:1	153n15
4:4–7	136	1:9	153n15
4:6	136	1:12–13	191
4:8	165	1:13	118n31
4:14	129	3:5	164n24, 165n26
4:24–25	30	4:5	141
5:11	70	4:12	153n15
5:16	141		
5:19	165n26	## 1 Thessalonians	
6:2	7n6		
6:12	70		2, 3, 4, 7, 8, 9, 10, 11,
			12, 14, 14n10, 14n12,
			15n12, 16n13, 17,
Ephesians
			18, 20, 22, 23, 24, 30,
			32, 33, 34, 34n7, 35,
1:1	153n15		36, 37, 42, 44, 45, 46,
1:5	153n15		47, 49n15, 50, 60,
1:9	153n15		61, 63, 64, 65, 75, 93,
1:11	153n15		97, 97n5, 100, 101,
2:10	141		101n8, 104n10,

1 Thessalonians (continued)

	109n20, 134, 135, 135n48, 137, 139, 143, 146, 146n2, 146n3, 149, 152, 156, 157, 174, 179n41, 181n43, 185, 193, 193n57, 198n62, 200, 201, 204, 205, 207, 208, 210, 211, 212, 213
1	123, 123n37
1:1	76, 98, 99, 101, 103
1:1—2:11	98
1:1—2:12	8, 91, 92, 97, 98, 144, 204
1:1–5	33n6, 105
1:1–10	104, 105, 116, 119, 216
1:1–12	99
1–2	145
1:2	174
1:2—2:16	37
1:2–3	105, 106n12
1:2—3:13	36
1:2–5	98
1:2–10	34, 46, 98, 99, 104, 122, 144
1:3	76, 97, 123, 150n10, 177, 198, 198n62, 210
1–3	3, 32n5, 37, 99, 121, 145n1
1:4	15, 65, 103, 104, 105, 107, 109n20, 110, 112, 139, 144, 193n57, 204
1:4–5	108, 210
1:4–6	110n23
1:4–8	112
1:5	31, 34n7, 76, 103, 108, 109, 109n21, 110, 110n22, 110n24, 115, 122, 123, 124, 144, 150n13, 151
1:5b	109n21
1:6	3, 15, 76, 110, 111n26, 112, 114, 123, 127n41, 170, 171, 204
1:6–7	32, 115
1:6–8	110
1:6–10	42, 98
1:6–11	33n6
1:6b	109
1:7	112, 113, 114, 116, 144, 204
1:7–10	112
1:8	114, 122
1:9	1, 15, 16, 65, 66, 79, 84, 103, 105, 123, 155, 168, 170, 199, 204
1:9–10	46, 83, 88, 116n29, 118n31, 142, 144
1:9b–10	116, 116n29
1:9c	117
1:10	118, 151, 210
1:10a	118
1:12—2:14	33n6
2	68, 121, 123n37, 133
2:1	32, 34n7, 99, 122, 123, 123n36, 124, 149, 150n13
2:1—3:10	46
2:1—3:13	98, 99
2:1–7	124
2:1–8	34
2:1–12	31, 32n5, 34n7, 67, 98, 100, 108n19, 119, 120, 121, 121n34, 122, 124, 126, 136, 137, 144, 217
2:1–16	122
2:2	31, 32, 34n7, 76, 122, 123, 150n13, 151
2:3	31, 32, 32n5, 124
2:3–4	122
2:4	76, 124, 126, 151
2:4a	126
2:5	31, 34n7, 122, 124, 125, 130, 150n13
2:5–6	122, 139
2:5–7	122
2:5–8	130
2:6	31, 125, 130

SCRIPTURE INDEX

2:7	126, 130, 131	3:7	32, 47
2:7–8	140n51	3:8	34n7, 103, 140n53, 212
2:7–12	15, 205		
2:7b	130	3:9	76
2:7c	130	3:10	36
2:7c–8	130, 131	3:11–13	36, 42, 98, 146n2
2:8	32n5, 76, 123, 131, 132, 139, 151	3:12	3, 32n5, 97, 210
		3:12–13	106n14
2:8–9	151	3:13	160, 181n43, 182, 207, 210, 212
2:9	32, 32n5, 76, 86n30, 123, 140, 140n52, 140n53, 151	4	150n13, 154
		4:1	32, 51, 99, 100, 141, 145n1, 149, 149n7, 149n8, 150, 151, 152, 176
2:9—3:13	34		
2:10	122, 140, 141, 181n43		
2:10–11	140		
2:11	31, 32n5, 122, 139, 140, 150n13	4:1–2	3, 65, 98, 146, 148, 149, 173
2:11–12	105, 139, 140, 141	4:1—5:11	205
2:12	32, 32n5, 47, 64, 105, 137, 139, 141, 142, 144, 151, 205	4:1—5:22	34, 88, 98, 99
		4:1—5:24	36, 37
		4:1–7	165n26
2:13	173	4:1–8	88, 218
2:13—3:10	122n35	4:1–12	48, 155, 156, 193n57, 199
2:13–16	34n7, 67, 70, 98, 100, 146n2		
		4:2	32, 100, 149, 150, 150n13, 168
2:14	68, 186, 193n57		
2:14–16	60n21	4:3	50, 100, 146, 146n2, 152, 153, 153n15, 153n16, 155, 157, 159, 162, 168, 170, 171, 181n43, 193n57, 205, 207
2:15	152		
2:15–21	33n6		
2:16	68, 210		
2:17	122, 139		
2:17—3:10	122, 146n2		
2:17—3:11	98	4:3–5	79
2:17—3:13	37	4:3–6a	156
2:17–18	47	4:3–7	155, 157
2:18	195n58	4:3–8	65, 80, 98, 146, 148, 152, 153, 154, 155, 157, 160, 164
2:19	15, 76, 182		
2:20	76		
3:1—4:31	33n6	4:3a	162
3:2	32, 76, 151	4:3b	160, 161, 161n21
3:3	32, 67, 122n35, 150n13, 212	4:3b–6	163
		4:3b–6a	155, 157, 160, 161
3:3b	144	4:4	100, 153, 153n15, 153n16, 157, 160, 161, 162n23, 167, 181n43, 207
3:4	31		
3–4	100		
3:5	122n35, 139		
3:6	3, 97, 139, 150n10, 210	4:4–5	166
		4:4–6	167

1 Thessalonians (continued)

Verse	Pages
4:4c–5	164
4:5	65, 155, 156, 160, 164, 165, 165n24, 166, 167
4–5	3, 8, 32n5, 37, 45, 47, 49n15, 50, 88, 121, 145, 145n1, 146
4:6	32, 32n5, 51, 100, 163
4:6a	160
4:6b	167, 168
4:7	32n5, 64, 65, 105, 122, 144, 153, 153n15, 153n16, 154, 156, 157, 168n29, 170, 181n43, 207
4:7–8	163
4:8	122, 146n2, 168, 169, 169n30, 170, 172, 175n34
4:8–9	50
4:9	32n5, 146, 156, 172, 173, 174, 175, 176, 179
4:9–10	206
4:9–12	98, 106n14, 146, 148, 172, 219
4:10	32, 51, 100, 174
4:10b	176
4:11	32, 32n5, 100, 176
4:11–12	50, 206
4:12	99, 155, 156
4:12a	156
4:13	37, 65, 76, 99, 146
4:13—5:11	43, 48
4:13–18	47, 84, 98, 146n2, 179
4:14	84, 85, 85n28, 97n5
4:15	76, 182
4:16	43, 76, 84
4:17	76, 103
4:17–18	42
4:18	32, 32n5, 37, 99
5	181n43, 183n44, 195
5:1	146, 179, 179n41, 183n44
5:1—6:10	33n6
5:1–11	65, 98, 146, 148, 179, 180, 181, 182, 191, 199, 206, 220
5:2	32, 43, 141, 146n2, 150n12, 181n43, 182, 183, 183n44, 183n45, 192
5:2–4	192
5:2–8	179n41
5:3	71, 76, 181n43, 183, 183n45, 184, 185, 192
5:3–4	180
5:3a	183n44
5:3b	183n44
5:4	180, 181n43, 183n45, 186, 186n49, 192
5:4–5	189, 190, 206
5:4–8	43, 181n43
5:4a	186n49
5:4b	186n49
5:5	15, 180, 181n43, 182, 188, 188n53, 193, 193n57, 199
5:5–6	183n44, 189
5:6	65, 122, 180, 197
5:6–7	183n44, 195
5:6–11	197
5:7	181n43
5:7–8	180
5:8	76, 97, 144, 195, 198n61, 198n62, 210
5:8–10	210
5:9	76, 122, 168, 180, 181n43, 193n57
5:9–10	181n43, 197
5:11	32, 32n5, 37, 99, 180n42, 181n43
5:12	32, 146
5:12–13	181n43
5:12–22	98
5:13	32n5, 97, 100, 210
5:13–22	99
5:14	32, 32n5, 178, 193n57
5:15	122
5:18	153n15
5:20	190

5:23	42, 47, 76, 100, 181n43, 182, 207, 212
5:23–24	32n5, 105
5:23–28	47, 98
5:24	144
5:25	100
5:27	97, 210
6:11–18	33n6

2 Thessalonians

	65, 135, 135n48
1:8	165
2:13	153n16
3:6–13	178

1 Timothy

2:15	153n16
5:5	140n53
6:14–15	179n40

2 Timothy

	39
1:1	153n15
1:3	140n53
2:11	141
2:11–12	141
3:16	39

Philemon

	135
1:2	101
1:10	139

Hebrews

2:11	136n49
2:12	136n49
2:17	136n49
3:1	136n49
3:12	136n49
10:19	136n49
10:28	168n29
12:21	169n30
13:1	175
13:22	136n49

James

1:2	136n49
1:9	136n49
1:16	136n49
1:19	136n49
2:1	136n49
2:5	136n49
2:14	136n49
2:15	136n49
3:1	136n49
3:10	136n49
3:12	136n49
4:11	136n49
5:7	136n49
5:9	136n49
5:10	136n49
5:19	136n49

1 Peter

1:1—2:3	155
1:5	179n40
1:13	198
1:20	179n40
1:22	175
2:11–12	155
5:8	198
5:12	136n49

2 Peter

1:7	175
3:10	182–83
3:15	136n49

1 John

2:9	136n49
2:10	136n49
2:11	136n49
3:10	136n49
3:12–17	136n49
4:20–21	136n49
5:16	136n49

3 John

1:5	136n49
1:10	136n49

Revelation

1:3	179n40
1:9	136n49
3:2-3	197
3:3	183
4:18	197n60
5:11-26	197n60
6:11	136n49
12:10	136n49
16:15	183
19:10	136n49
22:9	136n49
22:10	179n40

APOCRYPHA (NEW TESTAMENT)

Joseph and Asenath

11:7-11	116

Sibylline Oracles

3:591-9	165
5.495-9	118

EARLY CHRISTIAN WRITINGS

Ben Sira 148n6
Clement of Alexandria
 83
Exhortation to the Heathen
 83

Eusebius

Ecclesiastical History

6. xix. 5-9	41

Firmicus Maternus, Julius 83

Error of the Pagan Religions
 83

Justin Martyr

1 Apology

5-6	89n32

Origen	30
Suetonius	73n13
II	
25.4	73

Tertullian

Apology

10-11	89n32

GREEK AND ROMAN LITERATURE

Apuleius

Metamorphoses (The Golden Ass)

9.14	89n32

Aristotle

 36

Ars Rhetorica

3.9.1-3	141

Nicomachean Ethics

2.1	2n2
5.6.8	139n50
8.11.2	139n50
8.12.5	139n50

Politics

1.5.2	139n50

Arrian

Bitynica

frag. 1.2	40n11

Cassius Dio (Dio Cassius)

60.27.4	177

Roman History

VII	71, 74

Cicero

De Natura Deorum Academica

2.3.8	89n33

Epistulae ad Familiares

9.21.1	4

Dio Chrysostom 31, 121, 129, 130

Discourse
77/78.38   129
Oration
12.61   129
32:10   31
32.11   31
32.11–12   31
32.26   123n36
77/78.38   31

Diodorus Siculus
Library of History
20.72.2   129

Epictetus
Diatr.
2.14.12–13   111n25
Discourses
4.4.48   152
Enchiridion
15   142

Herodotus
2.144   81

Homer
Odyssey
7.1–13   132
15.437–453   132

Livy
2:36.6   89n33
3.6.5   89n33
5.14.3–4   89n33
6.1.12   89n33

Maximus of Tyre
129

Mithrasliturgie
29

Plato
Phaedrus
231a   177
Republic   177n37
4.441D–E   177
6.496D   177

Pliny the Elder
Ep.
2.6   34n7
7.7   34n7

Plutarch
129
Am. Prol.
469C   139n50
De Iside et Osiride
364D   81
On Fraternal Affection (On Brotherly Love or De Fraterno Amore)
    175n35
7 E   139n50
478 C   175n35
479C–D   175n35
479F   139n50
487 E   175n35
Lib. ed.
8F–9A   138
13D   138
14A   138
Moralia
527D   79
798E–F   177

Posidonius
30

Pseudo-Diogenes
129

Quintilian
Institutio Oratoria
8.3.30–37   173
12.73–74   123n36

Res Gestae Divi Augusti
    70n8

Seneca the Younger
De Providentia
  2.5   139n50

Epistulae Morales ad Lucilium
  6:5–6   34n7

Xenophon
Memorabilia Oeconomicus
  1.6.3   111n25

www.ingramcontent.com/pod-product-compliance
Lightning Source LLC
Chambersburg PA
CBHW071243230426
43668CB00011B/1560